THE CAMBRIDGE

OAKESHO

Each volume of this series of companions to ma... philosophers contains specially commissioned essays by an international team of scholars, together with a substantial bibliography, and will serve as a reference work for students and non-specialists. One aim of the series is to dispel the intimidation such readers often feel when faced with the work of a difficult and challenging thinker.

Michael Oakeshott (1901–1990) was one of the leading British philosophers of the twentieth century. He has been influential particularly as a political philosopher but his work reflects philosophical interests that have only gradually come to be appreciated. In this volume a broad group of scholars offers a comprehensive overview of Oakeshott's philosophy, including his moral and political philosophy, his philosophy of history, science and aesthetics, and his views on the role of education. They analyse Oakeshott's ideas in different intellectual contexts and assess his overall contribution to twentieth-century thought. Accessible and rich with new scholarly material, this volume will be an excellent guide for students and scholars alike.

New readers will find this the most convenient, accessible guide to Oakeshott currently available. Advanced students and specialists will find a conspectus of recent developments in the interpretation of Oakeshott.

EFRAIM PODOKSIK is Senior Lecturer in Political Science at the Hebrew University of Jerusalem. He is author of *In Defence of Modernity: Vision and Philosophy in Michael Oakeshott* (2003).

OTHER VOLUMES IN THE SERIES OF CAMBRIDGE COMPANIONS

ABELARD *Edited by* JEFFREY E. BROWER *and* KEVIN GUILFOY

ADORNO *Edited by* THOMAS HUHN

ANCIENT SCEPTICISM *Edited by* RICHARD BETT

ANSELM *Edited by* BRIAN DAVIES *and* BRIAN LEFTOW

AQUINAS *Edited by* NORMAN KRETZMANN *and* ELEONORE STUMP

ARABIC PHILOSOPHY *Edited by* PETER ADAMSON *and* RICHARD C. TAYLOR

HANNAH ARENDT *Edited by* DANA VILLA

ARISTOTLE *Edited by* JONATHAN BARNES

ATHEISM *Edited by* MICHAEL MARTIN

AUGUSTINE *Edited by* ELEONORE STUMP *and* NORMAN KRETZMANN

BACON *Edited by* MARKKU PELTONEN

BERKELEY *Edited by* KENNETH P. WINKLER

BOETHIUS *Edited by* JOHN MARENBON

BRENTANO *Edited by* DALE JACQUETTE

CARNAP *Edited by* MICHAEL FRIEDMAN *and* RICHARD CREATH

CONSTANT *Edited by* HELENA ROSENBLATT

CRITICAL THEORY *Edited by* FRED RUSH

DARWIN 2nd edn *Edited by* JONATHAN HODGE *and* GREGORY RADICK

SIMONE DE BEAUVOIR *Edited by* CLAUDIA CARD

DESCARTES *Edited by* JOHN COTTINGHAM

DEWEY *Edited by* MOLLY COCHRAN

DUNS SCOTUS *Edited by* THOMAS WILLIAMS

EARLY GREEK PHILOSOPHY *Edited by* A. A. LONG

EARLY MODERN PHILOSOPHY *Edited by* DONALD RUTHERFORD

EPICUREANISM *Edited by* JAMES WARREN

EXISTENTIALISM *Edited by* STEVEN CROWELL

FEMINISM IN PHILOSOPHY *Edited by* MIRANDA FRICKER *and* JENNIFER HORNSBY

FOUCAULT 2nd edn *Edited by* GARY GUTTING

FREGE *Edited by* THOMAS RICKETTS *and* MICHAEL POTTER

FREUD *Edited by* JEROME NEU

GADAMER *Edited by* ROBERT J. DOSTAL

GALEN *Edited by* R. J. HANKINSON

GALILEO *Edited by* PETER MACHAMER

GERMAN IDEALISM *Edited by* KARL AMERIKS

GREEK AND ROMAN PHILOSOPHY *Edited by* DAVID SEDLEY

HABERMAS *Edited by* STEPHEN K. WHITE

HAYEK *Edited by* EDWARD FESER

HEGEL *Edited by* FREDERICK C. BEISER

HEGEL AND NINETEENTH-CENTURY PHILOSOPHY *Edited by* FREDERICK C. BEISER

HEIDEGGER 2nd edn *Edited by* CHARLES GUIGNON

HOBBES *Edited by* TOM SORELL

HOBBES'S 'LEVIATHAN' *Edited by* PATRICIA SPRINGBORG

HUME 2nd edn *Edited by* DAVID FATE NORTON *and* JACQUELINE TAYLOR

HUSSERL *Edited by* BARRY SMITH *and* DAVID WOODRUFF SMITH

WILLIAM JAMES *Edited by* RUTH ANNA PUTNAM

KANT *Edited by* PAUL GUYER

KANT AND MODERN PHILOSOPHY *Edited by* PAUL GUYER

KANT'S 'CRITIQUE OF PURE REASON' *Edited by* PAUL GUYER

KEYNES *Edited by* ROGER E. BACKHOUSE *and* BRADLEY W. BATEMAN

KIERKEGAARD *Edited by* ALASTAIR HANNAY *and* GORDON DANIEL MARINO

LEIBNIZ *Edited by* NICHOLAS JOLLEY

LEVINAS *Edited by* SIMON CRITCHLEY *and* ROBERT BERNASCONI

LOCKE *Edited by* VERE CHAPPELL

LOCKE'S 'ESSAY CONCERNING HUMAN UNDERSTANDING' *Edited by* LEX NEWMAN

LOGICAL EMPIRICISM *Edited by* ALAN RICHARDSON *and* THOMAS UEBEL

MAIMONIDES *Edited by* KENNETH SEESKIN

MALEBRANCHE *Edited by* STEVEN NADLER

MARX *Edited by* TERRELL CARVER

MEDIEVAL JEWISH PHILOSOPHY *Edited by* DANIEL H. FRANK *and* OLIVER LEAMAN

MEDIEVAL PHILOSOPHY *Edited by* A. S. MCGRADE

MERLEAU-PONTY *Edited by* TAYLOR CARMAN *and* MARK B. N. HANSEN

MILL *Edited by* JOHN SKORUPSKI

MONTAIGNE *Edited by* ULLRICH LANGER

NEWTON *Edited by* I. BERNARD COHEN *and* GEORGE E. SMITH

NIETZSCHE *Edited by* BERND MAGNUS *and* KATHLEEN HIGGINS

NOZICK'S 'ANARCHY, STATE AND UTOPIA' *Edited by* RALF BADER *and* JOHN MEADOWCROFT

OAKESHOTT *Edited by* EFRAIM PODOKSIK

OCKHAM *Edited by* PAUL VINCENT SPADE

THE 'ORIGIN OF SPECIES' *Edited by* MICHAEL RUSE *and* ROBERT J. RICHARDS

PASCAL *Edited by* NICHOLAS HAMMOND

PEIRCE *Edited by* CHERYL MISAK

PHILO *Edited by* ADAM KAMESAR

THE PHILOSOPHY OF BIOLOGY *Edited by* DAVID L. HULL *and* MICHAEL RUSE

PIAGET *Edited by* ULRICH MÜLLER, JEREMY I. M. CARPENDALE *and* LESLIE SMITH

PLATO *Edited by* RICHARD KRAUT
PLATO'S 'REPUBLIC' *Edited by* G. R. F. FERRARI
PLOTINUS *Edited by* LLOYD P. GERSON
QUINE *Edited by* ROGER F. GIBSON JR
RAWLS *Edited by* SAMUEL FREEMAN
THOMAS REID *Edited by* TERENCE CUNEO *and* RENÉ VAN WOUDENBERG
RENAISSANCE PHILOSOPHY *Edited by* JAMES HANKINS
ROUSSEAU *Edited by* PATRICK RILEY
BERTRAND RUSSELL *Edited by* NICHOLAS GRIFFIN
SARTRE *Edited by* CHRISTINA HOWELLS
SCHOPENHAUER *Edited by* CHRISTOPHER JANAWAY
THE SCOTTISH ENLIGHTENMENT *Edited by* ALEXANDER BROADIE
ADAM SMITH *Edited by* KNUD HAAKONSSEN
SOCRATES *Edited by* DONALD MORRISON
SPINOZA *Edited by* DON GARRETT
SPINOZA'S 'ETHICS' *Edited by* OLLI KOISTINEN
THE STOICS *Edited by* BRAD INWOOD
LEO STRAUSS *Edited by* STEVEN B. SMITH
TOCQUEVILLE *Edited by* CHERYL B. WELCH
WITTGENSTEIN *Edited by* HANS SLUGA *and* DAVID STERN

The Cambridge Companion to

OAKESHOTT

Edited by Efraim Podoksik
Hebrew University of Jerusalem

CAMBRIDGE
UNIVERSITY PRESS

CAMBRIDGE UNIVERSITY PRESS
Cambridge, New York, Melbourne, Madrid, Cape Town,
Singapore, São Paulo, Delhi, Mexico City

Cambridge University Press
The Edinburgh Building, Cambridge CB2 8RU, UK

Published in the United States of America by
Cambridge University Press, New York

www.cambridge.org
Information on this title: www.cambridge.org/9780521764674

First published 2012

Printed in the United Kingdom at the University Press, Cambridge

A catalogue record for this publication is available from the British Library

Library of Congress Cataloging-in-Publication Data

The Cambridge companion to Oakeshott / edited by Efraim Podoksik,
Hebrew University of Jerusalem.
pages cm. – (Cambridge companions to philosophy)
Includes bibliographical references and index.
ISBN 978-0-521-76467-4 (Hardback)
ISBN 978-0-521-14792-7 (Paperback)
1. Oakeshott, Michael, 1901–1990. I. Podoksik, Efraim.
B1649.O344C35 2012
192–dc23

2011052385

ISBN 978-0-521-76467-4 Hardback
ISBN 978-0-521-14792-7 Paperback

CONTENTS

CONTRIBUTORS

JAMES ALEXANDER read history at Trinity College, Cambridge, and now teaches politics at Bilkent University, Ankara. He is the author of *Shaw's Controversial Socialism* (2009). Currently he is concerned with the fundamental categories of philosophy, and with dialectical definitions of concepts such as liberty, right, tradition and politics.

DAVID BOUCHER is Head of the School of European Studies, Deputy Pro Vice-Chancellor and Director of the Collingwood and British Idealism Centre, Cardiff University. He is also adjunct professor of international relations at the University of the Sunshine Coast, Australia. Among his authored books are: *The Social and Political Thought of R. G. Collingwood* (1989); *A Radical Hegelian: The Social and Political Thought of Henry Jones* (with Andrew Vincent, 1992); *Political Theories of International Relations* (1998); and *The Limits of Ethics in International Relations* (2009). His most recent book is *British Idealism: A Guide for the Perplexed* (with Andrew Vincent, 2011). He was taught by Michael Oakeshott at the London School of Economics (1976–7) and has published many book chapters and articles on Oakeshott.

ELIZABETH COREY is Assistant Professor of Political Science in the Honors College at Baylor University. She is the author of *Michael Oakeshott on Religion, Aesthetics and Politics* (2006) and has published on many aspects of Oakeshott's thought.

PAIGE DIGESER is Professor of Political Science at the University of California at Santa Barbara, and is author of *Our Politics, Our Selves?* (1995) and *Political Forgiveness* (2001).

RICHARD FLATHMAN is George Armstrong Kelly Professor Emeritus at Johns Hopkins University. He is the author of numerous articles and books, including: *Willful Liberalism* (1992); *Reflections of a Would-Be Anarchist* (1998); *Freedom and its Conditions* (2003); and *Pluralism and Liberal Democracy* (2005).

WILLIAM A. GALSTON is Ezra Zilkha Chair in Governance Studies and College Park Professor at the University of Maryland. From 1993 to 1995 he served as Deputy Assistant to President Clinton for Domestic Policy. His nine books include: *Liberal Purposes* (1991); *Liberal Pluralism* (2001); and *The Practice of Liberal Pluralism* (2005).

ANDREW GAMBLE is Professor of Politics and Fellow of Queens' College, University of Cambridge. He is the author of *Hayek: The Iron Cage of Liberty* (1996), *Politics and Fate* (2000) and *The Limits of Politics* (2009).

BYRON KALDIS is Professor of Philosophy at the Hellenic Open University. He is the general editor of the *SAGE Encyclopedia of Philosophy and the Social Sciences* (2013) and of *Mind and Society: Cognitive Science meets the Social Sciences*, Synthese Library.

TERRY NARDIN is Professor of Political Science at the National University of Singapore. He is the author of *The Philosophy of Michael Oakeshott* (2001) and editor, with Luke O'Sullivan, of Oakeshott's *Lectures in the History of Political Thought* (2006). He is also the author of *Law, Morality, and the Relations of States* (1983) and other writings on the political theory of international relations.

LUKE O'SULLIVAN is Associate Professor of Political Science at the National University of Singapore. He is the author of *Oakeshott on History* (2003) and general editor of *Michael Oakeshott's Selected Writings* (2004 to present).

EFRAIM PODOKSIK is Senior Lecturer in the Department of Political Science at the Hebrew University of Jerusalem. His publications on

Oakeshott include *In Defence of Modernity: Vision and Philosophy in Michael Oakeshott* (2003).

STEVEN B. SMITH is the Alfred Cowles Professor of Political Science and formerly Master of Branford College, Yale University. His books include *Spinoza, Liberalism, and the Question of Jewish Identity* (1997), *Reading Leo Strauss: Philosophy, Politics, Judaism* (2006), and he is the editor of *The Cambridge Companion to Leo Strauss* (2009). His book *Political Philosophy from Athens to America* will be published in 2012.

IAN TREGENZA teaches political theory in the Department of Politics and International Relations at Macquarie University, Sydney. He is the author of *Michael Oakeshott on Hobbes: A Study in the Renewal of Philosophical Ideas* (2003).

DANA VILLA is Packey Dee Professor of Political Theory at the University of Notre Dame. He is the author of *Arendt and Heidegger: The Fate of the Political* (1995); *Politics, Philosophy, Terror* (1999); *Socratic Citizenship* (2001); and *Public Freedom* (2008). He also edited *The Cambridge Companion to Hannah Arendt* (2000).

KEVIN WILLIAMS is Senior Lecturer in the Mater Dei Institute of Education, Dublin City University, and former President of the Educational Studies Association of Ireland. His books include *Education and the Voice of Michael Oakeshott* (2007) and *Faith and the Nation: Religion, Culture and Schooling in Ireland* (2005).

ABBREVIATIONS

CPJ	Michael Oakeshott, *The Concept of a Philosophical Jurisprudence: Essays and Reviews 1926–51* (Thorverton: Imprint Academic, 2007)
EM	Michael Oakeshott, *Experience and its Modes* (Cambridge: University Press, 1933)
EPW	Michael Oakeshott, *Early Political Writings 1925–30* (Thorverton: Imprint Academic, 2010)
HC	Michael Oakeshott, *On Human Conduct* (Oxford: Clarendon Press, 1975)
HCA	Michael Oakeshott, *Hobbes on Civil Association* (Oxford: Basil Blackwell, 1975)
LHPT	Michael Oakeshott, *Lectures in the History of Political Thought* (Thorverton: Imprint Academic, 2006)
NL	Michael Oakeshott, *Notebooks and Letters 1922–90* (Thorverton: Imprint Academic, forthcoming)
MPME	Michael Oakeshott, *Morality and Politics in Modern Europe: The Harvard Lectures* (New Haven, CT: Yale University Press, 1993)
OH	Michael Oakeshott, *On History and Other Essays* (Oxford: Basil Blackwell, 1983)
PFPS	Michael Oakeshott, *The Politics of Faith and the Politics of Scepticism* (New Haven, CT: Yale University Press, 1996)
RP	Michael Oakeshott, *Rationalism in Politics and Other Essays* (London: Methuen, 1962)
RP [1991]	Michael Oakeshott, *Rationalism in Politics and Other Essays*, new and expanded edition (Indianapolis, IND: Liberty Fund, 1991)

RPML Michael Oakeshott, *Religion, Politics, and the Moral Life* (New Haven, CT: Yale University Press, 1993)
VLL Michael Oakeshott, *The Voice of Liberal Learning: Michael Oakeshott on Education* (New Haven, CT: Yale University Press, 1989)
VMES Michael Oakeshott, *The Vocabulary of a Modern European State* (Thorverton: Imprint Academic, 2008)
WH Michael Oakeshott, *What is History? And Other Essays* (Thorverton: Imprint Academic, 2004)

CHRONOLOGY

1901	Michael Joseph Oakeshott born on 11 December in Chelsfield, Kent, second son of Joseph Francis Oakeshott and Frances Maude Oakeshott (née Hellicar).
1912	Begins to attend St George's School, Harpenden (Headmaster Revd Cecil Grant).
1914–18	First World War.
1920–3	History undergraduate at Gonville and Caius College, Cambridge.
1923–4	Awarded Christopher James Studentship at Gonville and Caius. Visits Germany.
1924–5	English teacher at King Edward VII Grammar School, Lytham St Anne's, Lancashire.
1925	Elected Fellow, Gonville and Caius College.
1927	Marries Joyce Fricker.
1931	Son, Simon, born. Oakeshott appointed College Lecturer.
1933	University Lecturer in History. Holds this position until his departure from Cambridge in 1949. *Experience and its Modes* is published.
1936	Publishes with G. T. Griffith a book on horse-racing: *A Guide to the Classics, or, How to Pick the Derby Winner*.
1938	Divorces Joyce Oakeshott and marries Katherine Alice Burton (previously Mrs Ian Cox).
1939	Compiles anthology *The Social and Political Doctrines of Contemporary Europe*. The Second World War erupts.

The editor would like to express his deep appreciation to Professor Robert Grant and Dr Simon Oakeshott, who were most generous in supplying bits of information for this chronology and correcting factual errors.

1940	Enlists in the British Army (Royal Artillery).
1944–5	Serves on the Continent in battlefield intelligence unit, 'Phantom' (GHQ Liaison Regiment). Adjutant of 'B' Squadron.
1945	War with Germany ends in May. Clement Attlee is appointed prime minister after the Labour Party wins the parliamentary election in July. War with Japan ends in August.
1946	Oakeshott edits a new edition of T. Hobbes's *Leviathan* and writes an introduction to it.
1947–54	Member of the editorial board of the *Cambridge Journal*; later, general editor.
1949–51	Fellow, Nuffield College, Oxford.
1950	Appointed Professor of Political Science at the London School of Economics after the death of Harold Laski.
1951	Takes up appointment at LSE and remains there until his retirement in 1968. Conservative Party wins the parliamentary election. Winston Churchill returns to serve as prime minister.
1952–3	Visiting Muirhead Lecturer at the University of Birmingham.
1955	Divorces Kate Oakeshott.
1958	Visiting Professor, Harvard University. His lectures are posthumously published as *Morality and Politics in Modern Europe* (1993).
1962	At the urging of his colleague Maurice Cranston, Oakeshott publishes ten of his essays as *Rationalism in Politics and Other Essays*.
1965	Marries Christel Schneider.
1968	Retires from LSE but continues to contribute to the MSc History of Political Thought programme until 1981.
1975	*On Human Conduct* and *Hobbes on Civil Association* published.
1979	Margaret Thatcher becomes prime minister after the Conservative Party wins the parliamentary election.
1983	*On History and Other Essays*.
1989	*The Voice of Liberal Learning* (a collection of essays on education) published.
1990	Oakeshott dies in Acton, Langton Matravers in Dorset, England during the night of 18/19 December.

EFRAIM PODOKSIK

Introduction

A few years ago a commentator referred to Michael Oakeshott as 'the greatest English philosopher of the twentieth century'.[1] This rather unremarkable suggestion provoked a small storm among the readers, including even some Oakeshottians. The idea that someone who was often regarded as a philosophical outsider could be more profound and interesting than his peers apparently offended, or at least peeved, many people. Their reaction showed that even after the tremendous surge in interest in Oakeshott's thought over the past decade, it is still a 'niche' interest.

One of the purposes of the current volume is to make it less so. This is not a book written exclusively by and for Oakeshottians. Rather, it is the enterprise of a diverse collection of scholars who wish to understand the broad meaning and impact of Oakeshott's philosophy and share their understanding with others. Not all contributors will subscribe to my conviction regarding the exceptional greatness of Oakeshott's philosophy (though all, I believe, would agree that it offers something of value to the modern mind); yet as the editor I feel obliged to confess that this is my view and to offer a few general accompanying remarks.

In philosophy, as in art, an opinion about greatness cannot be proven. The recognition of the value of a philosophy is in the final account always a matter of inner conviction, of immediate and sincere acknowledgement of the quality of thought displayed. Therefore, no text about Oakeshott (or any other philosopher) can ever offer an irrefutable demonstration of his alleged value. Commentary can never offer more than assistance in interpreting the philosopher's works. Only by reading Oakeshott himself can the reader make up his or her own mind regarding the value of his thought. Yet I believe that most of those who will take the advice to read him will not be disappointed. The growing popularity of Oakeshott's ideas is not, in my opinion, a matter of fashion. It is a sign of something inherent in his thought, of its inner vitality.

Oakeshott thought and wrote in a manner unusual among his contemporaries. This was a contingent historical circumstance, which prevented the significance of his ideas from being immediately recognized. It is due to this contingency that during his life he was often considered an 'unserious' thinker.[2] Historical circumstances made his thought appear 'untimely'. Yet circumstances can never abolish what is essential in every philosophy worthy of its name: drive, passion, a vital force that (to paraphrase Oakeshott himself) connects the personality of a philosopher with eternity. Whenever this vitality exists, the philosophy will in the end find its readers. And, indeed, this is what has been happening to Oakeshott's philosophy in recent years.

Not all philosophical enterprises in the history of European thought have suffered from such initial indifference. Many great philosophies have swept the intellectual life of their times apparently without difficulty. But it is wrong to assume that power and clarity of mind always enjoy an easy path to glory. In this respect, Oakeshott's case can be compared to those of Aristotle, Hobbes or Schopenhauer.[3] Hardly anyone who immersed himself in these three philosophers can deny their power of mind. Yet there were times when Aristotle's works fell into obscurity; Hobbes was always known and respected, but only in the twentieth century was his place in the major political philosophical canon ensured; Schopenhauer's ideas were notoriously ignored at the time of their publication, and even now his philosophy is often underestimated.

Like Oakeshott, all three were great stylists (though Aristotle's brilliance is less noticeable at first glance due to the fact that most of his extant writings seem to be fragments or notes). The sceptical observer often rightly mistrusts a philosopher who is also a rhetorician. Yet in these cases the style does not obscure the meaning; on the contrary, it is the effect of the clarity of the message. In true philosophy what is said and how it is said are one and the same thing.

Those who met Oakeshott often noted his modesty, his nonchalant attitude towards worldly recognition. But I would not necessarily interpret this indifference as modesty. Rather, its true spring appears to be a profound confidence in the vital powers of his own mind, combined with the awareness that these are undeserved. The ability to philosophize is often experienced as something not achieved, but rather bestowed. Oakeshott regarded philosophical accomplishment as entirely different from typical petty bourgeois personal achievement, from 'success' through hard work. For him, it is a result of the mind's own drive, the force of which makes the whole personality unable to resist it.

There was an element of daring in Oakeshott's philosophical modesty, which distinguished it from the timid modesty of the leading currents in British philosophy of the twentieth century, such as logical realism and analytical philosophy. This is what set his philosophy apart from the mainstream, but what also made it potentially greater. Whether this intellectual adventure paid off, whether Oakeshott achieved philosophical greatness, must remain a matter of personal judgement. I myself believe he did; others may disagree. But what cannot be denied is the unusual attraction of the challenge presented by Oakeshott's philosophy: the challenge of considering what it means to philosophize (in his own phrase) 'without reservation' in a philosophically timid and confused age.

The Companion is a cooperative enterprise. It brings together Oakeshott scholars and experts in other branches of study relevant to the subject; committed Oakeshottians and those who observe his ideas from a certain distance. Some articles are pieces of commentary; others conduct a dialogue, friendly or critical, with Oakeshott's ideas. Some deal with the texts themselves; others embark on contextual research.

Despite this variety of approaches, however, or perhaps informed by it, the book is designed as a coherent volume. It has a plan and a direction, and its chapters can be read in sequence. There are unavoidable overlaps between the chapters, yet on the whole each, taken individually, deals with its own specific question, whereas all the chapters taken together provide (one hopes) a more or less comprehensive outlook on the main aspects of Oakeshott's thought.

The volume is divided into three parts. It begins with an overview of Oakeshott's general philosophy. In the first chapter James Alexander presents his interpretation of Oakeshott's vision of philosophy and offers a general classification of worlds of experience at different stages of Oakeshott's intellectual development. The final (fifth) chapter in this part, written by Kevin Williams, also deals with the general notion of worlds of experience, but does so from the standpoint of Oakeshott's philosophy of education. For Oakeshott envisioned various worlds as coexisting in the condition of 'conversation' and emphasized the role of proper education in maintaining this conversation. Chapters 2 to 4 analyse three of these worlds: Luke O'Sullivan outlines Oakeshott's philosophy of history, arguing that his 'real achievement ... was to establish history as an autonomous mode of understanding'. Byron Kaldis focuses on the unjustly neglected topic of science. He asserts that Oakeshott's philosophy of science can be understood as a form of 'dialectical constructivism', and compares it to views of science in other philosophical currents, such as Neo-Kantiansim. Elizabeth Corey writes on the role of aesthetics in Oakeshott. She describes possible and actual criticisms directed against his view of aesthetics, and deals with the question of how Oakeshott's aesthetics relates to his philosophies of religion and practice.

The second part of the book discusses aspects of Oakeshott's theories of human conduct, society and politics. Steven Smith opens this part (Chapter 6) with an analysis of Oakeshott's notions of practice and practical experience. He also touches on the subject of politics, arguing that, in the light of Oakeshott's philosophy of practice, his politics appears 'not so much that of a Burkean conservative looking to the past than of a Cold War liberal hoping to disenthral his readers of the charms of perfectionism'. In the seventh chapter Andrew Gamble offers a somewhat different perspective. He analyses Oakeshott's notion of ideology in the context of what appears to be his most explicitly political period, marked by a considerable number of polemical essays and book reviews: the late 1940s and 1950s. In these writings, Gamble argues, Oakeshott clearly positions himself within the tradition of conservative thought. Terry Nardin, in turn, focuses on Oakeshott's relatively neglected essays from the late 1950s and 1960s (Chapter 8). These writings already contained the conceptual seeds that he later developed in *On Human Conduct*. At the same time, the essays are valuable in themselves, as it is in them that Oakeshott provides the most detailed account of his approach to political rhetoric. *On Human Conduct* itself is analysed in Chapter 9 by Paige Digeser and

Richard Flathman. The authors describe the theoretical framework of Oakeshott's major treatise on social thought, putting special emphasis on the notions of freedom, individuality, civil association and law. Finally, in Chapter 10 William Galston presents a general overview of Oakeshott's political theory. He addresses it from the standpoint of its contemporary significance and offers a number of criticisms regarding what he sees as its inadequacies.

The third and final part of the volume, unlike the first two, which deal mainly with Oakeshott's ideas themselves, attempts to place his ideas in their context (or contexts) so as to enrich our understanding of them and to examine parallels between Oakeshott and other thinkers. One way to understand Oakeshott is to locate him within the philosophical tradition of British Idealism. This is the subject of David Boucher's chapter (Chapter 11), which examines Oakeshott's debt to the British Idealists of previous generations. Boucher also sheds light on the debate between 'Absolutists' and 'Personalists' within the big family of British Idealism, arguing that Oakeshott took the side of Absolute Idealism. Another important context is that of German Idealism, which left an indelible mark on Oakeshott's thinking. This is the subject of Chapter 12, where I argue that Oakeshott's ideas are fully intelligible only in the context of German thought of the nineteenth and early twentieth centuries. I focus especially on the previously unexplored theme of Oakeshott's debt to Schopenhauer. The next chapter (Chapter 13), by Ian Tregenza, deals with Oakeshott as an interpreter of Hobbes. This subject can be seen as implying two contextual elements: first, Oakeshott's debt to Hobbes's philosophy; and second, Hobbes scholarship in the mid twentieth century. Tregenza examines Oakeshott's contribution to this scholarship and compares his interpretation of Hobbes with those of Strauss, Warrender and Brown. Finally, in Chapter 14 Dana Villa juxtaposes Oakeshott's critique of Rationalism with that of famous Cold War liberals such as Hannah Arendt and Isaiah Berlin. Villa argues that Oakeshott's understanding and critique of Rationalism differed in many important respects from those of Arendt and Berlin, and he finds their approaches more adequate than Oakeshott's in grappling with the demons of the twentieth-century past.

The volume, of course, cannot find room for a detailed exposition of all Oakeshott's writings or every topic in his philosophy. Yet one can hope that this cooperative work will become a useful guide for those who would like to acquaint themselves with the central themes of his philosophy.

NOTES

1 J. Alexander, 'Smooth Sailing on Endless Hostile Sea', *Times Higher Education Supplement*, 8 August 2005, 27.

2 A. Sullivan, 'Taken Unseriously', *New Republic*, 204 (6 May 1991), 42.

3 His fascination with the first two is well known, whereas the Schopenhauerian moment in his philosophy is addressed in this volume.

PART I

Oakeshott's philosophy

JAMES ALEXANDER

1 Oakeshott as philosopher

All understandings are conditional.[1]

INTRODUCTION: PHILOSOPHY

Philosophy now means more or less anything done by philosophers. But the history of philosophy suggests that there are four points of the philosophical compass, which I would like to call wonder, faith, doubt and scepticism. That is to say, any philosopher is likely to have an attitude that involves one or more of these views:

1. that there is a world and no words to explain it, so that words and world are part of one undifferentiated reality – and our response is wonder,
2. that there is a world, and one word to explain it, which is not itself of this world, and so explains it on authority – and our response is faith,
3. that there is a world, and many words which appear to explain it, of which we, by some method or other, must examine to establish the certainty we suppose is there – and our response is doubt,
4. that there is a world, or worlds, and many words which appear to explain it, or them, none of which have any greater authority or reason or status than any other, so that we are left with uncertainty – and so our response is scepticism.

All of these views were there at the beginning and will be there at the end. The classical philosophers established philosophies with all these orientations. But for the last five centuries or so philosophers have tended to ignore wonder, dismiss faith and rebut scepticism. Philosophy, in modernity, is doubt and nothing but doubt. There are modern philosophers who have not agreed: but they are usually errant figures – Heidegger, Jaspers and Arendt, say, or Barth, Brunner and Balthasar, or Chesterton, Weil and MacIntyre, or Nietzsche, Foucault and Rorty. Ever since Descartes, philosophers have been philosophers of doubt. Locke, Leibniz, Berkeley, Hume, Reid, Kant, Mill, Russell, Wittgenstein, Popper, and so on, all attempted to maintain the expectation that certainty of some sort could be established without collapsing into speechlessness (wonder), without falling back on religion (faith) and without admitting that any claim has as much truth as any other (scepticism). Most academic philosophers, especially in the twentieth century, have been philosophers of doubt. But Oakeshott was not.

Oakeshott was a philosopher of scepticism and faith. As we shall see, the scepticism was an axe that cut at the faith, until, by the end of his life, faith was cut down to the root.[2] So he was, above all, a sceptic. And this meant that he had no patience at all for epistemological questions, which come down to the question of whether we can know anything. (No philosopher of wonder, faith or scepticism would consider this an important question: the important question is what we know or do not know and what consequences this has for us.) After Descartes, philosophers supposed that certainty – that which could not be doubted – could only be found in a priori understanding or a posteriori experience. But when Berkeley and Hume doubted that our knowledge of the world a posteriori was certain, philosophy was left with what seemed a formidable difficulty. One way of avoiding it was to suggest, with Berkeley, that the existence of the world depends on God, but this was a capitulation to faith. Another way of avoiding it was to suggest, with Hume, that we could, despite scepticism, depend on probabilities and habits. Yet another way was to suggest, with Kant, that some third alternative to analytic a priori and synthetic a posteriori knowledge might give us certainty. Most philosophers since – including Russell and Popper – have hesitated between variants of Hume's and Kant's suggestions. But there was another possibility, which was that of Hegel: and this was to say, as Oakeshott said, that 'a priori and a posteriori are alike vicious abstractions' because 'it is impossible to think in advance of experience, and no experience is merely empirical'.[3]

Oakeshott took his conception of philosophy entirely from Hegel. 'Hegelian philosophy', scoffed Schelling, 'boasts of being a philosophy which presupposes nothing, absolutely nothing'.[4] This is a philosophy that has suffered the abuse of Schopenhauer, the mockery of Kierkegaard and the inversions of Marx. But, contrary to what is often thought, it is what Schelling said it was, an attempt to generate, for the first time, a philosophy without presuppositions – that is, a philosophy which was beyond scepticism because it began with a scepticism about all presuppositions.[5] Hegel thought that all earlier philosophers had mistakenly attempted to begin philosophy with certainty: some *logos* or *cogito* or *Grund* which, on consideration, was seen to be arbitrary – as arbitrary as the claim 'God exists'. Hegel thought that 'all presuppositions or assumptions' (*Voraussetzungen oder Vorurteile*) had to be abandoned. Philosophy, he wrote 'should be preceded by *universal doubt*, i.e. by total presuppositionlessness' (*die gänzliche Voraussetzungslösigkeit*).[6] What Hegel's critics found unacceptable about this conception of philosophy was not that it was presuppositionless, but that, despite this rather bleak beginning, it generated suppositions which seemed to resemble nothing so much as suppositions of faith. This was especially the case with the Absolute: which was, from one point of view, simply what was true, but, from another, seemed a vast objective summary soul, spirit or god. Controversy still reigns about this. Heidegger said, 'Hegel presupposes already at the beginning what he achieves at the end'.[7] Heidegger did not think this was a problem; but most other philosophers considered it was, because it blurred faith into scepticism. It was perhaps even more of a problem for Oakeshott, whose conception of philosophy, in its earlier form, presupposed its end in its beginning, yet, in its later form, presupposed only its beginning.

Hegel thought that Aristotle's logic was an imposition on the world from outside. 'Logic', he wrote, 'cannot *presuppose* any of these forms of reflection and laws of thinking, for these constitute part of its own content and have first to be established within the science.'[8] This meant that logic was, properly, onto-logic; and so the problem for philosophy was not epistemological but ontological: to explain how logic emerged from a unity of word and world, of experience and experienced, of understanding and understood.

Everything in Hegel's philosophy is the consequence of this. We need not agree with his dialectic of being, nothing and becoming, of logic, nature and spirit, of subjective, objective and absolute – that relentless thesis, antithesis, synthesis which for Hegel became what the iambic pentameter was for Shakespeare, a poetic structure he used with greater and greater mastery as he aged. It is not necessary for us to say that Hegel succeeded in writing a philosophy without presupposition; it is enough to say that he saw what was necessary if logic were to avoid arbitrariness.[9]

Oakeshott himself was indebted not only to Hegel's *Phenomenology of Spirit* but also to Bradley's *Appearance and Reality*.[10] The reason for this is that Bradley, in taking over Hegel's assumptions, had emphasized, in English manner, their scepticism. While Hegel perhaps incautiously had encouraged his critics to think that his philosophy was itself a recapitulation of all existence, Bradley more cautiously proposed that his was a mere sketch of it. His philosophy was not a 'system' but a 'sceptical study of first principles'.[11] But he agreed with Hegel that word and world could not be separated. 'Being and reality are ... one thing with sentience: they can neither be opposed and, nor even in the end, distinguished from it'.[12] Bradley called this unity what Hegel had called it – the Absolute – but he emphasized that it meant only 'experience where no contradiction can remain'.[13] 'Everything is experience' was the claim, and 'experience is one'.[14] Which explains why Copleston called Bradley's philosophy a 'mixture of scepticism and fideism'.[15] In Oakeshott's earliest writing, there was an even stronger emphasis on scepticism. Oakeshott did not refer to an Absolute at all. But he did, at first, use the term 'experience'.[16] And, as he perhaps realized later, this was still not as far as scepticism could go.

Oakeshott spoke successively of philosophy in three different ways. In the 1930s he referred to philosophy in terms of experience. It was

> experience without reservation or arrest, without presupposition or postulate, without limit or category; it is experience which is critical throughout and unencumbered with the extraneous purposes which introduce partiality and abstraction into experience. It is the attempt to realize the character of experience absolutely. And it is satisfied with nothing save an absolutely coherent and complete world of experience; it will accept only that which it cannot avoid without contradicting itself.[17]

In the 1950s, when he mentioned philosophy, which was not often, he referred to it in terms of conversation.

Philosophy, the impulse to study the quality and style of each voice, and to reflect upon the relationship of one voice to another, must be counted a parasitic activity; it springs from the conversation, because this is what the philosopher reflects upon, but it makes no specific contribution to it ... There is no body of philosophical 'knowledge' to become detached from the activity of philosophizing.[18]

And in the 1970s he referred to philosophy in terms of understanding. It was

an unconditional adventure in which every achievement of understanding is an invitation to investigate itself and where the reports a theorist makes to himself are interim triumphs of temerity over scruple. And for a theorist not to respond to this invitation cannot be on account of his never having received it. It does not reach him from afar and by special messenger; it is implicit in every engagement to understand and is delivered to him whenever he reflects. The irony of all theorizing is its propensity to generate, not an understanding, but a not-yet-understood.[19]

The differences between each conception of philosophy is the subject of the first three parts of this chapter. But it is important to recognize that his conception of philosophy did not change in two respects. Firstly, he always supposed that philosophy was thought without presupposition. And secondly, his writings indicate the continued ability of his conception or conceptions of philosophy to explain something about human experience, understanding or conduct in its entirety. Almost no other philosopher in the twentieth century – except perhaps Collingwood – found a way of using a conception of philosophy to say something of such relevance to the century. Oakeshott had an extremely original way of showing how a conception of thought without presupposition enables us to understand all other forms of thought. He had that rarest of theories: a theory of the significance of every element of human experience (art, religion, science, history, politics and philosophy) in relation to experience itself.

EXPERIENCE

The word 'experience' is associated with the Idealist conception of philosophy. If we assume, as many do, that the Idealist tradition is dead, then Oakeshott's Idealism can seem only the oddest of antiques. It is easy to forget, if we engage with the rather fragmentary traditions of contemporary academic philosophy, that almost every philosopher in the late nineteenth century was an Idealist.[20] The assumption of Idealism – that what can be known can only be known by us and therefore cannot be known as it is in itself – was taken to be fundamental by Berkeley, Kant and almost everyone afterwards; while the further assumption of Absolute Idealism – that what can be known can be known both by us and as it is in itself, for these cannot originally or eventually be distinguished – was taken to be fundamental by Hegel and everyone who followed him; which in England was Bradley, Green, Caird, Bosanquet and many others. But by the time Oakeshott came to write, it was rare for a philosopher to advocate an unambiguously Idealist philosophy.

The view one takes of modern philosophy comes down to the view one takes of the lineage that runs from Descartes through Berkeley to Kant and then either to Hegel or Schopenhauer.[21] If one goes beyond Hegel or Schopenhauer, then this history collapses; as it did for Kierkegaard and Nietzsche, whose importance in the history of philosophy is that they respectively articulated the consequences of venturing beyond Hegel's and Schopenhauer's philosophical Idealism – in the direction, significantly, in the first case, of a return to faith and, in the second case, of an advance to scepticism. Once the established tradition collapsed (by which I mean the conviction that the lineage embodied adequate developments of an argument), philosophers found that they had a new relation to the history of philosophy. Heidegger suggested philosophy should begin at the beginning, before Socrates; but most others settled for salvaging whatever could be salvaged from older philosophers. Interestingly, in the twentieth century this usually involved a return to Hume. To some extent modern philosophy still divides into those who think there is *something* in the Idealist lineage and those who ignore it on the ground that another lineage – which oscillates between realism and nominalism (oscillating partly because unwilling to discuss metaphysics) and which passes from Hume to Russell – despite all *its* difficulties, is far more important.

Although Oakeshott wrote after Moore and Russell, he thought there was something in the Idealist lineage, and this chapter will consider his successive attempts to restate it in such a way that even those of the other lineage would be unable to object to it.[22] In his first book, Oakeshott argued for an absolute conception of philosophy as thought without presupposition. This was taken, as we have seen, from Bradley, who, as much as Hegel, had insisted that philosophy should be not axiomatic but presuppositionless.

There is an idea [wrote Bradley] that we start, consciously or unconsciously, with certain axioms, and from these reason downwards. This idea to my mind is baseless. The method actually followed may be called in the main the procedure used by Hegel, that of a direct ideal experiment made on reality. What is assumed is that I have to satisfy my theoretical want, or, in other words, that I resolve to think. And it is assumed that, if my thought is satisfied with itself, I have, with this, truth and reality. But as to what will satisfy I have of course no knowledge in advance ...[23]

Philosophy was not, then, active but reactive; it took its content from 'experience'. If our experience rested on presuppositions about what the world was, then it was incomplete experience. This meant that there were, in effect, two sorts of truth. There was truth itself, absolute truth, which was, in Bradley's terms, 'the predication of such content as, when predicated, is harmonious, and removes inconsistency and with it unrest'.[24] Even if we could not achieve truth, and Bradley's scepticism made him reluctant to commit himself to the idea that we could, it existed nonetheless as the necessary postulate of complete experience. It followed, then, that there were the 'partial truths' found in incomplete experience. 'Every partial truth is but partly true,' declared Bradley, 'and its opposite also has the truth.'[25] Which, of course, was a classically sceptical utterance; with the ambiguity – which could also be classically sceptical – that there was a complete truth, of a different order to these incomplete truths, which might in principle not have an opposite.

In *Experience and its Modes,* Oakeshott attempted to make a definitive statement of the nature of philosophy understood as complete experience, or, in his own emphatic phrase, 'experience without presupposition, reservation, arrest or modification'.[26] This experience is not *our* experience, at least not in the first instance; it is 'not whatever I happen to think; it is what I am obliged to think'.[27] And what I am obliged to think is whatever is involved in all thought. Experience is one, it cannot be divided: there is nothing beyond it.[28] It is both 'experiencing' and 'what is experienced' together, for, these are, 'taken separately, meaningless abstractions'.[29] It *is* 'reality', and it *has* 'truth': where only 'coherence' (and not 'correspondence') can be an adequate 'criterion' of truth.[30] 'The only absolute in experience is a complete and unified world of ideas, and for experience to correspond with that is but to correspond with itself; and that is what I mean by coherence'.[31]

Oakeshott tended not to use the word 'absolute'. But even he sometimes had to use it to indicate that the categories of subjective and objective were derivative of something simpler.[32] He argued both that there is no objective world beyond experience and that experience cannot just be *my* subjective experience. 'To take my experience as merely mine is to take it as less than it is, and so as other than it is'.[33] This did not mean that subjectivity has no part to play in experience. Oakeshott repeated again and again that experience was absolute in the sense that when we experience the world we enhance its unity.[34]

What has to be noticed about this conception of experience is that it is beyond refutation: it is hard to see how, for instance, it could be shown to be incoherent, because its coherence is an inevitable consequence of its simplicity and its simplicity an inevitable consequence of the presupposition of all presuppositions, that philosophy be without presupposition. This conception is irrefutable because every attempt to refute it depends on presuppositions which themselves come from a limited, partial or arrested mode of thought. Indeed, everything, according to this view of experience, including one's own self, is an abstraction from the whole: so that *every particular can only be seen as particular* when seen in terms of one of the 'modes' or 'modifications' of experience by which complete experience is distorted and becomes incomplete experience.[35] Each mode is, by definition, 'defective' because it has abandoned the 'proper criterion of experience' through seeing the whole from a 'limited standpoint'.[36]

If the first concern of *Experience and its Modes* was to understand philosophy as complete experience, the second was to indicate how these 'modes' of incomplete experience should be understood.[37] McTaggart supposed that Hegel had wanted 'to establish the existence of a logical connection between the various categories which are involved in the constitution of experience'.[38] Hegel, like Kant and Aristotle, used 'categories' to mean the predicates of absolute experience, and Hegel, and Bradley after him, tended to write mostly about how these categories were manifest through all experience, culminating, in Hegel's case, in art, religion and philosophy. This was ambiguous because it saw every partial form of experience as part of absolute experience. Bradley had spoken explicitly of 'modes' or 'different regions of experience', which when compared to complete experience were 'found to be imperfect'.[39] But he wrote nothing systematic about them, and still supposed that they culminated in perfect experience. It was left to Collingwood and then Oakeshott to attempt to put these separate modes of experience into some order. Collingwood continued to write about them, in Hegelian manner, as if they were in some sense continuous. But Oakeshott wrote about them as if they were discontinuous.

Oakeshott considered three such incomplete forms of experience in his *Experience and its Modes*: history, science and practice, each with its own presuppositions about experience – and each, therefore, incomplete. The modes will be considered in more detail below. What is important here is that they were separate, they did not form a hierarchy or continuity, and they were not together exhaustive of experience. They were contingent rather than necessary, and there was no sense that there might not be others – indeed, later Oakeshott added another. And this is why his theory was not a system, but merely 'systematic as far as it goes'.[40] It could not be systematic because the whole was not the sum of its parts. Each mode, Oakeshott explained, is 'wholly and absolutely independent of any other; and ... each, in so far as it is coherent, is true for itself'.[41] Each has truths, but these truths are only the truths of an incomplete form of experience; and so none has absolute truth, which only exists in relation to the whole and is possible only for complete experience.[42] It followed that what is true in one form of experience, in terms of one set of presuppositions, is not true in another form of experience. So no truth can be carried from one mode to another without making a mistake.[43] This last doctrine is perhaps the one for which Oakeshott is most famous.

Oakeshott's conception of philosophy enabled him to be sceptical about the forms of incomplete experience, but only because he was not sceptical about the existence of complete experience. This was a certainty which critics of Idealism thought could only ever be a faith. According to Hegel, Bradley and Oakeshott, however, this certainty – that the world is a unity, and that it is no more and no less than experience – emerges from a sceptical conception of philosophy as thought without presupposition. Since this was not itself a presupposition but a lack of presupposition, it could not be destroyed by sceptical arguments. Hegel had followed the sceptics as far as saying that any attempt to define the One led one to a definition which also seemed to be a definition of Nothing, since it was a definition of the wholly indeterminate. But whereas a sceptic, or at least a modern sceptic, would take this to be the *reductio ad absurdum* of attempting to define the One, Hegel took it to be the first step of logic. It was, in Oakeshott's repeated phrase, what we are obliged to think. Our usual modes of thought may be arbitrary, but we can only know that they are arbitrary in relation to an absolute arbitrariness. And this is, I think, still an argument that can be made against any scepticism which is scepticism without faith – against, for instance, Oakeshott's later scepticism. A scepticism with faith postulates two sorts of truth: the truth of the complete and unconditioned, and the truths of the incomplete and conditioned. But a scepticism without faith postulates only one sort of truth: incomplete and unconditioned truths. It is not clear what to do with this form of scepticism. For even the most thorough sceptics in history – Buddhists and Pyrrhonists – have postulated some sort of unconditioned beyond what is conditioned: which can be experienced as *nirvana* or *ataraxia*. Bradley thought the need for an unconditioned was fundamental, and he laid it down as a challenge, saying that anyone who disputed any metaphysics, or disputed that metaphysics had any value, simply had yet another, perhaps unstated or unconscious, metaphysics.

There is no clear way of arguing one's way out of Oakeshott's paradoxical system. The only possibility is to step aside completely and say, as Baillie said, that 'a system of unrealities is not real because it is a system'.[44] And this is exactly what Oakeshott did in his subsequent writings. Earlier, in *Experience and its Modes*, philosophy was complete experience and so clearly higher, nobler, than any other form of experience – 'perhaps the only complete escape open to us'.[45] But later this was no longer the case. Oakeshott now claimed that philosophy was simply one form of conversation among others.

CONVERSATION

Conversation, unlike experience, is only words: it is not word and world together. To characterize philosophy as conversation rather than experience, as Oakeshott did in the 1950s, is thus to reduce its significance with some severity.

After *Experience and its Modes*, of course, Oakeshott was concerned with politics rather than with philosophy. His reputation now is as an unusual, but penetrating, political philosopher – perhaps the greatest of his century in English. He may have abandoned philosophy when contemporary philosophers adopted different methods – usually logical or linguistic, but always 'analytical' – for establishing the more minimal sorts of certainty or uncertainty they wanted to establish. Analysis laid emphasis on argument; on the steps of an argument, given certain presuppositions, rather than on the presuppositions themselves. It is not said often enough that philosophy became a bit boring. Only the achievements in the history of philosophy and in political philosophy indicate that philosophy in the twentieth century still occasionally had the same breadth as it had had in older centuries. Oakeshott certainly took no interest in philosophy as professional philosophers came to practise it. He may have considered it a waste of time to restate the position he had come to, especially since restatement would have required him to explain how his own position had changed.

Oakeshott wrote *nothing* about the apparent changes in his thought. Sometimes it is suggested that the change was a consequence of abandoning Hegel for Hobbes.[46] Oakeshott never said that he adopted Hobbes's ideas; but he must have been aware that they undoubtedly contradicted at least the manner in which he had expressed his own ideas. In *Experience and its Modes* he had identified philosophy and experience, while Hobbes, in *Leviathan* and elsewhere, had distinguished them.[47] Oakeshott's account of Hobbes's distinction could not have been clearer. Experience was a matter of images, whereas philosophy was a matter of words. Experience depends on sensation, recollection and imagination: especially on 'the ability to recall and turn over in the mind the decayed relics of past sensations'.[48] It works in images, which are always particular and never universal, and so cannot be doubted, as words can, because truth and falsity do not apply to them.[49]

Philosophy, on the other hand, is a consequence of reasoning made possible through the use of language. It imposes words on experience, introducing universals and enabling us to reason about causes and effects. For Hobbes, therefore, philosophy is 'about the name of things not the nature of things'.[50] It is, in Hobbes's words, 'conditional knowledge, or knowledge of the consequence of words'.[51]

Oakeshott called this 'at once a nominalist and a profoundly sceptical doctrine'.[52] According to Hobbes, philosophy was not complete experience, indeed, was not experience at all, but was simply knowledge of the words used about the images that make up experience. There is no reason to doubt that this became Oakeshott's view, although he never said as much. If we reconstruct what happened to the arguments of *Experience and its Modes* then we can see that what Oakeshott did in effect was to complete his scepticism by applying it to experience itself. It took Oakeshott back from Bradley to Berkeley. Bradley had assumed, as we saw, that philosophy was without presupposition, that whatever *is* has to be one, and that being and thought are therefore tied up together. The weakness of this form of Idealism is that it requires a surrogate for God. If experience is not simply subjective, that is, *our* experience, then it requires the positing of an entity which experiences whatever there is to be experienced. This was not the sort of philosophical argument that was likely to survive secularity.[53] In the twentieth century it was dismissed, as Schopenhauer dismissed it in the nineteenth century, with incomprehension and exasperation.[54] Barth once asked why Hegel had not 'become for the Protestant world something similar to what Thomas Aquinas was for Roman Catholicism'.[55] The answer is that Hegel had grafted a philosophy of faith on a root of scepticism. And the tree would not grow on the root.

It must be supposed that Oakeshott, at some stage in the 1930s or 1940s, completed his scepticism. But this came at the cost of abandoning his own metaphysical system: he never again wrote about complete experience. And there was a new levity, scorn and subtlety in his writing. This is particularly evident in an essay he wrote on conversation in the late 1940s. In this essay, Oakeshott characterized conversation as something carried out for its own sake. It is 'colloquial': admitting many styles; suited for 'minds disposed to intellectual adventure'; and never 'more than half serious'. It is not about winning arguments, but about pursuing one subject on to other subjects: it 'wanders'. It requires someone with 'an amused tolerance of himself; he will be sceptical about his own opinions; he will not take himself seriously; but he will be interested in what he finds himself to be'. Oakeshott suggested that it is not, perhaps, an activity suitable for a 'genius' – who will prefer a less dialectical form of expression. But most emphatically, as Oakeshott characterized it, and, indeed, as it is, it has no *telos*. It is a matter of 'choice and chance' – he likened it to a game of cards – and of 'ultimate inconsequence'.[56]

This essay itself would have been of little consequence had Oakeshott not, ten years later in 'The Voice of Poetry in the Conversation of Mankind', used conversation as the frame for explaining what he had formerly called the modes of experience. All the categories, now called the 'diverse idioms of utterance', including philosophy – although there was an ambiguity about this – were considered forms of conversation.[57] Whereas in *Experience and its Modes* he had begun with experience – what we are obliged to think – here he began with what *we* experience and what *we* think. So experience, now always the experience of a self, was spoken of as if it were experienced as conversation. Oakeshott supposed that a self is not an entity but an activity, an activity of imagining. When there is an encounter between a self and a not-self, there is a relation between this activity of imagining and images.[58] The term for the encounter between selves and images (which includes other selves) is 'conversation', and in any such encounter, or conversation, 'there is no "truth" to be discovered, no proposition to be proved, no conclusion sought'.[59] Oakeshott was somewhat reluctant to say that philosophy was a form of conversation. I have already quoted the comment that it is not strictly a form of conversation but is 'parasitic' upon it; 'it springs from the conversation, because this is what the philosopher reflects upon, but it makes no specific contribution to it'.[60] Yet there was ambiguity here, since he also commented that philosophy is eminently 'conversable' – as it undoubtedly is.[61] Perhaps Oakeshott was unsure of what to say about philosophy. But whereas formerly philosophy, as complete experience, had been the only complete escape, now each form of experience, including philosophy, reconfigured as a form of conversation, was said to be equally an 'emancipation' or 'escape' from the others.[62] Oakeshott could now say that the tendency in any conversation for a 'body of conclusions' or *dogmata* to emerge was a 'defect' in that conversation. He admitted that many would consider this opinion 'frivolous' and 'sceptical'. He then denied the frivolity but admitted the scepticism.[63]

Oakeshott never explicitly abandoned the arguments of *Experience and its Modes.* Instead he offered different arguments, or similar arguments in a different terminology. What was most significant was that the tension between a sceptical and a faithful orientation – the inclination to identify everything and nothing since everything was, in the absence of presuppositions, necessarily supposed to be identical with nothing – was resolved in a sceptical direction. The scepticism dissolved its own former reconciliations; the ladder was kicked away, and the absolute reconciliation of subjective and objective was lost almost without a word. There was no argument, but it is possible that arguments as such did not have so much to do with Idealism – or its 'refutation', for that matter.[64]

Oakeshott, although now fully sceptical, remained an Idealist. He never spoke of objects or realities; he always spoke of images. And, as we shall see, when he came to explain what philosophy was in his later writing, he still assumed that it was thought without presupposition.

UNDERSTANDING

If this were an Hegelian essay, it would suggest that Oakeshott's first statement was a thesis, the second statement an antithesis and the third a synthesis; for in Oakeshott's last reflection on philosophy, in *On Human Conduct*, there is a reconciliation of the first account of philosophy as complete experience, of word and world together, and the second account of philosophy as wholly separate from experience, of word separate from world. It was a partial reconciliation, clearly, but what Oakeshott held on to was, against Hobbes, that philosophy was in a sense an unconditional activity – because it was without presupposition.

Bradley said that philosophy was an 'experiment on reality'; and perhaps the vice of the Hegelian experiment was its virtue – its singularity. For Hegel had conducted the experiment of experiments on reality; and Bradley and the early Oakeshott had followed him in this. Then Oakeshott made a simple adjustment. Now, instead of one decisive experiment there were to be experiments as oft as ye shall make them. And, finally, in *On Human Conduct* he returned to an attempt at total statement. It was a work about what we now call politics, and what Oakeshott called 'civility', but Oakeshott always thought, as he had said about Hobbes, that every good political philosophy had a conception of philosophy running through it. So, something which is unknown in political philosophy since Sidgwick and Green, Oakeshott ran a conception of philosophy through his political philosophy. And *On Human Conduct*, as it stands, is perhaps the greatest modern statement of philosophy as an undogmatic *skepsis*.

Skepsis means 'inquiry'. In the *Outlines of Pyrrhonism*, Sextus Empiricus explained that scepticism was a matter of not only understanding but also living. Oakeshott, as we have seen, always spoke of philosophy as an escape, but did not suppose that the escape was any more true or real or ultimate than the ordinary activities which philosophy was an escape from. He was, in other words, sceptical even about the *ataraxia*, or tranquillity, which the ancient Sceptics thought followed from suspending belief. And he was also sceptical about Hume's epistemological scepticism. His view remained Hegelian in this sense: his scepticism was intended to enable us to say something about everything – but also to enable us to recognize the limits of what is said.

On Human Conduct considers philosophy in terms of understanding. Understanding is ubiquitous, since it accompanies all activity, but there is also a particular activity, which Oakeshott calls the 'engagement to understand', which has both unconditional and conditional forms. Any engagement to understand is a conscious attempt to make the world more intelligible, and this occurs through interrogation. There is some ambiguity in Oakeshott's argument here, however, which I think can be avoided if his account of understanding is stated in terms of a threefold distinction of conventional understanding, conditional understanding and unconditional understanding.[65]

Conventional understanding is part of all activity, and does not necessitate any particular engagement to understand; it is, simply, the natural accompaniment of all activity. Oakeshott claims that when we understand something conventionally, we see it not just as a particular, but in terms of what philosophers have called universals, that is, in terms of whatever 'characteristics' it has which can be distinguished from 'their contingent circumstances'. These characteristics are 'rudimentary ideal characters'; and Oakeshott was as convinced as Hegel was, that it is impossible to understand *anything* without abstracting from it, without discovering its ideal character, without generalizing it.[66] Every identity is continually 'related, correlated, juxtaposed, concatenated'; but conventional understanding 'excludes any interrogation which calls in question the conditional sufficiency of the identities themselves'. The result of such uninterrogative understanding is the 'satisfying and useful verdicts' of all human activity.[67] Oakeshott rightly, but perhaps at the cost of a certain ambiguity, considered this a form of conditional understanding, but he nonetheless distinguished it clearly from the form of conditional understanding that is part of the engagement to understand.

Conditional understanding is the relative activity associated with all particular forms of study (with the 'modes' of history, science and practice to be discussed below), that is, with any study of anything: a self, a state, a system, a species, a symbol, a set, a song and so on – in terms of what makes it what it is (i.e. in relation to what is universal about it). Oakeshott's concern in *On Human Conduct* is with this conditional understanding. It seeks to understand objects or events or identities not in terms of their characteristics – as conventional understanding does – but 'in terms of their postulates'.[68] Unlike conventional understanding, it explores the 'conditionality' of a something through interrogation. But, unlike unconditional understanding, it only takes interrogation so far. It is then arrested, because 'the unconditional engagement of understanding must be arrested and inquiry must remain focused upon a *this* if any identity is to become intelligible in terms of its postulates'.[69] And this is why Oakeshott says that all understandings are conditional. Whenever we attempt to understand something or anything – such as the conduct or civility Oakeshott himself attempts to understand in his book – we are committed to conditional understanding.

Unconditional understanding is the ultimate activity, the activity of understanding in its ideal form. If understanding is unconditional, it does not limit the understanding possible to an understanding of *this* but interrogates the identity of *this* to see *that* beyond it and interrogates *that* to see *yon* beyond it, and so on. Unconditional understanding, seen this way, could well end in the *Schweigen* of Wittgenstein, the *Verhaltenheit* of Heidegger, the *pistis* of Paul, the *ataraxia* of Sextus, the *epistemé* of Plato or the *thaumazein* of Socrates. But Oakeshott says *nothing* about where it might end; it is, for him, endless. The principle, he declares, is 'Never ask the end.'[70] The philosopher is engaged in an unconditional adventure in which every achievement of understanding is an invitation to investigate further and where any understandings achieved by the philosopher are merely 'interim triumphs of temerity over scruple'. This is *skepsis*, relentless interrogation: 'The irony of all theorizing is its propensity to generate, not an understanding, but a not-yet-understood'.[71] (An inelegant but necessary word. We still lack a word in English for something not yet understood.) This engagement is unconditional not because it has an unconditional *telos* but, on the contrary, because 'what constitutes its unconditionality is the continuous recognition of the conditionality of conditions'. It is 'perpetually *en voyage*'. And this endless unconditional activity is what Oakeshott means by philosophy.[72]

What Oakeshott shows us is that there are three stances we can adopt in understanding the world. Firstly, there is the stance of the philosopher, concerned with the adventure of endless understanding. Secondly, there is that of the theorist, who is committed to understanding *this* rather than *that*. He may be a scientist or an historian. And thirdly, there is that of the human, who can do no other than understand the world around him conventionally, since it is not only a condition of all activity that this is so, but also constitutive of what it is to be human that it is so. All of us are human; only some of us are theorists; and perhaps only one or two of us are philosophers. Or, to put it another way, and perhaps a better way: we are human at every moment, we are theorists at times, and we are philosophers only at certain rare times.[73]

Oakeshott does not say *anything* about what the philosopher can say, but it is likely that the philosopher can say only what is negative – like Pyrrho and Nagarjuna – allowing all positions to empty out into negations. But theorists are those who have achieved understandings of a *this* or *that*, and so, naturally, are most tempted to address humans as if their truths, derived from a conditional understanding, have some authority in the world of conventional understanding. Oakeshott declares bluntly that they have not. The theorist of conduct, he says, has a 'different concern' from 'those engaged in conduct', which is 'to investigate the conditions of their enterprises, not to engage in them'. Anyone who blurs these two activities together is not a 'theorist' but a 'theoretician', that is, a 'fraudulent tutor'.[74] This is the great negative doctrine of Oakeshott's writings: that we may say what we like, but we may not suppose that what we say has the consequences we hope it does.

Oakeshott's distinction of the categories of understanding is, as far as I know, wholly original. It is not objective but subjective. Popper, who sought 'objective knowledge', distinguished three worlds: a first world, of objects; a second world, of subjective experience; and a third world, of ideas. Like Frege, Popper ended making metaphysical claims his own philosophy could not warrant.[75] But Oakeshott, who supposes that only subjective knowledge is worth discussion, says nothing about objects or ideas: there is only what can be known by us, which is firstly what we understand about what we want; secondly what we understand about this and that; and thirdly what we understand about everything – where the last is not an understanding which can be achieved but is understanding as an endless activity. It is what we call philosophy.

CATEGORIES

It should be obvious that the changes in Oakeshott's conception of philosophy do not affect what he says about the modes or idioms – what I will call categories – in terms of their inner determination or in terms of their relation to each other. All it affects is the relative status of the categories of incomplete experience or conditional understanding to *complete* experience or *unconditional* understanding – that is, to philosophy. If philosophy is complete experience, then clearly incomplete experience is not only limited but in error; however, if philosophy is unconditional understanding, then conditional understanding is limited without being in error.

So, whether philosophy is complete experience or unconditional understanding does not affect the fact that it was always necessary for Oakeshott to ask what incomplete experience (or conditional understanding) is. Collingwood's *Speculum Mentis*, which was published in 1924, had already dealt with this question, and Oakeshott's *Experience and its Modes* was published in 1933.[76] It is perhaps worth commenting that these are two of the greatest theories of the categories of thought ever written, rivalling Bacon's *Instauration* and Hegel's *Encyclopaedia* in scale of conception. And yet they are usually ignored. Wittgenstein's *Tractatus* and Heidegger's *Being and Time* – usually taken to be the classics of the same era – are obscure, fragmentary and disappointing by comparison. Wittgenstein and Heidegger are still overrated; Collingwood and Oakeshott still underrated. Ayer dismissed Collingwood's philosophy as part of the 'debris of absolute idealism'.[77] But Ayer failed to see that it was only within the Idealist tradition that attention was paid not only to one's own philosophical activity – what one wants to think – but, as a consequence of the view that philosophy is thought without presupposition, to what one is obliged to think (as Oakeshott put it early on) or what it is possible in principle for anyone to think (as Oakeshott put it later on). One looks in vain to Wittgenstein or Heidegger, or any other modern philosopher for that matter, for a conception of human thought in its entirety.

For the sake of clarity, it is worth presenting the arrangement of the categories in *Speculum Mentis* and in Oakeshott's writings in a table. There is much that could be said about the categories. The major difference between Collingwood's arrangement and Oakeshott's is that Collingwood considered each form of thought to be inferior to its successor. As I have indicated in the table that follows, each flowed into the next until the argument reached a non sequitur with the failure of what seemed to be the most complete form of knowledge, history; at which point Collingwood had to state, without much argument, a case for saying that experience, in the end, was not of the world but of the experience of experiencing the world. That is, philosophy was the return of thought upon itself, mind in its own mirror, *speculum mentis* – 'the self-liberation of thought from uncriticized assumptions'.[78] The difficulty for Collingwood was that he ended his argument with a conception of philosophy that was meant to appear to be a result when it was clearly the conception – the Hegelian conception of presuppositionless thought – which had made his entire enquiry make sense from the beginning.

Table

Collingwood's *Speculum Mentis* (1924)	*Experience and its Modes* (1933)	'The Voice of Poetry in the Conversation of Mankind' (1959)	*On Human Conduct* (1975)
Master category: EXPERIENCE	Master category: EXPERIENCE	Master category: CONVERSATION	Master category: UNDERSTANDING
Starting point: the self	Starting point: the whole	Starting point: the self	Starting point: the whole
[Each category is an error which necessitates a more complete form of knowledge in its successor, so here there is a scale]	[Each category is discontinuous in relation to the others]	[Each category is discontinuous in relation to the others]	[Each category is discontinuous in relation to the others]
Five forms of experience:	Two levels of experience:	Four 'voices' or 'idioms' of conversation:	Three levels of understanding:
I. Question without answer i.e. ART	I. Complete experience, i.e. PHILOSOPHY	I. Considering images in themselves, i.e. POETRY	I. Unconditional Engagement to Understand, i.e. PHILOSOPHY
II. Question and unexplainable answer, i.e. RELIGION	II. Incomplete experience (the 'modes'):	II. Considering images for use, i.e. PRACTICE	II. Conditional Engagements to Understand:
	a. Experience *sub specie præteritorum*, i.e. HISTORY	III. Considering images independently of use	
	b. Experience *sub specie quantitates*, i.e. SCIENCE		

III. Question and explainable answer expressed in abstractions, i.e. SCIENCE	c. Experience *sub specie voluntatis*, i.e. PRACTICE	(hypothetically), i.e. SCIENCE	a. where what is understood is an exhibition of intelligence, i.e. HISTORY
	(POETRY: not discussed except in relation to practice)	IV. Considering images independently of use (actually), i.e. HISTORY	
IV. Question and explainable, concrete answer which is impossible, i.e. HISTORY		[non sequitur]	b. where what is understood is *not* an exhibition of intelligence, i.e. SCIENCE
[non sequitur]		V. PHILOSOPHY: not discussed (as it is 'parasitic') but mentioned as a form of conversation which considers the other forms of conversation	III. Conventional Understandings in relation to conduct, i.e. PRACTICE
V. The return of thought upon itself i.e. PHILOSOPHY			
			(POETRY: not discussed because it is not a form of understanding)

NB POETRY (or 'art) is only considered when Collingwood or Oakeshott begins with *our* experience as selves. RELIGION is distinguished by Collingwood, but always treated as a part of PRACTICE by Oakeshott: this in turn is never considered by Collingwood (who never distinguishes theory and practice).

In many respects their conceptions of the categories were similar. Collingwood derived his ordering of the categories from the 'natural order' of our lives (since we respond as children first to art, then religion, then thought) and from the history of humanity (where art emerged first, then religion, then science, and finally history only in the last few centuries).[79] What is interesting about Collingwood's characterization of each is that they are theorized in terms of question and answer. In short, summarizing the entire argument:

art is question without answer;

religion is question and answer, where the answer cannot be explained but only repeated;

science is question and answer, where the answer can be explained in other terms but is abstract, universal and does not deal with particulars; and

history is question and answer, where the answer is concrete and particular, but where the totality of answers about particulars can never be assembled.

Experience and its Modes differed from *Speculum Mentis* in two important ways. One was that it began with presuppositionless thought as its presupposition, which made it a simpler matter to show that all other thought was by definition, and through definition, incomplete. The other difference was that it stated emphatically that the categories were only errors in relation to philosophy, and not in relation to each other; but that, nonetheless, they were entirely separate forms of error. Each was treated as if it were constructed with a relative coherence, which, although defective when considered in terms of complete experience, meant that the truths of a form of incomplete experience were true only in terms of that incomplete experience. A truth derived from one category could not be transferred to another without what Oakeshott called 'irrelevance' or 'confusion' or *ignoratio elenchi*.[80] Even though Oakeshott had abandoned the conception of complete experience well before 1959, he continued to hold on to the view that the different forms of incomplete experience (or conditional understanding) were irreconcilable.

It should be clear from table that Oakeshott ordered the categories slightly differently in each incarnation of his argument. In *Experience and its Modes* history, science and practice were dealt with in their own terms. Each had its criterion of category. History was the experience *sub specie præteritorum*, the world seen under the category of the past.[81] Science was experience *sub specie quantitatis*, the world seen under the category of quantity.[82] Practice was experience *sub specie voluntatis*, the world under the category of change.[83] Each was incomplete experience for a different reason. History was incomplete because it is a contradictory form of experience: experience of the past that is also experience in the present of a past that cannot be known without the present.[84] Science was incomplete for the same reason Collingwood offered: because it is a contradictory form of experience that describes a world of events as if it is a world of instances. It ignores the fact that there is 'no valid inference from *some* to *all*' by offering a 'world of generalizations' as a surrogate for the 'real world'.[85] And practice was incomplete because it distinguishes two worlds, the world of what is and the world of what ought to be, which once distinguished can never be reconciled. 'Every achievement within the world of practice only reveals the incompleteness of that world: which is why the world of practice is a world of permanent dissatisfaction'.[86] In short, each mode seeks complete experience, but instead finds that experience is incomplete, because it offers not a world but two worlds that can never be reconciled. In history, experience is of the infinite contingent events of the past; in science, experience is of a nature rendered static in terms of hypotheses; and, in practice, experience is of a perpetual world of 'not yet'.

In 'The Voice of Poetry in the Conversation of Mankind' Oakeshott introduced a new category, poetry. This is the only change he ever admitted to making in his writings.[87] But it was not the only change, for he also framed the categories differently. They were no longer contrasted with complete experience, but compared to poetry itself, which was now considered the simplest form of experience. This poetry was what Collingwood called art and what we might call wonder: the simple experience of images in and for themselves. It is not a form of understanding at all – which is why Oakeshott never discussed it in *Experience and its Modes* (where experience and understanding were considered identical) or *On Human Conduct* (where understanding, distinguished from experience, was the subject). It is a form of complete experience, but experience without understanding, experience of images. In poetry, Oakeshott declared, there is no truth, no fact, no antecedent or consequent. 'Words are themselves images and not signs for other images'.[88] Poetry is, therefore, mere contemplation, and as an activity is only 'making images of a certain kind and moving about among them'.[89] This conception was certainly subversive of the conception of philosophy as experience, for now he said that this apparently complete form of experience was not philosophy but only poetry; which was, he said, 'all that can, in the end, survive of the Platonic conception of *theoria*'.[90]

In this essay there was an abstract ordering of the categories that had not existed in *Experience and its Modes*. Oakeshott repeated what he had said before: there was 'no fixed number' of categories, there was no 'hierarchical order' of them, and that they were not 'divergences from some ideal' but 'diverge only from one another'.[91] But writing of history, science and practice in terms of images, or conversation, had the consequence of introducing a categorical distinction between practice on the one hand and history and science on the other. Practice was now understood to be the *use* of images, and this now divided into two categories: the first was the category of 'desire and aversion', which is 'the world *sub specie voluntatis*' (a world of images of objects of desire and aversion); the second the category of 'approval and disapproval', which is 'the world *sub specie moris*' (a world of images recognized as other selves).[92] History and science remained more or less as they were, but they were now distinguished from practice on the grounds that while practice is the use of images for our purposes, science and history are attempts to understand images apart from any purposes we have.[93] This was a claim that was developed in the distinction in *On Human Conduct* between conditional and conventional understanding.

It should be clear that in *Experience and its Modes* each of the three categories Oakeshott discussed was incomplete because it could be shown to be incomplete even in terms of the criterion which establishes its world as a distinctive one. Interestingly, this would not have been so for poetry, since poetry, as far as it goes, is a form of experience which cannot recognize itself as incomplete – and this is where Collingwood's account is misleading in *Speculum Mentis*: a question without an answer is not a question, and so art could not make religion necessary unless religion were already necessary. A man who saw the world simply in terms of images would simply not recognize practice, history, science or philosophy as meaningful forms of experience. He would be, in Oakeshott's term, a truant: someone who thought that appearance simply was reality.[94] This is truancy because no one has ever supposed for very long that this is actually the case. Words are not just images, or not for long.

In Oakeshott's last statement of the relations of the categories in *On Human Conduct* philosophy was restored to its height as unconditional understanding, and poetry – which was not a form of understanding – was not discussed. What he had formerly called 'practice' was called 'conduct', and discussed at length, but always in such a way that the understanding appropriate to conduct, conventional understanding, was categorically distinguished from the conditional engagement to understand which was divided again into different 'idioms'. 'Every such idiom is an unambiguous system of theorems which has acquired (or which aspires to) the condition of a distinguishable "science"'.[95] His principle of division in *On Human Conduct* was external rather than internal to the idioms: here he only made a distinction between conditional understandings which understand identities as 'exhibitions of intelligence' and understandings which understand them otherwise in terms of natural causes.[96] The classic modern mistake, for Oakeshott, was a 'carelessness of categories' in which 'identities recognized as themselves exhibitions of intelligence' are 'reduced to the understanding of identities not so recognized'.[97]

Between *Experience and its Modes* and *On Human Conduct*, then, Oakeshott introduced an inner structure to his system. No longer was there a set of forms of incomplete experience that were equally arrested because incomplete; now, where everything was incomplete, there was a structure indicating the different sorts of understanding appropriate to whatever it is we want to do with images and identities.

Oakeshott saw as well as Collingwood did that in an obvious sense practical experience is prior to all others – but he thought it a mistake to assume that the practical world is the only real world. He acknowledged that the impulse to escape practical life is itself practical – that is, it seeks to change the world of what *is* to the world of what *ought to be* – but he insisted that it involves forms of experience, or conversation, or understanding which are wholly independent of practice.[98] There was no hierarchy; there were only forms of interrogation. But the ideal of interrogation was philosophy; which was an ideal for the philosopher who subjectively recognizes that when he understands a *this* or *that* his understanding is conditional. Oakeshott thought that this was an ideal of importance not only for philosophers, but for theorists and, indeed, for all of us.

PHILOSOPHER

Oakeshott never composed a complete system; and he never summarized the system in his thought. But it is evident that in his writings there are four different levels of experience or understanding. Since he himself theorized these in the 1950s in terms of an encounter between self and not-self, where a not-self was an 'image', we have:

1. an encounter where an image is what it appears to be,
2. an encounter where an image is understood to be what it is for our purposes,
3. an encounter where an image is what it is understood to be in relation to its postulates,
4. an encounter where an image is something which, when understood, reveals another image, which, when understood, reveals another image, *ad infinitum*.

The first is manifest as poetry, the second as practice, the third as the various sciences and the fourth as philosophy. These are distinguished – if we use Oakeshott's terminology of images – because the first involves nothing other than existing among images; the second involves using images; the third involves interrogating images; and the fourth involves the continued interrogation of images and the images behind images and so on endlessly. In his early philosophy all would have been forms of experience, where philosophy was complete experience, but in his later philosophy only poetry was experience as such; the others were forms of understanding. He did not say, as he could well have said, that this was a sort of circle; but there is no reason why philosophy, as the endless interrogation of images, could not in the end empty into the simple experience of images that is poetry, contemplation, *theoria*.

I happen to think that a finished Oakeshottian system of four categories does more to establish a clear understanding of the relation between different sorts of activity than any comparative system. But there remains a problem, which is whether the two major conceptions of philosophy he put forward – philosophy as complete experience and as unconditional understanding – are commensurable or not.

This is a very difficult question, and I do not have a clear answer to it. Certainly it is evident that Oakeshott abandoned in his later writings the monistic, apparently teleological metaphysics of Absolute Idealism. This meant, of course, a change in the status of philosophy, which, denied of its metaphysical *telos*, was no longer the highest form of experience, the only complete escape; it was now merely one escape among others. But it is also evident that he remained committed to the Hegelian assumption that philosophy was thought without presupposition and so, in some sense, prior to all other thought. And this is where a problem emerges. For it is possible that Oakeshott's later writings simply stated from the point of view of the thinker what was stated in the earlier writings from the point of view of thought itself. The later Oakeshott characterized philosophy as an endless activity – but so did the early Oakeshott, so did Bradley and so did Hegel.[99] The only difference is that the early Oakeshott postulated a limit to philosophy, which was called 'complete experience', whereas the later Oakeshott postulated no limit, no completion and no experience.

It is possible, then, that the only difference between the earlier and the later explanation of philosophy is that the earlier postulated *peirata* while the later postulated *apeiron*. But there is no difference between a bounded and unbounded world if there are limits to how far one can see; and if we suppose that Oakeshott, in his later writings, abandoned what-we-are-obliged-to-think for what-we-can-think, then this would explain why he abandoned the conception of philosophy of experience without abandoning its corollaries (that all other forms of understanding are separate and limited, that all major error is a consequence of mistaking a limited form of understanding for an unlimited one, and all minor error is mistaking a truth in one limited form of understanding for a truth in another limited form of understanding). Oakeshott's scepticism simply encouraged him to maintain a proper silence about anything ultimate.

The strength of this later conception of philosophy is that, because it is sceptical, it does not consider that anything – except perhaps totality itself – is beyond understanding, or, at least, beyond conversation. It does not attempt to find certainty in any this or that, and so attempts to establish how everything may relate to everything else. All understandings are conditional, and there is nothing under the sun that cannot be written about. This is why it does more to recognize all the categories of experience than any other modern rival. The *only* silence in the later Oakeshott is his silence about ontology.

But it is important to recognize that this silence leaves us with the riddle of any philosophy which completes itself by kicking away its own ladder. Eliot said of Bradley, 'His philosophy seems to give you everything that you ask, and yet to render it not worth wanting.'[100] Oakeshott's philosophy was always sceptical, but in its early Bradleyan form it had a metaphysics appropriate to scepticism, while in its late form it did not – or did not say it did. Scepticism, having established what it was *obliged* to think, denied the obligation to think it; for it was obvious that the truth that experience is one, which is obligatory, could then be opposed by an equal and opposite truth: that experience is not one. Thus did Oakeshott adjust, or appear to adjust, to the *Zeitgeist* which was, of course, relativistic, pluralistic, individualistic – and, above all, secular. The extent to which he recognized this is not at all clear. Oakeshott – unlike Wittgenstein or Heidegger – rarely, if ever, showed us the workings out of his ideas. He understood something, and then – with unparalleled elegance – reconstructed the steps backwards, as if ideally. So anything we say about what happened is mere supposition. All we know is that although he remained sceptical, his earlier philosophy resembled classical scepticism in postulating an unconditioned behind the conditioned; while the later philosophy resembled modern scepticism in postulating nothing other than its own activity.

Whether Oakeshott's later philosophy has to be understood in terms of his earlier philosophy is a question to which there is no certain answer. It is doubtless part of the secularizing of metaphysics, which has occurred over the last three centuries. God divided the world in two. The Absolute, which Kierkegaard called the 'invisible vanishing point' of the world, restored the unity of the world.[101] But, when the invisible vanishing point vanished, the world was no longer one, nor two, but many. Oakeshott's completed *skepsis* is the philosophy of this last stage. It is a masterpiece of sceptical lack of commitment, and is quite possibly the greatest philosophical system of the twentieth century. But in the end we have to ask ourselves whether this is enough, or whether some sort of *ataraxia* or *nirvana* or even *pistis* is necessary to complete the picture – whether we need an unconditioned behind the conditioned.[102] In which case, the problems of philosophy are far more the problems of the second century – the problems of Sextus and Tertullian – than we have yet to recognize.

NOTES

1 *HC*, p. 98.
2 For lengthy treatments of Oakeshott as philosopher see S. A. Gerencser, *The Skeptic's Oakeshott* (London: Macmillan, 2000); T. Nardin, *The Philosophy of Michael Oakeshott* (University Park: Pennsylvania State University Press, 2001); and E. Podoksik, *In Defence of Modernity: Vision and Philosophy in Michael Oakeshott* (Thorverton: Imprint Academic, 2003), pp. 35–125.
3 *EM*, p. 117.
4 F. W. J. Schelling, *On the History of Modern Philosophy*, trans. A. Bowie (Cambridge University Press, 1994), p. 148.
5 See the chapter on 'presuppositionless thinking' in S. Houlgate, *The Opening of Hegel's Logic: From Being to Infinity* (West Lafayette, IND: Purdue University Press, 2006), pp. 29–53. Westphal argues that Hegel's entire philosophy was a response to 'Skepticismus', about which he wrote in *c.* 1801, six years before he wrote the *Phenomenology*. See K. R. Westphal, *Hegel's Epistemological Realism: A Study of the Aim and Method of Hegel's Phenomenology of Spirit* (Dordrecht: Kluwer Academic, 1989), p. 11.
6 G. W. F. Hegel, *Encyclopaedia Logic*, 78, quoted in Houlgate, *Opening of Hegel's Logic*, p. 29.
7 M. Heidegger, *Hegel's Phenomenology of Spirit*, trans. P. Emad and K. Maly (Indianapolis: Indiana University Press, 1988), p. 30.
8 G. W. F. Hegel, *Science of Logic*, 1.35, quoted in Houlgate, *Opening of Hegel's Logic*, p. 31.
9 McTaggart suggested that there could be an Hegelian logic without being Hegel's logic: J. M. E. McTaggart, *A Commentary on Hegel's Logic* (Cambridge University Press, 1910), p. 311.
10 *EM*, pp. 6 and 8. Oakeshott, like many writers in the early twentieth century, did not cite authorities, on the grounds that there are no authorities in philosophy.

11 F. H. Bradley, *Appearance and Reality: A Metaphysical Essay* (London: George Allen & Unwin, 1925), p. xii.
12 *Ibid.*, p. 146.
13 *Ibid.*, p. 147.
14 *Ibid.*, p. 457.
15 Frederick Copleston, *A History of Philosophy*, vol. VIII, *Bentham to Russell* (London: Burns & Oates, 1966), p. 188.
16 Experience, of course, was an Hegelian word (*Erfahrung*). See *Phenomenology of Spirit*, 14, quoted in Westphal, *Hegel's Epistemological Realism*, p. 197. Indeed, it was Kantian. See H. J. Paton, *Kant's Metaphysics of Experience: A Commentary on the First Half of the Kritik der reinen Vernunft* (London: George Allen & Unwin, 1932).
17 *EM*, p. 347.
18 M. Oakeshott, 'The Voice of Poetry in the Conversation of Mankind', in *RP*, pp. 200–1.
19 *HC*, p. 11.
20 See D. C. Stove, *The Plato Cult and Other Philosophical Follies* (Oxford: Basil Blackwell, 1991), p. 97.
21 Schopenhauer saw this clearly. See his 'Sketch of a History of the Doctrine of the Ideal and Real', in *Parerga and Paralipomena: Short Philosophical Essays*, 2 vols., trans. E. F. J. Payne (Oxford: Clarendon Press, 1974), vol. I, pp. 1–28. See also Stove, *Plato Cult*, pp. 101–4, for the opposite judgement of exactly the same lineage.
22 Hegel's philosophy was itself an attempt to do this, since Absolute Idealism was in a sense an attempt to reconcile Idealism and Realism. See Westphal, *Hegel's Epistemological Realism*.
23 F. H. Bradley, *Essays on Truth and Reality* (Oxford: Clarendon Press, 1914), p. 311.
24 Bradley, *Appearance and Reality*, p. 165.
25 Bradley, *Essays on Truth and Reality*, p. 232.
26 *EM*, p. 2
27 *EM*, p. 59, repeated for history, p. 110.
28 'Pluralism or dualism ... are characteristic of any world when insufficiently known', *EM*, p. 33; 'Any thinker who demands a reality beyond experience is certain of disappointment', *EM*, p. 54.
29 *EM*, p. 9.
30 *EM*, p. 35.
31 *EM*, p. 40.
32 *EM*, p. 47.
33 *EM*, p. 68; cf. p. 196.
34 *EM*, p. 31.
35 *EM*, p. 85.

36 *EM*, p. 71.
37 *EM*, p. 4.
38 J. M. E. McTaggart, *Studies in the Hegelian Dialectic* (Cambridge University Press, 1896), p. 1.
39 Bradley, *Appearance and Reality*, pp. 457–8, 466.
40 Not a system, *EM*, p. 3; but systematic, p. 8.
41 *EM*, p. 75.
42 *EM*, p. 77.
43 *EM*, p. 76.
44 J. B. Baillie, *The Origin and Significance of Hegel's Logic: A General Introduction to Hegel's System* (London: Macmillan, 1901), p. 345.
45 *EM*, p. 3.
46 Gerencser's *Skeptic's Oakeshott* maintains that Oakeshott was originally Hegelian but became increasingly Hobbesian as his attention turned from philosophical to political concerns. For one consequence, see James Alexander, 'Oakeshott on Hegel's "Injudicious" Use of the Word "State"', *History of Political Thought*, 32 (2011), 147–76.
47 Oakeshott discusses Hobbes's philosophy in his 'Introduction' to T. Hobbes, *Leviathan* (Oxford: Basil Blackwell, 1946), pp. xviii–xxvii.
48 *Ibid.*, p. xxiii.
49 *Ibid.*, p. xxiv.
50 *Ibid.*, p. xxvi.
51 Hobbes, *Leviathan*, p. 40.
52 Oakeshott, 'Introduction', p. xxv.
53 The success of Idealism in offering philosophers the consolations of religion is part of Stove's criticism of it in 'Idealism: A Victorian Horror Story', *Plato Cult*, pp. 83–177.
54 Schopenhauer's abuse of Hegel is strewn throughout his works. His own philosophy had some difficulties, which, ironically, at least according to Nietzsche, would have required some sort of Hegelian correction. See F. Nietzsche, *Writings from the Early Notebooks*, ed. R. Geuss and A. Nehemas (Cambridge University Press, 2009), p. 7.
55 K. Barth, *Protestant Theology in the Nineteenth Century: Its Background and History* (London: SCM Press, 1972), p. 384.
56 M. Oakeshott, 'The Voice of Conversation in the Education of Mankind' (*c*. 1948), in *WH*, pp. 187–99, esp. 187, 189, 190, 191, 193, 198.
57 Oakeshott, 'Voice of Poetry', p. 198.
58 *Ibid.*, pp. 204–5.
59 *Ibid.*, p. 198.
60 *Ibid.*, pp. 200–1.
61 *Ibid.*, p. 200.
62 *Ibid.*, pp. 241–2.

63 *Ibid.*, p. 204.

64 See Stove, *Plato Cult*, pp. 114–18.

65 There is possible confusion because he distinguishes 'unconditional' from 'conditional' understanding, and then, without emphasis, distinguishes several 'platforms' of conditional understanding. I think that Oakeshott's line of thought can be better understood if we distinguish 'conventional' understanding (not part of an 'engagement to understand') from 'conditional' understanding (part of an 'engagement to understand'). Oakeshott's terminology is sometimes ambiguous because, for him, conventional understanding is a form, the simplest form, of conditional understanding.

66 *HC*, p. 4.

67 *HC*, p. 7.

68 *HC*, pp. 8–9.

69 *HC*, p. 11. For other uses of the familiar word 'arrest', see pp. 18–19.

70 *HC*, p. 2.

71 *HC*, p. 10.

72 *HC*, p. 11. He did not himself call it 'philosophy' in *On Human Conduct* – one of the most terminologically cautious books of all time – in order to avoid dragging in what he would have considered were unhelpful associations; but on p. 11 he identifies this form of understanding as the engagement of a 'philosopher'.

73 Again, this may *end* in contemplation (for Oakeshott 'poetry' and actually a form of what I call 'wonder'), but since contemplation is not a form of understanding it is not discussed in *On Human Conduct*. Compare E. Podoksik, 'The Voice of Poetry in the Thought of Michael Oakeshott', *Journal of the History of Ideas*, 63 (2002), 717–33.

74 *HC*, p. 26.

75 See Karl Popper, *Objective Knowledge: An Evolutionary Approach* (Oxford: Clarendon Press, 1972), pp. 73–4.

76 It has been said that Oakeshott did not read *Speculum Mentis* until after writing *Experience and its Modes*. See P. Franco, *Michael Oakeshott: An Introduction* (New Haven, CT: Yale University Press, 2004), p. 45. This seems highly unlikely. Oakeshott often used Collingwood's ideas without attribution. Compare Oakeshott's introduction to Hobbes, *Leviathan*, esp. pp xii and xxi, to R. G. Collingwood, *The Idea of Nature* (Oxford University Press, 1945), pp. 8–9. Oakeshott's claims about the three great traditions of political philosophy make almost no sense until one reads Collingwood.

77 A. J. Ayer, *Philosophy in the Twentieth Century* (London: Weidenfeld & Nicolson, 1982), p. 193.

78 R. G. Collingwood, *Speculum Mentis* (Oxford: Clarendon Press, 1924), p. 247.

79 *Ibid.*, pp. 50–3.
80 *EM*, p. 5.
81 *EM*, p. 118.
82 *EM*, p. 195.
83 *EM*, p. 273. 'Change' meant *both* the 'production' of and the 'prevention' of change, *EM*, p. 256.
84 See *EM*, pp. 105, 107, 111.
85 *EM*, pp. 205, 214, 215.
86 *EM*, pp. 257, 263, 304.
87 For the change see *EM*, p. 297 and *RP*, p. vii.
88 Oakeshott, 'Voice of Poetry', p. 235.
89 *Ibid.*, pp. 216–17.
90 *Ibid.*, p. 220.
91 *Ibid.*, pp. 200, 201, 206.
92 *Ibid.*, pp. 206–8. The distinction was not put like this in *Experience and its Modes*, but it was implicit. See esp. *EM*, pp. 278–80. The distinction was repeated in *On Human Conduct* in the discussion of morality as practices. See *HC*, pp. 62–8. Note: it is perhaps necessary to say that I use 'categorical' here as the appropriate adjective for 'category' in English. Oakeshott's 'categorial', e.g. in *HC*, pp. 12–14, is a late and an unnecessary refinement.
93 See Oakeshott, 'Voice of Poetry', pp. 215–16, and his 'The Activity of Being an Historian', in *RP*, pp. 137–67.
94 Oakeshott, 'Voice of Poetry', p. 247.
95 *HC*, p. 17.
96 *HC*, p. 13.
97 *HC*, p. 15. See the comments on 'psychology' and 'sociology', which he saw in part as 'a muddle', 'rubbish', 'a masquerade of categories'. See *HC*, p. 21–5.
98 *EM*, p. 297.
99 Indeed, Oakeshott's characterization of philosophy in *EM*, p. 347, as 'critical throughout' shows it is, in the abstract, identical to the characterization of philosophy in *On Human Conduct*.
100 T. S. Eliot, in 1924, quoted in L. Gordon, *Eliot's Early Years* (Oxford University Press, 1977), p. 54.
101 See S. Kierkegaard, *Fear and Trembling* (Cambridge University Press, 2006), Problem II, p. 59.
102 For philosophers who have raised effective questions about this sort of scepticism see the anti-Platonic arguments of D. C. Stove in *The Plato Cult* and the Platonic arguments of S. R. L. Clark in *God's World and the Great Awakening* (Oxford: Clarendon Press, 1991), pp. 1–30.

LUKE O'SULLIVAN

2 Worlds of experience: history

INTRODUCTION: THE LEGITIMACY OF HISTORY

Oakeshott once said he was 'more grateful for having been brought up to read history than for almost anything else'.[1] But he was always more interested in the philosophical problems raised by historical knowledge than in practising the historian's craft. One such problem was the need, as the French historian Marc Bloch put it, for history to 'prove its legitimacy as a form of knowledge'.[2] Assuming this sceptical challenge could be answered, what were the conditions of historical knowledge, and how did it resemble, and differ from, other forms of knowledge like science and common sense? Oakeshott's contribution was to establish philosophically that history really was an autonomous, distinctive and irreplaceable form of thinking about the past.

The most important sources for Oakeshott's philosophy of history are his first and last books, *Experience and its Modes* and *On History and Other Essays*; the essay 'On the Activity of Being an Historian' in *Rationalism in Politics*; and the first essay in *On Human Conduct*, 'On the Theoretical Understanding of Human Conduct', which identified history as *the* theoretical means of understanding human action. All these writings consistently rejected scepticism about historical knowledge and insisted that historical understanding was a unique and autonomous type of intellectual inquiry. They differed, however, in their accounts of the precise conditions or categories presupposed by historical thought, and of how history was related to other kinds of knowledge.

Readers of Oakeshott's early work in particular sometimes concluded that he himself was an historical sceptic. Gertrude Himmelfarb called *Experience and its Modes* 'an invitation to historical nihilism'.[3] The book caused J. W. Meiland to believe that Oakeshott thought historical knowledge 'impossible'.[4] In contrast, R. G. Collingwood, the writer on the problem of historical knowledge with whom Oakeshott is most often compared, saw no such sceptical entailments, and pronounced his treatment of the subject 'masterly'.[5] There are two reasons for this discrepancy.

The first is that the young Oakeshott espoused a Rationalist and Absolute Idealist philosophy, leading him to argue that genuine knowledge could only take the form of a complete rational definition of a concept.[6] He remained sufficiently committed to this view in the early 1930s for *Experience and its Modes* to argue that all the modes of experience, including history, were relatively inferior to philosophy: history was 'abstract and defective' when 'regarded from the standpoint of the totality of experience'.[7] There was thus a tension in Oakeshott's early philosophy between his desire to identify a 'system of postulates' or 'structural presuppositions' for historical explanation, and his inherited metaphysical position.[8]

The second reason is that even when Oakeshott ceased criticizing history for nothing worse than not being philosophy, he still held that all knowledge, historical or otherwise, depended on certain postulates or presuppositions. These logical presuppositions made it possible to tell one form of thought from another; to tell science apart from common sense, or history from philosophy. The exploration of these presuppositions, or in the technical language of *On Human Conduct* and *On History*, 'categories', already governed his approach to the philosophy of history in *Experience and its Modes*, and it was sufficient to confuse and mislead anyone who did not share his view that all knowledge necessarily rested on 'categorial' foundations.[9]

Critics thus failed to appreciate that Oakeshott was trying to occupy the middle ground between two extremes in the debate over historical knowledge. At one end lies the naive view of historical knowledge as unproblematic direct and immediate knowledge of the past. At the other is the sceptical view that genuine knowledge of past reality is impossible in principle. Oakeshott, by admitting that the past is not directly accessible (so that the first view cannot be right) but denying that this lack of immediate access to the past posed an insuperable problem (thus rejecting the second view), charts a course between these two poles.

THE HISTORICAL AND PRACTICAL PASTS

The exact nature of the past as a mode of time was a subject on which Oakeshott became increasingly agnostic; *On History* sometimes dropped the article altogether, writing simply of 'past' rather than *the* past.[10] There were different ways of conceiving pastness, each identifiable from its own distinctive assumptions. But even if we are going to insist that history treats the past as 'real' (as Oakeshott did in *Experience and its Modes*),[11] there was no disputing the fact that we have no direct access to it. Historical knowledge of past events therefore had to be indirect, or mediated, in order to be possible at all.

Moreover, historical knowledge had to be mediated in a particular way. While all relationships to pastness entailed certain conditions, the philosopher of history sought to identify those peculiar to the discipline. Oakeshott went about this by contrasting the historical perspective on the past with the attitude to the past characteristic of what *Experience and its Modes* called the 'practical mode'. For this practical perspective, adopted by daily life and common sense, the past is significant only in relation to our present actions and future plans.

On History distinguishes various ways in which this is so. There is, for example, a 'residual' past manifested in our current embodiment; the former ballet dancer now has pains in her ankles. There is a 'remembered' past which is essential to my identity and personality; if deprived of my memories, I will not know who I am or what to do next. And there is a 'recollected' past, which we may use as a source of advice or examples; last time these stocks declined in value they recovered quickly, so perhaps I should buy more now.[12]

For society, the practical past may take mythical, religious, folkloric or nationalistic forms. It is sometimes said that modernity is a peculiarly 'historical' era, but insofar as it is true that contemporary society is 'dominated' by history, we must be clear that for Oakeshott it is not history in the disciplinary sense that is meant. The reflexive self-consciousness about the past characteristic of modernity, its 'historicism', was for Oakeshott simply another form of the practical past which treats history as a 'living' past significant only in relation to the present and the future. Historicity is not identical with authentically historical understanding.

Although Oakeshott believed that 'each man is his own self-enacted "history"',[13] it did not follow from this conception of the historic nature of personal and cultural identity that we are all our own historians in the theoretical, technical sense. Historical discourse is sometimes presented by so-called 'post-modern' writers as no different in kind to other forms of discourse about the past,[14] but for Oakeshott this represents a failure to observe the qualitative distinction between historical understanding and the practical view of the past.

Though the practical past varies endlessly in content, formally it always consists of a 'vocabulary of symbolic characters' that 'contains emblems of ... virtues, vices and predicaments'. Its utility rests on the assumption that it is unproblematic, even if the meaning of a symbol diverges greatly from the historical understanding of events. So, for example, in England, King Canute has become a symbol of futility, even though his turning back of the waves was intended to demonstrate to his unctuous advisers the limits of royal power. Conversely, this didactic past may be unable to accommodate certain survivals, so that 'The removal ... of Trotsky from the official Bolshevik emblematic past ... was part of an undertaking to construct a symbolic vocabulary of practical discourse which would not prejudice an approved practical present'.[15]

Oakeshott did not mean to deprecate the practical past; quite the opposite. It was 'an indispensable ingredient of an articulate civilized life'.[16] Nor did he deny that past events viewed practically could be objects of complex scrutiny. In a legal context, for example, considerable research may be necessary to establish a property right. But the kinds of questions that historians would ask, about the author of the title deed, about the social and intellectual and economic contexts of its creation, about its relationship to other documents of its kind, and so forth, would always be subordinate to the aim of proving or disproving its authenticity.

For history, in contrast, the past is problematic simply as such, and the fake document is every bit as interesting as the real thing. The historian's interest is in understanding the events that gave rise to it, and the only future goal it serves is that of resolving some historical problem or other. Of course, in reality, the problem is never that of explaining the existence of a single piece of evidence, such as a legal document, in isolation. *On History* presents an ideal model in which the distinctively historical view of the past has its logical beginning, not in memory or recollection, but in a present understood as composed entirely as evidence.

CATEGORIES OF HISTORICAL THOUGHT

Like Goldstein, who arrived at a similar view via the Anglo-American tradition of analytical philosophy, Oakeshott emphasized that to see something as historical evidence is already an intellectual achievement, declaring the historical present 'the most sophisticated of all presents, difficult to achieve and difficult to sustain'.[17] Every object, for the historical gaze, is surviving evidence of past happenings, and as such, no piece of evidence stands on its own. Something recognized as 'a Roman coin' is a testament to the previous existence of an entire economy, indeed, an entire civilization.

If 'evidence' is one category of historical thought, the notion of a 'situation' is another. The coin, or the picture, or the book, comes into existence at a specific time and place; it forms part of a snapshot that reveals what the society we are studying was like at that moment. Oakeshott's philosophy of history is thus a form of contextualism in which all objects of historical knowledge acquire their identities in relation to other such objects. This was already implicit in the concept of a 'world' of experience in *Experience and its Modes*, which argued that no experience exists in isolation from other experiences: 'the given in experience is always ... a complex, integral whole or system'.[18]

The problem with the use of the category of a 'situation' to characterize the system of relationships in which all pieces of historical evidence are enmeshed is that it is static, whereas the past is dynamic. Historical works have certainly been written, as Oakeshott recognized, that use the device of a particular 'slice' of time. One might concentrate, for example, only on the year 1492, comparing the state of the European and the American continents from a synchronous perspective. But this point of view was an unstable one; what happened in 1492 was the outcome of many earlier happenings, some of which had their roots in things that took place many centuries before.

We require, then, some further categories, including the notion of an 'event', and, implicit in it, the idea of 'change'. Historical events, for Oakeshott, are understood as outcomes, products of a confluence of other events. In history we understand why something happened as it did by relating it to a series of preceding events. If this sounds obvious, it is worth pointing out that it contrasts with the practical view, which understands the past in terms of its significance for our own present or future. The historical past, however, is understood in terms of its own past. We grasp the French Revolution historically by understanding it as a result: the result of contingencies such as military defeat in the Americas, crushing national debt and bad harvests, Louis XVI's intransigence over constitutional reform, and so forth.

In other words, we do *not* form an historical understanding of why the French Revolution came about in terms of the events that succeeded it, that is, in terms of the elapsed time between it and ourselves. So, while the French Revolution continues to have an impact on us today, apprehending its significance and relevance for ourselves is not the same as understanding it historically. This is not to say that significance and relevance are exclusively practical criteria; if we ask about the significance or relevance for nineteenth-century Europe of the French Revolution, we may still be asking an authentically historical question (though we would then be asking it about the nineteenth century, and not the Revolution, of course). The real question is whether or not the understanding of the past is subordinated to present ends.

Oakeshott's conception of historical events also requires the category of 'change', because an historical event is a difference. Something is an event for historical understanding if, without it, things would not have turned out as they did. But this is clearly a judgement, and recalls the constructed nature of Oakeshott's historical events. While he never doubted that history was about 'facts',[19] he saw facts as the conditional outcomes of processes of historical reasoning. Meiland's label of 'constructionism' for Oakeshott's theory is apt, even if it does not have the sceptical consequences Meiland imputed to it. As Nardin observes, 'the entities of history, on this difficult theory, have become as elusive as the particles of the nuclear physicist. A historical identity, properly understood, is nothing other than its own circumstantial coherence understood as a contiguity of discernible differences'.[20]

The crucial thing to comprehend is that historical events, on this view, are not 'there' in advance. They are not, as Oakeshott put it, like pieces of a jigsaw puzzle that have a predetermined arrangement simply waiting to be discovered. 'What an historian ... composes is something more like a tune ... than a neatly fitted together, solid structure'.[21] At first sight, this does, indeed, sound like a sceptical view; but Oakeshott's point is that there can be no other possible basis for historical knowledge.

The naive view of historical knowledge holds that the criterion of the adequacy of an historical account is its resemblance to the events themselves. We compare the account to the events as we might compare a model to a technical drawing. But the problem is that whether or not 'the events themselves' continue somehow to exist in past time, they are utterly inaccessible. Even the existence in the modern era of photographic or video images does not alter this problem.

Visual media only capture particles of light and waves of sound; they certainly do not simply 'show us how it was'. As historical evidence, they need just as much, if not more, interpretation as the pottery shard or the papyrus fragment. Ironically, the insistence that only such a correspondence between the historical account and the event can validate historical knowledge itself becomes the unstated ground of much historical scepticism, because the belief that it is impossible to confirm whether or not the account does in fact match the event is often implicitly taken to render historical knowledge impossible.

Note that this is not a problem of historical *method*. It is a mistake to think Oakeshott was telling historians how to write history.[22] In fact, he regarded historical method as entirely dictated by the subject matter. Indeed, there was no such thing as *the* historical method; one might need numismatics, statistics, palaeography or any number of other techniques to carry out historical research. The problem that concerned him was not 'methodological' but philosophical, and is as follows: given that we can recognize a certain type of thinking as historical, what are the conditions that allow us to do so? But as he was fond of pointing out, historians do not need to wrestle with such questions in order to write good history. The conditions of historical thought do not need to be explicit in order to be observed.

HISTORY AND SCIENCE

This investigation of the conditions of the possibility of historical knowledge belongs ultimately to German Neo-Kantian thought.

The modern effort to explore the philosophical problems raised by historical knowledge had few precedents in nineteenth-century England; Oakeshott correctly identified F. H. Bradley's essay on 'The Presuppositions of Critical History' as the only effort by a writer to examine this problem in the later Victorian era.[23] In that period it was German authors, in particular Droysen, Windelband, Simmel, Rickert and Dilthey, who pushed the subject on to the philosophical agenda.[24]

These Neo-Kantians argued that the account of the conditions of the possibility of knowledge in Kant's *Critique of Pure Reason* was sound in claiming that all knowledge rested on certain fundamental categories. However, Kant's division of experience into distinct realms of phenomenal necessity and noumenal rationality needed modification if it was to accommodate Dilthey's desire for a 'critique of historical reason'. In particular, the idea that the phenomenal realm was exclusively the preserve of natural science needed reconceptualizing. Windelband, for example, proposed a distinction between 'nomothetic' natural science and 'idiographic' historical science, arguing that 'One kind of science is an enquiry into general laws. The other kind of science is an enquiry into specific historical facts'.[25]

This became broadly Oakeshott's own position. Scientific explanation involved identifying some lawlike relationship between types of events. Whether this relationship was conceived mechanistically or probabilistically, what was being related were not individual events but types of events, and the connection between them was a lawlike relationship ideally expressible in exclusively formal, quantitative terms. While this form of explanation was perfectly valid in its own terms, Oakeshott argued consistently that it could not provide a model for historical understanding.

Thus, while one could still talk about the 'explanation' of a 'cause' as a presupposition of historical thought, as Oakeshott did in *Experience and its Modes*,[26] such talk simply did not mean the same thing as it did in science. History invokes specific circumstantial reasons rather than generic physical factors as 'causes', and these reasons are ultimately themselves events, related to each other not in terms of external laws but only by other events, each of which is as unique as they themselves are. The French Revolution is not an instance of a type ('revolution'), but an absolutely individual, unrepeatable, phenomenon.

Here, Oakeshott had philosophers of science such as Carl Hempel in mind. Hempel had argued that all historical explanation involved demonstrating that given an event of a certain type, another event of a certain class could also be expected to have occurred. As physical science increasingly moved away from deterministic causation, Hempel adopted a more probabilistic view, according to which history aimed to show, not that given certain causes a certain kind of event must have occurred, but only that a quantitative value could be assigned to the probability of a certain kind of event having occurred.[27] But from either point of view history becomes a sort of retrospective prediction.

Oakeshott saw this account of historical causation as completely question-begging.[28] Imagine, he argued, that we took this view literally in relation to, for example, a piece of legislation. To 'explain' this statute historically, we would, according to Hempel, be able to entirely ignore what the statute is about, or how the problem to which it is a response arose. We would treat it as simply a member of the class of all statutes, and since all statutory enactments are preceded by other kinds of events such as parliamentary debates, multiple readings of the proposed legislation, votes and so on, we would then deduce that these kinds of events were also the causal conditions of this particular statute. We would not, at any point, have to look at what was said in the debates, or who voted for or against the legislation, or why. His scornful conclusion was that 'neither in the procedure it follows nor the conclusions it seeks is [Hempel's account] recognizable as even a parody of historical enquiry and understanding'.[29]

Oakeshott did acknowledge that social sciences such as sociology or economics could approach events as instances of types and formulate generalizations about them, but the social sciences ultimately remained more akin to history than to natural science. *On Human Conduct* insisted on a fundamental distinction between the scientific understanding of events as the outcomes of processes, on the one hand, and the historical perspective in which events were the results of the interactions of intelligent agents, on the other. Phenomena such as 'a rock formation, a wave breaking on the shore, a thunderstorm, a butterfly on the wing, the facial resemblances of children and parents, a chameleon changing colour, melting ice, etc.' belong to the category of casual processes in which intelligence plays no role.

They are an essentially different class of phenomena to those to which a symbol, or a work of art, or a religious ritual, belong.[30]

HISTORY AS THE SCIENCE OF CONTINGENCY

Phenomena of this latter kind are 'expressions of reflective intelligence'. This emphasis on intelligent agency as a postulate of historical thought is not meant to imply that historical events are to be understood as intentional outcomes. Indeed, it is crucial to Oakeshott's understanding of history that it offers an understanding of events unavailable *in principle* to any of the actors involved. This, incidentally, is a major difference between his philosophy of history and Collingwood's. Collingwood favoured the idea, also found in Dilthey, that the goal of historical understanding was the re-enactment of the subjectivity of historical actors, 'the present revival and reliving of past experiences'.[31]

For Oakeshott, in contrast, the recovery of the thoughts and intentions of past actors, insofar as it was possible at all, was at best a stage on the way to constructing whatever series of events the historian wished to understand. At worst, it implied a reopening of the possibility of historical scepticism, because successful re-enactment was impossible to verify against the original experiences themselves. In his view it was impossible to be at one and the same time an actor in events and have an historical understanding of them.

This notion of historical understanding is reminiscent of the Hegelian owl of Minerva; it is precisely because historical theorizing is exclusively retrospective and non-participatory that it can assemble an understanding of a past event that transcends the standpoint of anyone who figured in it. Historical thought is not subject to the spatio-temporal limitations of the particular historical actor, but the price we pay for the wisdom of this kind of hindsight is an appreciation of the past that is inherently inapplicable to our own practical ends. Paradoxically, 'history' in this sense is something that no one could ever possibly have taken part in, and that can only be 'made' by historians.

Since for Oakeshott the relationship between historical events was not constituted by the experiences of past actors, but by other events, he needed an account of the nature of this relationship. This he found in the concept of 'contingency', another fundamental category of historical understanding in his later work. In *Experience and its Modes* he treated it simply as a synonym for 'accident', and argued that the idea of an accident belonged to the vocabulary of the practical mode. 'The hard winter of 1812 which ruined Napoleon's expedition to Russia, the storm which dispersed the Armada ... from the standpoint of the participants, were distressing mischances ... But the attitude of the historian is not that of the eyewitness or the participant'.[32] In *On Human Conduct* and *On History*, however, 'contingent' is used to describe a kind of relationship between events that is itself composed of nothing but events.

Nardin neatly sums up Oakeshott's conception of contingency. 'First, a contingent relationship, like that between Spinoza's voicing unorthodox views and his excommunication, is a temporal or sequential one. Second, the acts or other events that are contingently related are congruent with one another', so that what comes after is understood as the outcome of what went before. Finally, 'the elucidation of this congruence ... depends upon an understanding of ... context. And because there are many possible contexts ... there are many ways of elucidating ... meaning'.[33] No historical event is restricted to being seen from only one point of view; indeed, each generation of historians finds different questions to ask about the past.

We must avoid implying that historical events have an independent quality that for Oakeshott they actually do not have. But this discussion of his notion of an historical event does help to bring out his point that for history there is no question of seeing the past as a necessary process. It also underlines that while his philosophy of history does not prescribe any particular method for historians, it does identify certain types of investigation of the past as non-historical. We have already seen that he distinguished the historical attitude to the past from the practical and scientific attitudes to the past, but he also drew a sharp line between historical and philosophical, or pseudo-philosophical, approaches to history.

CRITICAL AND SPECULATIVE PHILOSOPHIES OF HISTORY

'Philosophy of history' is actually an ambiguous designation, since 'history' may refer either to past events or to the discipline devoted to their study. We noted that the type of philosophy of history with which Oakeshott was concerned – the investigation of the foundations of disciplinary history – was a nineteenth-century development; but a far older type of philosophy of history was already in existence. This was the attempt to find some overall meaning in the historical process. The Graeco-Roman conception of political change as a repetitive and cyclical process, and the Judaeo-Christian belief that historical time is a progressive revelation of God's will leading to a final culmination, can be regarded as 'philosophies of history' in this sense.

More recently, Kant, Hegel and Marx all identified some necessity in the flow of events. For Kant, it was the movement of humanity towards a cosmopolitan federation of republican states; for Hegel, the growth of human freedom as first one, then a few, and finally, all, achieved political liberty; and for Marx, the overthrow of exploitative bourgeois society and the establishment of communism.[34] These very different visions were all influential, directly or indirectly, throughout the twentieth century, and still resonate today; all the prominent twentieth-century examples, from Spengler's *Decline of the West*, through Adorno's *Dialectic of Enlightenment*, to Fukuyama's *The End of History* and Huntington's *Clash of Civilizations*, were written in their shadow.[35]

The value of such works is not the issue here; it matters only that they are not works on 'philosophy of history' in the sense that interested Oakeshott. He vacillated somewhat in his assessment of this 'speculative' approach to the philosophy of history, the label usually used to distinguish it from the 'critical' Neo-Kantian investigation of historical epistemology to which his own work was a contribution. In his earlier writings he seems to have felt that speculative philosophy of history was genuinely a branch of philosophy; later, he leant more towards viewing it as a form of the practical past.[36] Regardless of the status he assigned it, however, he consistently argued that it was not to be confused with history of the sort written by historians.

This remains true even if one is concerned with 'world' or 'global' history; world history can be (and has been) written without either exhibiting the claim of historical necessity that unites the otherwise very different writings of Kant, Hegel and Marx, or claiming to predict the eventual outcome (something else that all three thinkers, with varying degrees of confidence, believed their theories could do). Oakeshott insisted that studying the past in an attempt to 'expose its teleology' was 'inherently impossible while the historian remains ignorant (as he must be) of both its beginning and its end'.[37]

Quite consistently, Oakeshott criticized any effort at historical writing that aimed to 'produce a story which is the ratification if not the glorification of the present'.[38] This 'Whig' approach, as Herbert Butterfield famously described it, had ruined E. H. Carr's attempt to write a history of the Russian Revolution. Carr's *History of Soviet Russia* had succumbed to 'the unfortunate enterprise of writing history backwards', making it 'the story of those who were "proved right" by success'.[39] It treated the victory of the Bolsheviks as predetermined, and abandoned the historian's critical perspective in favour of celebrating its success.

However, Oakeshott's own writings also include essays that exhibit the features, if not of speculative philosophy of history, then certainly of a practical outlook on the past. His later work in particular often displayed a kind of inverted version of the Whig perspective, pessimistic and condemnatory rather than celebratory. 'The Masses in Representative Democracy' is a good example.[40] It provides a thumbnail sketch of European history from the medieval era onwards in terms of the formation of certain types of character or personality. Following Jacob Burckhardt's *The Civilization of the Renaissance in Italy*,[41] Oakeshott argued that the gradual breakdown of the communal arrangements of medieval society from the late thirteenth century onwards resulted in a new sort of persona, the 'individual'.

The desire to decide for oneself rather than simply as a member of a collectivity gradually became so widespread that a new form of government was needed to accommodate it: representative democracy. But this change provoked a reaction. Many proved unable to adapt themselves to this new attitude to life, and demanded that the authorities assist them in coping with the alterations it produced. In the modern world, this hostility to the loss of the communal order had hardened, producing the type of the 'anti-individual'. Such characters had made up the bulk of the followers of totalitarian regimes, and they were the main threat to modern freedom. As Jay remarked, there is a similarity here between Oakeshott and the Frankfurt School, in particular Adorno's concept of the 'authoritarian personality'.[42]

Oakeshott did not follow Hegel or Marx in suggesting that the course of European politics displayed any necessity. Nevertheless, he clearly wanted to draw some implications for its future direction. While the conclusion reached by 'The Masses in Representative Democracy' was not entirely pessimistic, a later essay, 'The Tower of Babel', which appeared in *On History*, most certainly was.[43] In 1961 Oakeshott could still write that 'the moral prestige of individuality' remained intact, but two decades later he was no longer so sure.

'The Tower of Babel' is an allegory of a society that is utterly destroyed by its pursuit of a technological and materialistic utopia, and was presumably intended as a prophetic vision of modernity's likely future in a manner analogous to those speculative philosophies of history discussed above. However, it does not belong to the same sequence as the first three essays in *On History*, on 'Present, Future and Past', 'Historical Events' and 'Historical Change'. Its presence between the same pair of covers serves only to illustrate the great difference between the two senses of 'philosophy of history' that we have been discussing.

The question then arises of whether there is any logical relationship between them. That is, do Oakeshott's views on the autonomy of history as a form of understanding have any direct bearing on his beliefs about the direction of European history? The answer must be negative. One can consistently hold that history is an autonomous form of knowledge without accepting Oakeshott's portrayal of European history. The reverse is also true; one might find Oakeshott's narrative of the course of events attractive while adopting a very different conception of the nature of historical understanding.

HISTORY AND MORALITY

In fact, Oakeshott's critical philosophy of history and his literal and allegorical treatments of the European past actually appear inconsistent with one another. One crucial implication of the distinction between historical and practical conceptions of the past not emphasized thus far was that historical understanding excluded moral judgements about the past. That was not to say that moral judgements about the past were irrelevant in all contexts; far from it. They were intrinsic to legal and political action, for example. But precisely because they were characteristic of these forms of practical action, it was redundant to offer them in the context of historical study. A court, not a history book, was the appropriate place to reach a decision on war guilt.

This did not mean that Oakeshott thought historians were forbidden to recognize the moral dimension of past action in their work. His essay 'On the Activity of Being an Historian' was criticized for precisely this reason by the historian of France, A. J. Cobban, who felt that his conclusions licensed assimilating atrocities such as massacres 'into the norm of political events'. Oakeshott, he argued, was saying that 'we cannot help describing massacres as massacres', but that 'the important point is to avoid any suggestion that massacres are a bad thing, because this could be a moral judgment, and therefore non-historical'.[44]

Oakeshott's objection to extrinsic moral judgements in historical thinking was most fully worked out in *On Human Conduct*. There he argued that viewing any action in exclusively moral terms entailed seeing it only in relation to some set of conventions about what constitutes acceptable or unacceptable conduct, and thus to see it in less than its full individuality. If all that we know about what happened is that it was a massacre and that it was wrong, we actually know very little. Oakeshott's point is not that this judgement is incorrect, but that it says nothing, by itself, about the why, how, when, where or who of what took place; in other words, it tells us nothing about anything we need to know in order to grasp the event historically.

We are now more able to appreciate how Oakeshott's philosophy of historical knowledge and his writings on European history are in tension with one another. Even in an essay such as 'On the Character of a Modern European State',[45] his most authentically historical essay, he could not resist introducing the use of moral character types. Although the bulk of the essay deals with the tension between the two ideas of government that he contended were at the heart of the post-Renaissance European state, to each of these forms of government there corresponded a particular type of personality, and it was quite clear where his preference lay. But when Oakeshott argued that the form of government he identified with an instrumental, goal-directed conception of the state had its counterpart in the type of the anti-individual, his analysis remained at a typological level.

Thus, if the aim of historical writing is to treat events as fully individual, as Oakeshott argued repeatedly both in *Experience and its Modes* and *On History*, then the use of such personality types in historical understanding is inadequate at best. To be fair, he admitted that he was giving in to 'the temptation to seek a more general understanding than a historical understanding can provide' in speculating about the role that different types of moral character had played in European history.[46] Moreover, Oakeshott's theory of historical knowledge enables identification and criticism of the assumptions and statements in his own work that are inconsistent with authentically historical thought.

HISTORY AND AESTHETICS

Oakeshott's dislike of what he called 'anti-individualism', and of certain other trends in the modern world, perhaps had its root in a somewhat Nietzschean inclination to judge the world in aesthetic terms, a tendency he sometimes proved incapable of keeping at bay in his own attempts at historical narrative. Yet he was unwaveringly clear in principle about the difference between the historical view of the past and other views, including, we should now make clear, fictional narratives of the past.

One prominent twentieth-century approach to the philosophy of history was to try to assimilate it to the natural sciences. However, other thinkers have sought to establish the quite contrary view that history was in fact a form of art, and that, at the extreme, there was no difference between history and literature. Hayden White and Hans Kellner have both advanced versions of this position. Because in many examples of historical writing we can find historians making use of narrative conventions of various sorts in a manner akin to fictional narratives, so the argument runs, history must be a form of fiction.[47]

This is not a view Oakeshott shared. Although narration may be the form of literary presentation most often used to present the logical culmination of historical thinking, a series of contingently related events, this is not a necessary relationship. For one thing, some historical works may decide to occupy themselves with notionally static situations, in which case narrative will tend to be displaced by descriptive analysis. But Oakeshott's theory also leaves open the possibility of there being other ways to convey an understanding of a series of events that do not involve the use of chronological narrative. His philosophy of history did not dictate to historians the form in which they should present their findings any more than it told them how to do their research.

Even if one does believe that history is committed to reporting its findings in narrative form, Oakeshott's account still permits a distinction between historical and fictional discourses. There is a prior commitment in historical understanding to the notion of evidence; it is both a logical starting point and an ethical obligation, given that he always treated 'truth' as a presupposition of historical thought.[48] A novelist may make use of evidence in writing a story, but may freely ignore it if it is unhelpful to the demands of plot and characterization. Even if a sentence should occur in a novel that was identical to one in an historical work with respect to syntax, grammar and vocabulary, its logical status would nevertheless be distinct.

Moreover, whereas a novelist may make use of conventions of genre such as comedy and tragedy, these form no part of the evidence from which historical reasoning begins. Novelists are also free to construct a plot in which earlier events acquire significance only in the light of later ones; this is crucial to literary art. But as we have seen, the reasons for the occurrence of any given sequences of historical events cannot be explained in terms of the events that came after them, even if the subsequent changes in their meanings for the historical actors who lived through them (and perhaps even their descendants) forms part of the story.

Ultimately, then, Oakeshott's overall philosophical classification of the various modes of experience, to which 'poetry' (a synonym for art) was a belated addition, maintains as firm a distinction between the historical and the aesthetic perspectives as it does between historical, scientific and commonsensical ways of thinking. Tragedy, Oakeshott once observed, belongs to art and not life;[49] and since it is past life that forms the subject of historical inquiry, even where we are dealing with the history of art, this is not itself an artistic endeavour. There is nothing inherently impermissible in writing about the past as comic or tragic; it is only that doing so breaks with the conditions of historical thought.

HISTORICAL EDUCATION

Unfortunately, Oakeshott's exclusive concern with the ideal type of historical understanding and the grounds on which it could be distinguished from other forms of knowledge meant that he never went into detail concerning the ways in which different attitudes to the past can come into conflict with one another. His essays on the philosophy of education made clear that history was an essential component of a liberal education, but the exemplary instance of the tensions that can arise between historical and practical views of the past provided by the teaching of history in schools was something he never discussed.[50]

All governments desire to educate their citizens so that they have some understanding of their national past which will fit them for their adult lives, but in Oakeshott's sense of the term, this is an education in a practical rather than an historical type of past. As we noted, he considered the practical past essential to civilization; but unless it is supplemented by the historical perspective, it remains vulnerable to reduction to propaganda. Authoritarian societies are particularly prone to this problem, but even in free countries, the practical past, which in principle has the potential to be a valuable source of moral reflection and a means of self-knowledge, is not immune from transformation into an ideological caricature in which only what is approved of is to be counted as good, and everything else is suspect or outlawed.

It is, of course, not Oakeshott's fault if the conception of history that he believed integral to liberal education is commonly ignored in schools. His distinction between the practical and the historical past at least allows the identification of the problem in precise terms. However, anyone hoping to find in his writings an extended discussion of what is sometimes called 'the social responsibility of the historian',[51] or some insight into the place that historians have, or should have, in the modern world as public intellectuals, will be disappointed.

CONCLUSION

Oakeshott's real achievement in the philosophy of history was to establish history as an autonomous mode of understanding, akin to

Cassirer's identification of history as a unique symbolic form.[52] It was identifiable as such by its use of certain distinctive presuppositions or categories. Oakeshott's conception of these categories changed over time; *Experience and its Modes* highlighted the ideas of 'past', 'fact', 'truth', 'reality' and 'explanation', whereas *On History* emphasized the notions of 'evidence', 'situation', 'event', 'change' and 'contingency'. But both books see the aim of historical thinking as the establishment of an internally related and uninterrupted sequence of events, and insist that historical thinking is not to be confused with commonsensical, scientific or philosophical thinking.

Oakeshott was not the only thinker whose philosophy of history presented historical thought as actively constructing the past (but not therefore less capable of grasping the 'truth' or 'reality' of what went on in it). Collingwood, Cassirer, Goldstein and Croce could all be added to this list.[53] More recent writers have continued to advance the subject, for example Bevir by integrating it with the analytical philosophy of language, and Tucker by showing how Bayesian probability can be applied to the logic of historical judgement.[54] Nor, as a pioneer, is Oakeshott the best introductory guide.[55] Nevertheless, *On Human Conduct* and *On History* in particular set out the conditions of historical thought with exceptional clarity and rigor. They ensure Oakeshott will always have the distinction of having written not one but two of the very few classic works on the problem.

NOTES

1 M. Oakeshott, address to the London School of Economics History Society, n.d., unpublished, Oakeshott collection: 1/3, LSE Archives, London.

2 M. Bloch, *The Historian's Craft* (Manchester University Press, 1984), p. 9.

3 G. Himmelfarb, *The New History and the Old* (Cambridge, MA: Harvard University Press, 1987), p. 182.

4 J. W. Meiland, *Scepticism and Historical Knowledge* (New York: Random House, 1965), p. 62.

5 R. G. Collingwood, *The Idea of History* (Oxford University Press, 1946), p. 151. See also D. Boucher, 'Overlap and Autonomy: The Different Worlds of Collingwood and Oakeshott', *Storia, Antropologia e Scienze del Linguaggio*, 4 (1989), 69–89.

6 See the editorial introductions to *WH*, *CPJ* and *EPW*.

7 *EM*, p. 145.
8 *EM*, pp. 101, 144.
9 'Categorial', not 'categorical', foundations; the notion of knowledge as 'categorical', in the sense of absolutely fixed and definite, was exactly what Oakeshott's 'categorial' philosophy rebutted. Categorial presuppositions are themselves historic entities that have changed over the course of history, somewhat akin to Kuhn's paradigms in natural science.
10 *OH*, p. 14.
11 *EM*, p. 101.
12 *OH*, pp. 15–17.
13 M. Oakeshott, 'Place of Learning', in *VLL*, p. 21.
14 M. L. Davies, *Historics: Why History Dominates Contemporary Society* (London: Routledge, 2006).
15 *OH*, pp. 36–44.
16 *OH*, p. 44.
17 *OH*, p. 28. Compare L. Goldstein, *Historical Knowing* (Austin: University of Texas Press, 1976).
18 *EM*, p. 28.
19 *EM*, p. 101.
20 T. Nardin, *The Philosophy of Michael Oakeshott* (University Park: Pennsylvania State University Press, 2001), p. 159.
21 *OH*, p. 117.
22 See M. Stanford, *A Companion to the Study of History* (Oxford: Blackwell, 1994), p. 130.
23 F. H. Bradley, *The Presuppositions of Critical History and Aphorisms* (Bristol: Thoemmes Press, 1993). For Oakeshott's notice of Bradley's 'Presuppositions', see his review of Bradley's *Collected Essays* in *CPJ*, at pp. 140–1.
24 See for example J. G. Droysen, *Outline of the Principles of History*, trans. E. B. Andrews (Boston: Ginn & Co., 1875); G. Simmel, *The Problems of the Philosophy of History: An Epistemological Essay*, trans. G. Oakes (New York: Free Press, 1977); W. Windelband, 'Rectorial Address', *History and Theory*, 19 (1980), 169–85; H. Rickert, *The Limits of Concept Formation in Natural Science*, trans. G. Oakes (Cambridge University Press, 1986); W. Dilthey, *Hermeneutics and the Study of History*, 6 vols., ed. R. A. Makkreel and F. Rodi, vol. IV, *Selected Works* (Princeton University Press, 1996).
25 Windelband, 'Rectorial Address', p. 175.
26 *EM*, p. 101.
27 See C. Hempel, 'The Function of General Laws in History', *Journal of Philosophy*, 39 (1942), 35–48; C. Hempel, 'Reasons and Covering Laws

in Historical Explanation', in *Philosophy and History: A Symposium*, ed. S. Hook (New York University Press, 1963), pp. 146–63.

28 See *OH*, pp. 72–82.

29 *OH*, p. 82.

30 *HC*, p. 13.

31 Collingwood, *Idea of History*, p. 175.

32 *EM*, p. 140.

33 Nardin, *Philosophy of Michael Oakeshott*, pp. 138–9.

34 I. Kant, *Political Writings* (Cambridge University Press, 1991); G. W. F. Hegel, *The Philosophy of History*, trans. J. Sibree (New York: Dover Publications, 1956); K. Marx, 'Manifesto of the Communist Party', in *Selections*, ed. A. M. Wood (New York: Macmillan, 1988), pp. 141–68.

35 O. Spengler, *The Decline of the West*, trans. C. F. Atkinson (New York: Random House, 1962); T. Adorno and M. Horkheimer, *Dialectic of Enlightenment: Philosophical Fragments*, ed. G. S. Noerr, trans. E. Jephcott (Stanford University Press, 2002); F. Fukuyama, *The End of History and the Last Man* (New York: Free Press, 1992); S. Huntington, *The Clash of Civilizations and the Remaking of World Order* (London: Simon & Schuster, 1998).

36 Compare *WH*, pp. 201–5, and *OH*, pp. 102–6.

37 *OH*, p. 102.

38 H. Butterfield, *The Whig Interpretation of History* (New York: W. W. Norton, 1965), p. v.

39 M. Oakeshott, 'Mr Carr's First Volume', in *CPJ*, pp. 326–7.

40 M. Oakeshott, 'The Masses in Representative Democracy', in *RP* [1991], pp. 363–83.

41 J. Burckhardt, *The Civilization of the Renaissance in Italy*, trans. S. G. C. Middlemore (Harmondsworth: Penguin, 1990).

42 M. Jay, *The Dialectical Imagination: A History of the Frankfurt School and the Institute of Social Research 1923–1950* (Berkeley: University of California Press, 1973), p. 279.

43 M. Oakeshott, 'The Tower of Babel', in *OH*, pp. 165–94.

44 A. J. Cobban, 'History and Sociology', *Historical Studies*, 3 (1961), 1–4.

45 M. Oakeshott, 'On the Character of a Modern European State', in *HC*, pp. 185–326.

46 *HC*, p. 323.

47 H. White, *The Content of the Form: Narrative Discourse and Historical Representation* (Baltimore, MD: Johns Hopkins University Press, 1987); H. Kellner, *Language and Historical Representation: Getting the Story Crooked* (Madison: University of Wisconsin Press, 1989).

48 *EM*, p. 101.

49 M. Oakeshott, 'Scientific Politics', in *RPML*, pp. 107–8.

50 Oakeshott, 'Place of Learning', pp. 33–4.
51 F. Bédarida (ed.), *The Social Responsibility of the Historian*, Diogenes no. 168 (Oxford: Berghahn Books, 1994).
52 E. Cassirer, *An Essay on Man: An Introduction to a Philosophy of Human Culture* (New Haven, CT: Yale University Press, 1992).
53 B. Croce, *History: Its Theory and Practice*, trans. D. Ainslie (New York: Russell & Russell, 1960).
54 M. Bevir, *The Logic of the History of Ideas* (Cambridge University Press, 1999); A. Tucker, *Our Knowledge of the Past: A Philosophy of Historiography* (Cambridge University Press, 2004).
55 The best introduction is currently J. L. Gaddis, *The Landscape of History: How Historians Map the Past* (Oxford University Press, 2002).

BYRON KALDIS

3 Worlds of experience: science

> Scientific activity is not the pursuit of a premeditated end ... What holds science together and gives it impetus and direction is not a known purpose to be achieved, but the knowledge scientists have of how to conduct a scientific investigation. The particular pursuits and purposes are not superimposed upon that knowledge, but emerge within it.[1]

INTRODUCTION: PHILOSOPHY AND EPISTEMOLOGY

Oakeshott's writings on science are neither as extensive nor as well known as those on politics and history.[2] Throughout his life Oakeshott held a unitary position with regard to science. The Oakeshottian view of science may be called 'dialectical constructivism', whereby science constructs reality as its own domain by means of a dialectical interrelationship of method and content: 'science ... *must create* its own subject matter'.[3]

Oakeshott's principal writings on science are to be understood – as he himself insists in *Experience and its Modes* – from the vantage point of what he conceived to be philosophical inquiry. For him, philosophy stands or falls by its own self-assessment: it 'must stand upon its own feet'.[4] This is not the case with other, partial, forms of experience. But to approach these, one should first be clear about Oakeshott's distinctive conception of philosophy and about his depiction of the particular process by which human knowledge is formed.

I would like to thank Eugene Heath for his most helpful comments.

1. Sought for its own sake, philosophy is, for Oakeshott, irrelevant to practical interests, or any other application or guidance, and is definitely not '"the fusion of the sciences", "the synthesis of the sciences" or the *scientia scientiarum*'.[5] It is wrong to hope that 'philosophy has anything to learn from the methods of scientific thought or that the conclusions of philosophy "must be in harmony with the results of the special sciences"'.[6] Philosophy is self-conscious and auto-reflective; science is neither.

Yet Oakeshott's casting of science (and indeed of all other modes) in a subordinate role vis-à-vis philosophy should not be mistaken as entailing the negative view that science is wholly defective or that it merely draws its value from its applicability. On the contrary, science and history along with philosophy should 'be regarded as attempts to escape from the conduct of life, attempts to throw off the responsibility of living'.[7] This is a veritable Nietzschean *escape*, as Oakeshott calls it, in a thoroughly positive vein. This crucial notion, 'escape', commendable as a 'refuge from life',[8] is used in both the opening and the closing of *Experience and its Modes*.

A caveat, however, is in order at this point, especially because of a common misunderstanding, according to which Oakeshott snubs science. He held an elevated opinion of science as a cultural achievement, 'an intellectual adventure recognized as a component of an inheritance of human understandings and beliefs'.[9] What he actually rebukes is 'scientism'. In his view, it is wrong to conflate the pursuit of scientific inquiry with 'scientism'. Scientism is a 'corruption' of science, a 'superstition about scientific enquiry', 'the neo-Pelagian assumptions of scientism'.[10] It would be a wrong sort of 'escape', or spurious escape, to judge a mode of experience like science as merely invalid and thus to dismiss it in order to 'look for a philosophy beyond it in some other, different world; that is too easy an escape'.[11]

2. The second foundational element of the background against which Oakeshott's view of science must be understood is his general epistemological stance regarding knowledge. The epistemological backdrop against which scientific knowledge ought to be erected must eschew all barren dichotomies such as the myth of experience supposedly divided between experiencing and what gets experienced, experience versus reality, fact versus theory, method versus content and the like. Experiencing emerges as a whole, which is *not* immediate, non-conceptual or atomic. The attack

against the duality between the 'what' and the 'how' in experience assumes many forms revolving around the generic idea that the 'character' of experience is strictly correlative to the manner in which it is experienced.[12] In the case of science, this attack on dualities comes down to superseding the separation between the *method* and *content* of inquiry, forming the kernel of his 'dialectical constructivism'.

Although experience suffers arrests or abridgements (like science or history), it is ultimately one and homogeneous. It is always a single world taken as a whole. Analysis, however, abstracts (for various purposes) sides or epistemic regions. Thus for the purpose of neuroscientific studies of human vision analysis may distinguish between the epistemic region of sense experience and that of thought, thereby portraying thinking as a mode of knowledge distinct from other modes of sense experiencing. However, such a distinction or partition has no basis in reality, and it is the task of philosophical critique to disclose these as the abstracted partialities of what is primarily complete, individual and concrete. There is no categorial distinction between thinking in concepts and mere feeling or non-conceptual sensation, or between 'brute' sensation and perception. Knowing, in general, involves no separation between sensation and judgement. In the specific case of scientific knowledge, it involves abolishing the separation between purely observable data and theory-laden phenomena: 'there is no knowledge of "things" apart from concepts'.[13]

In completing his holist view of experience, Oakeshott also defends the thesis that truth, or reality, is not separate from experience. This constitutes another attack on epistemic dualities, consistent with his attack on the bare sense-datum conception of knowledge. For Oakeshott, what is always given in experience is a world of ideas rather than atomic facts or isolated things qua particulars. To the extent that experiencing approximates truth or becomes increasingly more 'satisfactory',[14] becomes increasingly 'more of a world', 'achieves' a greater degree of such internal unity, we can readily appreciate that neither 'truth' nor 'reality' is an outside, something over and against such a world of ideas. Rather, truth is within experience; it is an end towards which experience strives, yet not an external end. 'Truth is a result', an 'achievement', and so is reality.[15]

Science, too, as a mode of experience aims at 'achieving' such 'coherence' and therefore must be seen as 'system'. No part 'is more important than any other and *none is immune* from change and rearrangement'.[16] Oakeshott asserts this about all modes, yet this is specifically applicable to his view of science. The radical implications of this approach (that later came to be known as Quinean holism[17] or, more generally, as the Duhem–Quine thesis)[18] are echoed in Oakeshott's remark: 'no scientific generalization is ... beyond the possibility of revision'.[19] There is no rigid distinction between facts (as 'given' and protected from revision) and theory in science.[20] This attack on the 'given' will be placed within a wider intellectual context in the last section.

SCIENCE IN *Experience and its Modes*

The most sustained discussion of science as a mode of experience occurs in chapter 4 of *Experience and its Modes* (although scattered remarks on science can be found in other chapters). A mode of experience is an arrest or modification of experience, seen from the point of view of the totality of concrete experience. Central to Oakeshott's philosophy is his insistence that each mode is self-contained and absolutely detached from all others; thus attempting to travel from one to the other in this archipelago of isolated modes is equivalent to committing the 'most fatal of errors', that of *ignoratio elenchi*.[21] A mode is nevertheless not devoid of positive value; it is not a mere privation. Each mode, Oakeshott insists, is not 'merely separative, but also synthetic and integrative'.[22] It is not only a 'selective omission' but 'also and always the *construction* of a separate world of ideas at the point of the arrest'.[23] Observed from outside, namely from the standpoint of philosophical totality, each mode of experience appears incomplete and partial, constantly striving to 'achieve' more coherence or to become more 'satisfactory', 'more of a world'. Judged from inside, however, namely seen in itself as a separate mode contrasted with another (e.g. science as absolutely distinguished from historical understanding), each mode has a specificity, a 'character', of its own.[24] It is '*homogeneous*' and therefore relative to its own degree of coherence, 'true to itself', 'true if its postulates are accepted'.[25] Science, like all modes, 'organizes' reality relative to its own 'character' or from its own perspective and thus its truth is always relative.

Crucially, however, the notion that concrete reality (philosophy) supersedes science by 'destroying' it should be construed from a *logical* point of view only.[26] Such an overcoming must not be understood literally, historically or practically, since the concrete is only logically prior to the abstract. The totality of concrete experience is the logical ground of every mode of experience.[27] Philosophy shows each mode to be a self-contradiction.[28] Therefore, when science is analysed from the logical standpoint of concrete unconditional reality, its conditionality is revealed. Yet, to the extent that philosophical critique does not literally destroy science by superseding it altogether, it does not divest science from its positive character, from its relative truth.

These general epistemic commitments shape Oakeshott's view of what constitutes specifically the presuppositions of science. First, he attacks as absurd the position that scientific knowledge is the product of the mind and is altogether separated from a mind-independent reality (as 'given'). This subjective–objective chasm leads to the misconception that a world of ideas is forever barred from grasping the world of reality. Second, he underlines as his constant leitmotiv the idea that the 'what' and the 'how' are united in all human knowledge; therefore the subject matter and method of science are intertwined, being 'two aspects of a single whole'.[29] Third, scientific inquiry starts neither with a simplistic 'collection of data' nor with measuring, experimenting, observing and the like, but already with a world of ideas. One could say, scientific inquiry is already *in media res* or, better, *in media notionis*: 'from the beginning the world of scientific experience lies before the scientist in outline'[30] – meaning, from a *logical* beginning, not an historical point in time. These three epistemic features are central to Oakeshott's 'dialectical constructivism'.

The world specific to scientific experience is a world conceived *sub species quantitatis*, a world of instances sharply opposed to events (which make up history), and is thus amenable to causal explanation. Science deals with generalities, not individualities. Even if some modes may entertain the possibility of distinguishing singularities in their own world (say, historical events, though this is an oversimplification, too), what is distinctive of scientific experience is that it is a mode of experience dealing entirely with general instances or general laws. These generalizations of science, however, are not enumerative but *statistical generalizations* referring to *series* of observations. Statistical generalizations, the backbone of science, are quantitative mathematical generalities.[31] The statistical nature of scientific generalizations is supported by probability, thus allowing science to extend beyond observations.

The sophisticated yet gradual growth of science necessitates, at first, that it leave behind both common sense and particular observations (or personal testimony), replacing these with definite and demonstrable experience. This achievement plays the role of *Pisgah* in scientific thought, the biblical summit from which one may behold the Promised Land.[32] Oakeshott's definition of science is encapsulated in what he insists to be its explicit and sole criterion, namely that scientific ideas are 'absolutely stable' and 'absolutely communicable':[33] they form a world of purely quantitative experience and precise measurement.

Within this conception of scientific knowledge, Oakeshott identifies physics as its 'prototype' and, in particular, mechanics as the prototype of scientific explanation. With regard to the former, he detects the process of reduction of all other sciences to physics, 'the logical end of scientific experience'.[34] The latter, mechanical explanation, exhibits for Oakeshott certain specified characteristics: it is not only the simplest or most economical explanation, but is also general, quantitative and self-contained (its validity lies within itself, not beyond its own world). In the final analysis, it is always an explanation in terms of motion. This view of science excludes as irrelevant what today would be called an analysis of the context of discovery. Oakeshott considers his task to be the description of the logical features of explanation rather than an account of the psychological process by means of which scientists happen to come to their conclusions.

Scientific explanation, further, employs what Oakeshott calls '*structural concepts*'.[35] The world studied by science amounts to the relations that hold between these structural concepts. Oakeshott's constructivist view holds that these (quantitative) concepts of science can find their proper place only within scientific statements expressing generalizations that link those concepts with each other. They are called 'structural' in that they enter into relations that form the scaffolding of the world of science.

Yet this skeletal frame is not sufficient, as science (in its pursuit of a more comprehensive world for itself) goes on to formulate *hypotheses*. These are attempts to integrate further those structural concepts into a coherent system (of theories), in order to move from what is known partially at some stage to something more fully known at a subsequent superior stage.

Science cannot remain at the level of mechanical regularities. Oakeshott acknowledges the logical urge of science to move from mere empirical generalizations (e.g. Boyle's law) to explanations of the underlying mechanism (Bernulli's kinetic theory of ideal gases) responsible for the regularities empirically observed. He adds, unsurprisingly, that the explanatory hypotheses put forward must be further checked against observation and experiments. However, loyal to his epistemic commitments, Oakeshott insists that these observations and experiments are controlled by hypotheses; they are not just haphazard collections of data but always integrated *in media notionis*. Observations and experiments are not a process aiming at verification, and truth and falsity are not a matter of correspondence between theories and an unalterable 'outside'.[36] He emphasizes here a version of the Duhem–Quine thesis: no isolated generalization can be reformed or abandoned on the evidence of observations.[37]

Not resting on single observations means, then, that science must make use of *statistical* generalizations. Indeed, it is the statistical method for organizing observations rather than induction that furnishes the essential mark of scientific knowledge. Statistical generalizations are a necessary logical vehicle. They enable science to move beyond a certain world of ideas determined by the structural relations of concepts (e.g. 'mass' and 'gravity') towards further determinable relations. Here it is crucial to be clear: Oakeshott views the whole scientific experience as a *single* process, despite its different tools. Combining observation and experiment with hypothesis, and all three with scientific experience (ever considered as a seamless web of ideas), implies that any particular observation must be integrated within a systematic whole. This is how coherence – the mark of all knowledge – is satisfied (in degrees, of course, the measure of which is judged externally by philosophy). In other words, measuring, observing, experimenting, formulating statistical generalizations, developing hypotheses (whose assertions are subject to further checking and testing) are not so many distinct stages but 'a single act'.[38]

Related to statistical generalizations, induction and inference as elements of the 'logical structure' of scientific thinking and practice is the role of *hypotheses* we have met above, also called by him 'supposals'.[39] Since statistical statements are based on probability, all scientific generalizations are *hypothetical* and not categorical: they do not play an ontological role. They make no reference to an external world; they do not designate. What is asserted in a hypothesis is no more than a relation between two items.[40] It follows that scientific judgements cannot be 'apodeictic', meaning 'deterministic'. This does not jeopardize Oakeshott's basic thesis that science puts forward a world view the conclusions of which are valid and certain, insofar as mathematical quantitative generalizations are concerned.[41] A scientific proposition – qua *hypothesis* – asserts only a relation or the 'dependence of the consequent upon a condition not asserted to be realized'; in this sense, he proclaims, 'the life of science is not its own, but a borrowed life'.[42]

The final step brings us to a topic dear to British Idealism (and of course to German Idealism too, from which the distinction was inherited), namely a separate discussion of '*nature*'. Discussing 'nature' as if it were a semi-autonomous subject within a philosophical engagement with 'science' was once common, so much so that R. G. Collingwood, for instance, wrote an entire book on nature bearing that title.[43] We are nowadays accustomed to dealing with both 'nature' and 'science' as a single subject, not distinguishing the so-called philosophy of nature (indeed the appellation has disappeared almost entirely) from the philosophy of science. To the Idealists, for sure, the philosophy of nature was seen as a related subtopic, but more often than not they clearly felt the need to discuss nature ontologically while science was approached epistemologically. While sensing the need to introduce 'nature' as a topic in addition to 'science', Oakeshott merges the two analyses in a distinctive way. For him, 'nature' denotes reality and reality is one with experience, as we have seen. Experience being a world of ideas, it follows that 'nature' denotes a world of ideas, which in the case of science is revealed by the method specific to science. True to his epistemic commitments, Oakeshott is able to assert that 'nature' must not be seen as the given domain of science, but as its product. Once again, we see here evidence of the Oakeshottian 'dialectical constructivist' view of science: the method determines the subject matter, and at the same time the latter dictates the appropriateness of the former. Subject matter and method are thus interrelated. Or (since even describing them as interrelated is misleading): method and subject matter are not two separate items waiting to be related;

they are indeed one.[44] 'Dialectical constructivism' – whereby method constructs its domain and the latter, in turn, prescribes the appropriate method – is best encapsulated in the statement: 'without ... the method, there is no matter; without the instruments of measurement, nothing to measure'.[45]

'Nature' is therefore part of the scientific world view. This view is self-contained, and consequently 'nature' cannot denote anything other than this self-contained system itself: nature is a *postulate*, not an outside thing or physical condition waiting to be observed.[46] Nature is not 'planets, apples and stones'.[47] It is not a datum against which a scientific hypothesis is to be verified. Nature is 'the *creation* of the scientific mind for the sole purpose of satisfying that mind'.[48] We cannot, strictly speaking, use the expression 'the scientific view of nature', for 'nature' and 'science' are inter-defined. 'Nature' is what science says it is. In the context of how Oakeshott understands science, nature can be defined only by science itself, and must therefore be grasped by the principal vehicle of science: statistical generalizations.

The same constructivist position is also found in 'The Voice of Poetry in the Conversation of Mankind': science is said to construct a rational world of related concepts ('structural concepts' in *Experience and its Modes*), 'in which every image recognized to be relevant "fact" in the idiom of [an] inquiry is *given a place* and an interpretation'.[49] *Scientia* must be understood as 'a universe of discourse, a way of ... moving about among images ... an inquiry ... specified by the manner in which it was conducted'.[50] Science has its own vocabulary, whose distinctive logical character is, unlike that of poetry, entirely 'symbolic' – we may nowadays call it referentially extensional. And these scientific terms function as signs strictly governed by science's own rules. Such an activity *constructs* 'a rational world of consequentially related conceptual images'.[51] This is equivalent to the interrelated structural concepts in *Experience and its Modes*, whereby method and content intertwine.

SCIENCE AND THE SOCIAL SCIENCES

This view of science is carried on when Oakeshott deals with the social sciences, and particularly with economics and psychology. He dismisses as misconceived certain attempts to carve economics away from science.[52] In his view, it is useless to make the scientific status of economics depend on our answer to questions such as: is its subject matter part of the material world?; are the items of the human world unique, non-repeatable and non-quantifiable?; can there be laws of economic behaviour? Economics *is* a science in the distinctive Oakeshottian terms. For what scientific statements refer to is not an independently existing reality (e.g. a felt emotion or a human being acting in economic transactions, and the like) but *abstractions*. Economics is indeed a 'science of man', yet it deals not with actual humans but with 'scientifically conceived man, scientifically abstracted man'.[53] Economics is scientific if it concerns itself with scientific abstractions and measurements, employing generalizations that are analytical, that is, lack referential extension to concrete particulars. Moreover, economics is a purely analytical science, and, in this sense, it goes further than natural science, which retains a kind of limited referentiality to a physical world.[54] Economics – like every science – is an attempt to organize or integrate its structural concepts and their mutual implications into scientific (statistical) generalizations expressing a coherent relational whole.[55] It does not refer directly to particular human desires or specific economic transactions, and does not concern itself with observing, or with generalizations extracted from observing, actual economic behaviour. Like every branch of science, it *constructs* its own domain. Oakeshott emphasizes that 'science is one' and that what he has to say about the social sciences is a 'further determination of the character of scientific experience'.[56]

The same goes for psychology.[57] Adjectives such as 'physical' or 'mental' that allegedly qualify reality 'as it is' are in fact foreign to science, for it forms its own self-contained world of structural concepts (abstractions) and their relations (generalizations). Psychology cannot be excluded from the purview of science because it allegedly deals with 'inscrutable mental events' (erroneously so conceived), with singularities of mental states or with personal introspection. For in fact it deals with its own concepts and quantitative generalizations. Thus, to the extent that any discipline conforms to the character of scientific experience as 'stable and communicable', it should count as 'science'.

The relationship between natural and social sciences receives subtle treatment in Oakeshott's later writings. In both his earlier and later writings, despite a change in terminology, Oakeshott conceives of social sciences as dealing with generalizations or ideal types and thus as distinct from a different kind of understanding required to theorize concrete actions in their historical contingency and contextual specificity.

In the first chapter of *On Human Conduct* Oakeshott deals with science under the general heading of 'theoretical understanding'. The discussion is phrased in terms of 'theorizing' rather than 'experience', and theorizing is understood as an 'engagement'. It involves the never-ending 'adventure' of reflective consciousness, that is, a 'theorist' engaged in an activity, a 'going-on': this activity is an 'understanding' that issues in 'theorems'. Theoretical understanding is unconditional engagement aiming at securing a less mysterious comprehension of the world by removing as much as possible the conditional presuppositions on which all inquiry inevitably rests. That the world becomes less mysterious, or the presupposed conditions are reduced, is analogous to what *Experience and its Modes* repeatedly characterized as the 'achievement' of experience 'becoming more of a world'. Again, as in the earlier book, where method and subject matter intertwine, so here too, understanding and the very instrument of understanding are said to 'emerge together'.[58]

An 'arrest in the unconditional understanding' represents the starting point of scientific inquiry by *abstracting* a certain identity or 'ideal character' out of contingent characteristics. Each specific understanding of a certain domain is an autonomous inquiry with its own distinctive postulates supporting it, 'insular ... resistant to "reduction"', and this is analogous to the separability of the modes of experience.[59] Inquiries can be distinguished in terms of the 'categories', in respect of which they identify unambiguously the items of their domain, and hence in terms of the appropriate kind of questions they pose about these items. There are two 'orders' of inquiry. One order identifies the goings-on in its domain as falling under the category of intelligibility, that is, activities themselves exhibiting intelligence: human actions, moral sentiments and so forth. The other order of inquiry attempts to understand rock formations, thunderstorms and the like, that is, 'processes' or 'causal conditions' that exhibit no intelligent behaviour. The former category contains items that involve self-understanding, the latter contains items devoid of it.[60]

It appears that here we have reached the distinction between natural and social sciences. The chief difference between the two is that the requisite postulates supporting each order of inquiry must be different: postulates relevant to the items of natural processes require that those are understood as 'determined', while in the case of human action the relevant postulates demand that activity is understood as a procedure or performance, as something that itself involves understanding.[61] The identities of each category are 'exclusive of each other'; hence each inquiry must remain distinct.[62] Explanation of human action requires its own type of theoretical understanding categorially distinct from that of natural phenomena. The exclusivity of each order of inquiry is undergirded by the corresponding exclusivity of theoretical language. Furthermore, each of the two orders can be subdivided into distinct special 'sciences' (e.g. economics or psychology, on the one hand; physics or biology, on the other). Each such subtype of an order of inquiry has its own 'idiom' or 'system of theorems'.[63]

Now, two misconceptions should be avoided here. First, this distinction does not imply that one order stands somehow closer to the concrete reality of particulars than the other. Oakeshott points out that no theorizing can 'escape' the 'prison' of conditionality. It rests on a platform of postulates and operates by abstracting a 'character', or ideal type, from contingent characteristics. The theorist of 'human conduct' departs from everyday understanding, for his business is not to re-enact empathetically an agent's concrete performance. Even when dealing with a substantive performance by an assignable agent, as we shall see again at the end of this section, theoretical understanding still rests on a platform of postulates that '*endow* it with conditional intelligibility of which he [the theorist] is the *author*'.[64] It is always an active, creative and therefore conditional engagement, for it *creates*, by means of its distinctive concepts, its own domain.

Second, Oakeshott emphasizes that we are not dealing with the distinction between the 'mental' and the 'physical' or between intentional human action and causally moving inert bodies, conceived of as ontological categories, as 'entities' identified independently of the order of inquiry appropriate for each.[65] The distinction between the 'mental' and the 'physical', or between 'intentionality' and 'mechanical motion', must be understood as specifically designated by 'science'. It is significant that throughout the discussion Oakeshott chooses to keep 'science' in inverted commas, wishing to indicate that he is working his way towards a definition of it, not unlike what he did in *Experience and its Modes*, using, though, a different terminology. In *Experience and its Modes* the scientific mode of experience was described in terms of conceptual abstractions (structural concepts) and their relations (statistical generalizations). In *On Human Conduct* each subdivision of an order of inquiry is said to employ its own idiom in order to understand categorially distinct identities within its domain. These identities are not those of everyday pre-scientific reality, they are not 'given'; rather, they are 'necessarily the creature'[66] of each science's own system of theorems. 'Science' signifies an 'instrument of understanding' informed by a system of theorems analogous to the system of structural concepts in *Experience and its Modes*. The instrument (earlier called 'method') 'itself *designates* the identity investigated and gives it the required unambiguous character by *endowing* it with the categorial and idiomatic unambiguity'.[67]

Maturity of a 'science' is assessed by its success in combating categorial ambiguity and equivocality. The task now becomes more complex and frustrating, as the theorist turns away from employing a 'science' to gain understanding of a going-on, towards a self-reflection on the nature of these 'sciences' themselves.[68] The theorist examines the 'instruments'. As we have seen, each subdivision of an order of inquiry must frame distinctly its domain by its own idiom without categorial muddle. But what is crucial is to keep the principal division between the two orders of inquiry intact. Accomplishing this is far from straightforward, and some social sciences may content themselves with less than completely unambiguous items in their domains, that is, without 'well-articulated' items 'composed of … theorems available' to them.[69] But this is preferable to a futile attempt to construct an 'alleged all purpose science' that defies the principal division between orders, one that mixes natural phenomena with intelligent activity, a 'masquerade of categories'. To illustrate how such misunderstandings fail to eradicate idiomatic confusion, Oakeshott invokes the examples of what he considers to be still (in his time) underdeveloped and hybrid 'sciences': psychology and sociology. The commendable urge to direct psychology away from contingent characteristics towards abstract ideal types is muddled by the misconception that the identified characters are, absurdly, in the heads of actors. Abstracted theorems of psychology, in which 'mental' processes are understood as 'psychological mechanisms' (as, for example, in neurophysiology), are erroneously taken to be actual causes or 'laws' operating on human conduct, which is an exhibition of intelligence.[70] Psychology may indeed use scales and measurements, graphs and the like, but it should not fall prey to the illusion that it turns into an allegedly superior 'scientific' understanding of phenomena that are exhibitions of intelligence.

The same goes for sociology and its alleged 'laws', out of which a system is pretentiously construed. Such 'laws' cannot do justice to the real nature of social practices, for these are exhibitions of intelligence and rule following rather than 'law-like relations between the components of social systems'.[71]

In *On Human Conduct* Oakeshott thus distinguishes between two categorially different types of 'science' corresponding to the two orders of inquiry. But what should be made of the unity of scientific experience, espoused in *Experience and its Modes*? There he argued that science must be seen as one, and regarded the separation between the so-called special sciences as contingent imperfection. In my view, this position does not contradict his later approach in *On Human Conduct*. For the unity he ascribed to science was a 'logical' one, as he called it.[72] The 'unifying principle' of scientific experience is that it conceives of the world as 'stable and absolutely communicable'. What matters is that social sciences comply with this essential postulate of scientific experience. 'Scientific' is not synonymous to 'material' or 'physical', and does not bar the study of human action.[73] In both works, 'scientific' inquiry involves *abstracting*.

However, once we move beyond this abstracting of 'human conduct' as ideal type in order to offer thick descriptions of particular substantive performances as individual occurrences embedded in social practices, we move beyond social sciences and 'theorize contingency', as Oakeshott calls it.[74] A substantive performance is an individual occurrence bearing characteristics specific to itself. It thus resists being assimilated to types as their token. After identifying a going-on generically as an exhibition of human conduct (an act of intelligence and not a movement of tectonic plates or a biological phenomenon), there must come its elucidation as a specific act performed by an assignable agent.[75] When theoretical understanding moves beyond identification of types towards elucidating unique performances, it must construe each such action as a unique '*eventum*',[76] not as an instance falling under a covering law. Oakeshott stresses that even though a specific performance is always embedded in social practices, the task should be to 'understand it without explaining it away', as social science would do.[77] In accomplishing this, theoretical understanding should avoid committing two mistakes: being content with (a) a 'science of human nature' and (b) a 'science of society'.[78] Explaining an agent's particular performance in terms of theorems of 'natural' human behavior or in terms of an action's 'social determinants' (i.e. by means of the two alleged 'sciences', respectively) misses altogether an act's substantive specificity. To understand a particular performance as a mere token of a type is therefore a 'categorial confusion', even if social sciences have been 'too eager to be seduced' in this way.[79]

Insisting on the unity of science and therefore on the social sciences being 'scientific' in the precise sense explained so far, does not amount to assimilating them to natural science. As Oakeshott stresses in 'Scientific Politics', the problem is not the faith in the method of natural science, nor even the attempt, like that of J. S. Mill, to find in this method a model for social sciences. Rather, what is wrong is to regard the domain of political and social action as comprising problems on a par with scientific problems.[80] Elsewhere, he repeats the same apropos of Hobbes's distinction between a permissible description (a model) of civil association in terms of inertial motion and believing wrongly that its actual operation is such a motion.[81]

INTELLECTUAL KINSHIP

'What in an age of science is the task of philosophy?' According to Oakeshott, this question was already found in Hobbes.[82] Oakeshott's answer is that philosophy's aim is rational knowledge surpassing experience as brute sensation. He distinguishes between knowledge of phenomena (science) and a theory of knowledge (philosophy), assigning to philosophy a *critical* role: philosophy (when juxtaposed with science) provides science with the compass that allows it to avoid epistemological misconceptions as to what kind of mode of experience science is: misconceptions such as that there is a subject–object or method–content duality, or that there is an absolute, mind-independent 'given', a theory-independent physical reality.

Oakeshott shared this view of the critical role of philosophy with other philosophers and philosophical schools. Two of them display especially strong affinities with his approach: Marburg Neo-Kantiansim and the philosophy of science of Wilfrid Sellars. I will conclude this chapter by elucidating these affinities.

Oakeshott's 'dialectical constructivism' comes closest to the work of Hermann Cohen and Ernst Cassirer. There are striking similarities between Cohen's 'critical idealism', a position centring on the 'constructive character of thought', and Oakeshott's construction of a world of experience. In this respect Cohen's remark that 'stars are not *given* in the sky, rather, it is within the science of astronomy that we designate such objects as *given*'[83] reminds us of Oakeshott's similar statement quoted above: that nature is not planets, apples or stones but the creation of science.

Unlike these Neo-Kantians, Oakeshott does not regard mathematical natural science as the epitome of knowledge par excellence. But he shares with them the idea of searching for a critical standpoint that would allow for a study of the postulates of science. Similar to them, he rejects the notion of the 'given', espousing the *constructive* character of knowledge.

It is true that Neo-Kantians used the expression 'fact of science', signifying the bedrock of knowledge, whereas no such 'fact' is acceptable to Oakeshott, for whom science is an ever continuing dialectical activity in search of more coherence – perpetually *en voyage*.[84] Yet Neo-Kantians employ the expression 'fact of science' mainly to deny – specifically in the form of infinitesimal calculus – the opposition between sensibility and concepts. They repudiate the simplistic dichotomy between science as a stock of theories and an external reality that provides data to science. They do not look at science as a true picture of objective reality, considering such a view naive. Science, for them, is rather the epistemological achievement that closed the gap between sensible intuition and conceptual understanding. Similar to the dialectical interplay of method and content in Oakeshott, Cohen underlines the interdependence of 'facts' and 'laws' in science, repudiating Kant's orthodox assimilation of the Newtonian scientific laws to rigid categories of understanding.

Further, Cassirer, a Neo-Kantian philosopher of the younger generation, shares with Oakeshott the view of science as a network of concepts and hypotheses, arguing that in science 'the "thing" of the popular view of the world ... no longer remains isolated ... but is connected inseparably by logical threads with the totality of experience'.[85] And 'in the scientific construction there appears as connected by continuous conceptual intermediates, what in the ... naive view appears ... unrelated'.[86]

Moreover, Cassirer shares with Oakeshott the assessment that the task of philosophy in an age of science is to furnish a *critical* theory of knowledge for the conduct of science. According to Cassirer, 'the true object of philosophy is ... [to] determine and bring to light ... the "organization" of the cognition of nature'.[87]

Cohen, Cassirer and Oakeshott, then, all share the view of experience as devoid of false dichotomies, principally between concepts and sense impressions. This rejection of dualities leads to the dialectical interplay of method and content in science. Philosophy 'constructs' the concept of experience beyond the dichotomy of empiricism–rationalism: experience is seen as a cognitive 'achievement'.

This view of science and experience, which demolished the belief that reality could be separated from knowledge, had its counterpart in twentieth-century analytical philosophy. Sellars's famous criticism of what he calls the empiricist framework of experience, and especially his attack on 'the myth of the given', can be seen as complementary to the false dichotomy between empiricism and rationalism that Neo-Kantians exploded.[88] They all share a view of cognition that rejects foundational 'givens', namely free-standing observational reports. Sellars argued that this myth rests on wrong premises – tacitly assumed but in the end untenable and self-contradictory – that preclude formation of any plausible framework for empiricism. The empiricist view of the 'given' presupposes the following process: there are, allegedly, non-verbal episodes of direct ('self-authenticating') awareness, possessing intrinsic credibility, which gets transmitted to subsequent observational reports that express this awareness. The unsatisfactory character of such a framework is expressed in Sellars's eloquent simile: 'these self-authenticating episodes would constitute the tortoise on which stands the elephant on which rests the edifice of empirical knowledge'.[89] Tortoise signifies the ultimate foundation, a *terminus*, meant to support the entire edifice without itself being supported. Hence the 'myth' of it being 'an unmoved mover': 'the *given*, in epistemological tradition, is what is *taken* by these self-authenticating episodes. These "takings" are, so to speak, the unmoved movers of empirical knowledge'.[90] This framework, however, fails to take into account that in order to be able to enunciate observational reports of such allegedly autonomous cognitive episodes the speaker is required to know 'a lot of other things' or to '*presuppose* knowledge of general facts' of a certain sort.[91] And no such epistemic autonomy is forthcoming. Empirical statements may seem to rest on what is customarily called a foundation. Yet Sellars reminds us that this is not a one-way dependence. The reverse is also the case, for observational reports presuppose further empirical knowledge.

Sellars's emphasis on the two-way dependence is analogous to what I called 'dialectical constructivism' in Oakeshott, for whom the view that science may hope to be 'given' (or 'take') support from without would be just a misconception. Moreover, Sellars's rejection of empiricist foundationalism as 'static'[92] parallels Oakeshott's view of experience as a flow, process or movement.[93]

Sellars argues: 'empirical knowledge, like its sophisticated extension, science, is rational, not because it has a foundation but because it is a self-correcting enterprise which can put any claim in jeopardy, though not all at once'.[94] This is similar to how Oakeshott conceives of the self-remedying activity of understanding in *On Human Conduct*. In his early writings the view is the same. As he says in *Experience and its Modes*: 'this so-called necessity of finding a beginning for thought outside the region of judgement is no necessity at all'.[95]

We are already familiar with Oakeshott's critique of naive foundationalism (the misconceived urge to find an external beginning) and his overall view that scientific inquiry starts with an already formed world of ideas. On my interpretation, Oakeshott's anti-foundationalism, which others have discerned, too, is not merely nor mainly his belief in the never-ending series of ascending unconditionality adumbrated in *On Human Conduct*. Rather, his most poignant anti-foundationalist stance is contained within the cluster of his epistemic commitments proclaimed in *Experience and its Modes*. In this section, I have shown briefly how these commitments go back to Neo-Kantian views and receive a more detailed analysis by Sellars. Oakeshott, armed with these epistemic commitments, mounted a sustained attack on the positivist conception of science understood in the precise sense I adopt from Sellars, and according to which, 'the framework of theoretical objects (molecules, electro-magnetic fields, etc.) and their relationships is merely an *auxiliary* framework'.[96] On this positivistic view, theories in science are supposed to be dependent on a more important axis of non-scientific observational reports: the self-authenticating 'tortoise'. Both Sellars and Oakeshott reject this cognitive geography that separates the inner experiential core from a derivative theoretical appendix. For Oakeshott, too, the network of relations between structural concepts forming science is never a secondary or derivative outpost governed by the centre: everyday sense experience and its language.

What makes such a view of science permissible and convincing (against the positivist position) is the role assigned to philosophy. In all the philosophical instances encountered in this section, philosophy plays a *critical* role. It refuses to regard science as merely an outpost of ordinary language and experience. Sellars castigates such a positivist map of knowledge as a misconception: the positivist mistake in dealing with science philosophically is to construe it as 'a mode of discourse which is, so to speak, a peninsular offshoot from the mainland of ordinary discourse'.[97] The mistake amounts to trying to solve epistemological problems triggered by the language of scientific theories in such a way as if this language were a replica of the everyday naive way of describing and explaining 'empirical fact with the presuppositions of *givenness*'.[98] Such an assimilation of scientific language to ordinary language and, what is more, inheriting the latter's bankrupt framework of givenness, is what Sellars calls the 'positivistic or peninsular conception of scientific discourse'.[99] Science for Oakeshott, too, is no such an appendix to ordinary experience. It is a theoretically robust mode of experience that constructs reality as its domain in its own distinctive mode.

NOTES

1 M. Oakeshott, 'The Idea of a University', in *VLL*, p. 104.
2 The very few exceptions to the norm, papers dealing with Oakeshott on science, are E. Podoksik's 'The Scientific Positivism of Michael Oakeshott', *British Journal for the History of Philosophy*, 12 (2004), 297–318, and B. Kaldis's 'Oakeshott on Science as a Mode of Experience', *Zygon*, 44 (2009), 169–96.
3 *EM*, p. 245, italics the present author.
4 *EM*, p. 7.
5 *EM*, p. 2.
6 *EM*, p. 354.
7 *EM*, pp. 296–7.
8 *EM*, pp. 3, 297, 355. 'Escape' reappears later, in *HC*, p. 28: the theorist is obliged to '*escape*' from the everyday understanding of the 'cave-dwellers', building a theory based on postulates.
9 M. Oakeshott, 'Education: The Engagement and its Frustration', in *VLL*, p. 88.
10 M. Oakeshott, 'Scientific Politics', in *RPML*, pp. 99, 105.
11 *EM*, p. 3.
12 *EM*, p. 9.
13 *EM*, p. 51.
14 'Satisfactory' is Oakeshott's favourite notion for approximating the condition of totality or 'completeness' whereby ideas form themselves into a 'system' that is internally related.
15 *EM*, p. 48.
16 *EM*, p. 33, italics the present author.
17 Compare Quine's well-known attack against the two positivist pillars of logical empiricism, analyticity and reduction of meaningfulness to logical construction out of immediate experience: 'our statements about the external world face the tribunal of sense experience not individually but only as a corporate body'. W. Quine, 'Two Dogmas of Empiricism', in *From a Logical Point of View* (Cambridge, MA: Harvard University Press, 1980), p. 41. Oakeshott remarks that 'each advance [in knowledge] affects retrospectively the entire whole', *EM*, p. 41.
18 Compare 'In scientific experience … no single observation is … by itself, important, and certainly not … conclusive', *EM*, p. 208.
19 *EM*, p. 212.
20 *EM*, pp. 42–3, 111.
21 *EM*, p. 5.
22 *EM*, p. 73.
23 *EM*, p. 73, italics the present author.
24 *EM*, pp. 74, 76.

25 *EM*, pp. 75, 76–7, italics the present author.
26 *EM*, pp. 81, 82.
27 *EM*, pp. 79, 82.
28 *EM*, p. 80.
29 *EM*, pp. 175, 192, 198.
30 *EM*, p. 182.
31 *EM*, pp. 164, 185–8, 205.
32 *EM*, p. 171.
33 *EM*, p. 171.
34 *EM*, p. 178.
35 *EM*, p. 182, italics the present author.
36 *EM*, pp. 199–201, 239.
37 *EM*, pp. 185, 187, 201.
38 *EM*, p. 186.
39 *EM*, p. 210.
40 *EM*, p. 211.
41 *EM*, p. 204.
42 *EM*, p. 215.
43 R. G. Collingwood, *The Idea of Nature* (Oxford: Clarendon Press, 1945).
44 *EM*, p. 190; cf. pp. 175, 198.
45 *EM*, p. 191; cf. M. Oakeshott, 'The Concept of a Philosophy of Politics', in *RPML*, pp. 128–9.
46 *EM*, p. 191.
47 *EM*, p. 194.
48 *EM*, p. 193, italics the present author.
49 Oakeshott, 'Voice of Poetry', p. 214, italics the present author.
50 *Ibid.*, p. 213.
51 *Ibid.*, p. 216.
52 *EM*, pp. 222–8.
53 *EM*, pp. 229–30.
54 *EM*, p. 231.
55 *EM*, p. 221.
56 *EM*, p. 220.
57 *EM*, pp. 234–43.
58 *HC*, p. 4.
59 *HC*, p. 11.
60 *HC*, pp. 12–16.
61 *HC*, p. 13.
62 *HC*, p. 15.
63 *HC*, p. 17.
64 *HC*, pp. 27–8, 106; italics the present author.
65 *HC*, p. 14.

66 *HC*, p. 17.
67 *HC*, pp. 17–18, italics the present author.
68 *HC*, pp. 19–25.
69 *HC*, p. 20.
70 *HC*, pp. 21–3.
71 *HC*, pp. 24–5.
72 *EM*, pp. 220, 227, 229, 243, 246.
73 *EM*, p. 229.
74 *HC*, p. 101.
75 *HC*, pp. 91–107.
76 *HC*, p. 101.
77 *HC*, p. 101.
78 *HC*, pp. 93–8.
79 *HC*, p. 97. A similar position was held in his 'Science and Society', in *CPJ*, pp. 244–6: a 'science of society' was dismissed, pejoratively, as 'technology of human control'.
80 Oakeshott, 'Scientific Politics', p. 99.
81 M. Oakeshott, 'Logos and Telos', in *RP* [1991], p. 359.
82 M. Oakeshott, 'Introduction to *Leviathan*', in *HCA*, pp. 20–1.
83 Hermann Cohen, *Das Princip der Infinitesimal-Methode und seine Geschichte* (Berlin: Ferd. Dümmler, 1883), p. 127. Cohen insists that the world of things is not given as such but is based on the 'laws of thought'.
84 *HC*, p. 11.
85 E. Cassirer, *Substance and Function and Einstein's Theory of Relativity* (New York: Dover Publications, 1953), p. 166.
86 *Ibid.*, p. 307.
87 E. Cassirer, 'Hermann Cohen and the Renewal of Kantian Philosophy', *Angelaki*, 10 (2005), 97–8.
88 W. Sellars, 'Empiricism and the Philosophy of Mind', in *Science, Perception and Reality* (Atascadero, CA: Ridgeview, 1963), pp. 127–96.
89 *Ibid.*, p. 167.
90 *Ibid.*, p. 169.
91 *Ibid.*, p. 168.
92 *Ibid.*, p. 170.
93 *EM*, pp. 66, 70, 75, 81, 122.
94 Sellars, 'Empiricism and the Philosophy of Mind', p. 170.
95 *EM*, p. 18.
96 Sellars, 'Empiricism and the Philosophy of Mind', p. 173.
97 *Ibid.*, p. 174.
98 *Ibid.*
99 *Ibid.*

ELIZABETH COREY

4 Worlds of experience: aesthetics

INTRODUCTION: THE IMPORTANCE OF AESTHETICS FOR OAKESHOTT

Why did Michael Oakeshott include an essay about aesthetics in his collection of political essays, *Rationalism in Politics*? This question has puzzled many readers. One commentator described the inclusion of 'The Voice of Poetry in the Conversation of Mankind' as 'esoteric in connection with the main theme' of the volume.[1] Others simply pass it by, preferring to focus on the more overtly political topics of the book, which include Oakeshott's famous 'Rationalism in Politics' essay and his work on Hobbes. Still others read 'The Voice of Poetry' but walk away shaking their heads, finding Oakeshott's ideas about aesthetics foreign to any understanding of art they have ever encountered.

These approaches to Oakeshott's work on aesthetics fail to take account of its fundamental importance to his philosophy as a whole. 'The Voice of Poetry' is not a diversion from the serious work of theorizing morality and politics but rather a definitive expression of Oakeshott's philosophical outlook. Here he restates his theory of modality and carves out a place for a mode he had formerly omitted: the poetic mode, which he designates 'the voice of poetry'.[2] Poetry for Oakeshott was not a mere embellishment, a leisure activity engaged in so that one might return to work refreshed. To listen for the voice of poetry was rather to cultivate a certain detachment from all the mundane things that ordinarily, and unavoidably, concern human beings. Although Oakeshott saw quite clearly that no one could live a fully poetic life, he also thought aesthetic appreciation offered satisfactions that could prove extraordinarily valuable in their own right.[3]

Careful readers will note that Oakeshott's emphasis throughout the essay falls heavily on the subject doing the appreciating rather than the object appreciated. Indeed, he makes a startlingly expansive statement about what can qualify as a poetic image: 'any scene, shape, pattern, pose or movement in the visible or audible world, any action, happening or event or concatenation of events, any habit or disposition exhibited in movement or speech, any thought or memory is a poetic image if the manner in which it is imagined is what I have called "contemplating"'.[4] Thus aesthetic appreciation may emerge anywhere and at any time. The view out one's back door, the habitual expression of a friend, the look of the sky in winter – these images are potentially aesthetic. To state the point quite radically, the implication is that all of life may be approached aesthetically, if one is so disposed. This means that we cannot divide experience into 'political' matters and 'poetic' matters. Rather, the whole world may be viewed according to different modes of understanding. And when we do so – view the world in different modes – we learn something important about the nature and limits of each mode.

OAKESHOTT'S VIEW OF AESTHETICS

Although his views developed over many years, Oakeshott's 1959 essay, 'The Voice of Poetry in the Conversation of Mankind', is his definitive statement on aesthetics.[5] Here Oakeshott returned to the theory of modality he had originally developed almost thirty years earlier in *Experience and its Modes*. But before he restates the features of the modes or 'voices', Oakeshott sets out the philosophical presuppositions upon which the remainder of the essay depends.

First, he maintains that the distinctive mark of being human is an ability to participate in conversation. Conversation is a metaphor, a recognition that the diverse voices of human experience (here: science, practice and poetry) must somehow interact without one claiming dominance over the others.[6] At the level of individual persons, those who participate in this 'conversation of mankind' ideally possess both education and the moral habits of patience, energy, self-restraint and tolerance. They must have something to say as well as an inclination to listen. Thus the scientist attends to the businessman, the businessman to the poet, the poet to the scientist. None of the conversation partners desires to dominate because each recognizes the distinctive mode in which the others speak. If this seems an unduly optimistic and civilized model of human intercourse, Oakeshott recognizes quite clearly that it is. In fact, he thinks the conversation has fallen into a 'bog' from which rescue is nearly if not entirely impossible. He thus claims only that poetry has a specific and limited place in the conversation 'which it may from time to time command but in which it is never alone'.[7]

Second, Oakeshott sets out a particular conception of the human self and its relationship to the world. A self, he claims, is constituted in activity. There is no primordial stuff that stands behind this active self: to be active but engaged in no particular activity is a contradiction in terms. Thus the self always partners with 'images', which it conceives in particular ways according to the manner or mode in which it is active. These images constitute the 'not-self'. In practical activity, images (words, gestures, expressions, physical objects) are understood as useful or useless. Each is 'the reflection of a desiring self engaged in constructing its world and in continuing to reconstruct it in such a manner as to afford it pleasure'.[8] The practical self therefore uses tools for building, eats cabbages for energy and nutrition, and employs colleagues as assistants in accomplishing desired ends.

The person engaged in the mode of science, on the other hand, sees images (the not-self) primarily as ways of illuminating and explaining the invisible world of mass, volume and number. Words in scientific discourse designate an unseen reality. And when these words 'can be refined no further, they give place not to gestures but to technical expressions, to signs and mathematical symbols which can be more exactly assembled ... because they have been purged of the last vestiges of ambiguity'.[9] If there is beauty in a scientific formula, it lies not in the particular numbers and letters chosen but in the ideas they represent. In *scientia* 'colleagues' are the subjects of physiological or psychological study, 'cabbages' not things to be eaten but chemicals and compounds awaiting differentiation and analysis. Oakeshott does recognize that science is not always undertaken with this purely theoretical focus and that very often scientists set out to solve some problem in the practical world. However, science as a mode is not concerned with these particular problems but with illumination according to scientific categories.

'Self' and 'not-self' therefore assume different kinds of relationships depending on the mode in which one is active. In both practical activity and science, words and images are *essentially* symbolic markers, not things to be valued as ends in themselves. Thus the vocabulary of practical activity consists of 'so many agreed signs which, because they have relatively fixed and precise usages, and because they are *non-resonant*, serve as a medium for confident communication'.[10] Practical language conveys desire and aversion as well as approval and disapproval; we care about meaning, not evocativeness. Communication in this mode aims at satisfactions that may or may not result from asking, entreating, questioning, commanding and complimenting. The language of practice is 'like a coinage, the more fixed and invariable the value of its components, the more useful it is as a medium of exchange'.[11]

The austerely symbolic vocabulary of *scientia* conveys information that is in principle available and communicable to everyone. But this vocabulary also refers to something beyond itself. Indeed, it is an even more severely symbolic language than the language of practice, and 'the range of its utterance is both narrower and more precise'. Scientific symbols, writes Oakeshott, are like chessmen; 'they stand for what can be done with them according to known rules, and the rules which govern the use of mathematical symbols are stricter than those which govern the use of words'.[12] The goal here is always clarity – not surprise, poignancy, or charm.

Against these voices poetry emerges as distinct because it refuses the invitation to put language in the service of anything else. The words of a poem or the brushwork of a painter are not ways of procuring a future satisfaction or of designating something other than the work itself.[13] Unlike those of science and practice, poetry's images are not arranged consequentially. Poetry does not call us to action but asks that we look and enjoy. It is in this sense that Oakeshott can designate poetic contemplation a 'complete' activity. Whereas in science and practice we begin to perform operations on images almost as soon as we perceive them, initiating a goal-oriented process, poetry uses images as resting places. The images in poetry are to be enjoyed entirely for their unique qualities and an unusual and close relationship exists between the self and its images, which are emphatically *not* symbolic. In poetry 'words *are themselves images* and not signs for other images'.[14] They are immediately present, inviting 'contemplation' and providing a temporary respite from the practical and scientific pursuits of virtue, pleasure and knowledge. 'Cabbages' here are no longer food or chemicals but the objects of poetic imagining:

> In the night the cabbages catch at the moon,
> the leaves drip silver,
> the rows of cabbages are a series of little silver waterfalls in the moon.[15]

An image of this kind invites its reader to reflect and to look, not to act or desire. The self here is leisurely in the Aristotelian sense, and this leisure 'springs from the self-sufficiency enjoyed by each engagement in the activity and by the absence of any premeditated end. At whatever point contemplation is broken off it is never incomplete'.[16] Time and duration have no meaning for the contemplating self and a sense of wholeness inheres in the activity.

Oakeshott adopts a specific technical vocabulary to designate this relationship between the self and its images in poetry. The term of approbation is emphatically not pleasure but 'delight'. The activity in poetry is 'contemplating' or again 'delighting', words which Oakeshott employs interchangeably throughout the essay. Works of art are neither used nor desired but 'enjoyed'. The images in poetry are 'permanent' and 'unique'. No work of art can substitute for another; they are not to be valued like banknotes, but like human beings. Poetic images are, strictly speaking, incapable of being replicated. They are instead 'recognized as individuals, not concretions of qualities that might appear elsewhere'.[17] Poetry is said to be neither pleasurable nor painful; it has no antecedents or consequents. The essence of poetic activity is therefore not to represent, symbolize, exhort, teach or admonish: it is to make images and to engage in acts of imagination. The activity of the poet, as of the person who appreciates the poetic voice, is to contemplate, to delight and to wonder. Aesthetic experience is a world in which consequences are put aside in favour of present enjoyment.

None of this denies that artistic images may be, and very often are, put in the service of symbolic meaning – a woman's shoe in a Dutch still-life painting 'symbolizes' the erotic, and passages in 'Winter' from Vivaldi's *Four Seasons* unmistakably evoke the cold.

Christian art is likewise saturated with symbolic meaning. Indeed, it is primarily understood as important not for its images but for the messages and meanings these convey.[18] Still, Oakeshott classifies such intentions and effects as irrelevant to the aesthetic experience he is describing here, which evokes only contemplation and delight.

What sorts of images does Oakeshott think may be understood poetically? All of the standard 'aesthetic' pursuits appear: visual art, written verse and fiction, and musical composition. But this is by no means an exhaustive list, for (as it happens) the boundaries of contemplative experience are quite difficult to specify, as I have suggested above. Nevertheless, certain images are more likely than others to be seen as poetry, because they resist being read symbolically. 'A work of art is merely an image which is protected in an unusual degree from being read (that is, imagined) in an unpoetic manner, a protection it derives from its quality and from the circumstantial frame within which it appears'.[19] Oakeshott's example of 'a loaf of bread in paint' provides a vivid example of this sort of frame. No one would mistake the loaf for food; and thus the image is transformed from practical to contemplative. In the same way other images may be 'ambiguously' practical: a porch that provides shelter but also charm, a silver pitcher, a page from a medieval Bible now framed and displayed in someone's living-room. Poetry emerges when the links to practical activity are broken.

The poetic voice, however, is neither particularly stable nor strong, which accounts for its vulnerability with respect to the other modes. Poetry is especially unprotected against the voice of practice, which tends to insert itself at every opportunity. 'What does this work of art have to *teach* us?' it asks. Is this poem suitable? Is it useful for society? Does this work provide an appropriate model for moral behaviour? Thus practical questions are asked about the moral content of aesthetic images. The voice of poetry, Oakeshott maintains, does not respond to these questions because it is unconcerned with pleasure and pain, approval and disapproval. Of course these categories may be brought to bear on poetry, as they often are. But they are not essentially within its purview. The danger for the conversation as a whole lies in its tendency to forget that poetry has a voice of its own, one which blithely disregards practice and prefers to speak in terms of delight. Just as a girl may interrupt a conversation she finds tedious, turning it towards a topic she finds more pleasing, poetry playfully interrupts more 'serious' pursuits for the sake of enjoyment and diversion.

Throughout 'The Voice of Poetry' Oakeshott emphasizes the categorical distinction between poetry and practical activity, in part to distinguish his view from one he had advanced nearly thirty years earlier in *Experience and its Modes*. There he argued that the most 'thoroughly and positively practical life is that of the artist or the mystic ... [A]rt, music and poetry ... are wholly taken up with the practical life'.[20] In a candid statement of his change in view – indeed the only such statement he ever made – Oakeshott introduced the first edition of *Rationalism in Politics* by admitting that he wished to retract the 'foolish sentence' he had written in *Experience and its Modes*, which placed poetry within the mode of practice.

CRITICISMS OF 'THE VOICE OF POETRY'

Several criticisms are commonly made of this essay. The first of these, often voiced by poets and artists themselves, is that the essay's description of 'poetry' does not accord with accepted notions of creative activity – that Oakeshott is describing something, to be sure, but not art or poetry in any recognizable form. Oakeshott is not unaware of this potential objection, commenting somewhat cryptically near the beginning of the essay that '[n]either the poet nor the critic of poetry will find very much to his purpose in what I have to say'.[21] Second, some readers find the essay incomplete since it fails to consider many important questions of aesthetics.[22] Those who approach it with questions about what ought to be considered art and why, or about the relative value of different kinds of art, or about the attitude or intention of the artist, will likely be disappointed that Oakeshott does not engage these topics. Third, and perhaps most compelling as a criticism, is the observation that an Oakeshottian response to poetry itself seems to require an elaborate education or initiation. 'Contemplation', writes one critic, 'must now be understood as a learnt response to art, a form of appreciation that must be continually reinforced by a "theoretical" concept of art; the "poetic" and the "non-poetic" have to be continually separated from each other'.[23] As such, practical activity lurks around the edges of contemplative experience because the notion that there might be a particular 'desired' or 'approved' conception of art *is itself practical*.

Responses to these criticisms should be made only after first reiterating the purpose of Oakeshott's essay, which is to provide a modally distinct explanation of aesthetic experience and to protect aesthetics thus understood from the incursions of practice. The essay is therefore simultaneously an explication and a defence, or *apologia*.[24] As an explication, it aims at defining the scope and limits of the 'voice' or 'mode' of poetry. As a defence, the essay protects this conception of poetry against misunderstandings, which tend to be expressed with practical considerations in mind. It is true that the essay invites many of these misunderstandings, for Oakeshott uses common words to describe a kind of experience (poetry) in a way that is quite unconventional. Still, several replies are worth making to the objections articulated above.

The first and second criticisms – that readers do not recognize the 'poetry' Oakeshott describes and that he does not give a complete account of art – may be addressed together. The essay does in fact invite both these objections, because in using the terms 'poetry' and 'art' Oakeshott is engaging a subject on which many people already have opinions. Indeed, most of us have a notion that art is a certain kind of object, something special that can be described, categorized and distinguished from things that are 'not-art'. Thus many readers will be inclined to compare Oakeshott's account with their own, judging it deficient or praiseworthy to the degree it accords with ideas they already hold.

However Oakeshott is not describing a concept we already know and understand. He is engaged in something much more radical than this. Although he uses familiar terms, throughout the essay he redefines and delimits these terms quite idiosyncratically. 'Contemplation' is no longer the contemplation of Aristotle or of Bonaventure; it is an altogether different activity that involves seeing familiar things in an unusual way.[25] 'Poetry' is not essentially written verse or paint on canvas, but a mode of human activity that belongs alike to the 'poet' and to the viewer who is inclined to see things poetically. Oakeshott emphasizes again and again that 'poetry' is an experience, a 'voice' that stands alongside the voices of practice and science. As such, the locus of the activity is not outside human consciousness (an artefact) but within it. Thus the emphasis of the essay falls on all the ways in which human beings tend to overlook, ignore or corrupt this way of seeing (call it 'poetry' or whatever one likes; the name matters less than the manner of viewing the world). And the most common way of getting poetry wrong is to demand that it answer our practical needs, which include our desires for pleasure, moral instruction, expression of emotion, and so on.

R. G. Collingwood observes in his *Autobiography* that in order to discover an author's meaning 'you must also know what the question was (a question in his own mind, and presumed by him to be in yours) to which the thing he has said or written was meant as an answer'.[26] Until one has done this one has not understood an author; and, of course, the most common mistake is for us to put our own questions to a text and then to complain that its author has failed to answer them. The question to which Oakeshott's essay most directly offers an answer is: how might we describe a mode of human *experience* that apprehends images solely to delight in them? His question is not: what is poetry or aesthetics as these are commonly understood?

The third criticism, as I have observed, is perhaps the most interesting and compelling of the group. It is the notion that an aesthetic attitude of contemplation, delight and enjoyment is somehow unnatural or artificial; or indeed that Oakeshott himself is being practical in recommending a 'correct' way of appreciating art. Two responses to this criticism are worth making. First, if we pause to consider it, the aesthetic attitude Oakeshott describes is the most natural of all human responses to the world. To spend any time at all with small children is to learn, sometimes to one's chagrin, that they care nothing for practical considerations. Time and duration have no meaning for them; they do not worry at all about lateness or promptness or about our endless adult lists of obligations. Enjoyment and play are their operative categories. They are content to delight in the beauty of a piece of glass found on the sidewalk or a long-abandoned snail shell. The language children speak is 'an heroic [one] of [their] own invention ... because [they] are moved not by the desire to communicate but by the delight of utterance'.[27] What Oakeshott describes as aesthetic is therefore a natural but easily lost human response to the world. It is difficult only because we have allowed practical experience to overtake us. Second, implicit in this final criticism is the notion that Oakeshott himself is moralizing about art – that he is 'recommending' or 'exhorting' readers to approach aesthetic experience 'in the right way'. The tone of the essay as a whole is not a moral exhortation; it is, as I have argued, explication and defence. It aims, like a confident hostess, at introducing a shy, demure voice (poetry) that nevertheless has something distinctive and vital to say.

However, although the essay is not a moral exhortation it does contain hints that there is some kind of connection between poetry and practice. This final criticism is therefore worthy of further consideration. Oakeshott maintains that there are 'links', 'connections' and 'channels' between poetry and practice even as he is also at pains to disentangle the two voices throughout most of the essay. This tension is one of the most intriguing parts of the essay, about which I shall say more below after a brief consideration of religion.

THE AESTHETIC CONSCIOUSNESS AND THE RELIGIOUS DISPOSITION

A primary purpose of Oakeshott's essay is thus to set out the essential characteristics of the poetic voice, as different as this may be from many ordinary conceptions of 'poetry'. As I have already stressed, Oakeshott places little emphasis on art as product and artist as maker. He is instead concerned with what has been called 'the aesthetic consciousness', that is, the person who does the seeing.[28] It is worth pointing out that in principle an artist (using the term loosely) need not even inhabit the mode of poetry to produce his 'art'. He may well be simply an excellent craftsman, producing woven baskets for money – baskets that are later recognized for their quality and placed in a museum. The baskets become 'poetry' only because the spectator's aesthetic consciousness deems them worthy of contemplation.

Oakeshott's emphasis on this aesthetic consciousness provides an important connection to his view of religion. He wrote about religion extensively as a young man in the 1920s and 1930s, but from then on was silent about it until he considered it once more in *On Human Conduct*. In his early writings the religious person is someone who possesses just this aesthetic consciousness, a person who can see the beauty of the world as it is without looking to the future for fulfilment. Such a person is content with present reality. To engage life with this aesthetic or 'religious' disposition requires that one reject the worldliness inherent in career and achievement. It asks, rather, for the cultivation of 'insight' and a 'personal sensibility'.[29] Both art and religion represent Oakeshott's way of negotiating an ever-present tension between permanence and contingency, between our desire for permanent fulfilment and our inability to attain it. Aesthetics and religion help us to negotiate this tension by supplying experiences that are complete in themselves.

In a certain sense one can claim that for Oakeshott aesthetic consciousness had replaced religious consciousness, while simultaneously adopting its main features. In this sense, the change went parallel to a change that occurred in the English consciousness in general. This is sometimes seen as a result of the decline of orthodox religion in England during the late nineteenth century and a replacement of religion with aesthetics, as in the writings of Walter Pater. I do not doubt that all of this plays a part in the development of Oakeshott's views, and it is worthwhile to trace his intellectual influences. But most interesting of all is the *nature* of the felt experience that generated these differently named ideas in Oakeshott's thought. The core of it was a poignant sense that human life was limited in the satisfactions it could offer, that death was the central fact of life, and that little, if anything, could rise above the temporal and transitory. Oakeshott longed for something permanent and stable, which he found in a certain way in poetic experience. Thus one can observe the striking language in 'The Voice of Poetry', language partly drawing on the work of Edward Bullough, but also, perhaps, echoing Augustine in the final line quoted below:

> In practical activity an image may be said to be impermanent because it is always a temporary resting-place in a necessarily endless process which is concluded only in death; it is a step in the execution of a policy or a project; it is something to be made use of, to be improved or transformed ... The images which partner contemplation, on the other hand, have the appearance of being both permanent and unique. Contemplation does not use, or use-up or wear-out its images, or induce change in them: it rests in them, looking neither backwards nor forwards.[30]

From a critical perspective, this attitude of 'enjoyment' looks to be an agnostic's replacement of the divine with something man-made – either a poetic artefact or a consciously willed disposition to view the world poetically. Oakeshott's youthful essays indeed seem at times to approach something like this in his attempt to overcome the world through 'living in the present'. But poetic contemplation is not 'doing' in any practical sense; it requires a willingness to be acted upon, to receive and to cherish. It also demands a certain kind of humility in not claiming to know the things that lie beyond human experience. It is at once Socratic and Augustinian, but also distinctly modern.

AESTHETICS AND MORALITY

The implication of the preceding sections is that somehow the aesthetic attitude may inform all of life. But this clashes quite obviously with Oakeshott's idea of modality, where each mode is separate from the others – practice from science, science from poetry, and practice from poetry. If indeed the modes or 'voices' are radically independent, as Oakeshott asserts throughout most of his writing, then this idea of an 'aesthetic view of life' would be a misunderstanding of his main thesis and a conflation of the poetic and practical modes. Yet Oakeshott himself gives hints that these two modes may at times approach each other. To return to the question I touched on above: if there is some relationship between these modes, how might it be described and what are the implications for Oakeshott's thought as a whole? The fundamental issue may be set out in two parts. First: is Oakeshott's view of moral conduct informed by aesthetic considerations, or is the mode of practical activity radically separate from aesthetics? Second: if practical life and aesthetics are related, exactly *how* do they relate?

With respect to the first question, there is evidence on both sides. Since poetic images are not subject to moral approval or disapproval, and since they do not inform or guide us in any way, they would seem utterly irrelevant to moral conduct. Far from forging connections, Oakeshott seems intent upon '[driving] a wedge between the experience of art and … the nature of experience in the Practical Mode'.[31] On the other hand, friendly and hostile critics alike have long observed that a certain aesthetic outlook pervades Oakeshott's work, including his reflections on practical matters. J. G. Blumler, writing in 1964, thought that Oakeshott's conservative 'reverence for tradition' was *merely* an aesthetic preference. According to

Blumler, conservatism could be supported in one of two ways: either by appeal to a religious foundation – some conception of natural law that undergirds the tradition – or by 'an appreciation of the elegance of traditional politics'.[32] Oakeshott, he thought, chose the latter, which was ultimately grounded in nothing except a notion of good taste. Aesthetic preference meant, for Blumler, superficiality and arbitrariness. Others, however, have described the aesthetic basis of Oakeshott's thought as something rich and positive. A recent study concludes that his view of aesthetics is definitely relevant to his moral philosophy and that '[i]nsofar as every performance enacts a self, in so far as a self is responsible for the self it becomes, every individual is a poet'.[33] Much in Oakeshott's work confirms this. In his essay from 1948 entitled 'The Tower of Babel', Oakeshott claims that all human activity has a poetic character.[34] Likewise, the concluding pages of 'The Voice of Poetry' make similar connections between aesthetics and morality.

How can these contradictory impulses be reconciled? Is the only choice either absolute modal independence or some kind of 'Aesthetic Primacy', which asks that *all* experience be seen through the lens of the aesthetic so that practical (moral) experience is subordinated?[35] Neither of these options is entirely satisfactory on its own, because Oakeshott argues for both positions at different points in his writing. At times he observes that there are indeed links between practical activity and poetry: 'we may', Oakeshott writes, 'find in practical activity itself intimations of contemplative imagining capable of responding to the voice of poetry'.[36] In other places, however, he is quite clear about poetry's modal independence from practice: 'poetry is an escape ... from the considerabilities of practical activity'.[37] Still, the concluding pages of 'The Voice of Poetry' suggest undeniable, if indirect or 'oblique' links between these two modes. Thus we must conclude that aesthetics and morality relate in some way. Oakeshott does not systematically spell out the nature of this connection, but there are several ways one might characterize it based on the statements he does make about it.

First, we might consider the possibility that certain kinds of relationships or activities are somehow exempt from the full implications of their positions within the practical mode. These include love, friendship and 'moral goodness', which Oakeshott characterizes as 'ambiguously practical'. In love and friendship, for instance, we appreciate the 'uniqueness of a self'; and a friend evokes 'interest, delight, unreasoning loyalty, and ... (almost) ... contemplative imagination'. The relationship of friends is 'dramatic, not utilitarian'.[38] Likewise, in moral goodness there is a 'release from the deadliness of doing and a possibility of perfection, which intimates poetry'. It is a 'private and self-sufficient activity, not accommodated to the world, emancipated from place or condition, in which each engagement is independent of what went before and of what may come after'.[39] One way of specifying the relationship between poetry and practice might thus be to create a special category of experience that bridges the two modes.

But what kinds of experience would fall into this category, and why? Of course not all friendships intimate poetry. Some friendships aim primarily at pleasure or utility and thus lie squarely within the mode of practice, as Aristotle helps us to see. By the same token, ordinary relationships of utility may at times take on a poetic aspect. Perhaps a better way of specifying this intermingling of these modes is to observe that, depending on inclination, one might choose to view all of experience from the point of view of *either* practice or poetry. If one inclines towards practice, then even the most poetic images might be seen as useful or inimical to some ulterior goal: 'each image [would be] recognized as something to be made use of or exploited'.[40] On the other hand, seeing the world poetically would yield an inclination to enjoy and delight in images of moral conduct (and anything else) as primarily aesthetic. The danger here would be a tendency towards a certain kind of 'aestheticism' for which many thinkers have been rightly criticized. An *exclusively* aesthetic approach to the world neglects the seriousness and purpose that is often called for in moral life. But Oakeshott does not demand that we abandon practice; he asks, rather, that we respect the integrity of all the modes and recognize the diversity of their claims upon human beings. 'To listen to the voice of poetry is to enjoy, not a victory, but a momentary release, a brief enchantment', he maintains. 'And perhaps, obliquely, it is something more. Having an ear ready for the voice of poetry is to be disposed to choose delight rather than pleasure or virtue or knowledge, a disposition which will reflect itself in practical life in an affection for its intimations of poetry'.[41]

These two modes may interpenetrate, it would seem, in one additional and interesting way that is implied but unstated. If one has the experience of poetic contemplation and realizes its delights, one might try to maximize those delights – to order one's life so as to prioritize aesthetic experience. At this point the desire for such priority might become the premise of a practical syllogism as follows: if the contemplative (aesthetic) life is good and should be maximized, and if buying a luxury car, say, would inhibit my ability to engage in such contemplation because of anxiety and expense, then I should not buy this luxury car. This syllogism is 'practical' all the way down, but its initial premise is the product of an aesthetic insight. Thus the aesthetic might again have an indirect effect on practice. Poetry would not then be merely a contribution that richens or deepens the 'flavour' of practice, leaving the priority of practical life untouched. Instead, the poetic experience might have a transformative effect that would be capable of bringing about a fundamental change in disposition. A person who has been thus transformed might begin to prefer sympathy to criticism, reflection to action. Perhaps not coincidentally, this might also mark the beginning of the philosophic life, which demands a similar retreat from the world of practical activity.

AESTHETICS AND POLITICS

To return at last to the question with which this essay began: why should a political philosopher have been so concerned with aesthetics? Is the inclusion of 'The Voice of Poetry' in *Rationalism in Politics* inexplicable, the essay itself esoteric? Is Oakeshott's view of politics really 'anti-politics', as Crossman has put it disparagingly, merely 'the posture of an aesthete whose true delight is in love and poetry'?[42] I have argued above that a connection exists between the aesthetic world and the moral world, such that receptivity to the aesthetic may become dispositional. Such a person is unlikely to be ruled by the current gods of achievement and acquisition. He will live 'with' his age, but not as its creation, to paraphrase Schiller.[43] Still, what does all this have to do with the political philosophy for which Oakeshott is famous?

One misconception should be disposed of at the outset. In focusing on poetic experience, Oakeshott did not espouse some kind of aesthetic politics that valued doing grand deeds on a national stage. He did not, after all, regard politics as even remotely close to man's highest activity; indeed, he thought it quite impossible to find human fulfilment in politics. A footnote in 'The Voice of Poetry' makes this point forcefully. There Oakeshott distinguishes, perhaps with a nod to Hannah Arendt, modern 'practical' politics of the last four centuries from the 'poetic' activity of politics in ancient Greece.[44] Further confirmation of his views about the dissatisfactions inherent in politics may be found in the many places throughout his corpus where he describes the profound limitations of politics, as well as the illusions of those who wish for it to provide more than it does. Indeed, Oakeshott's sense of political activity is in a certain sense the *antithesis* of aesthetic appreciation. It aims not at beauty and wonder but at achieving a reasonable measure of coherence and success in practical life.

In one sense, then, Crossman (quoted above) is right. Oakeshott did genuinely value love and poetry more highly than practical political and moral activity, and this, in our modern ideological age, is something to be admired, not disparaged. A vitally important, though often overlooked, statement of Oakeshott's perspective on the relative unimportance of politics compared to other human activities is found in an essay entitled 'The Claims of Politics' (1939). This essay is a provocative refutation of the common, moralistic argument that political activity is the most important way of taking part in the life of a society. 'Politics,' Oakeshott writes, 'is a highly specialized and abstracted form of communal activity; it is conducted on the surface of the life of a society and except on rare occasions makes *remarkably small impression* below that surface.'[45] The rejuvenation of a society comes not from those engaged in politics but from artists, poets and philosophers – people whose distance from 'the world' is not merely accidental but essential to their work: the 'emotional and intellectual integrity and insight for which they stand is something foreign to the political world'.[46] Politics requires not just immersion in the practical world, as one would expect, but even spiritual callousness, an inability to see the subtleties of various positions, and an unwillingness to re-examine one's own positions once they have been formed. A 'limitation of view', Oakeshott writes, 'which appears so clear and practical, but which amounts to little more than a mental fog, is inseparable from political activity'.[47] Similarly, Oakeshott ends his famous essay 'On Being Conservative' by observing that the world of politics is appropriate not for those who are poetic, youthful and energetic, but for sober adults who have learned how to navigate the commonplace and even tedious world of fact. Politics is an activity suitable for those who 'are so inclined and have nothing better to think about'.[48]

But of course the implication of Crossman's remark is that love and poetry are less serious pursuits than politics, and that to be an 'aesthete' is a trivialization of life. No doubt there are numerous examples of this tendency in those who advocated an aesthetic approach to experience, but I do not think that Oakeshott falls into this category. His attachment to aesthetics, as central as I have argued that it is, represents merely one small though vitally important contribution to a larger philosophical output that was, indeed, taken up with practice and particularly with modern politics. His polemical essays in *Rationalism in Politics*, as well as his philosophical examination of civil association in *On Human Conduct*, are attempts to characterize practical life more accurately against many modern (and not so modern) misunderstandings of it: Pelagianism, Rationalism and the politics of faith, to name just a few. Many modern approaches to politics and to practical life are not merely a threat to the aesthetic sensibility but are also utopian, which is the real ground upon which Oakeshott attacked them. While much of his work, therefore, attempted to preserve a space for those activities that were truly important to him, such as self-enactment, love, friendship and philosophy, Oakeshott also (*pace* Crossman) had a political philosophy in the strict sense of the term. Although what he often called conservatism is a disposition that overlaps with an aesthetic sensibility, it has political implications that go well beyond aesthetics. These implications relate, quite simply, to what politics must do if it wishes to facilitate human flourishing. Oakeshott's emphasis on what *presently* exists undergirds a view of politics as civil association that would eschew the grand projects and reforms handed down by an all-powerful state.

But the 'conservative disposition' is also worth cultivating as an attitude towards the world in general – not just towards politics. Such an attitude, Oakeshott maintains, requires that one 'be equal to one's own fortune . . . live at the level of one's own means . . . [and] be content with the want of greater perfection which belongs alike to oneself and one's circumstances'.[49] Such an attitude is, in Christian terms, the antithesis of pride – a rejection of all grand projects that are so aptly symbolized by the tower of Babel. The picture of the conservative disposition that emerges in 'On Being Conservative' is particularly notable for its aesthetic overtones, given the emphasis on terms I have already noted in 'The Voice of Poetry'. In 'On Being Conservative' conservatism appears as a remarkably countercultural moral orientation. It is a propensity, above all, to *enjoy* rather than to seek. Friendship, the most conservative of all relationships, is 'dramatic, not utilitarian', and the friend is someone 'who excites contemplation'.[50] This conservative disposition rests not on reverence for the past; rather 'what is esteemed is the present' and happiness consists in *enjoying* 'what is available' and *delighting in* what is present.[51] Oakeshott's pronounced emphasis on living in the present, on enjoyment and on the contemplative disposition all describe the essence of the aesthetic consciousness. And here it is called 'conservatism'.

All this supports the conclusion that Oakeshott's thought on aesthetics ought to be seen as central to his philosophy as a whole. I have implied throughout that something about 'The Voice of Poetry' demands greater attention, that it is not merely a diversion or departure from his serious thought about politics, but is instead central to his philosophical outlook. Insofar as it is the clearest expression of his view of life in general – of human experience understood not as a series of trials or achievements but as something to be enjoyed and appreciated – these ideas inform all of his thinking. Any true and practicable politics must get to grips with the various modes in which free human beings engage the world in which they live and find value where they will. A politics that refuses to consider Oakeshott's insights on this score is an ideological politics that takes its bearings from something other than a full understanding of human possibilities. '[T]o know only one's own tradition is not to know even that', remarks Oakeshott in his essay 'Political Education'.[52] This remark is strikingly similar to Oakeshott's conception of modality: being conversant only in one's favoured 'voice' is a failure to have understood the whole. In our modern ideological age, preoccupied as it is with politics and practical activity, Oakeshott's aesthetic emphasis thus appears extraordinarily attractive. It stands as a corrective to all the doctrinaire, bellicose and preservative brands of conservatism that are so popular today. His view will not be embraced or even understood by many; but for those who retain some sense of life's richness and diversity, it represents a profound account of life's possibilities.

NOTES

1 G. Catlin, review of *Rationalism in Politics, and Other Essays*, in *Western Political Quarterly*, 16 (1963), 259–61.
2 In *Experience and its Modes* (Cambridge University Press, 1933) Oakeshott had designated the modes as science, history and practice. I use the terms 'modes' and 'voices' interchangeably throughout this chapter.
3 I also use the terms 'poetry', 'poetic experience', 'art' and 'aesthetics' interchangeably.
4 M. Oakeshott, 'The Voice of Poetry in the Conversation of Mankind', in *RP*, p. 224. R. Grant remarks in 'Oakeshott on the Nature and Place of Aesthetic Experience', in C. Abel and T. Fuller (eds.), *The Intellectual Legacy of Michael Oakeshott* (Thorverton: Imprint Academic, 2005), p. 298: 'anything may be viewed aesthetically by one so minded', and this puts the 'spectator, rather than the author or object, in the driving seat'.
5 The piece was originally published as a free-standing work and later included in *Rationalism in Politics*. Oakeshott's one other significant statement on poetry, unpublished until quite recently, is an essay entitled 'An Essay on the Relations of Philosophy, Poetry and Reality', in *WH*, pp. 67–116.
6 Practice or 'practical experience' here should not be confused with his use of the term 'practices' in *HC*.
7 Oakeshott, 'Voice of Poetry', p. 204.
8 *Ibid.*, p. 207.
9 *Ibid.*, p. 216.
10 *Ibid.*, p. 211; italics the present author.
11 *Ibid.*, pp. 211–12.
12 *Ibid.*, p. 216.
13 E. Podoksik, 'The Voice of Poetry in the Thought of Michael Oakeshott', *Journal of the History of Ideas*, 63 (2002), 718–23, places Oakeshott in the tradition of Ruskin, Pater and Wilde, a tradition that valued 'art for art's sake'.
14 Oakeshott, 'Voice of Poetry', p. 235; italics the present author.
15 C. Sandburg, 'Nocturn Cabbage', in *Rainbows are Made: Poems by Carl Sandburg* (Orlando, FL: Harcourt, 1982), p. 55.

16 Oakeshott, 'Voice of Poetry', p. 221.
17 *Ibid.*, p. 220.
18 Oakeshott recognizes that his notion of aesthetic experience is particularly modern. Only the emancipation of objects from their practical uses allows for the kind of contemplation he describes. See 'Voice of Poetry', pp. 238–9.
19 *Ibid.*, p. 225.
20 *EM*, pp. 296–7.
21 Oakeshott, 'Voice of Poetry', p. 203.
22 See H. Davis, 'Poetry and the Voice of Michael Oakeshott', *British Journal of Aesthetics*, 15 (1975), 67: 'Perhaps the most that could be said is that Oakeshott's view focuses on *only one* of the interesting or significant aspects of art, and is a positive inducement to disregard or not to seek for others'.
23 *Ibid.*, 66.
24 Oakeshott acknowledges the purpose of the essay as an apology for poetry in 'Voice of Poetry', pp. 239–42.
25 See Oakeshott's discussion of this distinction, *ibid.*, pp. 218–24.
26 R. G. Collingwood, *An Autobiography* (Oxford University Press, 1939), p. 31.
27 Oakeshott, 'Voice of Poetry', p. 246.
28 'Aesthetic consciousness' comes from E. Bullough, *Aesthetics* (Stanford University Press, 1957), pp. 69–79.
29 Oakeshott uses both of these terms repeatedly in his essay 'Religion and the World', in *RPML*, pp. 27–38.
30 Oakeshott, 'Voice of Poetry', p. 218; cf. Bullough, *Aesthetics*, p. 74.
31 Davis, 'Poetry', 62.
32 J. G. Blumler, 'Politics, Poetry and Practice', *Political Studies*, 12 (1964), 36.
33 G. Worthington, 'The Voice of Poetry in Oakeshott's Moral Philosophy', *Review of Politics*, 64 (2002), 306.
34 M. Oakeshott, 'The Tower of Babel', in *RP*, p. 72.
35 See Podoksik, 'Voice of Poetry', 720, for a summary of what is meant by Aesthetic Primacy, a term Podoksik borrows from Monroe Beardsley.
36 Oakeshott, 'Voice of Poetry', p. 243.
37 *Ibid.*, p. 242.
38 *Ibid.*, p. 244.
39 *Ibid.*, p. 245.
40 *Ibid.*, p. 207.
41 *Ibid.*, p. 247.
42 R. Crossman, review of *Rationalism in Politics*, in *Times Literary Supplement*, 28 September 1962, 753–4.

43 'Live with your age, but be not its creation; labour for your contemporaries, but do for them what they need, and not what they praise'. F. Schiller, *Aesthetical and Philosophical Essays* (Boston: Francis A. Niccolls, 1902), p. 33.
44 See Oakeshott's footnote in 'Voice of Poetry', p. 202.
45 M. Oakeshott, 'The Claims of Politics', in *RPML*, p. 93.
46 *Ibid.*, p. 95.
47 *Ibid.*, p. 93.
48 M. Oakeshott, 'On Being Conservative', in *RP*, p. 196.
49 *Ibid.*, p. 169.
50 *Ibid.*, p. 177.
51 *Ibid.*, p. 168.
52 M. Oakeshott, 'Political Education', in *RP*, p. 131.

KEVIN WILLIAMS

5 Education as conversation

INTRODUCTION

The metaphor of conversation underpins Oakeshott's entire philosophy to such an extent that Bhikhu Parekh refers to his account of human agency as 'a conversational theory of action'.[1] It has been described as 'rich and capacious' and as a 'root metaphor' for education by John B. Bennett,[2] and its potential has been used by other scholars to illuminate the activities of teaching and learning. The value of the metaphor is a feature of an essay by Marc O. DeGirolami that draws substantially on what he calls Oakeshott's 'conversational theory of education' in the elaboration of a framework for a philosophy of education.[3] Of course, the metaphor, which Oakeshott takes from Hobbes and Montaigne, is not a new one. It also appears in the work of Cardinal Newman and Matthew Arnold, two important theorists of the concept of a liberal education in the nineteenth century. The metaphor is reflected in Arnold's characterization of culture as made up of multifaceted 'voices of human experience' represented by 'art, science, poetry, philosophy, history, as well as of religion'.[4]

This chapter aims to analyse what exactly Oakeshott means by his characterization of education as a conversation. It endeavours to tease out the implications of Oakeshott's use of the term and to explore ways in which the metaphor can take on life in the business of teaching and learning. The chapter also considers the plausibility of the two principal strands of criticism of the metaphor of

This text of this chapter has benefited from the comments of Colm Lennon and Caitríona Williams.

conversation, finding that much of this criticism is ill founded. Yet the tendency of Oakeshott's educational conversation to resist the accommodation of disagreement in respect of moral, political and religious convictions is acknowledged. The metaphor of education as conversation is shown, nevertheless, to be susceptible of development in a way that supports a more nuanced pedagogy that will allow for such disagreement.

What, then, is meant by conversation in the educational context?

OAKESHOTT'S EDUCATIONAL CONVERSATION

Firstly it is necessary to outline the contours of Oakeshott's philosophy of education. To understand this philosophy it will help to draw on a distinction that is developed in a posthumously published essay entitled 'Work and Play'.[5] This is a distinction between 'work' or practical experience and 'play' or the scientific, historical and aesthetic modes of experience. He maintains that genuine education, that is, as conducted in schools and colleges, consists in the initiation of young people into the metaphorical conversation made up of the languages of human understanding (including that of art) that are rigorously set apart from the world of 'work' or practical experience. The world of practical experience evolves from being one mode alongside others in *Experience and its Modes*, assuming in the later works its status as a *bête noire*, potentially subversive of the true remit of education. This remit is to enable young people to use the explanatory languages of human understanding.

The link between learning these languages and learning to participate in the 'conversation of mankind'[6] is made very explicit. The title of the essay 'The Voice of Conversation in the Education of Mankind', written *circa* 1948, reflects this very clearly.[7] In 'The Voice of Poetry in the Conversation of Mankind', written in 1959, the point is developed: 'Education, properly speaking, is an initiation into the skill and partnership of ... conversation in which we learn to recognize the voices, to distinguish the proper occasions of utterance, and in which we acquire the intellectual and moral habits appropriate to conversation'.[8]

For Oakeshott, therefore, education involves learning to join in the special form of play constituted by the 'conversation of mankind' as convened by teachers and educational institutions. The conversational playfulness associated with education can be said to be liberal in two ways. In the first place, it is liberal in terms of where it is conducted, that is, in an arena that is a 'place apart'[9] from the rest of society. This arena is free from intrusion by the demands of the language of practical activity, the 'language of appetite',[10] or from the world *sub species voluntatis*, 'from the here and now of current engagements'.[11] In the second place, it is liberal in what it does, that is, it liberates learners by emancipating them from servitude to this 'language of appetite'. Accordingly, through their education, young people are offered 'a release from the immediacies, the partialities and the abridgements of the local and contemporary world'.[12] This 'release' constitutes 'an emancipation from the mere "fact of living", from the immediate contingencies of place and time of birth, from the tyranny of the moment and from the servitude of a merely current condition'.[13] Education as 'release' into a world of play is related to conversation because the essence of a conversation is to be playful and to offer its participants no greater pleasure than the pleasure of conversing.

Closer examination of the concept shows how conversation as a pre-eminently playful activity fits well with this conception of education. To quote Oakeshott's words:

> As civilized human beings, we are the inheritors, neither of an inquiry about ourselves and the world, nor of an accumulating body of information, but of a conversation, begun in the primeval forests and made more articulate in the course of centuries. It is a conversation which goes on both in public and within each of ourselves. Of course there is argument and inquiry and information, but wherever these are profitable they are to be recognized as passages in this conversation, and perhaps they are not the most captivating of the passages. It is the ability to participate in this conversation ... which distinguishes the human being from the animal and the civilized man from the barbarian.[14]

Before even embarking on formal education, it is via conversations with parents or primary care-givers that children enter into the world of human feeling and ideas. As the common conduit to becoming a person, conversation is, then, as Efraim Podoksik observes, more than just a metaphor.[15] Participation in practical and non-instrumental conversations is an inescapable feature of becoming a human being. It is not possible to become part of a community without such participation, and equally impossible to divest oneself of the culture thus acquired. As learning is constitutive of human identity, Oakeshott indicts the aspiration expressed by Bacon to 'throw myself into the river Lethe' in order 'to erase completely from my soul the memory of all knowledge, all art, all poetry' and 'to reach the opposite shore, naked, like the first man'.[16] The impossibility of discarding culture and the destructiveness of the attempt to do so are imaginatively communicated with a chilling persuasiveness by André Gide. Michel, the protagonist of *L'Immoraliste*, aspires to discover his 'authentic self' that had been 'hidden' by 'books, teachers, relatives' and to destroy the 'secondary, acquired self' that had been 'superimposed' by his education and 'childhood morals'.[17] The endeavour results in his serious psychological impairment and leads to the death of his wife. What Oakeshott explains, and what Gide shows, is that human learning is not a replaceable cultural filling or a series of discrete, detachable accomplishments, but rather it is a vital part of what makes human beings who they are. An essential ingredient of the human personality, culture is like the very air that we breathe.

Two points regarding the specifically educational dimension of conversation must be noted at this stage. In the first place, as with conversations proper, learning in Oakeshott's terms is open in that it is not conducted in the pursuit of some transcendent, absolute truth, of which the various modes of experience are a reflection. The inquiries of scientists or historians must not be expected to yield the definitive 'truth'. Rejecting all claims to absolute knowledge, Oakeshott envisages the conversation of mankind as a contingent, continuing dialogue between those willing to participate in it. With intellectual pursuits, as in political activity, there is neither a 'safe harbour' nor 'a destination to be reached'.[18] Each of the voices in Oakeshott's conversation, as Richard Rorty notes, is a 'cultural genre ... which centres on one topic rather than another at some given time not by dialectical necessity but as a result of various things happening elsewhere in the conversation'.[19]

In the second place, though the conversation is open-ended, Oakeshott does not envisage it as an adversarial enterprise where people argue about their ideas. It may well have 'passages of argument', but these are not the 'most captivating' of its features.[20] Oakeshott would seem to conceive of the discourse of argument as, in the words of a character in a novel by Ian McEwan, 'that old business of theorizing, taking up a position, planting the flag of identity and self-esteem, then fighting all comers to the end'.[21] For Oakeshott, conversation has an open character that makes it consistent with a conception of teaching and learning as a non-circumscribed shared search for knowledge. The conversation is conducted by equals or by teachers willing to engage learners in this exploration at the age-appropriate level. This elaboration of the implications of the notion of conversation is probably more child-centred than Oakeshott would have wished to endorse, yet conversation is of central relevance not only in much moral and civic education and but also in the teaching of many subjects across the curriculum. Conversation can play a positive role in promoting understanding within the major school subjects and it is an essential feature in the teaching of literature, history, geography, economics, religion and social studies.

STAGES OF LEARNING

What, then, are the stages in learning to participate in the educational conversation as elaborated by Oakeshott?

Language and literature

Underpinning his conception of these stages is a further language-related metaphor. This is to be found in a distinction that Oakeshott makes between what he calls the 'language' and the 'literature' or 'text' of a mode of thought.[22] This distinction allows Oakeshott to discriminate between different kinds and levels of education and should be considered more a conceptual tool than an epistemological truth. By 'language' he means the 'manner of thinking' appropriate to a particular mode of experience, and by a 'literature' or 'text' he means 'what has been said from time to time in a "language"'.[23] The literature consists in the facts, information, discoveries, conclusions or disclosures provided by the appropriate explanatory language. A textbook of geology, for example, contains some part of the current state of geological knowledge, but this compilation need make no reference to the way in which geologists came to establish this knowledge. The textbook represents the literature or text of geological knowledge, while the investigatory procedures whereby geologists have established this knowledge represent the language of the discipline. Oakeshott believes that learners need to be familiar with the literature of human understanding before they can master its languages. Facility or fluency in the language of any skill must be acquired by trying to speak or practise it rather than by studying dictionaries or grammar books about it. Much of this learning takes place within the context of a personal relationship between teacher and learner on an apprenticeship basis. In his pedagogy Oakeshott lays particular emphasis on the personal nature of the educational transaction, and this confirms the appropriateness of the conversation metaphor.

Early education

In terms of the language–literature distinction, early education involves, literally and metaphorically, a preparation to read the literatures of knowledge.[24] In primary school children learn reading, writing and arithmetic, to play musical scales and simple pieces of music, and they also begin to study foreign languages. Such activities involve much mechanical exercise to improve the children's dexterity at them. Oakeshott also makes the dramatic claim that the content of what primary school children read and of what they write is not important; it is enough that they become able to recognize and reproduce words.[25] This disregard for the content of what children should read and write may well be another rhetorical rebuff to proponents of 'relevance' within the curriculum. Most teachers and experts in literacy, however, would wish to argue that learning is facilitated where content connects in some way with children's interests.[26] Whatever his considered attitude to teaching and learning the enabling skills of literacy, Oakeshott does not believe that these are all that children's early education should consist of. He explicitly acknowledges the place within the school curriculum of the activities of singing, drawing and dance, pointing out that they prepare the way for the next stage of education.

In Oakeshott's account of the matter no sharp division exists between the early and the second stages of education. It is through a gradual and imperceptible transformation that children progress to the second stage. At this stage children begin to read the literatures of knowledge and to understand the information that these contain. To the pupils, therefore, the languages of mankind represent repositories of information about humankind and the world. In his similes, the world of learning 'appears much more like a stock of ideas, beliefs, perceptions, images and so on, than a capital'.[27] For Oakeshott, the curriculum at second level should be non-specialist in nature. Without 'significant orientation', it is not designed to cultivate 'individual talents and aptitudes'.[28] As school is the only institution specifically concerned with initiation into our cultural inheritance, it is, he believes, appropriate that it should provide for its pupils the full range of this inheritance. In his view, the ends of neither vocational nor university education are served by prematurely exposing young people to specialist studies. It is time next to consider, in more detail, the post-school dimension of education. Here his main concern is with the character and content of university education.

University education

Firstly, what is learned in a university is learned for the sake of the interest that it offers on its own account, rather than for the sake of the use to which it may be put. Even theology, law and medicine, studies that are directly related to professions, are included only because they represent branches of scholarship. Moreover, as apprenticeship elsewhere has to be added to studies in these areas, what occurs in university is, therefore, a 'preludial' form of education.[29] Secondly, university education is an education in the great explanatory languages of human understanding, and not merely in the literature generated by these languages. The university student does not simply learn to read the literature of knowledge but rather learns to manage the explanatory languages in which this literature is inscribed in order to gain an understanding and an appreciation of what it is like to think within the terms appropriate to these languages.[30] A text is not treated as an organization of information, as it is in vocational education, but rather as the paradigm of a language. In university education the text is considered an expression of how a particular explanatory language functions, and this is something that cannot be taught on its own as an abstraction from substantive texts.

The principal aim of Oakeshott's university curriculum is to teach the student to recognize and to distinguish between the different explanatory languages and to become 'familiar with the conditions each imposes upon utterance'.[31] Through acquiring the necessary familiarity some students will be enabled to speak one of these languages, that is, to express themselves in terms of its characteristic manner of thinking in a way that displays 'genuine understanding of the language spoken'.[32]

In respect of this purpose, we must ask how it is possible that students, who normally enjoy specialized initiation into a single language, can come to understand how their discipline fits into the map of knowledge and to appreciate how the other disciplines contribute to this map. This constitutes a particular version of a general problem in Oakeshott's epistemology that has been posed both by Bhikhu Parekh and Tariq Modood. Parekh wonders how Oakeshott can speak of conversation between voices where each uses a distinct, autonomous and self-contained language that shares nothing in common with the others.[33] In the terms of Oakeshott's discursive universe therefore, as Modood argues, there would appear to be 'no point of contact for conversing'.[34]

In considering how such a point of contact might be promoted, Oakeshott scornfully dismisses the project of widening curricula to include a course or courses of 'integrating' lectures.[35] To be accessible to non-specialists, such a course would be superficial and trivial. No 'sticky mess called "culture"'[36] can impose integration on the world of knowledge that he conceives of as radically differentiated. A culture is composed not of a 'set of abstract aptitudes' but rather of a conjunction of 'substantive expressions of thought'.[37] It is as impossible to think outside the terms of the individual language of a specific universe of discourse as it is to speak without using a particular language. As Oakeshott puts it, there exists no 'ideal non-idiomatic manner of speaking'.[38] This means that people cannot join in the educational conversation between the languages of mankind unless they speak one such language for themselves. According to Oakeshott, therefore, integrated courses or general courses in culture are misconceived attempts to teach the 'art of conversation ... to those who ... [have] nothing to say'.[39]

How, then, does he envisage that a student will come to understand and to appreciate the contribution of other voices to the educational conversation through the specialist study of one particular language or mode of thought? What Oakeshott believes is that the in-depth study of one particular discipline will offer some perspective on other disciplines by virtue of the fact that each discipline when studied in this manner will necessarily reveal something of its 'limits' and its 'presuppositions'.[40] Though he fails to provide more precise content to his argument, it seems reasonable to presume that Oakeshott means that any inquiry, pursued in depth, must demarcate subject matter, elaborate method and establish criteria of relevance, truth and validity. Such a procedure will inevitably require some familiarity with the different contexts in which knowledge is pursued and, as a result, students will acquire an understanding of the place of their discipline on the map of knowledge and of how it can be seen as a 'reflection' of the 'whole' of human knowledge.[41] Mary Midgley makes a similar point when she argues that a thorough understanding of the presuppositions of any discipline will enable the student to 'relate' these presuppositions to 'those needed for other inquiries'.[42] It is for this reason Oakeshott believes that each discipline, branch of scholarship or language of human understanding 'has within itself – when we drink deeply of it – a power to educate'.[43] Thus it is that 'no true and profoundly studied *techne* raises the distinction between acquiring a knowledge of some branch of learning and pursuing the general objects of education'.[44] The study of an area of knowledge, where this is sufficiently sustained, searching and sensitive to its wider context, should not result in a merely narrow, specialist mentality but should rather contribute to a genuinely educated frame of mind.

It may be argued, however, that knowledge of the presuppositions and context of her or his own discipline or area of expertise does not, *ipso facto*, enable an individual to understand other disciplines. Assuming that a university does provide an opportunity for informal contact between students and teachers of different disciplines, how can they understand each other without a common language? Oakeshott does not address this issue directly and indeed he may consider that the problem of creating points of contact between the languages arises only if, like Parekh and Modood, we take an extreme and exaggerated view of the level of expertise required to converse in the metaphorical languages of mankind. The ability to use these languages is not restricted to university dons and their students, but is to be found in embryonic, relatively undifferentiated form in the ordinary, everyday discourse of pre-school children. As noted earlier, it is via conversations with parents or primary caregivers that children enter into the world of human feeling and ideas. In this informal discourse lies the genesis of the sophisticated languages of the voices in the conversation of mankind. Moreover, before engaging on a particular course of study, students will already, from their school education, have learned something of a more formal nature not only about their chosen disciplines but also about other branches of scholarship.[45]

Perhaps each of Oakeshott's languages should be understood as having a pedagogic as well as a discursive idiom. The discursive idiom is that used in the pursuit of knowledge whereas the pedagogic is the idiom appropriate to teaching the discipline. This idea finds an echo in Newman's work where the teacher is conceived of as the 'living embodiment' of the universe of knowledge.[46] At university, students have the opportunity to study only a limited number of subjects but the teachers, as living embodiments of learning and expertise, also allow students to enjoy insights into the disciplines that they are not studying. This situation engenders a learning environment whereby 'the conversation of all is a series of lectures to each'.[47] In order to elucidate and to make accessible the character of their subjects, specialists will address their audience in the idiom of the teacher. In conversing with others from outside their discipline, those who wish to be understood will speak in this pedagogic idiom. And it is by means of such conversations in the literal sense that those disposed to do so may join in the metaphorical conversations between the great languages of humankind.

This leads to the questions of what counts as making an utterance that displays 'genuine understanding of the language spoken'.[48] Unfortunately, on this matter there is a lack of definition and precision about what Oakeshott actually means. He does, however, make clear that facility in managing one of the languages of human understanding does not necessitate being able to make an original contribution to the world of knowledge. This, he writes, 'can only be a rare achievement'.[49] Precise clarification of what counts as genuine understanding might shed light on the following matters. For example, it might explain whether there is a difference in the kind of understanding of physics that can be expected from a graduate in the subject and that of a graduate in engineering. Provision of such clarification might also tell us something about how Oakeshott conceives of the distinction between the level of understanding to be expected in history, for example, from an able student in the final year of secondary school and that to be expected from a university student of history. Perhaps, too, this clarification might explain in what sense a student of Classics, who has to deal with several universes of discourse (literary, philosophical and historical), can acquire a fluency in a particular language equivalent to that of the student of a single discipline. Doubtless, it would be unrealistic to expect of Oakeshott a graded taxonomy of levels of achievement in respect of each of the languages of human understanding. Moreover, his philosophy of education is profoundly antipathetic to any attempt to provide a rigid specification of predefined learning outcomes. Yet it would be helpful to find in his work some general indications regarding the nature of different levels of understanding within the pursuit of knowledge.

THE PEDAGOGY OF CONVERSATION?

Reference to a pedagogic idiom raises a general issue about learning to participate in the conversation of mankind. Oakeshott argues, quoting Antisthenes, that the 'chief advantage' to be derived from education is the ability 'of being able to converse with myself'.[50] He envisages conversations with oneself as being grounded in and sustained by conversations with others, because it is in conversations with others, especially with teachers, that ideas are explored and tested. Without exposure to the criticism of others, conversations with oneself risk being mere self-indulgence.

Oakeshott does not offer an elaborated pedagogy of the educational conversation in his writings about teaching and learning at university and seems to attribute to the teacher a strangely passive role.[51] What he seems to have in mind is a model of apprenticeship learning based on the university practice of medieval times whereby students were admitted merely as spectators to the great debates between Masters and Doctors. In *Rationalism in Politics*, medieval undergraduates are described as 'spectator-learners of a mystery' and in 'The Character of a University Education' he refers to contemporary students as 'spectators at performances'.[52] But the *disputatio* is not a teaching situation. In the *disputatio* the role of the disputants is primarily polemical rather than pedagogic and, consequently, they exercise no direct pedagogic function in respect of the student spectators. Accordingly, the relationship between students and disputants is not in fact a direct teaching situation at all. Oakeshott's pedagogy of university education appears therefore to accommodate only the attenuated notion of a learner imitating the teacher's example and overlooks the idea of supervised initiation into a skill of a learner by a teacher.

Wishing to resist the reduction of teaching skills to instruction in propositions, Oakeshott neglects that feature of apprenticeship whereby the learner gets a chance to practise a skill under the critical direction of a teacher proficient both at the activity and at initiating others into it. Judgement, which is made manifest as knowledge only in practice, is also best learned through graduated supervised practice. In his resistance to the idea that the teaching of skills can be reduced to instruction in propositions, it could reasonably be argued that the notion of supervised practice is assumed in Oakeshott's theory of learning. His observation that 'we come to penetrate an idiom of activity in no other way than by practising the activity; for it is only in the practice of an activity that we can acquire the knowledge of how to practise it' is consistent with such a theory.[53] But Oakeshott fails to make this explicit and this remains an omission in his philosophy of university education.

CONVERSATION AND ITS CRITICS

This absence of an elaborated pedagogy of initiation into conversation is an omission in Oakeshott's writings, but his critics concentrate more on the very use of the notion of conversation itself. This criticism is made up of two claims. According to the first claim, the metaphor is associated with elitism and, according to the second, conversation is linked to an unquestioning conservatism. Let us consider the charge of elitism.

A common conversation?

John White finds that Oakeshott's conception of conversation suggests 'the wide-ranging, unfocused atmosphere of an upper class dinner party'.[54] Yet I believe that the association of the notion of conversation with the 'upper class' is misguided. The charge of elitism is also seriously at odds with Oakeshott's strong conviction that the conversation of mankind is the patrimony of everyone regardless of social class background and that initiation into this emancipatory conversation is the right of every citizen and not just that of a cultural or social aristocracy. Though Oakeshott's views on liberal education were formed at a time when only a minority completed second-level schooling, the curriculum that he advocates has in principle the same purchase in the context of extensive current participation rates at this level in many western countries. In 'A Place of Learning' he insists that the invitation to become educated is extended equally to, for example, the child of 'a Neapolitan slum' as to the child of 'the better off'.[55] Oakeshott's curriculum is therefore not elitist, and indeed he is passionately committed to making available to everyone the curriculum traditionally restricted to the well-to-do.

The value of Oakeshott's metaphor of education as initiation into a conversation has been invoked to telling effect in an essay by Maxine Greene on the future of the American public school. She suggests that the Oakeshottian conversation can be interpreted broadly enough to include colonialist, female and working-class voices as well as popular and folk arts.[56] This is not a suggestion to be found anywhere in Oakeshott's writing, but these forms of literature are as capable of nurturing the imagination of learners as the more standard classical texts. What Greene proposes is a perfectly reasonable development of his essential ideas. Furthermore, although this is not an argument made by Oakeshott, it is my view that his educational conversation can in principle accommodate the teaching of practical subjects. Practical pursuits should not be identified with a crude instrumental 'language of appetite' because they can have a purely aesthetic dimension. Identity creation, 'learning to make something of ourselves'[57] or learning to make 'the most or the best'[58] of oneself can also assume an embodied quality. Learning to master a craft involves learning to participate in metaphorical conversation with its tradition. In several places, Oakeshott draws on a distinction made by A. N. Whitehead that is applicable to the teaching of non-classical literary texts and to the teaching of practical subjects: both forms of learning contribute to the 'quality' rather than to the brute 'fact of life'.[59]

Oakeshott's philosophy of education is consistent with making available within the curriculum at every level, from primary school to university, a wide range of cultural expression. There is also a pedagogic task to be undertaken, to which Oakeshott does not allude, in finding a way of making accessible to young people from backgrounds of socioeconomic disadvantage, especially in secondary schools, the traditional content of high culture that he quite rightly values so highly. This is necessary both in order to enable such young people to join in the conversation that is conducted in the language in which this content is inscribed and also to enable them constructively to challenge the social order wherein conditions of social deprivation are tolerated. Only by gaining access to the language of high-status knowledge and discourse will the socially disadvantaged come to exercise political control in their societies. Moreover, even young people who come from backgrounds of real poverty can engage in lively conversations with great literary texts and this can occur long before they reach university.[60] The capacity to engage in the educational conversation is not suddenly ignited when students attend university and, as DeGirolami with reference to Oakeshott correctly notes, it can well be 'salient in the elementary and secondary school context'.[61]

Conversation and conservatism

Michael Matthews and Joe McCarney have made an even more trenchant denunciation of the metaphor of the conversation on account of its alleged association with rigid conservatism and unquestioning traditionalism. Matthews claims that underlying the essay 'The Voice of Poetry in the Conversation of Mankind' is 'the world view which inspired the English ruling class to carry on their (*sic*) conversational diplomacy with European fascism in the 1930s'.[62] Unsurprisingly this tendentious, extravagant and false statement is not supported by any arguments. McCarney, by contrast, does elaborate on the grounds for his hostility towards Oakeshott. His criticism arises in the context of a trenchant denunciation of Richard Rorty for the latter's appropriation of Oakeshott's metaphor of the 'conversation of mankind'. McCarney takes his attack even further by indicting use of the metaphor as evidence of an ideological collusion by Rorty with the political right. McCarney then continues to reprove Rorty in an idiom that is as misguided as it is racist in respect of Oakeshott. 'Why', he wonders, 'should a sophisticated, contemporary Mid-Westerner assume the persona of a fake eighteenth-century English gentleman?'[63] The answer, he alleges, lies in Rorty's endorsement of Oakeshott's conservative ideology, which informs the metaphor. Underpinned by notions of 'aesthetics' and 'etiquette', this metaphor, argues McCarney, is 'precious and vapid' and 'sponsors a contemplative acceptance of the perennial riches of the human condition'.[64] Such 'acceptance' would be clearly inimical to any critical endeavour.

But careful perusal of his writings reveals why this attribution to Oakeshott of an uncritical traditionalism or unquestioning 'acceptance of the perennial riches of the human condition' is unjustified. In 'The Universities' can be found the somewhat impatient assertion that 'nobody would be so foolish as to deny the value of a critical attitude towards things'.[65] Quite explicitly in the essay 'The Political Economy of Freedom', in an observation that has escaped the attention of his critics, Oakeshott disparages the form of traditionalism that 'consists in merely doing what was done "last time"'.[66] This is why he insists that 'a morality in which reflection has no part is defective'.[67] In fact, Oakeshott makes the questionable claim that the most habitual form of moral conduct develops an element of 'selective conformity' that accommodates minor adjustments within the context of the tradition in which this form of conduct has its place.[68]

More generally, Oakeshott's conversation can be acknowledged as a rich account of the acquisition of a cultural inheritance, but the extent to which it can be said to accommodate a critical awareness of this inheritance is unclear. He certainly argues most emphatically that initiation into any of the languages of mankind must not be understood as initiation into static received doctrines. His conception of education as initiation into a cultural inheritance cannot, therefore and in fairness, be described as a 'process of socialization into a given intellectual identity'.[69] A culture, writes Oakeshott, is 'not a doctrine or set of consistent teachings or conclusions about a human life'.[70] Rather, it is a 'conversational encounter' composed of 'feelings, perceptions, ideas, engagements, attitudes and so forth, pulling in different directions, often critical of one another' but not at same time, causing us 'to be dismayed by the inconclusiveness of it all'.[71] Oakeshott then conceives of our culture as constituted, in the words of Podoksik, by 'radical plurality'; plurivocal rather than univocal, it is, in Stephen Prickett's term, a 'polyphony'.[72]

Further probing of Oakeshott's writings shows an openness to critical inquiry in the university. Oakeshott says that staff and students in a university should be 'critical of one another' and is very incisive in his treatment of the intellectual equipment necessary to engage in critique.[73] To be critical, 'it is not good enough to have a "point of view" ... what we need is *thoughts*'.[74] Nor is it enough, he argues, for a person to be 'in possession of an armoury of arguments to prove the truth of what she or he believes'; rather, what is required is the intellectual capacities to put her or him 'beyond the reach of the intellectual hooligan'.[75]

Yet although Oakeshott's emphasis on the intellectual qualities required in order to engage in critique is indeed appropriate and insightful, the metaphor of education as a conversation hardly implies a robust critical enterprise. In a conversation, insistence of the correctness of one's point of view represents 'bad manners' and is inimical to the conduct of congenial social intercourse.[76] Accordingly, it is hard to see how a voice such as that of Paulo Freire, speaking with passion and anger on behalf of the poor and oppressed, would fit into Oakeshott's conversation. Oakeshott acknowledges that the educational conversation may have 'passages of argument', but this conversation would not appear capable of accommodating systematic disagreement on moral, political and religious matters.[77] As Arcilla delicately notes, Oakeshott seems keener that students listen to, rather than join in, the educational conversation.[78] And my reservation here is that students who accept the invitation to be critical in order to challenge conventional moral and political values might find that criticism of certain values is in reality less than welcome within Oakeshott's academy. It is true that 'discussion of ideologies'[79] can indeed be tiresome, but the presentation of challenging argument does not have to be the preserve of self-serving ideologues of Left and Right.

So it could be said that Oakeshott recognizes, in principle, the place of critical debate, but that, personally, he is less than sympathetic towards it. His endorsement of the promotion of 'critical self-understanding'[80] as an educational aim does not appear to extend to social critique. Reasonably enough, he might say that arguments about moral and political values are not ones that he himself would wish to join. It is perfectly understandable why someone would wish to avoid encounters with the assertions of 'critical theorists' and of their conservative counterparts. Oakeshott has no enthusiasm for adversarial argument and there are good grounds for this lack of enthusiasm, because such argument can become a dialogue of the deaf. But agenda-driven theorizing represents one rationalistic extreme, and Oakeshott's attitude could be said to represent another. If his educational conversation is to be an honest engagement, then young people must be allowed to be critical without incurring the polite, civilized indifference of those adults whose values they are invited to criticize.

A certain tension, then, is to be found at the heart of Oakeshott's idea of conversation, when it comes to the political sphere and to criticism of prevailing sociopolitical arrangements. His account of political education neglects the anger and apathy towards, rather than respect for, political institutions that are common among young people who grow up in conditions of gross economic and cultural deprivation. Understandably, many readers of Oakeshott will feel that for these young people, political education can hardly be described as 'learning how to participate in a conversation'.[81] Some may be able to turn the invitation into an argument, but others will refuse the invitation and express their refusal in recourse to violence, vandalism and drugs. It is a pity that the situation of the poor and dispossessed features so little in his work. In this respect, there is a certain failure in Oakeshott's writing to take sufficiently into account the situation of the poor and the contexts of their lives.

To sum up, though the two criticisms of Oakeshott's metaphor of conversation cannot be sustained by an extensive, generous and nuanced reading of his work, his conception of conversation seems to resist the accommodation of significant and deep-rooted disagreement in the moral, political and religious areas. The final section of this chapter will consider how his notion of conversation needs to be developed to accommodate constructive critical dialogue in the moral, political and religious spheres.

CULTIVATING THE CONVERSATIONAL DISPOSITION

As noted earlier, Oakeshott seems to attribute to the teacher a strangely passive role in promoting conversation. The main burden of the argument of the conclusion to this chapter is that the conversational disposition must acquire a more active dimension and come explicitly to incorporate a capacity to decentre. What does this capacity mean? In psychology there are two concepts, called 'egocentricity' and its opposite, 'decentring'. 'Egocentricity' means that a person sees everything from her own point view and cannot make a connection with the world as perceived by others. 'Decentring' refers to the capacity mentally to step outside the individual's own universe and see things from the point of view of other people. Oakeshott does refer positively to this capacity. For example, he endorses the views expressed in a famous passage by the Eton master, William Cory, who 'understood education as a preparation for participation in conversation' and who emphasized the importance of the art of being able to assume 'at a moment's notice, a new intellectual position' and of 'entering quickly into another person's thoughts'.[82]

Cory's account of the intellectual disposition proper to the educational conversation resonates with the views of other important thinkers. It is, for example, consistent with the disposition identified by Kierkegaard in his well-known description of what it means to be a teacher: 'to be a teacher in the right sense is to be a learner. Instruction begins when you, the teacher, learn from the learner, put yourself in his place so that you may understand what he understands and in the way he understands it'.[83] It is also consistent with the disposition that Newman, whose writings on education resonate so much with Oakeshott's, identifies as a feature that a gentleman brings to his conversation.

> Nowhere shall we find greater candour, consideration, indulgence: he throws himself into the minds of his opponents, he accounts for their mistakes. He knows the weakness of human reason as well as its strength, its province and its limits. If he be an unbeliever, he will be too profound and large-minded to ridicule religion or to act against it; he is too wise to be a dogmatist or fanatic in his infidelity.[84]

The spirit of Oakeshott's writing is compatible with these views, but the connection between the conversational disposition and the activity of education stands in need of more searching development.

Oakeshott is well aware that where the disposition is absent, the pursuit of truth can degenerate into the mere exchange of assertions. André Gide astutely demonstrates the psychology of the process that Oakeshott rightly abhors whereby a scholarly hypothesis becomes a 'doctrine' in which 'stubbornness' comes to dominate the quite legitimate and, indeed, 'natural need' to affirm an argument.[85] Among the areas where it is difficult to avoid this defensiveness and to achieve a conversational disposition are two that people are traditionally advised to avoid in polite conversation, namely, religion and politics. It is true that no one could be more acutely sensitive than Oakeshott to the role of education in expanding the boundaries of human understanding. Yet more needs to be said about the role of conversation in enhancing human sympathies in order to avoid a possible situation where, in the words of Fred Dallmayr, 'no voice would be willing or able to listen to others'.[86] 'In genuine conversation', as Chris Lawn argues in his article on Gadamer and Oakeshott, we 'learn something about ourselves as we enter sympathetically the horizon of the other'.[87] One task of the educator is to encourage the sympathetic imagination required to enter into conversation with others even where there is resistance to entering 'the horizon of the other'.

In summary, therefore, it can be said that, in the notion of conversation, Oakeshott has bequeathed a valuable educational metaphor that is neither elitist nor rigidly conservative. Yet there is more work to be done on understanding how the conversational disposition can be best cultivated and how it can come to be embedded in the activities of teaching and learning. Part of Oakeshott's educational bequest is his provision of a conceptual platform on which this work can build.

NOTES

1 B. Parekh, 'The Political Philosophy of Michael Oakeshott', *British Journal of Political Science*, 9 (1979), 500.

2 J. B. Bennett, 'Liberal Learning as Conversation', *Liberal Education*, 87 (2001), 34 and 36.

3 M. O. DeGirolami, 'The Problem of Religious Learning', *Boston College Law Review*, 49 (2008), 1233.

4 M. Arnold, *Culture and Anarchy* (Cambridge University Press, 1966), 47; see also E. Podoksik, *In Defence of Modernity: Vision and*

Philosophy in Michael Oakeshott (Thorverton: Imprint Academic, 2003), pp. 214–15.
5 M. Oakeshott, 'Work and Play', in *WH*, pp. 303–15.
6 M. Oakeshott, 'The Voice of Poetry in the Conversation of Mankind', in *RP*, pp. 197–247.
7 M. Oakeshott, 'The Voice of Conversation in the Education of Mankind', in *WH*, pp. 187–99.
8 Oakeshott, 'Voice of Poetry', p. 199.
9 M. Oakeshott, 'Education: The Engagement and its Frustration', in *VLL*, pp. 69, 71–2, 76.
10 *Ibid.*
11 M. Oakeshott, 'Place of Learning', in *VLL*, p. 41.
12 *Ibid.*, p. 37.
13 *Ibid.*, p. 93.
14 Oakeshott, 'Voice of Poetry', p. 199.
15 See Podoksik, *In Defence of Modernity*, p. 218.
16 Oakeshott, 'Education: The Engagement and its Frustration', p. 73.
17 A. Gide, *The Immoralist/L'Immoraliste* (New York: Dover Publications, 2003), pp. 61, 63.
18 M. Oakeshott, 'Political Education', in *RP*, p. 133.
19 R. Rorty, *Philosophy and the Mirror of Nature* (Oxford: Blackwell, 1998), p. 264.
20 Oakeshott, 'Voice of Poetry', pp. 198–9.
21 I. McEwan, *The Child in Time* (London: Picador, 1988), p. 80.
22 M. Oakeshott, 'The Study of "Politics" in a University', in *RP*, pp. 308–9.
23 *Ibid.*, p. 308.
24 *Ibid.*, pp. 305–7.
25 *Ibid.*, p. 305.
26 See, e.g., M. Donaldson, *Children's Minds* (London: Fontana, 1978).
27 Oakeshott, 'Study of "Politics" in a University', p. 305.
28 *Ibid.*, pp. 305–6, 315.
29 M. Oakeshott, 'The Universities', in *VLL*, p. 125.
30 Oakeshott, 'Study of "Politics" in a University', pp. 313–14.
31 Oakeshott, 'Place of Learning', p. 38.
32 *Ibid.*
33 Parekh, 'Political Philosophy of Michael Oakeshott', 488n.
34 T. Modood, 'Oakeshott's Conceptions of Philosophy', *History of Political Thought*, 1 (1980), 316.
35 Oakeshott, 'Universities', p. 123.
36 M. Oakeshott, 'The Idea of a University', in *VLL*, p. 98.
37 Oakeshott, 'Place of Learning', p. 32.

38 Oakeshott, 'Voice of Poetry', p. 206.
39 Oakeshott, 'Universities', pp. 133–4.
40 *Ibid.*, p. 134.
41 *Ibid.*, p. 132.
42 M. Midgley, *Beast and Man: The Roots of Human Nature* (London: Methuen, 1980), p. 23.
43 Oakeshott, 'Idea of a University', pp. 100–1.
44 Oakeshott, 'Universities', p. 133.
45 See Oakeshott, 'Idea of a University', p. 102, and 'Universities', p. 127.
46 See D. G. Mulcahy, *The Educated Person: Toward a New Paradigm for Liberal Education* (Lanham, MD: Rowman & Littlefield, 2008), p. 45.
47 J. H. Newman, *The Idea of a University: Defined and Illustrated* (London: Longmans, Green & Co., 1901), p. 146.
48 Oakeshott, 'Place of Learning', p. 38.
49 *Ibid.*
50 Oakeshott, 'Universities', p. 133.
51 Oakeshott provides a more dynamic account of pedagogy when writing of the teacher–pupil relationship in the school context. See K. Williams, *Education and the Voice of Michael Oakeshott* (Thorverton: Imprint Academic, 2007), pp. 165–7.
52 Oakeshott, 'Study of "Politics" in a University', p. 312, and M. Oakeshott, 'The Character of a University Education', in *WH*, p. 386.
53 M. Oakeshott, 'Rational Conduct', in *RP*, p. 101.
54 J. White, 'Wellbeing and Education: Issues of Culture and Authority', *Journal of Philosophy of Education*, 41 (2007), 26.
55 Oakeshott, 'Place of Learning', pp. 39 and 40.
56 M. Greene, 'Imagining Futures: The Public School and Possibility', in W. Carr (ed.), *The Routledge Falmer Reader in Philosophy of Education* (London: Routledge, 2005), pp. 161–3.
57 Oakeshott, 'Study of "Politics" in a University', p. 303.
58 Oakeshott, 'Education: The Engagement and its Frustration', p. 47.
59 Oakeshott, 'Place of Learning', p. 41, and Oakeshott, 'Education: The Engagement and its Frustration', pp. 71, 83, 89, 91. The distinction between the quality and fact of life is made by A. N. Whitehead in *Religion in the Making* (Cambridge University Press, 1926), p. 80.
60 See Williams, *Education and the Voice of Michael Oakeshott*, pp. 80–4.
61 DeGirolami, 'Problem of Religious Learning', 1227n.
62 M. R. Matthews, *The Marxist Theory of Schooling* (Brighton: Harvester, 1980), p. 160.
63 J. McCarney, 'Edifying Discourses', in R. Edgley (ed.), *Radical Philosophy Reader* (London: Verso, 1995), p. 400.

64 *Ibid.*, pp. 400–1.
65 Oakeshott, 'Universities', p. 115.
66 M. Oakeshott, 'The Political Economy of Freedom', in *RP*, pp. 48–9.
67 M. Oakeshott, 'The Tower of Babel', in *RP*, p. 73.
68 *Ibid.*, p. 62.
69 This is precisely what Fred Inglis implies with reference to the views of both R. S. Peters and Oakeshott. See F. Inglis, 'Ideology and the Curriculum: Value Assumptions of System Builders', in M. Golby, J. Greenwald and R. West (eds.), *Curriculum Design* (London: Open University Press, 1975), pp. 41, 47n.
70 Oakeshott, 'Place of Learning', p. 28.
71 *Ibid.*, p. 39.
72 Podoksik, *In Defence of Modernity*, p. 228; S. Prickett, 'Polyphony, the Idea of Education and Social Utility', in S. Prickett and P. Erskine-Hill (eds.), *Education! Education! Education!: Managerial Ethics and the Law of Unintended Consequences* (Thorverton: Imprint Academic, 2002), p. 85.
73 Oakeshott, 'Study of "Politics" in a University', p. 310.
74 Oakeshott, 'Universities', p. 102.
75 *Ibid.*, pp. 102–3.
76 Oakeshott, 'Voice of Poetry', p. 201.
77 *Ibid.*, p. 198.
78 R. V. Arcilla, *For the Love of Perfection: Richard Rorty and Liberal Education* (New York: Routledge, 1995), p. 3.
79 Oakeshott, 'Universities', p. 122.
80 Oakeshott, 'Place of Learning', p. 26.
81 Oakeshott, 'Political Education', p. 129; see also Oakeshott, 'Political Economy of Freedom', p. 41.
82 Oakeshott, 'Voice of Poetry', p. 200n.
83 S. Kierkegaard, *The Point of View for my Work as an Author: A Report to History*, trans. W. Lowrie (New York: Harper, 1962), pp. 29–30.
84 Newman, *Idea of a University*, p. 210.
85 Gide, *Immoralist*, p. 112.
86 F. Dallmayr, 'Conversation Across Boundaries: Political Theory and Global Diversity', *Millennium: Journal of International Studies*, 30 (2001), 332.
87 C. Lawn, 'Adventures of Self-Understanding: Gadamer, Oakeshott and the Question of Education', *Journal of the British Society for Phenomenology*, 27 (1996), 272.

PART II

Oakeshott on morality, society and politics

STEVEN B. SMITH

6 Practical life and the critique of Rationalism

'Experience', of all the words in the philosophic vocabulary, is the most difficult to manage.[1]

INTRODUCTION

The entire work of Michael Oakeshott can be considered as a sustained reflection on a single problem: the relation of reason and the moral life. The question (or questions) that inform Oakeshott's wide and diverse body of writings are: is the aim of reason to describe the most general features of moral life as it presents itself to the ordinary understanding, or does reason aim to revise our ordinary beliefs and practices in order to offer a philosophically more cogent picture of the world? Is reason descriptive or revisionary?[2] At bottom, this is a variant of perhaps the oldest of all philosophical problems, namely, the problem of theory and practice. Is the task of philosophy to lead us out of the cave of received opinion and affect a transformation of the moral life, as Plato vividly affirmed? Or is the aim of philosophy largely to reaffirm established opinions and beliefs leaving 'everything as it is' as Wittgenstein maintained?[3]

At the core of Oakeshott's moral theory is the concept of experience. Experience remains for him the touchstone for philosophy. He appeals to an underlying core of common-sense beliefs and practices from which philosophy departs at its peril. From his early *Experience and its Modes* to the essays composing *Rationalism in Politics* to his magnum opus *On Human Conduct*, Oakeshott appealed to words like 'tradition' and 'practice' to set limits to the scope of philosophic inquiry. His goal is twofold. He wants to protect the world of practice and practical experience from the unwanted intrusions of the theorist, but just as important he wants to protect philosophy as well as other specific modes of experience from the attractions of practice.

Oakeshott has also been called a philosopher of practice for the centrality he has attributed to human experience, but this is not completely true, at least not without further stipulation. The term 'practice' may connote many different meanings. It may suggest a Marxian conception of praxis as a form of revolutionary activity; it may suggest a kind of instrumentalism, as in Dewey's philosophy of pragmatism; it may imply a Husserelian sense of a pre-theoretical 'lifeworld' that provides the ground for all later philosophical concepts and abstractions; or it may even suggest an Arendtian conception of action as a sphere that combines freedom, excellence and self-revelatory striving. Oakeshott's term means none of the above. Although his goal, we will see, is to examine the postulates of practical experience, he is never guilty of idealizing practice as providing the solution to philosophical problems. Perhaps most controversially, he seeks to keep philosophy as far as possible removed from the demands of practice and the practical life. There is even something slightly decadent in his insistence that philosophy is useless for any practical purpose. The task of philosophy is not to change the world, but to interpret it.

PHILOSOPHY AS THE QUEST FOR COHERENCE

Oakeshott's first attempt to theorize the world of practical experience occurs in Part 5 of *Experience and its Modes*.[4] From the beginning of his work, Oakeshott regarded the world of practice as the most difficult or problematic of his various modes of experience. The danger that he seeks to resist is the tendency to reduce all experience to practice or to view practice as the 'ground' or 'foundation' from which philosophy arises. Practice, he insists, remains one, but only one, form of experience along with science and history – he would later add aesthetics – which must be examined in terms of its own internal postulates and principles of intelligibility. No one form of experience takes precedence or priority over the others. As Paul Franco has keenly observed, Oakeshott reacted not only against the dominance of science but against 'the despotism of practice'.[5]

The most formidable objection Oakeshott must consider is whether practice constitutes an intelligible mode of experience at all. Against intuitionism (Bergson) or *Lebensphilosophie* (Dilthey) that regards all experience as a continual flow of sensation and perception, Oakeshott insists that practice constitutes a stable 'world of ideas'.[6] And against materialist or 'realist' philosophers who believe that practical activity consists of so many units of discrete, observable behaviour, Oakeshott denies the validity of the distinction between an external or 'objective' world of action and an internal or 'subjective' world of thought. Thought and action do not belong to two separate worlds of activity, but constitute a whole. At the same time and in a manner that anticipates his later epistemological critique of Rationalism, Oakeshott denies that thought precedes action as a cause precedes its effect. Thought and action are not externally or causally related. Rather, actions express thought and thinking is, so to speak, embodied in action. When it comes to practical experience, there is no 'inside' and 'outside', no 'before' and 'after'. Thought and action are conceptually related aspects of the same whole.[7]

At the same time that Oakeshott defends the unity of thought and action, he regards the world of practical experience as one of perpetual change. All action deals with the production or prevention of change.[8] When we act we either seek to make a change for the better or prevent a change for the worse. Even the prevention of change is a kind of action. All action, therefore, presupposes a distinction between 'what is' and 'what ought to be'. It may appear, then, that the world of practical experience is torn between the 'to be' and the 'not yet', that it constitutes not one but two separate worlds. But these two aspects of experience are actually two sides of the same coin. There are no fissures or breaks in experience, but only an ongoing principle of change ('Nought may endure but mutability').[9]

It is because the world of practical experience constitutes perpetual change that Oakeshott designates it as a world *sub specie voluntatis*.[10] It is the world viewed under the categories of will and volition. From his earliest writings, Oakeshott's conception of practice was tied to a strong sense of individualism. The principle of change is not something that merely happens to us, but something that we bring about or cause to happen as the result of our choices and decisions. It follows, then, that the world of practical experience is composed of individuals endowed with the capacity for will and choice and who confront the world as an object of ceaseless change. The self is said to be free, 'self-determined', an 'end in himself', thus giving a quasi-Kantian ring to Oakeshott's understanding of practical experience.[11] There are, of course, as Oakeshott admits, 'moods' where we might imagine ourselves other than we are. We might imagine ourselves as moved along by the inexorable tide of history or see ourselves as causally determined by a range of sociological, psychological or genetic forces. But to think this way is 'to violate the integrity of the self'; it is already to sow 'the seeds of disintegration' within the practical world.[12]

The fact that the world of practical experience is internally divided between the *is* and the *ought* does not mean that this distinction corresponds to two separate realities like the Platonic worlds of becoming and being or the Kantian phenomenal and noumenal realms. Both are aspects of practical experience as a whole. Uniting the two worlds of practical experience is the quest for coherence, the desire to bring into harmony the *here and now* with the *yet to be*. 'Practice,' Oakeshott writes, 'is the reconciliation, in detail and in practical fact, of "what is here and now" and "what ought to be"; it is this and all that it presupposes and involves.'[13] By coherence he does not mean the imposition of a rule or code of conduct, a kind of road map for living, nor does he mean blind, unswerving obedience to a moral law. Rather, a coherent world is one where there are no breaks, gaps or caesuras in moral experience, where all the parts ideally fit together like the pieces of a jigsaw puzzle.

Oakeshott's notion of the coherence of practical experience is perhaps best illustrated in a verse by Crabbe used by Churchill to express his understanding of 'consistency in politics':

> Minutely trace man's life; year after year,
> Through all his days let all his deeds appear,
> And then, though some may in that life be strange,
> Yet there appears no vast nor sudden change;
> The links that bind those various deeds are seen,
> And no mysterious void is left in between.[14]

To be sure, Oakeshott recognizes that the quest for coherence is always partial and never complete. The very possibility of morality requires the always-unfinished character of practical experience. The desire to reconcile all the competing and contradictory features of life remains forever a work-in-progress. Practice is and can never be more than 'a partially integrated world of experience', a world that can never be more than 'partial and inadequate'.[15] Every synthesis becomes by definition the occasion for a new antithesis. To achieve a final or permanent reconciliation of opposites would lead to the dissolution of morality and thereby the very presuppositions of practice. Life, as he would argue later on, is not a plan but an adventure.[16]

It is the perpetually unfinished character of practical experience – its 'permanent dissatisfaction' with itself – that ultimately distinguishes it from philosophy. Practical experience is always the quest for, never the achievement of, coherence. Philosophy, as Oakeshott defines it, is 'experience without presupposition, reservation, arrest, or modification'. It is 'knowledge that carries with it the evidence of its own completeness'.[17] Practice, just like science or history, remains an 'abstract' or defective mode when seen in the light of the philosophical pursuit of knowledge of experience as a whole.

But if practice cannot serve as a ground for or justification of philosophy, just as importantly – perhaps even more importantly – Oakeshott insists that philosophy cannot serve as a guide, much less a surrogate, for practical life. Philosophy and practice must be kept categorially distinct. While practical experience may contain elements of judgement, thought and reflection, it is most definitely *not* philosophy by other means. The central thrust of *Experience and its Modes* is to protect philosophy and the other modes of experience from the blandishments of praxis. 'A philosophy of life,' Oakeshott avers, 'is a meaningless contradiction.'[18] Life – practical experience – and philosophy – the quest for intellectual coherence – remain fundamentally inimical to each other:

> Philosophy is born an outcast, useless to men of business and troublesome to men of pleasure. But then, the pursuit of what affords unlimited satisfaction in experience for its own sake is something irrelevant to practical life, is an escape from living; and a philosophy which pretended to offer something practically useful would be a philosophy living beyond its means.[19]

Like Plato, Oakeshott recognizes that the philosopher's task is not an easy one, but not because the philosopher will stand accused of corrupting the young, but precisely because philosophy offers no alternative to the demands – and the delights – of practical experience. There is something about the restless pursuit of coherence for its own sake that puts philosophy beyond the ordinary moral world of good and evil.[20] Although Oakeshott denies that the various modes of experience express some order of rank, he cannot help but present philosophy's quest for knowledge of 'experience as a whole and for its own sake' as superior to the partial and incomplete character of practical experience. There is even something 'esoteric' about philosophy. 'To popularize philosophy is at once to debase it', he writes. 'Few, perhaps, will be found willing to surrender the green for the grey, but only those few are on the way to a philosophy.'[21]

PRACTICE AS TRADITION

In *Experience and its Modes* Oakeshott's main concern was to maintain the autonomy of philosophy from the dominance of practice, the understandable but misplaced desire to make philosophy useful. The book was written under the influence of the Idealist metaphysics of Hegel and F. H. Bradley, although Oakeshott's use of the language of 'modes' suggests an unacknowledged debt to Spinoza as well. The tone of the work seemed almost a throwback to the earlier Edwardian age.[22] The same cannot be said of his second major work, *Rationalism in Politics*, in which not only does Oakeshott express a tone of greater moral urgency but, as the title suggests, he turns to the problem of politics that was altogether absent in his earlier book.[23]

The central problem to which the essays composing *Rationalism in Politics* are addressed is no longer the defence of philosophy from the intrusions of practical life, but the defence of practical experience – now described as 'tradition' – from the threat of Rationalism. It is for his defence of tradition that Oakeshott has been widely described as a conservative in the style of Hume and Burke, but typically he offers his own highly individual, not to say idiosyncratic, defence of tradition. Oakeshott was by no means a traditionalist and he would have resisted the attempt to turn tradition into a kind of cure-all for the various modern pathologies that he diagnoses. He was not interested in restoring lost or endangered political traditions, but in restoring the traditional understanding of politics. His was an epistemological, not a political, traditionalism.

In the title essay of his book, Oakeshott distinguishes between two kinds of knowledge that, following Aristotle, he calls the practical and the technical.[24] Practical knowledge is knowledge acquired through doing; it is the kind of knowledge involved in riding a bicycle, driving a car or hitting a baseball. Technical knowledge, by contrast, is knowledge of rules, rules that can be read in a book or manual, memorized by heart and applied. Technical knowledge is based on an abstraction from the concrete practices and activities that make up human experience. Technical knowledge is to practical knowledge what knowing the traffic code is to driving a car or what knowledge of a legal textbook is to the practice of law. These two forms of knowledge may be inseparable from one another, but in every instance Oakeshott wants to say it is practical knowledge that forms the ground from which a tradition of thought and practice arises.

It is the practical character of our experience that is threatened by a certain attitude that Oakeshott describes as Rationalism. Rationalism is not the same thing as reason, much less reasonableness, and should not be mistaken for philosophy. The kind of Rationalism with which he is concerned is specifically modern rationalism, by which he means the belief that all knowledge must be susceptible to expression in propositional form. 'Rationalism,' he writes, 'is the assertion that … practical knowledge is not knowledge at all, the assertion that, properly speaking, there is no knowledge which is not technical knowledge.'[25] The sources of modern rationalism can be traced back to the early modern writings of Bacon and Descartes, both of whom attempted to establish a universal method by which new knowledge could be tested and that could provide a foundation for intellectual progress. What cannot stand up to the test of methodological rigor is no longer to count as knowledge.

For Oakeshott, it is the very 'sovereignty of technique' that endangers the stability and continuity of political traditions and the moral practices out of which they arise. The triumph of Rationalism has created a new kind of politics, the 'politics of the book', in which traditions of behaviour have been replaced by the rule of ideology.[26] Ideology is the antithesis of tradition. Ideologies are precisely the kinds of abstractions from political experience that can be neatly summarized into doctrines and put into book form.

Ideologies are 'abstracts' of political experience in which all the complexities and subtleties have been squeezed out.[27]

The rise of ideological politics can be traced back to the emergence of a new and inexperienced political class who lack traditional forms of political expertise and find themselves in need of some kind of shorthand knowledge. One of the first great expressions of this kind of ideological politics was Machiavelli's *Prince*, which Oakeshott describes as a 'crib' for the political education of a new prince, 'a technique for the ruler who had no tradition'.[28] Similarly he describes Locke's *Second Treatise* as 'a brilliant abridgement of the political habits of Englishmen' for the benefit of the newly enfranchised middle classes.[29] Nor to the consternation of American conservatives did Oakeshott spare the American political founding from his critique of modern rationalism:[30]

For the inspiration of Jefferson and the other founders of American independence was the ideology which Locke had distilled from the English political tradition. They were disposed to believe, and they believed more fully than was possible for an inhabitant of the Old World, that the proper organization of a society and the conduct of its affairs were based upon abstract principles, and not upon a tradition which, as Hamilton said, had 'to be rummaged for among old parchments and musty records' ... The Declaration of Independence is a characteristic product of the *saeculum rationalisticum*. It represents the politics of the felt need interpreted with the aid of an ideology. And it is not surprising that it should have become one of the sacred documents of the politics of Rationalism, and, together with the similar documents of the French Revolution, the inspiration and pattern of many later adventures in the rationalist reconstruction of society.[31]

The most destructive impact of Rationalism, however, has been reserved for the twentieth century with the rise of Marxism-Leninism and the claims of the industrial working class to rule. From its beginnings, Rationalist politics have been revolutionary and perfectionist. Such a view of politics takes wartime or other moments of national crisis as the norm and attempts to use them as a model for times of peace. No matter whether such ideologies took the form of 'life, liberty, and the pursuit of happiness', *'liberté, egalité, fraternité'* or 'workers of the world unite', they have sought to impose an ideal order of their own imagination on the less than perfect materials of actual human conduct. Like Isaiah Berlin, Oakeshott was deeply aware of 'the crooked timber of humanity'.[32]

His politics were not so much that of a Burkean conservative looking to the past than of a Cold War liberal hoping to disenthral his readers of the charms of perfectionism.

PRACTICE AS MORAL SYMPATHY

It is easy to regard Oakeshott's defence of tradition as a form of romantic nostalgia or his critique of Rationalism as an endorsement of irrationalism in politics. Both of these views are false. As suggested above, Oakeshott was not interested in restoring a world that is lost. A tradition once lost is lost forever. In this he would have agreed with Lady Bracknell from Oscar Wilde's *The Importance of Being Earnest*: 'I do not approve of anything that tampers with natural ignorance. Ignorance is like a very delicate exotic fruit. Touch it and the bloom is gone. The whole theory of modern education is radically unsound'.[33] Nor is Oakeshott's critique of Rationalism a rejection of reason *tout court*. Reason is not the antithesis of tradition but is bound up with traditional practices and habits. Rationalism is a corruption of reason, a specific aberration from which moral and political reason needs to be rescued.

In 'The Tower of Babel' (1948) Oakeshott considers two forms of moral experience that to some degree map on to his distinction between practical and technical knowledge. One is described as a morality of affection and behaviour and the other a morality of reflective thought.[34] Each of these moralities is a kind of ideal type. Neither is intended as a description of an existing moral practice. A morality of affective ties is based upon custom and unreflective experience. Oakeshott compares learning such a morality to the acquisition of a vernacular language that can be mastered and applied without ever having studied the rules of syntax or grammar.[35] We learn morality like we learn most things, not through rule books and guides but through practice.

It is the morality of reflection, however, that he believes has become dominant in the modern world. This kind of morality has roots in the early Greek and Christian worlds, but has only received full expression since the seventeenth century. By contrast to a morality of custom, a morality of reflection grows out of self-conscious deliberation over the first principles of moral behaviour. Oakeshott is by no means opposed to reflection on moral principle.

What he denies is the Rationalist's claim that moral reflection constitutes the best part of morality. Habit and reflection are parts of moral conduct and to elevate the reflective component above the customary and habitual is to do violence to the integrity of moral experience. A morality of principle not only tends towards dogmatism and inflexibility, allowing little room for accommodation and adjustment to circumstance, it is also guided by a vision of moral perfectibility that in a stunning remark he compares to 'idolatry'.[36]

It is not, then, moral reasoning as such, but only a certain understanding of moral reason that Oakeshott wants to resist. The rationality of morality is not to be discovered in general principles of conduct, whether these be the principles of natural law, the categorical imperative, or the greatest happiness for the greatest number. Morality cannot be compressed into a principle, but is an 'idiom of activity' that he defines as 'knowledge of how to behave appropriately in the circumstances'.[37] Rational activity is not a matter of applying a rule of conduct to a situation in which we find ourselves, but 'acting in such a way that the coherence of the idiom of activity to which the conduct belongs is preserved and possibly enhanced'.[38] Rationality is not so much adherence to a premeditated scheme or plan but fidelity to a way of life:

> No action is by itself 'rational', or is 'rational' on account of something that has gone on before; what makes it 'rational' is its place in a flow of sympathy, a current of moral activity. And there is no ground here upon which we may exclude *a priori* any type of action ... 'Rationality' is the certificate we give to any conduct which can maintain a place in the flow of sympathy, the coherence of activity, which composes a way of living.[39]

Oakeshott's use of the term 'flow of sympathy' puts him in the same moral sense tradition of Hume, Burke and Jane Austen that regards rationality as embedded in our habits, manners and moral sentiments.[40] Moral education is necessarily sentimental education. It consists of immersion in a way of life in all its detail. 'And since a tradition of behaviour is not susceptible of the distinction between essence and accident', Oakeshott writes, 'knowledge of it is unavoidably knowledge of its details; to know only the gist is to know nothing'.[41] All morality, like all rationality, is 'municipal' rather than universal in character. Such a conception of rationality may seem relativistic, but Oakeshott is above all a moral pluralist.

He values different moral voices and resists the tendency to impose uniformity on diverse practices. Moral traditions are always complex and to privilege one feature over others – Justice, Equality, Happiness, even Liberty – would be to reduce the whole to one of its parts and to impose an intolerable dullness and uniformity on the richness and variety of life.

The image of tradition as a 'flow of sympathy' is related to another one of Oakeshott's famous and most controversial metaphors for moral education as 'the pursuit of intimations'.[42] That a moral or political tradition may consist of a variety of 'intimations' suggests a complex whole that is never complete and rarely consistent. The various parts of a tradition – rules, decisions, precedents, principles – may hang together as a whole but not as a logical system. The relations of the parts to the whole is one of consanguinity rather than logical deduction:

> [A tradition of behaviour] is neither fixed nor finished; it has no changeless centre to which understanding can anchor itself; there is no sovereign purpose to be perceived or invariable direction to be detected; there is no model to be copied, idea to be realized, or rule to be followed. Some parts of it may change more slowly than others, but none is immune from change. Everything is temporary.[43]

This description of a tradition as 'the pursuit of intimations' was met with considerable resistance. In an appendix added to the original version of 'Political Education' Oakeshott responded to a number of his critics, who regarded him as having eliminated rational standards for political decision making. If moral and political practice consists of pursuing intimations, by what standards do we choose which intimations to pursue? In the case of competing moral traditions, how do we distinguish good choices from bad? Does his theory not fall prey to endorsing irrationalism when it comes to matters of moral choice?

These are legitimate questions, although they are not exactly the ones that Oakeshott set out to address. His reply, while not without difficulty, is that he is not seeking to recommend one moral tradition over others, but rather to inquire into what is involved in understanding any tradition. He is seeking to recover the traditional understanding of tradition from the rationalistic misunderstanding of politics. To repeat: his traditionalism is epistemological, not political. Oakeshott takes it as a given that moral and political life always takes place within a tradition and asks only how should that tradition be understood. His question is not whether this or that tradition is a good one, but whether a choice makes sense given the standards of moral reasoning within a particular tradition. Oakeshott is a moral particularist: moral reasoning is always reasoning about particular cases. A judge seeking guidance for the damages to be awarded in a civil case will consult similar cases of judicial reasoning; no amount of appeal to general principles such as Natural Law or the Greatest Happiness for society will provide an answer. The standard to be pursued is not conformity to some general rule but coherence with the tradition in question.

The problem with Oakeshott's understanding of a tradition is not that it denies rational standards for making moral choices, but that it assumes the traditional character of all behaviour. The ubiquity of tradition at times ceases to be a descriptive statement and becomes something like an analytical truth. Even moments of supreme political crisis and revolution are interpreted as more tradition-bound than they often appear. 'The Russian Revolution,' he asserts, 'was a modification of *Russian* circumstances. And the French Revolution was far more closely connected with the *ancien régime* than with Locke or America.'[44]

Oakeshott here wants to make the idea of tradition account for too much. While there is an obvious truth to the claim that the Russian Revolution was a Russian event, it is deeply misleading to call Stalin's Gulag a 'modification' of Russian practices, just as it is false to call the Holocaust a 'modification' of German circumstances. Were genocidal anti-Semitism and forced collectivization simply 'intimations' of existing traditions?[45] There was little in the practices of Wilhelmine Germany or Czarist Russia that could help an historian understand the fanatical cruelty, unknown in modern history, of National Socialism and Soviet Communism. The Final Solution and the Five Year Plans were conceived of and carried out as self-conscious efforts to remake politics in accordance to a plan and to argue otherwise is to understate their profound radicalism. To describe these policies as somehow part of a seamless web of tradition is not only to misdescribe their history but to underestimate their radical evil. Oakeshott seems to have had a greater faith in the power of tradition to mould the fate of mankind than seems warranted now.

PRACTICE AS PERFORMANCE

Oakeshott's third and final effort to define the character of practical experience occurs in *On Human Conduct.* This was a work of systematic political philosophy that rivals anything that had been produced in the twentieth century. *On Human Conduct* is often seen as representing a break with some of Oakeshott's earlier formulations. While in *Experience and its Modes* he remained faithful to the Idealist project of trying to capture experience as a whole, his goal now is the more limited one of attempting to describe or 'theorize' the 'postulates' of human conduct. And while in *Rationalism in Politics* he tried to grasp practical experience under the broad rubric of tradition, in *On Human Conduct* the language of tradition is dropped – the term does not even appear in the index – in favour of the generic term 'practice' to describe all human relations that have achieved a determinate or settled form.[46]

Oakeshott provided no explicit reasons for this change of vocabulary. Unlike the earlier works that had been written in a leisurely, deliberately non-technical style, *On Human Conduct* adopted a more formal manner and swarmed with Latinate vocabulary whose major concepts were *cives, civitas, lex, societas* and *universitas*. Although in the preface Oakeshott noted that the themes of the book 'have been with me nearly as long as I can remember', he seemed to give these themes new expression.[47] While in *Rationalism in Politics* he had stressed the dependence of rationality on certain pre-existing sentiments, manners and moral habits, in *On Human Conduct* he is at pains to emphasize the deliberative and intentional character of our activities. And while earlier he had made our moral choices dependent on traditions of thought and behaviour, he now emphasizes the way our practices are the result of certain intentional choices and actions.

What, then, characterizes a practice in terms of its postulates? At the core of Oakeshott's theory of human conduct is a distinction between understanding a practice and a process.[48] A practice is a 'going-on' conceived of as an expression of human intelligence. Practices are always intelligent responses to understood situations. Every situation, insofar as it is a human situation, is predicated upon understanding. There are no 'brute facts' in experience, only degrees of understanding. Practices – religious rituals, legal procedures, sports or politics – all need to be learned and understood as preconditions for participation in the practice itself. Such practices may be understood well or ill and this will determine the character of the individual 'performance', but the crucial point is that such practices always express 'an engagement to understand'.

A process, by contrast, may also be an intelligible happening but is not itself an exhibition of intelligence. Processes can be identified in terms of their causal conditions and as such specify certain law-like or functional characteristics, but they are not expressions of intelligent design. The movement of the tides or the rotation of the planets can be understood as intelligible happenings, but they are not an expression of understanding or will. A wave does not need knowledge of the laws of gravitation to crash upon the shore. While practices are an accumulation of individual choices over time, processes express causally related happenings.

Practices and processes represent two ideal 'platforms' of understanding, each with its own distinct set of postulates. The distinction maps to some degree the difference between the human and the natural sciences (*Geisteswissenschaften* and *Naturwissenschaften*), but the main target of the distinction is not physics or chemistry but the social sciences – mainly psychology and sociology – that have attempted to introduce a process idiom into the understanding of human conduct.[49] For Oakeshott, the confusion or conflation of practices and processes is the first and most fundamental category mistake. Some of his harshest statements are reserved for the attempt to view purposive or intelligent human behaviour as an expression of a person's biological, genetic or environmental make-up. Similarly, he rejects any effort to designate practices as 'systems' or 'structures' that exhibit laws of development, evolution or adaptation. This is to understand the human in terms of the subhuman and therefore to render it categorially unintelligible. In a wry aside, Oakeshott notes that when a geneticist offers an explanation of human behaviour, he says nothing more than everything is done by the genes and that 'this theorem is itself his genes speaking'.[50]

A further feature of a practice on which Oakeshott insists is its 'adverbial' character. Practices designate 'conditions to be subscribed to' rather than any specific performance ('The requirements of a practice are not obeyed or disobeyed; they are subscribed to or not subscribed to').[51] There is a formal character to practices that designate procedures not results, conditions not outcomes. The emphasis on the conditional character of practices is intended to indicate an element of choice and reflection and not simply habitual obedience to rules. While Oakeshott had distinguished a practice from a process, he now makes a further distinction between a practice and an individual performance. A practice does not determine in advance what a performer may or may not do within the limits of its rules, but reveals a certain open-ended quality as to how practices may be shaped by individual creativity and craftsmanship.[52]

Practices are, therefore, adventures in 'self-disclosure' in which the practitioner reveals his or her character through the quality of the performance. This holds true not only for highly skilled performances like playing a piano sonata or performing Hamlet, but for a countless range of quotidian activities. 'A practitioner,' Oakeshott insists, 'is always a performer, and this holds even in the extreme case where the practice is a ritual.'[53] But if practices are adventures in self-disclosure, they are also exercises in 'self-enactment'. By this term, Oakeshott alludes to the motive or 'sentiment' – actually certain 'nodal densities of sentiment' – in which an act is performed. These motives, he is clear, are not somehow the hidden cause of the action, like the Cartesian ghost in the machine, but specify the manner in which an action is performed, whether it is performed out of anger, pride, jealousy, kindness, pity and so on. These motives, no less (but also no more) than the act itself are constitutive of moral conduct.[54]

There is one final distinction that characterizes a practice and it is between practices that are instrumental to the achievement of some particular end and practices that are ends in themselves. 'The practice of all practices' – the practice whose goal is the acknowledgement of the authority of practice – is called by the comprehensive name 'morality'. Oakeshott defines this as 'the practice of agency without further specification'.[55] Moral conduct consists, for Oakeshott, not in some specific domain of practice, but in the element common to all practices. Morality consists not so much in what is done but in whether what is done is done well or not. It does not describe what is performed but how it is performed. Morality is more an exercise in virtuosity than the performance of any particular type of act.[56] As such, morality concerns the purely formal or conditional character of action and not the attainment of some substantive goal. The attempt to identify morality with the achievement of some end – human excellence, virtue, the good will, general utility – is to mistake the means for the ends. There is throughout Oakeshott's writings a general aversion to abstract proper nouns ('I cannot *want* "happiness"; what I want is to idle in Avignon or to hear Caruso sing').[57]

In *Rationalism in Politics*, Oakeshott had distinguished between a morality of affective behaviour and a morality of reflection; he now distinguishes between the practice of morality and the rules of morality. The practice of morality is like the practice of a living language. In identifying moral practice with a living language, Oakeshott hopes to bring out its non-instrumental character. Language can certainly allow us to achieve our particular ends and purposes ('Can you tell me how to find my way to Sterling Library?'), but language as a whole has no end or purpose. To ask what is the point of language is to ask a non sequitur. The same is true of morality. Morality, like language, may be bound by certain rules but still allows for a range of individual expressions. Just as there is no one correct way to use a language, so does morality allow for improvisation and almost infinite variability:

> There is room for the individual idiom, it affords opportunity to inventiveness, it may be spoken pedantically or loosely, slavishly or masterfully; it has rhythms which remain when the words are forgotten. It allows ambages as well as decisive utterance and response. Expressions in it harden into clichés and are released again; the ill-educated speak it vulgarly, the purists inflexibly; and each generation invents its own moral slang.[58]

It would be hard to find a passage that so deftly conveys Oakeshott's sense of moral pluralism. Not only is morality compared to a language, but Oakeshott also resists the establishment of a kind of moral Esperanto. The old speak this language differently from the young, parents from children, and men from women ('They [women] are apt to get along without any profound respect for rules and they are both more obstinate and generous').[59] Moral languages also have their 'professional custodians' and 'connoisseurs of moral style', but it is 'the unprofessional guardians of this vernacular' who are its most reliable protectors precisely for 'their intimations of balance, sobriety, and exactness'. It is they who make possible 'the stylist, the hero, the saint, the aristocrat, and the vagabond' who care only for morality's 'intimations of magnificence'.[60]

The practice of morality is not to be confused with the rules of morality any more than speaking English is identical to its grammatical and syntactical rules. 'Moral rules,' Oakeshott asserts, 'are abridgements.'[61] However beneficial rules may be, the abridgement of a practice is not a living practice any more than spoken English can be learned by reading a dictionary. There is a libertarian, not to say antinomian, streak in Oakeshott that resists the language of rules. Rules tend to ossify and coagulate a practice by turning it into a body of doctrine or set of duties:

> Where the relationships of a moral practice are articulated in rules they lose some of their characteristic expansiveness. The 'play' between agents is diminished; loyalty becomes legality, *obsequium* supersedes *fides*. And this strictness is magnified where rules become duties. The idea of 'duty' is that of a moral practice articulated, not in terms of rules which denote obligations generally owed, but in terms of *officia*; that is, obligations specified in respect of the occupation of 'positions'.[62]

It is often claimed, with a certain justice, that there is an Hegelian *sittlich* quality to Oakeshott's concept of a practice.[63] But more than anything else, this passage brings out the strong sense of moral individuality that underlies all of Oakeshott's writings, his resistance to viewing the moral life under the guise of reason alone, to reducing it to a set of rules or laws, or treating it as an instrument for social improvement. In the end Oakeshott's idea of moral experience defies categorization. It is his alone.

PHILOSOPHY IN PLATO'S CAVE

On Human Conduct not only provides Oakeshott's deepest and most compelling account of practical experience, it finalizes his views on philosophy and its relation to the world of practice. The theory–practice problem, as we have seen, was a central theme of *Experience and its Modes*, where philosophy and life were presented as virtual antitheses. To embrace philosophy means to escape life. The early Oakeshott seems to have accepted Hegel's dictum: 'When philosophy paints its grey in grey, then has a shape of life grown old'.[64] The question is whether this dualist vision of philosophy and the world of practical moral experience has survived into *On Human Conduct*.

Oakeshott begins the work with some reflections on the vocation of philosophy that he now calls by the terms 'theory' (*theoria*) and 'theorizing' (*theorein*).[65] It is one of the few times where he substitutes a Greek vocabulary for a Latin one. To theorize means to identify intelligibles or classes, to distinguish one set of likenesses from another. While in *Experience and its Modes* Oakeshott had defined philosophy as 'experience without presupposition', he now presents theory as 'the critical engagement of understanding'.[66] What distinguishes theorizing from other forms of understanding is its perpetually restless, unsettled character. Theorizing is 'an unconditional adventure in which every achievement of understanding is an invitation to investigate itself'.[67] The theorist is a person who is 'perpetually *en voyage*', never fully at home in the world and never content with his or her understanding. There is a Socratic, open-ended quality to Oakeshott's understanding of theory. The 'principle' of the theorist is simple: 'Never ask the end.'[68]

In one of the most engaging sections of the work Oakeshott illustrates his understanding of the theory–practice problem by a rereading of Plato's allegory of the cave from the *Republic*. On Oakeshott's telling of the story, the cave dwellers are 'like ourselves' in that they occupy a limited and conditional platform of understanding. This understanding may be sufficient to navigate the parameters of the cave, even if 'leaving no room for mystery' and 'asking no questions'. It is the theorist who first comes to realize the insufficiency of this understanding that constitutes practical experience. The inhabitants of the cave come to appear as 'prisoners' and the Platonic philosopher 'in some accounts at least' as an emancipator. The danger comes when the theorist's knowledge is presented not just as something different from but superior to that of the ordinary cave dweller, that is, when philosophy is presented as not merely 'useful' but as 'a gift of inestimable value to mankind'.[69]

On Plato's account the philosopher confronts the almost visceral hostility of the ordinary citizens among whom he finds himself. His claims to 'unconditional understanding' are invariably met with scepticism and even the threat of death. But Oakeshott takes an initially more benign view of the cave. Those who occupy the cave are not mere troglodytes. Among the cave dwellers, he says, are 'sagacious map-makers and adept diagnosticians' whose 'only serious intellectual defect is to be unaware of what they do not understand'.[70] They are inclined to treat the returned philosopher as a '*revenant*' from whom they have much to learn. It is not the true philosopher or theorist who needs to fear the jealousy of the crowd. Such people may even be respected for their 'fresh, questioning, unconventional intelligence'. The ordinary cave dwellers may even be inclined to accept 'the intellectual superiority' of the philosopher 'even where they cannot quite follow it'.[71]

Oakeshott maintains a severe, even self-denying, conception of philosophy. His philosopher is not a king, a legislator or a prophet bringing new codes of law, but a spectator, an observer and an inquirer seeking to understand experience in terms of its postulates. The task of philosophy is to understand the possibility of experience and not to offer an alternative to the practical knowledge of the artisan, the lawmaker or the judge. To use theory as a surrogate for practice is a betrayal of philosophy. When philosophy oversteps its limits, as it often does, when the theorist claims a monopoly of knowledge, when he seeks to usurp the place of ordinary understanding in practical life, and when he seeks to become useful to the city, the philosopher ceases to be a philosopher and becomes a moralist, a busybody and a scold:

> In short, what the cave-dwellers resent is not the theorist, the philosopher (him they are inclined to admire even if they have not much use for his concern with postulates), but the 'theoretician', the *philosophe*, the 'intellectual'; and they resent him, not because they are corrupt or ignorant but because they know just enough to recognize an impostor when they meet one.[72]

Oakeshott uses Plato's parable of the cave not only to protect philosophy from the lures of practice, but to protect practice from the intrusions of theory. His is a philosophy ultimately written from inside the cave. Like Wittgenstein, he wished to validate the ordinary languages of human intercourse. It is ultimately experience that remains the most effective defence against the hubris of theory. The best check on the limits of theory remains the common sense and ordinary judgement that constitutes practical experience at its best.

NOTES

1 *EM*, p. 9.
2 P. F. Strawson, *Individuals: An Essay in Descriptive Metaphysics* (London: Methuen, 1959).
3 L. Wittgenstein, *Philosophical Investigations*, trans. G. E. M. Anscombe (New York: Macmillan, 1968), § 124.
4 *EM*, pp. 247–321.
5 P. Franco, *The Political Philosophy of Michael Oakeshott* (New Haven, CT: Yale University Press, 1990), p. 56.
6 *EM*, p. 251.
7 The source for Oakeshott's ideas about the unity of thought and action could well be Spinoza; see *The Ethics*, in E. Curley (ed.), *A Spinoza Reader* (Princeton University Press, 1994), Book II, P7 (p. 119): 'The order and connection of ideas is the same as the order and connection of things'.
8 *EM*, p. 256.
9 *EM*, p. 273; the quote is from Shelley's 'Mutability'. See P. B. Shelley, *Shelley's Poetry and Prose: A Norton Critical Edition* (New York: W. W. Norton, 2002), p. 92.
10 *EM*, p. 258.
11 *EM*, p. 270.
12 *EM*, p. 271.
13 *EM*, p. 303.
14 George Crabbe (1754–1832), 'The Parting Hour', II, 1–6; quoted in W. Churchill, 'Consistency in Politics', in *Thoughts and Adventures* (Wilmington, DE: ISI Books, 2009), p. 44.
15 *EM*, p. 304.
16 *HC*, pp. 235–42.
17 *EM*, p. 2.
18 *EM*, p. 354.
19 *EM*, p. 355.
20 *EM*, p. 356.
21 *EM*, p. 3.
22 E. Podoksik, *In Defence of Modernity: Vision and Philosophy in Michael Oakeshott* (Thorverton: Imprint Academic, 2003), p. 141.
23 In all of *EM* only a single paragraph (p. 316) is devoted to politics and here only to show how political actors misuse history.
24 Aristotle, *Nicomachean Ethics*, trans. M. Ostwald (Indianapolis, IND: Bobbs-Merrill, 1962), VI.1140a–b (pp. 151–4).
25 M. Oakeshott, 'Rationalism in Politics', in *RP*, p. 11.
26 *Ibid.*, p. 22.

27 M. Oakeshott, 'Political Education', in *RP*, pp. 122–3.
28 Oakeshott, 'Rationalism in Politics', pp. 24–5.
29 Oakeshott, 'Political Education', p. 121.
30 For Oakeshott's critical reception by those on the neo-Conservative right, see P. Franco, *Michael Oakeshott: An Introduction* (New Haven, CT: Yale University Press, 2004), pp. 15–16, 111–12.
31 Oakeshott, 'Rationalism in Politics', pp. 27–8.
32 The phrase actually comes from Kant, 'Idea for a Universal History with a Cosmopolitan Purpose', in *Political Writings*, trans. H. B. Nisbet and ed. H. Reiss (Cambridge University Press, 1979), p. 46; see I. Berlin, *The Crooked Timber of Humanity* (Princeton University Press, 1998).
33 O. Wilde, *The Importance of Being Earnest*, in *The Major Works*, ed. I. Murray (Oxford University Press, 1989), act 1, part 2 (p. 493).
34 M. Oakeshott, 'The Tower of Babel', in *RP*, p. 61.
35 *Ibid.*, pp. 62–3.
36 *Ibid.*, p. 69.
37 M. Oakeshott, 'Rational Conduct', in *RP*, p. 101.
38 *Ibid.*, p. 102.
39 *Ibid.*, p. 109.
40 For Oakeshott's connection to Hume see W. J. Coats, Jr, *Oakeshott and his Contemporaries* (London: Associated University Presses, 2000), pp. 89–102.
41 Oakeshott, 'Political Education', pp. 128–9.
42 *Ibid.*, pp. 124, 133–6.
43 *Ibid.*, p. 128.
44 *Ibid.*, p. 126n.
45 In attempting to characterize the uniqueness of Hitler's Germany, Leo Strauss once referred to it as 'the only German regime – the only regime that ever was anywhere – that had no other clear principle except murderous hatred of the Jews'. See 'Preface to *Spinoza's Critique of Religion*', in *Liberalism Ancient and Modern* (New York: Basic Books, 1968), p. 226.
46 A word search reveals that 'tradition' appears only twice in *HC* and in neither case does it figure prominently: on page 24 Oakeshott speaks of the analysis of a poem in relation to a 'literary tradition' and on page 286n he uses it to distinguish the unlikeness of Russia and the West. I owe this information to Joshua Cherniss.
47 *HC*, p. vii.
48 *HC*, pp. 12–19.
49 *HC*, pp. 19–25.
50 *HC*, p. 15n.
51 *HC*, p. 58.

52 *HC*, p. 56.
53 *HC*, pp. 58–9.
54 *HC*, pp. 70–8.
55 *HC*, p. 60.
56 *HC*, p. 62.
57 *HC*, p. 53.
58 *HC*, p. 65.
59 *HC*, p. 65.
60 *HC*, p. 66.
61 *HC*, p. 66.
62 *HC*, p. 67.
63 Franco, *Political Philosophy of Oakeshott*, p. 151; J. L. Auspitz, 'Individuality, Civility, and Theory: The Philosophical Imagination of Michael Oakeshott', *Political Theory*, 4 (1976), 272.
64 G. W. F. Hegel, *Philosophy of Right*, trans. T. M. Knox (Oxford University Press, 1967), p. 13.
65 *HC*, p. 3n.
66 *HC*, p. 2.
67 *HC*, p. 11.
68 *HC*, p. 2.
69 *HC*, p. 29.
70 *HC*, pp. 29–30.
71 *HC*, p. 30.
72 *HC*, pp. 30–1.

ANDREW GAMBLE

7 Oakeshott's ideological politics: conservative or liberal?

INTRODUCTION

Michael Oakeshott has always been hard to characterize in terms of political doctrines and ideological persuasions. Everyone agrees he is a sceptic, but there is much less agreement as to what his scepticism implies for politics. Is he a sceptical liberal in the line of Tocqueville and Acton? Or a sceptical conservative in the line of Hume? Or is he sceptical of all politics? He constantly refused conventional political labels, whether Left or Right, liberal or conservative, regarding them as the product of that rationalism in politics he so deplored. He firmly declared that his thought had nothing to do with ideology, the most common form of Rationalist doctrine. Ideology was intellectually empty and had corrupted politics. Ideologies, according to Oakeshott, have supplanted traditions of behaviour, providing cribs for behaviour rather than an education in the activity itself. An ideology is an 'abstract principle or set of related abstract principles which has been independently premeditated'.[1]

Despite these strictures, however, Oakeshott is still regularly claimed as a conservative political philosopher, regarded by many as the most significant conservative philosopher of the twentieth century, and regularly cited by conservative politicians and commentators as an important influence. He was even offered a knighthood by the Thatcher government in the 1980s, but declined it. In many of his reviews and articles Oakeshott appears to be sympathetic to the conservative tradition, at least in England.[2] Some of his contributions to the *Cambridge Journal* in the 1940s, and several of the essays collected in *Rationalism in Politics*, feature strong attacks on collectivism in general and the British Labour Party in particular, as well as disparaging remarks about prominent standard-bearers of liberalism, including F. A. Hayek.

Yet on the other side are those who claim Oakeshott for liberalism because of his deep attachment to the English liberal political tradition, his apparent sympathy for many of the ideas of nineteenth-century economic liberalism,[3] and his understanding of the state as a non-purposive association. Oakeshott distinguishes between two understandings of modern European states as forms of association, libertarian and collectivist, nomocratic and teleocratic, whose basis is whether the state exists to promote many purposes or a single purpose.[4] There are many books in the secondary literature on Oakeshott that place him firmly in the liberal rather than the conservative tradition, for example Paul Franco, and more recently Efraim Podoksik, who has argued that Oakeshott is best understood as a liberal writer and that the tensions found in his writings are between the Whig and the romantic elements of the liberal tradition.[5]

These questions are connected to the broader issue of what it means to be a political writer on politics, or a political philosopher, and whether these activities are distinct from political ideology in the manner that Oakeshott supposed them to be. Is it possible to write about politics without adopting a political position, and if it is possible, did Oakeshott succeed in keeping the two separate? This chapter will explore these questions, mainly through an engagement with some of Oakeshott's key political essays and reviews in the 1940s and 1950s, although it will also briefly discuss *On Human Conduct*. Oakeshott published relatively little during his long life, and very seldom addressed contemporary political issues and concerns. The publication since his death of his many book reviews, as well as occasional papers and lectures, has added to the material on which an interpretation can be based, but much remains obscure, as Oakeshott no doubt intended that it should. This chapter will argue that there is a strong ideological character to some of Oakeshott's writing on politics, despite his denials, and that the ideological persuasion that is revealed is predominantly conservative, although what he understands by conservatism in the English context incorporates important elements of classical liberal thought.

IDEOLOGY

At the heart of these issues lies Oakeshott's conception of knowledge, and most specifically of ideology. Since Oakeshott's epistemology was an Idealist one that places great weight on the role of ideas and thought in constructing reality, it is puzzling why he would not admit ideology in certain of its forms at least to be a legitimate and unavoidable mode of experience in modern societies. David Manning explored this idea at some length, setting out what an ideological mode of experience in Oakeshottian terms would be like,[6] but never succeeded in persuading Oakeshott of its merits.[7] Oakeshott never abandoned his view of ideology as an expression of Rationalism. Ideology was responsible for much of the political and moral confusion of the modern world, introducing a range of concepts that were not just misleading but false. Oakeshott included in the list 'proletariat', 'nation state', 'popular sovereignty', 'social justice', indeed most of the categories in which modern political thought has been conducted. The terms 'Liberal' and 'Conservative' are acceptable as party labels, but Oakeshott does not speak of 'Conservatism' or 'Liberalism'. That would be to accept Rationalist abridgements of complex traditions of behaviour. Instead he talks of the conservative *disposition*, which is similar to Irving Kristol's characterization of neoconservatism as a *persuasion* rather than a doctrine.[8]

Oakeshott's belief in distinct modes of experience has led some interpreters to argue that he has nothing to say about politics conceived of as a mode of practice, but only as a mode of philosophy or of history.[9] On this reading, using historical or philosophical knowledge in practical politics is illegitimate because by moving between the two modes of experience the knowledge becomes abridged and a form of Rationalism. It is transformed into an ideology and as such destroys the original knowledge and understanding. From this standpoint the gulf between philosophical and historical understanding on the one side and practical understanding on the other can never be bridged, and should not be attempted. It follows that those seeking to be active in politics have nothing to learn from Oakeshott, and he has nothing to teach them. He is entirely remote from their concerns. His own interest in politics is to understand it in philosophical or historical terms, but those worlds, although satisfying in themselves, are quite disconnected from practice. To ask whether Oakeshott belongs more to conservatism or to liberalism is therefore a fundamental error. Oakeshott has no practical advice to give.

This interpretation is an entirely coherent and plausible understanding of Oakeshott's thought. It certainly captures something of what Oakeshott believed himself to be doing and the defences he erected around himself. But it is not convincing as an account of Oakeshott, because Oakeshott himself does not always adhere to it. Reading Oakeshott's early essays in particular, what is striking is not his detachment but his partisanship. There are many passages in which he writes as an ideologist. He is passionately engaged in political debate, clearly preferring one pattern of society and politics over another. He often does not write as a detached historian or philosopher whose only concern is to provide the most complete account of the phenomenon under investigation. Advocacy is never far below the surface and accounts for some of the fascination his writings have exerted. The difficulty is that it appears to contradict his epistemological stance on the radical separation of the different modes of experience. As an Oakeshottian, he should not be intervening in debates in the way that he does, and should not be making his own ideological persuasion so clear. Anti-ideology turns out on examination to be an ideological position itself, and only intelligible in an ideological framework. A comparison can be drawn with Leo Strauss.[10] He also appeared detached from the problems of contemporary politics, focusing on purely historical studies, particularly of classical political thought. But his approach inspired a Straussian school, many advocates of which drew lessons for the practice of contemporary politics. Oakeshott, too, had followers, but where he differs from Strauss is that on occasion he draws the lessons himself.

This can be seen clearly in the essays. Oakeshott is not even-handed between political parties or political traditions. For him there is truth and error in politics, and contemporary politics is characterized by increasing amounts of error. In his essay 'Contemporary British Politics' Oakeshott reviews Quintin Hogg's *The Case for Conservatism* and John Parker's *Labour Marches On*. He is disapproving of the suggestion that both these two political parties are inspired by 'a philosophy', the philosophy of the Mandate, in the case of Labour, and the philosophy of natural law for the Conservatives.[11] Oakeshott likes neither of them – both are Rationalist doctrines, remote from British political experience. He particularly dislikes the doctrine of the Mandate, which first raised its 'ugly head' in the seventeenth century during the civil war, and which he argues has no basis in political reality or British political tradition, because if accepted it would attribute absolute authority to the will of a temporary majority. He commends Hogg for rejecting this doctrine, but argues that the doctrine of natural law although superior suffers also from being an ideological construction rather than one based on British political experience. Natural law reproduces the separation between the individual and the state, and treats the individual as prior to the state, instead of understanding the state and the individual as a unity.[12] Hogg is also too fond of planning, making promises that the Conservatives will plan better than Labour. Oakeshott comments: 'The Rationalist bug has bitten the Conservative'. To defend conservative principles what is required, Oakeshott thinks, is to defend the customary way of doing things. It is a mistake to adopt the mode of Rationalist reasoning of their opponents, because to do so is to concede crucial intellectual ground. If all institutions have to be rationally justified, if all government becomes about planning, then the distinctive British form of understanding what it is to be free will be lost:

> It is the great merit of Conservatism that it has resisted the pressure of circumstances and a misled electorate to embrace the project of a centrally planned society. Its present weakness is that it has not resisted that pressure with the absolute conviction with which it should be resisted. If there ever comes a time when two parties compete for power on the basis of rival plans, an even larger lunacy than that from which we at present suffer will have established itself.[13]

Oakeshott is mildly reproving about Quintin Hogg. If Hogg reflects more, Oakeshott seems to be saying, he will see that there are stronger grounds on which to defend the things they both believe in. Towards Parker he is much more vitriolic. His review becomes an ideological polemic against collectivism and the Labour Party, which is presented as a thoroughly malign and alien import into British politics. Parker advocates the refashioning of the British constitution and British government, because, he says, 'the people wanted a purpose in peace as cogent as that given them in war'.[14] This will be achieved by creating a centrally planned society, which for Oakeshott is 'the ideal of all rationalistic politics'.[15] To this end, conference decisions of the Labour Party are to be made binding on the Labour government, which Oakeshott claims will mean that 'Parliament is demoted to the position of an executive body for carrying out the items of a programme determined each year by an irresponsible body'.[16] Oakeshott acknowledges that this position has not yet been reached, but 'it is the character of British Government implicit in the structure of the Labour Party'.[17] It promises a constitutional revolution besides which the introduction of central planning pales into insignificance. Nor is this the only danger. Labour also owes allegiance to the trade unions, and the Trades Union Congress (TUC) is an irresponsible body that appears to exercise a powerful influence over the decisions of a Labour administration. The repeal of the 1927 Trades Disputes Act at the behest of the TUC, according to Oakeshott, threatens to turn the House of Commons into a syndicalist assembly, in which a large number of MPs will owe primary loyalty not to their constituents but to the trade unions that nominated them.

Oakeshott had a low opinion of the Labour government elected in 1945. He talks about the 'incompetence' of their administration of departments, 'the delay and folly' of their foreign policy, and the 'grand stupidity' of their finance, and chastises the Conservatives for not being a more effective opposition.[18] But he also believes that the government is pursuing an underlying purpose, which is to concentrate much of the power that was still dispersed throughout society in the hands of the government. Nationalization is pressed not because it is necessary or because private enterprise is inefficient or monopolistic, but because without it a planned economy cannot be created. Oakeshott asks rhetorically, 'Why is not all this recognised by its promoters as despotism, and by those who suffer under it as tyranny?'[19] The answer Oakeshott believes is firstly because of the 'vast emotional and intellectual confusion' among British citizens about the nature and conditions of freedom, secondly because the changes were not preceded by a *coup d'état*, and thirdly because of the 'mediocrity' of the planners: 'Suspecting a tyranny, we look for a Strafford, and find only a Cripps, we look for a Cromwell and find only Clem Attlee'.[20]

Oakeshott is not comforted by this. In 'Contemporary British Politics' he suggests that the conclusions to be drawn from Parker's *Labour Marches On* are conclusions reinforced by the government's actions, namely 'that the Labour party has an *incentive* to become despotic ... that it has the *means* to become despotic ... and that it has the *intention* to become despotic'.[21] This makes a big contrast with Hogg's *The Case for Conservatism*. Here the conclusion is that 'Conservatism has no incentive to promote despotism and the aim of conservative politics is to guard society against all those concentrations of power which are liable to result in despotism'.[22]

What is the status of these judgements? Are they empirical? Historical? Philosophical? To those not of a conservative ideological persuasion they must appear ideological, interpreting a political situation through a particular ideological discourse, a set of general beliefs invoked to justify or criticize proposals for political action.[23] They clearly do not stem from any kind of even-handed assessment of the actual intentions and policy of the Labour government, of the kind which historians provide. They take the form of a political and ideological intervention, in which Oakeshott makes use of a number of familiar conservative ideological tropes, in particular perversity, futility and jeopardy, to attack his ideological opponents.[24] His main concern is to issue a warning about the dangers Labour poses to British democracy. By attempting to govern in accordance with an abstract idea of central planning, Labour threatens the freedom of British citizens. For Oakeshott, 'British democracy is not an abstract idea. It is a way of living and a manner of politics which first began to emerge in the Middle Ages'.[25] He feels passionate about defending it, but in order to defend it he has to become partisan, and he makes use of historical knowledge to fashion ideological arguments about the desirability of his view of British democracy as opposed to the Labour Party view. The historian as historian, according to Oakeshott, can have no opinion about the merits of one policy or development compared to another. Historians study how contingencies, events and circumstances explain why one outcome emerged rather than another. This is not Oakeshott's position here. He is fully engaged, as a partisan, on one side of the argument. The political language he uses is that of friends and enemies. The Labour Party cannot be accommodated within the British political tradition because its policy threatens to destroy it. Labour is guilty of a form of treason. The doctrine of the Rights of Man, which was based on common law practices and exported around the world, has now come back to 'confound our politics and corrupt our minds'.[26]

Oakeshott's more polemical writings might be defended on the grounds that since he never justified his views by reference to an abstract principle independently premeditated, but always to a concrete manner of living, he can be absolved from the charge of ideology. This depends on accepting an extremely narrow concept of ideology that is not shared by modern scholarship.[27] Ideologies can come in many forms, and the general beliefs they invoke can take the form of abridged historical arguments as well as abstract principles. But even if Oakeshott's narrow definition of ideology is accepted, it does not dispose of the problem. In many of his essays he still appears to be making a political intervention of the kind his account of experience rules out. He is using his historical knowledge to justify attacking the plans of the Labour Party as revealed in *Labour Marches On*, while giving qualified support to Hogg's conservative position.

The argument in 'Contemporary British Politics' is not an aberration. The ideological assumptions and preferences on which it is based recur throughout Oakeshott's writings. While there is a philosophical Oakeshott, and an historical Oakeshott, there is also an ideological Oakeshott. It is complicated because he is never simply an ideologue, and relatively little of his work is overtly presented in that way. But his willingness on occasion to engage in ideological disputes and to furnish ideological arguments is a distinctive and revealing aspect of his thought, and helps account for its appeal and its influence. Oakeshott has a vision of politics and of modernity that is a compelling one and which is not best served by pretending it is something else. An anti-ideology can be a potent form of ideology, and that is what Oakeshott provided. But what form does this ideology take? Is Oakeshott best placed within liberalism or conservatism? There are arguments on both sides, and it is the evidence for these that now needs to be considered.

OAKESHOTT AND THE CONSERVATIVE DISPOSITION

There is a strong prima facie case for seeing Oakeshott's primary ideological persuasion as conservative. In many of his reviews

Oakeshott appears to identify himself as a conservative. His comments on *The Case for Conservatism* indicate that he shares many of the same political assumptions as Quintin Hogg, even if they have some disagreements. He criticizes Hogg and Parker for agreeing that the basic categories of British politics are 'Left' and 'Right', because this involves imposing the categories of Continental politics on to Britain, where they do not belong, and would deprive Britain of much of its 'individuality'. While he concedes that Labour might be thought of as part of a Continental 'Left' to some extent, he disputes that the Conservatives are part of a Continental Right: 'There is nothing whatever in common between British Conservatism and any of the categories of continental politics'.[28] Talk of this sort is dangerous. It liberates 'a fog of unreality, and lost in this British politics may become detached from their real root in British society and its history'.[29]

This hints at the main reason why Oakeshott has most often been described as a conservative. His reverence for the British manner of doing things, the British political tradition, emphasizes the individuality and particularity of this tradition. The British political tradition is liberal in many respects, particularly as regards the diffusion of power, the rule of law and the protection of individual rights, but Oakeshott rejects the universal claims of liberalism, because he is only interested in claims that are grounded in the English political experience. He pours scorn on notions such as the Declaration of the Rights of Man and the American Declaration of Independence. These are abridgements of other political traditions and experiences: in the case of the United States, they are abridgements of British political experience, solidified into an eternal document. Oakeshott opposed the idea of the abstract individual, existing before the creation of the state and acting as the fount of all authority. Hobbes is preferred to Locke precisely because his theory of the state does not indulge the conceit of the sovereign individual.[30] Sovereignty is established once the people agree the covenant to end the war of all against all. Oakeshott has a conception of the authority of the state that is uncompromising in its implications for the obligations of citizens. The state is the condition for civil life, for peace and for all kinds of human flourishing. It is not a negative limit on the freedom of individuals. He rejected the 'metaphysical' conception of the individual. The 'individual' was an historical achievement in which 'government' had played a decisive part.[31]

Oakeshott is also a noted critic of liberal thinkers. While he is disapproving of lapses by English Conservatives towards Rationalism,[32] he is even more severe on the Rationalism in much liberal thought, particularly that of F. A. Hayek. Oakeshott never joined the Mont Pelerin Society, which Hayek established after 1945 as a kind of liberal international to lead the fight back against collectivism. Oakeshott approved strongly of the need to resist collectivism, but he disapproved of many of the intellectual means proposed. 'A plan to resist planning may be better than its opposite', he wrote about Hayek's *Road to Serfdom*, 'but it belongs to the same style of politics'.[33] He always opposed the subordination of politics to a purpose external to it, and emphasized the divide between a libertarian conception of politics,which was part of the conservative disposition, and the Rationalist conceptions of liberals and neoliberals.

The most important source however for Oakeshott's conservatism is generally held to be his essays in *Rationalism in Politics*, particularly 'On Being Conservative', a celebration of the conservative disposition in politics. It is not a conservatism to please everyone. Oakeshott rejects not just natural law but any transcendental justification for the existing order. Conservatism arises as a disposition within a settled tradition of behaviour. It seeks to preserve that way of life from external and internal attack. Reforms should only be undertaken to help it stay resilient. Politics involves more than technical knowledge about how to do things, it involves practical knowledge about a way of life. Abstract ideas are quite inadequate to grasp the particularity of a way of life, and in mistaking its character they encourage the adoption of inappropriate and often damaging policies to reform it. Abstract ideas, wherever they come from, do not travel, hence Oakeshott's scorn for imported Continental ideas. The British have no need for external guidance on how to run their affairs.

Oakeshott never called himself a nationalist. This is another Rationalist term that has no place in English politics. He disputed that Britain or any other country in Western Europe should be described as a nation state.[34] But in rejecting such terms he also rejects much of the terminology of modern liberalism. Oakeshott can be seen as belonging to a conservative tradition which emphasizes the gradual historical emergence of the institutions and customs which define the nation, and although he acknowledges that there are broad currents of thought at work here, and can speak quite confidently of the European mind, and the European conception of the modern state, he mostly resists generalization and talks of different national traditions, experiences and understanding, which make every state different. He has no patience with that strand in liberalism that regards the preservation of exclusive national jurisdictions as the main cause of war and conflict. Oakeshott celebrates states and national traditions.

'On Being Conservative' is one of Oakeshott's most elegant essays. Some have pointed out that it speaks only of a conservative disposition, which might be attached to a variety of political projects and attachments, liberal, conservative and socialist. It is at best situational conservatism rather than any kind of doctrinal conservatism.[35] What gives it substance, however, is its linking to definite national ways of life. What is most important in the conservative disposition is the desire to enjoy the world and its inheritance as we find it, and this means cherishing the traditions received from the past. For Oakeshott, the past conceived of in this way is intensely liberating because it is a repository of a wealth of practical knowledge, which is needed to live the good life.

This essay appears to endorse a strong version of the precautionary principle. 'Innovation', Oakeshott writes, 'entails certain loss and possible gain, therefore the onus of proof, to show that the proposed change may be expected to be on the whole beneficial, rests with the would-be innovator'.[36] He also argues that a change is more likely to be accepted if it 'resembles growth'. The change has to be 'intimated' in the situation and not imposed on it. If the innovation is 'a response to some specific defect', then it will be more desirable than one generated by 'a vision of perfection'. A person of conservative disposition, says Oakeshott, prefers innovations that are small and limited rather than large and indefinite, which proceed at a slow rather than a rapid pace, and when 'the projected change is most likely to be limited to what is intended and least likely to be corrupted by undesired and unmanageable consequences'.[37] These are quite stringent conditions for innovations to surmount, and most would fail the test, including universal suffrage or reform of the House of Lords. It is redolent of the conservative arguments against change set out by F. M. Cornford in his satirical guide to academic conservatism in Cambridge,[38] including the principle of unripe time and the principle of the dangerous precedent: nothing should ever be attempted for the first time.

Oakeshott examines the argument that the conservative disposition is deeply rooted in human nature. Human beings are risk averse, they prefer safety to danger, they accept change not because they like it but, as with death, because it is inescapable. He agrees that it is one of the strongest, perhaps the strongest of human preferences. Yet he also notes that in the last few centuries it has not been particularly strong in Europe. In a passage that echoes some of the sentiments in *The Communist Manifesto*, Oakeshott provides his own disquisition on the theme of 'all that is solid melts into air'. The conservative disposition has been eclipsed by the desire for novelty and change. 'There is a positive prejudice in favour of the yet untried'.[39] Risk-taking of an increasingly reckless kind has become rife. 'We are acquisitive to the point of greed' and everything is undergoing 'incessant improvement'. We are willing to try anything once, regardless of the consequences. One activity vies with another in being up to date. Religious and moral beliefs are discarded as casually as cars and televisions.

Oakeshott observes the passion of contemporary culture for the new and the untried with amused detachment. He does not think it can be arrested, and he does not recommend imposing the constraints of the conservative disposition on the restless, progressive bent of the modern individual. But he does not think this means that the conservative disposition is no longer relevant. On the contrary, he thinks that there are still certain spheres where it is supremely relevant. There are those activities that can only be engaged in with a conservative disposition, activities outside the sphere of the market, activities where a conservative disposition is uniquely appropriate because what is sought is 'present enjoyment and not a profit'.[40] He uses the example of friendship. It depends on the loyalties and attachments that proceed from familiarity, which would be destroyed if the economic calculus of the market were applied to them. He considers other activities such as fishing and craftsmanship. But Oakeshott concedes that it would be foolish and ineffectual to attempt to use this as an argument to impose conservatism across the whole of modern social life. He would like to protect as many of these traditional spheres as possible, but accepts that they are not and cannot become dominant.

There is another sphere, however, where Oakeshott thinks the conservative disposition is not only desirable but absolutely essential if the character of the activity is to be preserved; rules of conduct and by extension, politics. There are many activities, Oakeshott believes, in which a conservative disposition has a part to play, some in which it should be the 'senior partner' and some in which it should be master. For Oakeshott, there is no inconsistency in being radical in commercial, cultural and even private life, and conservative in politics. Indeed, radicalism is only tolerable in commercial and cultural life if politics is conducted according to conservative principles. Oakeshott carefully distinguishes the conservative disposition in politics from a set of conservative beliefs about organic principles, such as Royalism or Anglicanism, on which society should be founded. To be a conservative in this sense is to seek to defend those principles as the only legitimate principles for the organization of society. Oakeshott argues strongly against this interpretation of conservatism as implying a particular set of beliefs. For him, the conservative disposition 'is not necessarily connected with any particular beliefs about the universe, about the world in general or about human conduct in general'.[41] It only implies certain beliefs about the activity of governing and the instruments of government, not about morals or religion or natural law.

Is this a conservatism, then, without content? This is not Oakeshott's intention. There is a very serious content. He celebrates the apparent disorder of modern life, the absence of a plan, the chaotic process of human beings making choices and expressing themselves in a multitude of ways: 'We know as little and as much about where it is leading us as we know about the fashion in hats of twenty years time or the design of motor cars'.[42] Oakeshott acknowledges that some observers, including many conservatives, recoil from this character of modern life, deploring its wastefulness, its dissipation of energy, its excess, its lack of any clear direction, and seek to impose an order upon it. The worst offenders are socialists and collectivists who believe in the possibility of a 'collisionless manner of living proper to all mankind'[43] and seek to remove all the causes and occasions for conflict. This is a vision of human activity coordinated and directed from the centre towards a single centrally defined end. Oakeshott agrees that this is a coherent and intelligible political vision and even that 'there is much in our circumstances to provoke it'. But he regards it as inimical to a conservative disposition in politics, whose central purpose should be to preserve the diversity of human choices and activities.

The contrast Oakeshott draws here is between purposive and non-purposive forms of association. Those of a conservative disposition in politics he thinks should favour non-purposive association because this accepts the current condition of human circumstances and does not attempt to impose a pattern upon it. On this understanding of politics, the office of government is simply to rule. It is an indispensable activity, but also one that is inherently limited and specific, and difficult to preserve as such. He uses the analogy of the ruler as the umpire whose function it is to uphold the rules of the game, or the chairman of a meeting who governs the debate according to established rules but does not himself participate.

The emphasis is on understanding and enforcing the rules of the association, and this implies a very conservative attitude to those rules. They may gradually evolve and be amended, but only incrementally and only after much reflection and discussion. Politics becomes an activity which is inherently conservative, maintaining intact and handing on the rules which make the chaotic, turbocharged, expanding and constantly changing civil societies of modernity possible. If politics tries to embrace innovation and direct it, then it only succeeds by destroying the dynamism of civil society. To defend this position it is not necessary to ground it in a Rationalist doctrine about free markets or private property. It is sufficient merely to understand the function politics needs to perform in the kind of societies that are characteristic of modern times, and that function is a conservative one. Governments do not, therefore, do nothing. They have a great deal to do, because activities and circumstances are changing so much all around them, but the aim of all their actions is to maintain the rules which make possible 'the enjoyment of orderly and peaceable behaviour',[44] rather than to prescribe what that behaviour should be or to adopt a managerial conception of government. Oakeshott criticized the Conservatives for embracing 'productivity' as the prime object of policy in the

1960s and the Thatcher government for seeking to 'roll back the frontiers of the state' as a near disastrous blunder. In his view Conservative governments should have no place for managerial activity.[45] Oakeshott sums up his argument by noting that the disposition to be conservative in government is rooted in the belief that 'where government rests upon the acceptance of the current activities and beliefs of its subjects, the only appropriate manner of ruling is by making and enforcing rules of conduct'.[46] The state is a neutral arbiter and commands the loyalty of its citizens because it does not proclaim one version of the truth, but allows all its citizens the freedom to choose how they live their lives within the rule of law. The tools of government have to be periodically renewed to adjust to new circumstances, but only occasionally and only in response to a perceived need, and then only after careful deliberation. Politics, for Oakeshott, is more about conservation than innovation. There is a bias towards preserving the rules that exist rather than amending them. The onus is always on the proposers of change.

Oakeshott adds one further argument. Those who understand government in terms of rational planning typically imagine it to be a 'vast reservoir of power', which they seek to capture and use to pursue their favourite projects and which they believe to be for the benefit of mankind. They use politics to inflame passions and raise expectations about what government might accomplish for a particular group or class. They make promises they cannot keep, and treat governing like any other commercial activity, such as making and selling soap. The disposition to be conservative in respect of politics goes in the other direction. It seeks not to inflame passion and give desire new objects to feed upon, but to lower expectations and inject moderation into political debate, 'to restrain, to deflate, to pacify and to reconcile'.[47] This is not, Oakeshott explains, because he is opposed to passion in ordinary life; far from it. But he, like Hobbes, is opposed to it in politics because rival passions breed civil discord, and the conflict can destroy orderly and peaceable life.

This is a very distinctive conservative attitude to governing and to politics, which treats governing as a secondary activity but a necessary one and which aims all the time at preserving the established order of status and privilege by seeking to defuse sources of discontent and to reduce the intensity of politics, rather than increasing it. The task of government is to be sceptical about the passions of its citizens, and by being sceptical to encourage its citizens to moderate their demands on it. Oakeshott finds, therefore, no paradox for a people to be conservative in politics but adventurous and enterprising in most of their other activities. Indeed he thinks that the more adventurous and enterprising a society, the more necessary it is for it to be conservative in politics. If our circumstances were different, if the people were unadventurous and slothful, then he concedes a conservative disposition in politics might not be appropriate, although he personally thinks that a conservative disposition would be important for any conceivable set of circumstances. His key conclusion is that 'it is not at all inconsistent to be conservative in respect of government and radical in respect of almost every other activity'.[48] At the heart of this attitude is the need for scepticism in politics to counterbalance passion in the rest of life, which is why he thinks there is more to be learnt about the conservative disposition in politics from Montaigne, Pascal, Hobbes and Hume than from Bentham or Burke. Burke, in particular, is responsible for the confusion in modern conservatism that the conservative disposition should extend to all areas of life.[49]

He also thinks politics is not an activity for the young, because the sceptical attitude it enjoins means eschewing passion, optimism and commitment, and instead understanding politics as concerned with limits and trade-offs, acknowledging realities, favouring indifference, controlling desire, 'feeling the balance of things in our hands',[50] accepting many things that are distasteful or disagreeable or morally obnoxious. Only people with a certain maturity, or those like Pitt the Younger born prematurely old, have the talent to engage in politics. Oakeshott makes it clear that he himself would never consider it. To have a vocation for politics you must have both a feel for 'the commonplace world', the world of practice, and an inclination to engage with it but only if you have nothing better to think about.[51] During most of his academic career Oakeshott studied politics and wrote about politics, but he never chose to become directly engaged in politics, and retained his other-worldly stance.

OAKESHOTT AND THE LIBERAL DISPOSITION

Oakeshott wrote eloquently about the conservative disposition in politics, but he never wrote an essay on the liberal disposition and was often disparaging about thinkers associated with the liberal tradition, including John Stuart Mill[52] and even John Locke,[53] as well as New Liberals and neoliberals. Yet many have argued that Oakeshott is primarily a liberal rather than a conservative thinker. The main grounds for doing so depend on a particular reading of *On Human Conduct*, and on his approval of certain liberal thinkers, such as Constant, who understand non-purposive forms of association and who oppose managerial conceptions of government and Rationalism applied to politics.[54] Since Oakeshott objects to all ideologies such as Rationalism, and since he believes almost all contemporary politics has become rationalistic and supports the understanding of the state as an association with a single purpose, he is equally dismissive of modern conservatism as well as modern liberalism, while socialism is beyond the pale. His revival of the distinction between *societas* and *universitas*, civil association and enterprise association, as the most fundamental distinction in modern European consciousness, much deeper than the distinction between Left and Right,[55] is accompanied by a clear ideological preference for *societas*. Those who characterize him as a liberal claim his arguments for *societas* reflect a liberal rather than a conservative disposition. It aligns him with the classical liberal tradition in its emphasis on the non-instrumental rule of law which, in prescribing no common purpose, permits the greatest possible diversity of purposes and activities.[56]

Oakeshott's understanding of the state as a *societas* is extremely rich and seductive. The growth of individuality and personal autonomy from the late Middle Ages made this new understanding possible, allowing the state to be seen as an association which could claim to be free and sovereign insofar as it was not subject to an external authority, and possessed the authority and the procedures 'to emancipate itself continuously from its legal past'.[57] These laws are general laws, they lay down conditions of conduct rather than providing devices to satisfy substantive preferences and desires of the members of the association. Oakeshott contrasts this sharply with the state as a *universitas*, which he defines as 'an association of intelligent agents who recognise themselves to be engaged upon the joint enterprise of seeking the satisfaction of some common substantive want'.[58]

The modern state, according to Oakeshott, is formed through a tension between these two dispositions – *societas* and *universitas*, which are irreconcilable. They are not two aspects of the modern state but deadly rivals: 'They are both characteristic of a state not because they have an inherent need for each other, indeed they deny one another, but because they have become contingently joined by the choices of human beings in the character of a modern European state'.[59] *Universitas* may be a path that is more crowded with travellers, but *societas* is morally superior, and greatly to be preferred, since it permits the free development of individuality. *Universitas* by contrast involves slavery, the exercise of 'lordly rule' over subjects too fearful to assert their own individuality.

Oakeshott on a number of occasions praises libertarianism, while linking collectivism and Rationalism to despotism. He sees the great achievement of the modern world in Nietzschean terms as the liberation of individuality, the 'limitless process of self-transformation without self-destruction'.[60] Proteus rather than Prometheus is the model for the modern individual, and human life is understood as an adventure in personal self-enactment, with no guarantee of salvation or perfection. Oakeshott's enthusiasm for the kind of personality that has emerged in the modern world, and the particular understanding of politics and the state which supports and advances it, makes him an unusual conservative. He celebrates the autonomous individual, the society of enterprise and continuous change. He notes the destruction of communal ties, but is not nostalgic for them. Modernity is a set of circumstances to be enjoyed, and what is chiefly enjoyable is precisely the freedom to choose between a bewildering variety of beliefs, values and activities, to invent and reinvent oneself, to gain personal autonomy and moral responsibility.

Oakeshott's libertarianism in *On Human Conduct* is undeniable, and reflects his commitment to certain liberal values, of tolerance and choice and individualism, the endless adventure of self-creation. But at no point does it contradict the conservative view of politics outlined in 'On Being Conservative'. There is a profound pessimism in Oakeshott about politics, because the virus of Rationalism is so vigorous and contagious. He believes in rules of conduct that promote liberal outcomes, in the sense of allowing individuals to be as radical as they choose in the way they live their lives, but this requires a conservative rather than a liberal disposition in politics. He wants a political class that understands and respects the state as a non-purposive association and which will therefore govern cautiously and sceptically. He has a very low opinion of democracy, regarding universal suffrage as a disaster, a Rationalist project which assisted the trends towards the state being understood as an 'economy' rather than as a non-purposive association, and therefore as an enterprise to be managed to provide prosperity, jobs, welfare and security for its citizens. The spread of democracy has brought into government new elites that lack the experience and knowledge of the political tradition of their state to govern wisely and prudently. 'The generation of Rationalist politics is by political inexperience out of political opportunity'.[61] Oakeshott distinguishes between the state as a source of authority, the state as a source of power and the state as a mode of association. The state must be constituted in a way that protects non-purposive association, but this does not require a representative or democratic constitution. Democracy has repeatedly failed to protect non-purposive association, by encouraging rationalistic politics that constantly threatens it. Oakeshott is against 'lordly rule', except in special circumstances such as dealing with the poor[62] and external security, but he is strongly in favour of the rule of law, and a state that has the proper authority to uphold the rule of law with whatever force is required.

Non-purposive forms of association would be much more secure if all citizens were modern individuals, prepared to take responsibility for their lives. But the modern world has created two distinct personalities, the individual and the individual manqué.[63] Oakeshott's argument here is not philosophical or historical in the way in which he uses and applies these terms in his writing; instead, it is highly schematic, the kind of ideological reasoning typically found in the Rationalist ideologies he so deplores. The individual manqué is the 'mass man', the anti-individual, all those who refuse to be autonomous and who demand security from the state. Anyone who supports redistribution through the state belongs to the anti-individuals, and collectivist parties thrive by appealing to them. This simple ideological device provides Oakeshott with a key dividing line to separate those policies that pursue intimations from the inherited political tradition and those that are rationalistic and born of inexperience and intellectual error. Most of modern government comes within this second category, and constantly threatens to infantilize citizens and undermine the foundations of non-purposive association.

The conservative nature of Oakeshott's politics can be seen in another early essay, 'The Political Economy of Freedom'. Despite its title, this essay is much more about politics than about economics. The task of a political economy of freedom is to define the political conditions that can make economic freedom possible. Chief among these conditions is the diffusion of power. The idea that power should be dispersed throughout the community has roots in both liberal and conservative thought. In the economic sphere, it means that the state should not tolerate any monopolies, either of capital or of labour, although Oakeshott, in a characteristic ideological flourish, regards labour monopolies as more dangerous than any others.[64] This principle ensures competition, but it is diffusion of power, not competition, which Oakeshott emphasizes. If power is diffused, then competition will naturally follow. Oakeshott regards economic freedoms – property, free trade, competition and a stable currency – as much more important than political freedoms, such as freedom of speech, since, as he puts it, 'the major part of mankind has nothing to say'.[65] The economy of the nineteenth century, with state spending below 10 per cent of national income, no welfare state and minimal redistribution and protections for labour, is the society Oakeshott says we had learned to enjoy, and it is this society he seeks to defend against the encroachments of governments elected under universal suffrage, with their Rationalist schemes. Oakeshott's ideological preferences set him apart from New Liberals like Hobhouse or Keynes or Beveridge; they set him apart from social democrats like Durbin or Tawney or Cole; they even set him apart from many Conservatives, such as Harold Macmillan or Quintin Hogg – but they chime with familiar, mainstream twentieth-century conservative arguments about the dangers of collectivism, the welfare state, big government and democracy.

Does Oakeshott not still have resonances with the classical liberal tradition, as John Gray has argued?[66] In his essays, Oakeshott's attachment to the liberal principle of the rule of law does align him with a central liberal tradition. But he rejects all forms of doctrinal liberalism, aimed at promoting either democracy and human rights or economic laissez-faire. His conservatism resides in his endorsement of whatever has emerged from traditions of behaviour, and too much of nineteenth-century liberalism took the form of premeditated abstract ideas. Oakeshott did not share the radical political passions of John Bright or Richard Cobden. He thought the conservative thinkers of the nineteenth century had been justified in many of their fears about the prospects for western civilization.[67] Nineteenth-century liberalism was associated with the rise of democracy, the cause of political reform and the undermining of traditional political authority. Oakeshott was sceptical of all three.

Although Oakeshott was highly critical of the way Rationalism had invaded British politics and obscured the British political tradition, he still regarded the British understanding of their state as a civil association as superior to that of other nations. In *On Human Conduct* he derided the attempts of other nations to sustain representative forms of government.[68] Britain almost alone had preserved the continuity of its institutions, and succeeded in creating for long periods of its modern history a state that understood itself as a civil association rather than an enterprise association.[69] But even in Britain, the ability to protect the traditional British understanding of the state as a civil association was gravely under threat. Oakeshott's strong sense of national identity, his disparagement of other nations,[70] his references to 'foreign claptrap', his disdain for the European Community, are all part of his political vision. It is a very distinctive vision, and a very eloquent one, and it borrows from other traditions. But it is hard to dispute either its ideological or its predominantly conservative character.

NOTES

1 M. Oakeshott, 'Political Education', in *RP*, p. 116.

2 See for example his reviews of *The Conservative Opportunity* (1965), *Conservative Essays* (1978) and *Conservative Thoughts* (1988), in *VMES*, pp. 187–9, 280–2 and 295–7.

3 J. Gray, 'Oakeshott as a Liberal', in *Post-Liberalism: Studies in Political Thought* (London: Routledge, 1983), pp. 40–6.

4 W. H. Greenleaf uses this same distinction in his reconstruction of the British political tradition: W. H. Greenleaf, *The British Political Tradition* (London: Methuen, 1983), vols. I and II.

5 E. Podoksik, *In Defence of Modernity: Vision and Philosophy in Michael Oakeshott* (Thorverton: Imprint Academic, 2003); P. Franco, *The Political Philosophy of Michael Oakeshott* (New Haven, CT: Yale University Press, 1990).
6 D. J. Manning and T. J. Robinson, *The Place of Ideology in Political Life* (London: Croom Helm, 1985).
7 Personal information.
8 I. Kristol, *The Neoconservative Persuasion: Selected Essays 1942–2009* (New York: Basic Books, 2011).
9 M. Oakeshott, 'The Study of "Politics" in a University', in *RP*, pp. 301–33.
10 R. Devigne, *Recasting Conservatism: Michael Oakeshott, Leo Strauss, and Conservative Political Thought's Response to Postmodernism* (New Haven, CT: Yale University Press, 1994).
11 M. Oakeshott, 'Contemporary British Politics', in *CPJ*, p. 203.
12 Oakeshott moves away from this Hegelian understanding in his later writings.
13 Oakeshott, 'Contemporary British Politics', p. 208.
14 *Ibid.*, p. 206.
15 *Ibid.*, p. 207.
16 *Ibid.*, p. 209.
17 *Ibid.*
18 *Ibid.*, p. 211.
19 *Ibid.*, p. 213.
20 *Ibid.*, p. 214.
21 *Ibid.*
22 *Ibid.*
23 M. Oakeshott, 'Preface to *The Form of Ideology*', in *VMES*, p. 294.
24 A. Hirschman, *The Rhetoric of Reaction: Perversity, Futility, Jeopardy* (Cambridge, MA: Harvard University Press, 1991).
25 Oakeshott, 'Contemporary British Politics', p. 218.
26 *Ibid.*, p. 219.
27 Michael Freeden, *Ideologies and Political Theory: A Conceptual Approach* (Oxford: Clarendon Press, 1996). Freeden writes of Oakeshott (p. 328): 'It is only through denying that conservatism is an ideology, bearing a systematic morphology and armed with a novel conceptual map of its own, that Oakeshott evaded realizing that he himself was a conservative ideologist who had justifiably become an object of inquiry on the part of analysts of conservative ideology'.
28 Oakeshott, 'Contemporary British Politics', p. 208.
29 *Ibid.*, pp. 208–9.
30 M. Oakeshott, 'Introduction to *Leviathan*' [1975], in *HCA*, pp. 56–7.
31 M. Oakeshott, review of H. E. Read, *Anarchy and Order*, in *VMES*, p. 73.

32 See his reviews of *The Conservative Opportunity* and *Conservative Essays*.
33 M. Oakeshott, 'Rationalism in Politics', in *RP*, p. 21; see also A. Gamble, *Hayek: The Iron Cage of Liberty* (Cambridge: Polity, 1996), pp. 188–9.
34 *HC*, p. 188.
35 S. Huntington, 'Conservatism as an Ideology', *American Political Science Review*, 51 (1957), 454–73. Oakeshott noted in one of his last reviews that such is the corruption and ambiguity which has overtaken our political vocabulary that the name conservative has lost its meaning since even Stalinists are called conservatives. Oakeshott, review of *Conservative Thoughts*, p. 295.
36 M. Oakeshott, 'On Being Conservative', in *RP*, p. 172.
37 *Ibid.*
38 F. M. Cornford, *Micro-Cosmographia Academica* (Cambridge: Bowes and Bowes, 1908), pp. 15, 16.
39 Oakeshott, 'On Being Conservative', p. 174.
40 *Ibid.*, p. 175.
41 *Ibid.*, p. 183.
42 *Ibid.*, p. 185.
43 *Ibid.*, p. 186.
44 *Ibid.*, p. 188.
45 Oakeshott, review of *The Conservative Opportunity*, p. 188; review of *Conservative Essays*, p. 282.
46 Oakeshott, 'On Being Conservative', p. 189.
47 *Ibid.*, p. 192.
48 *Ibid.*, p. 195.
49 See Oakeshott's review of R. Kirk, *The Conservative Mind*, in *VMES*, p. 83.
50 Oakeshott, 'On Being Conservative', p. 195.
51 *Ibid.*, p. 196.
52 Oakeshott, 'Political Education', pp. 130–1.
53 *Ibid.*, pp. 120–1.
54 Oakeshott, review of *Conservative Thoughts*.
55 *HC*, p. 320.
56 Gray, 'Oakeshott as a Liberal'.
57 *HC*, p. 229.
58 *HC*, p. 205.
59 *HC*, p. 323.
60 *HC*, p. 241.
61 Oakeshott, 'Rationalism in Politics', p. 30.
62 *HC*, p. 305.

63 *HC*, pp. 276–8.
64 M. Oakeshott, 'The Political Economy of Freedom', in *RP*, p. 53.
65 *Ibid.*, p. 43.
66 Gray, 'Oakeshott as a Liberal'.
67 M. Oakeshott, review of *The Conservative Mind*, p. 82.
68 *HC*, p. 191.
69 Oakeshott acknowledges the importance of war and foreign policy in making all modern states, including Britain, enterprise states. But generally he has little to say about international relations, or the argument that it was British imperial expansion and 'lordly rule' abroad which made possible the cultivation of the rule of law and civil association at home. On this, see P. Anderson, 'The Intransigent Right', in P. Anderson, *Spectrum: From Right to Left in the World of Ideas* (London: Verso, 2005), pp. 3–28.
70 See for example his remark that 'Russians and Turks have never enjoyed the experience of freedom, and therefore can only think in abstractions': 'The Political Economy of Freedom', p. 40.

TERRY NARDIN

8 Rhetoric and political language

> Aristotle was wrong (and for a Greek characteristically wrong) when he said that the *ti estin* of 'politics', what it is and what makes it possible, is the power of speech. Polis-life is certainly impossible without 'speech', but this is not its sufficient condition ... What distinguishes 'men' from 'animals' is not speech but a *geistige Welt*. And this entails a past relationship. Men, and not animals, live in a world which is past, present, and future; men have a civilization to inherit, and they become men in so far as they possess what they have inherited, not merely in so far as they can communicate with one another in words.[1]

INTRODUCTION

Human beings are distinguished from other animals by living in a world of ideas. They are distinguished from one another by having different ideas, and their words mark these differences. But words can obscure as well as express meaning. Oakeshott's writings give evidence of close attention to the meanings of words and especially to political words and their persistent ambiguities. Moving between historical interpretation and philosophical examination, he provides an anatomy of modern European political discourse by distinguishing its characteristic questions and argumentative idioms. He unscrambles the inherited vocabulary used to describe the modern

Thanks to Luke O'Sullivan for helpful comments on this chapter, and the Faculty of Arts and Social Sciences at the National University of Singapore for supporting my work on it.

state and to define the authority, power and purposes of government, and he considers how competing views of the state as an association have shaped political activity and reflection since the Renaissance. And he is concerned throughout to distinguish political discourse, which is persuasive and therefore inherently rhetorical rather than a matter of proof, from discourse *about* politics – that is, to distinguish the practical arguments of rulers and citizens from the explanatory inquiries that are (he thinks) the proper business of the political theorist.

These themes appear in many of Oakeshott's writings but they are most prominent in several essays he wrote between the publication of *Rationalism in Politics* (1962) and *On Human Conduct* (1975). It is worth noticing what Oakeshott has to say about rhetoric and language in politics because little has been written about this aspect of his work and, more substantially, because these writings contain interesting ideas that are overlooked if one focuses on the major books. In particular, his discussion of rhetoric and political language is more fully developed in the essays than in *On Human Conduct*, where it is subordinated to the larger philosophical project of that book. It is in the neglected essays of this period that Oakeshott focuses most sharply on political discourse, its rhetorical character, and the effects of that character on the political vocabulary of the modern world.

THE AMBIGUITY THESIS

Paying attention to historical vocabularies of political speech is a hallmark of what has come to be called the Cambridge School of political thought, whose members – John Pocock, Quentin Skinner, Anthony Pagden, Richard Tuck and others – have reshaped the study of political thought by identifying distinct traditions, languages or ideologies of political argument.[2] Oakeshott, too, distinguishes historical languages, but he is concerned with how these languages inflect a *shared* political vocabulary to generate the conceptual tensions characteristic of modern politics. He does so most explicitly in the third part of *On Human Conduct* and in two essays written around the same time, but his interest in the ambiguities of modern political speech goes back several decades and is evident in other writings since the mid 1950s. Oakeshott's approach in these writings, though historically grounded, is often in the style of mid-century conceptual analysis rather than historical recovery.[3] It aims to clarify and repair terms that have been misapplied, obfuscated and turned into slogans, rendering them unfit for rational argument.

An early example of such analysis can be found in an unpublished paper, 'The Idea of "Character" in the Interpretation of Modern Politics', which seems to have been written around 1955. A tradition or language of discourse is a 'practice', which for Oakeshott in this essay is a 'diurnal' activity, one 'considered in respect of its known propensities' and which can be said, by virtue of those known propensities, to have a 'character'.[4] Modern European politics, he thinks, displays such a character. It is one that allows it to 'be recognized in terms of known and established dispositions' – dispositions that are evident in familiar political practices and styles of political argument. To discuss this politics, which is no longer confined to Europe, is to use a vocabulary composed of words such as 'law', 'state', 'authority', 'obligation', 'justice', 'rights', 'liberty', 'equality', 'community' and 'democracy'. These words are used to say different things and their meanings change as a result of how they are used. But the European vocabulary was never displaced by one of a different character (a Muslim vocabulary, for example) and has in fact 'been diffused outside Europe to such an extent that there is room for doubt whether there is a second political character of any significance now to be found in the world'.[5]

Oakeshott identifies Montesquieu as an early and acute theorist of the character of modern European politics, one who saw its vocabulary as allowing a range of meanings and (most boldly and originally) as displaying a polarity that determined these meanings. For Montesquieu, the words 'monarchy' and 'republic' (or 'democracy') identified not distinct constitutions but distinct activities of governments. The most important reason why a new kind of political discourse emerged, Oakeshott thinks, is that the governments of modern Europe were much more powerful than those of the medieval past – they could do more, so what they should do with their power became a practical question.[6]

The possibility that a government could effectively pursue ends of its own devising enabled Montesquieu to see that the question of its proper end – the question of what government is for – is distinct from questions about its constitution and authority, and that answers to those questions are irrelevant to the question of ends. Similarly constituted governments might pursue quite different ends and differently constituted governments similar ones. Most modern European states have representative assemblies, for example, but these bodies do different things, in one state mobilizing support for government policy, in another serving as a check on executive power. As Europeans realized the power of governments so their political discourse acquired a new character. It was increasingly concerned 'with what governments do and not with how governments are constituted and authorized'.[7] And the poles that determined the range of meanings of the associated words were not *more* or *less* activity of the same kind but different *kinds* of activity.

Oakeshott's later contrasts between 'teleocracy'[8] and 'nomocracy' or between enterprise and civil association are foreshadowed here, though the distinction (which is between what he unilluminatingly calls 'first' and 'second' orders of activity) is drawn less skilfully than in subsequent writings. Notably, he insists that these alternative views of the ends of government are not necessary but historic modes of activity; they emerged in response to a circumstance (the growth of state power), and in other circumstances different modes, or combinations of modes, might have become dominant.[9] Whether the distinction between enterprise and civil association is helpful in grasping the character of politics in, say, China is therefore an historical question, not a philosophical one – though by the time he came to write *On Human Conduct* it had become evident that his aim was to provide a statement of the possible range of human relationships as well as an historical account of how these relationships have found expression in the experience of particular peoples. But where there is such a division, the result will be an ambiguous vocabulary in which the meanings of political words change according to whether government is conceived of as a substantive venture or a procedural framework. Even if one is not persuaded by Oakeshott's argument that a tension between enterprise and civil association explains the ambiguities in modern political discourse, one might nevertheless agree that the character of modern politics is complex and its vocabulary ambiguous, and that there is something to be learned by paying attention to political words and how they are used in political arguments.

Oakeshott pursues the theme of ambiguity in another essay from the mid 1950s, 'The Concept of Government in Modern Europe'. Designed as a lecture in English for a Spanish audience, it makes for odd reading since the available English version translates the Spanish text, which is itself a translation of the English original (which has been lost). But the main points that Oakeshott makes are clear enough. 'Governing' can become an enterprise of pursuing ends beyond those of maintaining order and administering justice when the power of governments increases dramatically, which it did at the beginning of the modern period. So although the question of how the authority to govern should be constituted – whether it should be rule by one, a few, or many – had been discussed since the ancient Greeks, the question of the proper function of government is a modern one.[10] The constitutional question, he suggests, is now dead because it is widely agreed that 'the appropriate constitution of government has to be such that the governed may feel satisfactorily governed by themselves'[11] – even though how to realize such a constitution remains contested. But the question of function – of what governments, whatever their constitution, should be doing – remains very much alive. Oakeshott restates his thesis that there are two distinct orders of governing, which he calls 'primary' and 'secondary', the first prescribing substantive ends to be pursued by the governed, the second merely regulating whatever activities the governed are engaged in with an eye to ameliorating possible conflicts.

What is of interest here is the effect this disagreement about the proper ends of government has had on the political vocabulary of the modern world. It explains why most of the words in that vocabulary – 'liberty', 'justice', 'democracy' and so on – have two different, even contradictory, meanings. These differences are signalled by the adjectives that commonly precede those words, such as 'ancient' versus 'modern' liberty, 'political' versus 'economic' justice, or 'liberal' versus 'social' democracy. These ambiguities reflect no mere corruption of words but a deep ambivalence regarding the purpose of government.[12] It is, moreover, an ambivalence that generates expectations that governments should simultaneously engage in and avoid substantive activity, which is impossible.

Sketching a theme he will develop in subsequent writings, Oakeshott traces these contradictory expectations back to their medieval origin in the distinction between a monarch as the lord (that is, owner and manager) of a landed estate and at the same time the ruler of a people whose activities need to be regulated for the peace and good order of the realm – people who are not serfs to be managed and exploited for lordly ends but legal subjects with ends of their own. When the medieval realm gave way to the modern state, Europeans inherited these incompatible conceptions of the role of government and put them to use in their overseas colonies as well as at home, adopting equivocal approaches to war, religion, economics and welfare. Briefly and roughly sketched in this lecture, these are themes he develops later into a full-blown theory of modern politics.

Oakeshott dissents from Skinner's view that 'the modern concept of the state' emerged during this period in efforts to justify the claims of various rulers. What these centuries produced, he argues, was not a single, dominant conception of the state but alternative conceptions whose historical fortunes were and continue to be uncertain.[13] The unresolved tension between these conceptions imposed on the modern European political vocabulary an ambiguity in which political words often have two discrepant meanings. This tension is far more important than the contrast between Left and Right, terms that Oakeshott thinks 'merely represent an insignificant squabble about the common purpose to be imposed upon a state already assumed to be a purposive association'.[14]

POLITICS AND PERSUASION

If the ambiguous character of modern political discourse is one concern that emerged after the publication of *Rationalism in Politics*, its inherently rhetorical character is another. This feature of political speech arises because politics is a practical activity in which decisions have to be made, recommended to others and defended before or after the event. The arguments devised in weighing, recommending or defending a political decision – one contemplated or made by a government – draw upon a stock of words that may be organized in different idioms of discussion or 'ideologies'. To this extent, Oakeshott's interest in the rhetorical character of political discourse is paired with his interest in its vocabulary. But he is also interested in what, besides its subject matter, distinguishes political from other kinds of discourse. And the answer he suggests is that political talk is a 'persuasive' discourse of contingencies, probabilities and conjectures, not a 'demonstrative' discourse of necessities, certainties and proofs. If demonstrative reasoning cannot in fact prove anything when applied to politics, persuasive reasoning may also fail to persuade. But it is the only kind of reasoning, Oakeshott thinks, that is appropriate to political affairs.

Though there are passing references to the topic of persuasion in earlier writings, it is first developed in a Radio Free Europe broadcast in 1963.[15] Oakeshott's subject in this talk is the Communist claim to be able to derive practical guidance from laws of history. The claim is that once one has scientifically ascertained laws of historical change, one would be able to choose correct policies. Leaving aside the question of whether there are any such laws or whether, if there were, knowledge of them would enable us to make correct decisions, Oakeshott suggests that this 'scientific' pretension is in fact a rhetorical device – an effort to persuade by purporting to prove.

In this device, the word 'correct' has lost the meaning it has in the context of mathematical proof, which is that the conclusion (a theorem) can be shown to follow necessarily from a set of premises (axioms). The argument that an unprovable conclusion is correct may still be persuasive given the right audience – for example, an audience that believes that there are such laws. Such an audience might also be persuaded to endure the unpleasant consequences of a government's policies if it believes that they are dictated by necessary laws of historical change, that history will eventually deliver the promised benefits and that history, not government, is responsible for the present hardships. But an argument of this kind can work only if there is an audience that believes it. Once that audience disappears, the 'closed real-imaginary world' within which the argument makes sense – in this case, Stalin's world – is likely to disintegrate.[16]

Oakeshott examines the contrast between persuasive and demonstrative discourse again in his response to a critical review of *Rationalism in Politics* and, more closely, in a subsequent essay, 'Political Discourse'.[17] The argument of this essay is that it is futile to search for certainty in politics. Politics is the activity of making decisions in situations that call for a response by government. It is therefore shaped by the character of such situations, which are always complex and need to be interpreted so that the situation can be diagnosed and alternative responses to it deliberated. Despite frequent claims to the contrary, such interpretations and the diagnoses to which they lead do not determine the responses that governments make.

No response to a political situation can be said to be a 'necessary' response, in the sense that it is either 'inevitable' (a matter of natural necessity rather than human choice) or 'indispensable' (the desired goal cannot be achieved without it). If a response is considered in relation to its consequences, the decision maker must not only estimate the likelihood of various outcomes but also evaluate them according to a standard of better or worse. And if it is considered in relation to a principle (such as honour or justice), the decision maker must decide how the principle should be interpreted in the situation to which it is being applied. For all these reasons, interpretations of the situations to which governments may have to respond are inherently contestable and usually contested. The arguments to which they give rise are 'political discourse'. This discourse draws upon a stock of words – such as 'necessary', 'honourable', 'just', 'lawful', 'responsible', 'democratic' and 'peaceful', along with many others and their contraries – that compose not only a general vocabulary of political discourse but may also compose different special vocabularies or 'ideologies'.[18] An ideology, in this sense, consists of ideas and words used in framing arguments that invite certain ways of interpreting political situations and deciding how to deal with them.

Both persuasive and demonstrative argumentative designs have roots in antiquity, the first having been analysed by Aristotle in the *Rhetoric* and the second used by Plato in his Socratic dialogues and later on by European philosophers who looked to Euclid's *Elements* or to syllogistic logic as a model for rational political argument.

Oakeshott disagrees with Aristotle that speech distinguishes men from animals, but when it comes to discussing the features of political speech, he follows Aristotle closely. The persuasive design is illustrated by Pericles' speech (reported by Thucydides) advising the Athenians to reject a Spartan ultimatum. The speech diagnoses the situation, proposes a response and defends the proposal in terms of the consequences of adopting or not adopting it. An argument of this kind cannot be refuted, only shown to be less convincing than some other argument of a similar kind. Because an argument that rests on judgements about consequences involves possibilities, the probabilities asserted can be disputed and other probabilities urged. If the argument invokes an analogy, the identified similarities can be challenged as being non-existent or exaggerated. Such arguments, in short, involve contingencies, probabilities and guesses, not necessities, certainties and proofs. Their aim, as Aristotle explains, is to persuade by appealing to beliefs generally held among a given audience to be true and values generally regarded as important.

The second type of logical design springs from efforts to remedy what is taken to be a fatal deficiency of the first, which is that it does not yield certainty. A logical design that guarantees certainty generates a truly demonstrative political discourse. The certainty postulated in such discourse is thought to arise from indisputable axioms or indisputable information on the basis of which the proper or best response can be reliably chosen. An axiom is a single, universally valid standard or criterion according to which one can judge the correctness of a political proposal: Plato's 'justice', Bentham's 'utility', or some set of 'natural' or 'human' rights. The problem, however, is that if there is more than one criterion – if there are different definitions of justice, different ways of measuring utility, different lists of rights – one must rely on casuistry to balance the claims of each, and this means persuasive rather than demonstrative argument. Indisputable information on which to base a correct diagnosis of the situation and therefore be able to choose a correct response was once thought to be provided by oracles or prophecy, both of which were imagined to deliver specific predictions. But oracles are notoriously ambiguous and the information provided by prophets is always incomplete. And even if they were reliable, such predictions would be incapable of suggesting, much less demonstrating, a uniquely correct course of action.

More recently, the burden of providing certainty has fallen on science, which is expected to generate predictions based on laws of human behaviour or historical change. But before these laws can be used to make predictions they have to be translated from the abstract world of scientific theory to the contingent world of human actions. And as David Hume famously argued in calling attention to the logical leap in moral philosophy from *is* to *ought*, this cannot be done. Like statements of fact, statements of empirical regularity or historical tendency cannot generate moral or political prescriptions because those prescriptions also require judgements about which states of affairs are desirable or undesirable and how a desirable state of affairs might be brought about or an undesirable one avoided.

Oakeshott illustrates these points about the necessary failure of demonstrative political discourse in a discussion of Marx that builds upon his earlier radio talk. Marx's 'science' of 'history' is modally incoherent, he suggests, but even if it were coherent as a scientific theory it could not generate the practical prescriptions Marx claims to derive from it. Political deliberation involves making decisions that depend not only on the outcomes of actions but also on judgements of the value of those outcomes, and science cannot, on its own, provide standards of evaluation. To hold otherwise is to transgress the modal boundary between science and practice.

Some of these points are repeated in the first part of *On Human Conduct*, which can be read as an effort to support them by closely examining the idea of human action. Persuasion is treated here both as action itself and as auxiliary to action: a persuasive act is 'a recommendation to choose and to perform an action in terms of the alleged merits of its likely outcome'.[19] It follows that persuasive speech, which respects the agency of those it addresses, must be distinguished not only from outright coercion – the use of physical constraint or methods like hypnotism or torture that produce compliance in others without their understanding and therefore their agency – but also from threats or promises. Efforts to gain compliance by threatening harm or promising a reward (as in the case of blackmail or bribery) are not 'persuasion', even though they recognize agency and may be effective, because the considerations they advance are unrelated to the merits (either consequential or intrinsic) of the proposed course of action. Persuasive speech, Oakeshott reiterates, 'does not pretend to demonstrate its conclusions and consequently it cannot be refuted' but it may be 'resisted or rebutted by arguments of the same sort'.[20] And what applies to persuasive speech in general applies to political speech. Oakeshott's conclusion, then, is that because political discourse deals with contingencies, beliefs, values and possibilities, the reasoning on which it depends always involves weighing the pros and cons of alternative courses of action. It involves persuading oneself and others that a chosen course of action is best, on balance, while acknowledging that it cannot actually be proven to be best or known to be correct. This is the only kind of reasoning that is appropriate to practical affairs and therefore to politics.

Persuading oneself – reasoning with oneself in making a decision – is not quite the same as persuading others. In deciding what to do, we look for cogent reasons to choose one course of action rather than another. But when it comes to persuading others, a gap opens up because we must provide reasons that seem cogent to this new audience. Where the audience is large, miscellaneous, ignorant, stupid or venal, persuasive speech can be corrupting. This was Plato's complaint against 'rhetoric'.[21] But the real problem is not that those who must be convinced in politics are deficient in some way but that they believe different things and must be addressed in a way that is responsive to their beliefs. This can be seen with particular clarity in arguments over the grounds of authority, which may appeal to divine right, lawful inheritance, free and fair elections and the like. Speakers may be constrained, if they wish to persuade, to appeal to beliefs that differ from their own. And this may be hard to do credibly, reinforcing the impression that political speech is often just a pack of lies.

THE VOCABULARY OF MODERN POLITICS

Despite its various idioms, political discussion in modern Europe has relied on a shared general vocabulary in which the same words are used for distinct concerns. The states of modern Europe, Oakeshott contends, were always 'mixed and miscellaneous collections of human beings precariously held together'.[22] Each came into being as rulers acquired authority and power. And each was the ambiguous outcome of endless debate about the proper uses of authority and power, debate shaped by competing ideas about the kind of human association a state was or should be: a relationship of individuals recognizing the authority of common rules of conduct or a purposive enterprise.

A modern state, then, has three distinguishable features: a recognized office of *authority* (a title to rule invested in the office and resting on recognition by subjects); an apparatus of governing attached to this office (composed of instruments of *power* by means of which to exercise this authority); and a mode of *association* to be governed authoritatively.[23] Each of these features has generated a tradition of discourse; a tradition of justificatory argument concerning the constitution of a state and the authority of its government; a tradition of instrumental reflection concerned with gaining and using power; and a tradition concerned with determining the character of the state as a mode of association and, related to this, with specifying the purpose and therefore the duties or responsibilities of its government. Oakeshott's primary concern – because he thinks it has been the primary concern of modern politics – is with the debate over what a government should be doing, not with how its authority to rule should be constituted or legitimized or its power to rule could be effectively used.

One can approach each of these discourses as either a participant or an observer. Oakeshott distinguishes between philosophical and justificatory talk about authority, for example. The first aims to distinguish authority (and its corollary, obligation) from other ideas and to uncover its presuppositions. Philosophical inquiry, in this sense, has nothing to do with judging the authority of any actual government. The same is true of historical inquiry, which if it is to be genuinely historical must detach itself from the politics of a past it seeks to recover and comprehend.

Philosophical inquiry shows that the authority of a government depends on formal considerations, not substantive ones. Public officials are 'authorized' to act or speak only by a rule of some kind, not by non-formal considerations such as their persuasive skill or the truth of what they assert. Their decisions or orders get their authority from the office – the formal position within an institution – they occupy: 'authoritative utterance, in respect of its authority, is always official'.[24] In some cases, the authority of a statement may be unimportant (such as when we evaluate the cogency of an argument), but where what is stated is presented as obligatory, its authority *is* important. Whether a pronouncement is authoritative cannot be decided by examining what it prescribes, only by determining its relation to an office or procedure. (What it prescribes may count in assessing its justice or desirability, however.)

If we shift from philosophy to history, then we see that the vocabulary of authority is a rhetorical one consisting of words used to challenge or defend authority claims. Such a vocabulary is needed most where people's beliefs and interests are so different that the only plausible basis of association is mutual acknowledgement of a ruling authority. This, Oakeshott argues, was certainly the case in early modern Europe, where agreement about authority 'might be difficult to sustain, but agreement about anything else was manifestly impossible'.[25] The difficulty arises in part from the existence of competing authorities. In modern Europe what has been thought to distinguish the government of a state was that its authority is 'sovereign', that is, independent of and superior to the authority of any other office in or beyond the state.

By the end of the sixteenth century the state had come to be understood as a non-voluntary territorial association under the authority of a single government understood to have custody of its laws and the right to defend it against internal and external threats. But the idea of sovereignty was an unstable achievement. Sovereign or *supreme* authority was taken to mean *unlimited* authority and unlimited *power*. But because power is always contingent it can never be unlimited: there is no such thing as 'total' power. Nor can authority be unlimited or 'absolute': it is always conditional because conferred by law.[26] Defining sovereignty in terms of power suggests that the authority (or right) to govern depends on a government's power (or ability) to govern, which in turn suggests that this right is diminished if the government's power is resisted.

For Oakeshott, this was manifestly confused. The authority of a law does not depend on a government's ability to enforce it, nor does a subject's obligation to obey the law vanish if he or she can evade it. Relationships of power are instrumental; they are concerned with outcomes, not with obligations. But because such relationships rarely exist apart from relationships defined by law, power is commonly exercised by those who are recognized as having a right to make demands. Power, though distinguishable from authority, may therefore be contingently linked with it. But the possession of power cannot itself endow a person with authority, and although power can be used to secure obedience, it creates no obligation.[27]

Oakeshott is interested not only in the concept of authority but also in the arguments used to justify political authority and in the rhetoric of such arguments. Sometimes these are particular claims made on behalf of a ruler. But the argument can also proceed at a deeper level, concerning itself with general ideas about the grounds on which laws or offices are authoritative. The search for the foundations of authority in a state is related to its constitutional history and relies upon an inherited vocabulary for attributing to it a constitutional 'shape' in virtue of which its government is alleged to be authoritative. This vocabulary includes nouns such as 'monarchy', 'aristocracy' and 'democracy', and their corresponding adjectives, each indicating, if vaguely, the constitutional structure of a regime while suggesting reasons for recognizing or denying its authority.

Democracy, for example, is 'rule (*kratein*) exercised by an office identified in terms of its occupants (*demos*) and deriving its authority from that occupation'.[28] Such words once marked distinctions that have since been lost: 'despotism', 'dictatorship', 'autocracy' and 'tyranny' once referred to distinct ways of constituting a government. In a despotism the claim to authority rests on ownership of land and people, in a dictatorship on a supposed ability to rule in an emergency, and in an autocracy on self-appointment, while a tyranny makes no claim whatever to authority. Kant could distinguish a republic, which rests on separating legislative, judicial and executive power, from a democracy, which does not. But in passing from theoretical to political argument, these words cease to mark the distinctions they originally identified and degenerate into terms of praise or abuse.

Even where their precision has not been lost, none of these ancient constitutional terms (or subsequently invented compounds such as 'constitutional monarchy', 'mixed regime' and 'representative democracy') is adequate to describe modern states, which are arranged in ways too diverse to be summed up in a word or two. These expressions are, in any case, merely rhetorical because the task of justification they have been asked to accomplish is impossible: a government's authority can never be definitively justified. This authority rests neither on the beliefs, like the will of God, that are asserted as reasons for recognizing it, nor on a founding act, but (Oakeshott argues) on the continuous acknowledgement by subjects of an obligation to subscribe to its laws. Slogans such as 'divine right', 'majority rule' and 'national self-determination' may help to sustain faith in the authority of a government, but they are not its actual ground.

The rhetorical use of arguments about authority invites the mistaken conclusion that authority is unimportant and that a constitution is simply an apparatus of governing, a device for accomplishing whatever needs to be done. This confusion is concealed in ambiguous justificatory expressions concerned not with a government's authority but with its desirability, which in turn is often equated simply with its 'propensity to favour certain interests'.[29] A constitutional 'covenant' or 'contract', once understood (by Hobbes, for example) as an agreement to establish an authoritative civil government, is now taken as an agreement to comply with rules believed to be advantageous for as long as this belief lasts. 'Consent' has come to mean not acknowledgement of a government's authority but approval of its policies, ascertained through plebiscites, electoral propositions or public opinion polls. And where 'democracy' once stood for a particular kind of constitution, the word has been used to identify and legitimize arrangements as diverse as constitutional monarchy, the welfare state, communist rule, the rule of law or any state with a market economy. More confusion arises when the word is used for a method of rule ('democratic procedures') or to characterize policies in terms of their results ('democratic tax reform'). As a result the word 'democracy' now stands, ambiguously, for a constitutional shape, a source of legitimacy, a method of governing and a mode of association.[30] Such confusion may enhance its rhetorical power but can only diminish its analytical utility.

The effort to construct, maintain and use tools of governmental power constitutes a second major aspect of a modern state. This activity has produced a largely instrumental tradition of reflection. But the vocabulary in which concerns of this sort are discussed is similar to that employed in discussing the use of power outside politics. The instruments of government resemble those used in business and other areas of life: those who exercise power must collect information and revenue, employ agents and follow standard practices of communication, accounting, personnel management and the like.

From the standpoint of a concern to use power effectively, there are evident similarities between governing a state and managing a corporation. The result, Oakeshott thinks, is to assimilate governing to management, which has set in motion strong forces towards resolving the ambiguous character of the modern state in favour of enterprise association. But because government and business are not the same, the word 'power' is abused and the ideas of authority and power confused when a state is seen simply as an apparatus of power and governing as nothing but the exercise of this power. The shared vocabulary makes it hard to distinguish between power used to enforce obligations and power used to satisfy desires.[31]

This brings us to the question of the proper use of governmental power, and, more generally, to the proper activities of a government: questions that relate to the character of the state as a mode of association. The third and in Oakeshott's view most distinctive aspect of modern political discourse concerns alternative understandings of the state as a mode of association and related beliefs about the purpose of government. If a state is organized to pursue an overarching substantive end – if it is what Oakeshott calls an 'enterprise association' – the proper concern of its government is to adopt policies instrumental to achieving that end. But if it is viewed as an association of persons related on the basis of non-instrumental rules that respect their character as independent persons – a 'civil association' – then the concern of its government cannot be to pursue an overarching end, for there is no such end. Governing an association that has no substantive purpose cannot be the management of an enterprise; there are no choices to be directed, resources to be exploited or results to be produced. Governing in civil association is 'ruling', that is, the care and custody of the non-instrumental laws that are the terms of association.

Oakeshott had argued that European political discourse is pulled between two conceptual extremes or 'poles' long before he came to characterize these extremes as alternative views of the state as a mode of association. In an unpublished manuscript that was probably written a few years before the essays from the mid 1950s discussed earlier, he suggests that the European political vocabulary displays an understanding of the aims of government that is divided between 'faith' and 'scepticism' regarding these aims. The first is a view of government as an instrument for realizing perfection in human affairs, the second of governing as a limited and remedial activity. It has also been hard to avoid discussing the aims of government in terms such as 'social' or 'liberal', which are used too loosely to bear any consistent meaning.[32]

Nevertheless, as Oakeshott made clear in later writings, civil association should not be confused with free enterprise, private enterprise, capitalism or laissez-faire. Although the classical economists did not identify a state as a corporate enterprise, they did imagine it to be 'an association of would-be consumers' and 'an association for mutual benefit'.[33] Some thought a managed economy would mean more efficiency, and others, less, but all viewed governments as providers of 'public goods' that could not be so efficiently provided in any other way. By linking the classical economists with theorists of a planned economy, Oakeshott separates himself from Friedrich Hayek and other free-market liberals, with whose views his own are often compared.[34] Properly speaking, civil association is 'no enterprise' association: 'it is not relationship in terms of the pursuit of any enterprise whatever, "public" or "private"'.[35] Nor is civil association the same as 'limited government' or the libertarian's 'minimal state', for to distinguish states according to the amount of government interference they permit is to make civility a matter of degree, whereas the distinction between civil and enterprise association is one of kind.

Another mistake is to confuse an inquiry into the associational character of a state with an inquiry into the authority of its government. In the 'enlightened government' of the eighteenth century, for example, a ruler's superior knowledge was thought to give direction to his policies while at the same time justifying his authority to rule. The effort to connect a government's authority with the ends it pursues is also evident in expressions such as 'socialism', 'national socialism' and 'communism', which have been used to identify a state as a corporate enterprise. All are implicitly 'teleocratic' – that is, they suggest that the *purpose* pursued by a government is also the *ground* of its authority. Strictly speaking, the authority of a government cannot be derived from the purposes it pursues, because authorization is by definition antecedent: a government can be authorized to rule by an actual or implied constitutive act but not by a purpose. A purpose may suggest reasons for approving of a government, but not for acknowledging its authority to rule. As Oakeshott observes, the word 'telcocracy' confuses the purposes of government with certain beliefs about its authority; his own use of it might, therefore, be taken as ironic.

In short, it has proved hard to keep the inquiry into the character of the state as an association separate from inquiries into its constitution, authority and administration. Like discussions of authority and power, this discussion, too, has often been confused and insignificant.

'POLITICS'

If politics is deliberative, one of the matters to be deliberated is the proper scope of politics itself – that is, the proper boundary between public and private affairs. And if political arguments are not demonstrative, there is no definitive criterion for delimiting that boundary. Just as other political words have been obscured and debased by misuse, the words 'politics' and 'political' have suffered a similar fate and are now, Oakeshott thinks, 'merely rhetorical expressions, powerless to identify anything in particular'.[36] There is 'politics' not only in government but also in private affairs, and it is concerned not only with how authority should be constituted or how it can be justified but also with the purposes it should be made to serve and with predictions about who is likely to be deciding those purposes.

The question 'What is politics?' is therefore one that calls for basic inquiry, and it is not surprising that Oakeshott should tackle it at the beginning of the course of lectures on the history of political thought he gave annually at the London School of Economics during the 1960s. Political activity, he explains there, is not primordial, like eating and drinking, but an invention, like accounting or astronomy. It is possible only when there exists a multiplicity of human beings who are associated with one another in terms of common rules of conduct that give unity to their association. But politics also assumes some degree of diversity, for where (as in a tribal society) diversity is minimal, custom is king and there is not much scope for collective discussion of the terms of association.

Politics emerges only with the emergence of a distinction between 'public' and 'private' affairs along with an office of authority specifically concerned with matters regarded as public. Moreover, the laws and institutions of the community must be seen as an outcome of human choices and therefore as alterable, not as determined by natural necessity. Politics, then, is an activity concerned with deliberating alternative courses of action and alternative arrangements for making collective decisions. 'It is thinking about what should be done and persuading . . . those who have the authority to act to make certain choices and not others'.[37]

But the ambiguity thesis, which affects the meaning of all political words, also affects the meaning of 'politics' itself. Since we have words for specific activities of government, such as legislating, adjudicating or administering, the word 'politics' is best reserved for an activity that is not identified by these more specific words. That activity is to consider the desirability of the terms of association (which, in a modern state, are the laws that constitute and regulate it) and therefore it is to be concerned with the proper purpose of government. But if political discourse is concerned with the ends of government and the desirability of the laws it adopts to advance those ends, that discourse will be different depending on whether the state is viewed as an enterprise or a civil association.

In an enterprise state, politics concerns enforcing orthodoxy or distributing benefits. Only when a state is understood to be a civil association does politics emerge as deliberation about the desirability of laws apart from the advantages or disadvantages of having them and solely in relation to the terms of association, which in civil association are constitutive and not instruments for distributing benefits and burdens.[38] In civil association, whether an actual or proposed law is desirable depends on considerations such as its moral propriety, compatibility with other laws and enforceability. There is a 'categorial' distinction between recognizing a law as desirable and approving of its distributive consequences.[39]

One might conclude, from Oakeshott's efforts to reform political language, that he thinks we would be better off if linguistic carelessness could be suppressed and verbal and conceptual uniformity enforced. That this is not his view is perhaps most vividly illustrated by the 1983 version of his retelling of the story of the tower of Babel. In the familiar versions, God punishes the people of Babel for their assault on heaven by 'confounding the tongues' of the people so that they are unable to understand one another and coordinate their actions. Their ambitions are thwarted because they speak many languages. In Oakeshott's version, they come to grief because they speak only one language.

> Where there was only one subject of talk, imagination and language became impoverished. Newspapers degenerated before they were replaced by thrice-daily official bulletins on the progress of the Tower ... All conduct was recognized only in its relation to the enterprise. The words 'good' and 'bad', 'justice' and 'injustice' acquired restricted meanings appropriate to the circumstances: to each was affixed the adjective 'social'.[40]

With every activity, including speech, now subordinated to the enterprise of conquering heaven, a barbaric monomania replaces civilized diversity and the tower collapses not through divine intervention but of its own unbalanced weight to become 'the tomb of an entire people, not perished in a confusion of tongues, but the victims of a delusion'.[41] Part of that delusion is that one can achieve general and permanent agreement in human affairs and, in doing so, erase all ambiguity. Oakeshott's writings on political discourse illustrate not only a respect for conceptual clarity but also a conviction of the inevitability of ambiguity and its constructive possibilities.

NOTES

1 M. Oakeshott, notebook 18, in *NL*, forthcoming.
2 See for example J. G. A. Pocock, 'The Concept of a Language and the Métier d'Historien: Some Considerations on Practice', in A. Pagden (ed.), *The Languages of Political Theory in Early Modern Europe* (Cambridge University Press, 1987), pp. 19–40.
3 The more scholarly of these essays is 'The Vocabulary of a Modern European State', in *VMES*, pp. 232–66; the other, 'Talking Politics', in *RP* [1991], pp. 438–61, goes over the same ground in a more informal way. Both were first published in 1975, as was *On Human Conduct*.
4 M. Oakeshott, 'The Idea of "Character" in the Interpretation of Modern Politics', in *WH*, p. 256.
5 *Ibid.*, pp. 261, 263.
6 *Ibid.*, pp. 267–9. See also, *inter alia*, *MPME*, pp. 33–4, and *LHPT*, pp. 385–6, 399.
7 Oakeshott, 'Idea of "Character"', p. 270.
8 Oakeshott refers to 'telocracy' – one 'e' – in writings of the mid 1960s, but later spells it 'teleocracy'.
9 *Ibid.*, p. 273.
10 In writings of the 1950s Oakeshott speaks of the purpose of government as its 'function' or 'role', in the 1960s (*LHPT*, p. 469) as its 'business' or 'office', and in the 1970s as the 'office' or 'engagement' of government (*HC*, pp. 189, 193).
11 M. Oakeshott, 'The Concept of Government in Modern Europe', in *VMES*, p. 97.
12 *Ibid.*, pp. 100–1.
13 M. Oakeshott, review of Q. Skinner, *The Foundations of Modern Political Thought*, in *VMES*, pp. 287–92.

14 Oakeshott, 'Talking Politics', p. 459.
15 M. Oakeshott, 'Political Laws and Captive Audiences', in *VMES*, pp. 168–77.
16 *Ibid.*, pp. 172–3, 175.
17 M. Oakeshott, 'Rationalism in Politics: A Reply to Professor Raphael', in *VMES*, pp. 181–6; M. Oakeshott, 'Political Discourse', in *RP* [1991], pp. 70–95. The latter essay was written long before 1991, however. A clue to its date of composition is found in the fact that the essay compares Marx to Merlin. In a notebook dated 'Jan. 1966' in his own hand, Oakeshott discusses the nature of Merlin's knowledge of the future. M. Oakeshott, notebook 19, in *NL*, forthcoming.
18 Oakeshott, 'Political Discourse', p. 74.
19 *HC*, p. 46. Alternatively, it may recommend an action 'in terms of its being a subscription to a rule', p. 46n, but rules are no more conclusive than consequences. Like skill in assessing consequences, skill in using rules is deliberative, not demonstrative (*HC*, p. 68).
20 *HC*, p. 48.
21 *HC*, pp. 48–9.
22 *HC*, p. 188.
23 Oakeshott, 'Talking Politics', p. 441; *HC*, pp. 188–9.
24 Oakeshott, 'Vocabulary of a Modern European State', p. 235.
25 *Ibid.*, p. 236.
26 *Ibid.*, p. 237.
27 Oakeshott, 'Talking Politics', pp. 445–6; *HC*, p. 195.
28 Oakeshott, 'Vocabulary of a Modern European State', p. 242.
29 Oakeshott, 'Talking Politics', p. 444.
30 Oakeshott, 'Vocabulary of a Modern European State', pp. 247–8, 256; *PFPS*, pp. 130–1.
31 Oakeshott, 'Talking Politics', pp. 447, 458–9.
32 *PFPS*, p. 15.
33 *HC*, pp. 293, 294. This view of the state reappears in Rawls's definition of political society as 'a cooperative venture for mutual advantage'. J. Rawls, *A Theory of Justice* (Cambridge, MA: Harvard University Press, 1971), p. 84.
34 See, for example, C. Kukathas, *Hayek and Modern Liberalism* (Oxford University Press, 1989), pp. 175–91.
35 *HC*, p. 318; Oakeshott, 'Talking Politics', p. 457.
36 Oakeshott, 'Vocabulary of a Modern European State', p. 234.
37 *LHPT*, p. 37.
38 Oakeshott, 'Vocabulary of a Modern European State', pp. 259–66; Oakeshott, 'Talking Politics', p. 455.

39 'A complicated Finance Act provides a living for accountants and a system of law provides substantive satisfactions for lawyers. But neither the Act not the system may properly be recommended for these reasons'. Oakeshott, 'Vocabulary of a Modern European State', p. 262.

40 M. Oakeshott, 'The Tower of Babel', in *OH*, pp. 183–4.

41 *Ibid.*, p. 193.

PAIGE DIGESER AND RICHARD FLATHMAN

9 Oakeshott's *On Human Conduct*

INTRODUCTION

Michael Oakeshott published two book-length treatises during his lifetime: *Experiences and its Modes* (1933) and *On Human Conduct* (1975). The first of these, discussed in earlier chapters of this volume, presented and defended an idealism that was out of step with the philosophical currents of the time. The second offered a somewhat different understanding of philosophical reflection and a much narrower focus. Instead of seeing philosophy as a concern for the whole of human experience that can be divided into various modes, *On Human Conduct* takes philosophical reflection to entail 'a disclosure of the conditions of understanding'.[1] Instead of focusing on the character of experience, *On Human Conduct* offers a theoretical exploration of human agency and civil association.

In whatever other ways his perspective may have changed in the course of the forty-two years between the publication of these two books, Oakeshott remained deeply sceptical of philosophy's capacity to direct or govern our practical activities.[2] He also remained profoundly committed to a deep form of pluralism, individuality and the capacity of human beings to devise traditions or practices that did not merely regulate but, more importantly, enabled an extraordinary diversity of ways of life. These themes, explored below, provide the backdrop for the vision of political association that forms the core of *On Human Conduct*.

The book is composed of three essays: the first considers the character of theory, human agency and practice; the second focuses on civil association and how it resembles and differs from what he calls an enterprise association; and the last offers an account of the emergence of the modern European state, the rise of individuality and the tension between two diametrically opposed understandings of governing. Because Oakeshott saw the work as an engagement in theory, he began it with an account of what it means to theorize. In this 'adventure', Oakeshott writes, the philosopher does nothing more and nothing less than to seek 'to understand in other terms what he already understands'.[3] For most readers of *On Human Conduct*, this rather disarming and seemingly innocent beginning is quickly dispelled by the realization that getting to those 'conditions of understanding' and presenting an understanding of something that is already understood is a rather complicated affair. In considerable part, the complexity of the project is a function of Oakeshott's language. We are immediately faced with such terms as 'a going-on', 'intelligibles', 'identifying', 'orders and idioms of theoretical inquiry', 'practices', 'self-disclosure', 'self-enactment', 'adverbial conditions', 'civil association', 'enterprise association', 'individual manqué', *societas* and *universitas*. Moreover, when the discussion explicitly turns to political things, the reader is faced with terms such as *civitas*, *cives*, *lex* and *respublica*. The postulates, the jargon, the Latin and the economic (but for the most part elegant) writing style have discouraged many and impeded others from understanding the book's purpose and structure.

Part of what is going on can be understood only by considering Oakeshott's account of theory and how that account is played out in the organization of the book. It will therefore be useful to say a few things about his theory of theory. First, from Oakeshott's perspective, all forms of understanding rest on presumptions and presuppositions that are not (and generally cannot be) called into question when one is using them to understand something else. For example, asking someone the time of day, presumes, and does not call into question, the idea of 'time'. To try to settle on an adequate conception of time before telling the time (that is, to call the postulated idea of 'time' into question) would probably mean that we would never get an answer to the question of the time of day. This does not mean that we do not have an understanding of the question regarding the time of day. Rather, it means that in most of our day-to-day interactions we possess a level of understanding that is perfectly adequate to the task, even though those understandings and practices rest on things that we do not fully understand. As such, all of our understandings rest on postulates that create what he calls a 'platform of understanding' – a platform that is used to launch our understanding but is not itself called into question. If we ever become inclined to consider the meaning of the struts and supports that constitute that platform, we may quickly discover that we understand very little about them. Any attempt to understand them, however, will require an additional set of postulates and assumptions that create yet another platform of understanding in which we use (and not call into question) additional presuppositions and assumptions. All understanding, including theoretical understanding, rests on what is used and not understood. As Oakeshott notes, 'The irony of all theorizing is its propensity to generate, not an understanding, but a not-yet-understood'.[4] On this view, theorizing abates but does not entirely lift the mystery of the world.[5]

How does his understanding of theory and theorizing help illuminate his own project? The heart of *On Human Conduct* is the second essay, where Oakeshott sets out many of the key elements to and conclusions of his political theorizing. More specifically, this essay outlines a form of civil association that he believes is most consistent with seeing ourselves as free agents capable of a high degree of individuality. In contrast, the first essay of the book sets out 'some of the terms and presuppositions' that support and constitute the second essay. While the second essay rests on a platform of understanding in which such terms as 'free agency', 'practice' and 'morality' are used to understand something about civil association, the first essay explores those postulates and hence must rest on another platform of understanding. For example, his notion of human conduct, discussed in the first essay, postulates 'reflective consciousness', but it does not itself offer a theory of consciousness. In order to discuss the postulate of consciousness, one would have to set out yet another platform of understanding that would depend on another set of not-yet-understood assumptions.

If the second essay rests on a platform of understanding whose postulates are explored in the first essay, does the second essay explore the postulates that compose a platform of understanding for the third essay? In many respects the second essay seeks to understand what Oakeshott already understands in the third essay's discussion of the historical emergence of the European state (hence the feeling of repetition one sometimes gets in the discussion). The philosophical engagement of the second essay does not displace or in any way improve upon the historical understanding of the third essay, but takes a number of terms that constitute the third essay (*societas*, *universitas*, ruling, lordship, law, individuality) and seeks to refine them in a manner that allows a clearer, closer theoretical analysis. By shifting gears, the second essay discards historical ambiguities that would occlude our understanding of what these terms mean. For example, a central theme of the third essay is that the state has always been understood ambiguously. For some thinkers, it is an association in which the subjects are tied together by their loyalty to one another and by the recognition that they share 'a common linguistic or moral condition', and not a substantive purpose.[6] Oakeshott, who favours this conception of the state, identifies it as a *societas*.

Alternatively, others understand the state as a *universitas*. From this perspective, the state is composed of members who are joined together in a manner that seeks to secure some shared substantive purpose or purposes. It is the view of the state as a corporation in which the role of government is to manage and seek to achieve its common purpose, however that may be understood. These two historical understandings of the state coexist despite the fact that, in theory if not in practice, the one excludes the other. Between them lies a tension that infuses all actual political and legal institutions that came to compose the modern state. In Oakeshott's view, 'it is this tension, and not any of the others celebrated in current political discourse, which is central to the understanding of the character of a modern European state and the office of its government'.[7]

In the second essay, Oakeshott is not concerned with the ambiguity of a state that is torn between the terms of *societas* and *universitas*. Rather, he focuses on the conditions for these human associations as well as identifying their distinguishing characteristics. In so doing, he offers not a *societas* (which is an historical identity) but a civil association (which is a theoretical construction), not a *universitas* but an enterprise association. In short, the second essay takes up the question of what is presumed in order to make sense of an association in which individuals are joined by a common linguistic or moral condition as opposed to a substantive purpose. In other words, the book begins with what could be seen as the most abstract of considerations in the first essay and eventually makes its way to the more concrete historical discussion of the third essay. The theoretical engagement, however, moves in the other direction. Consequently, there is something to be said for the claim that a better starting point for the book is really the third essay.

What follows is a thematic discussion of some of the central elements in the book. Among the enduring attributes of Oakeshott's work, however, is a deep understanding of the concepts of pluralism and of freedom that his theoretical work both exhibited and fiercely defended. It is to these themes that we now turn.

OAKESHOTT'S DEEP PLURALISM

Echoing, and influencing, views widely held among recent political and social theorists, in *Political Liberalism* John Rawls wrote about 'the fact of pluralism', that is, the fact that in virtually all actual moderately developed political societies, or rather in all such societies that allow a modicum of freedom to their citizens and subjects, there develops an abundant plurality of groups, associations, clubs, parties, ideologies, creeds and the like.[8] This being an uncontested fact, the task of the theorist – and of course also the practitioner – is less to explain it than to consider its consequences and the best ways of coping with them. From this perspective, Oakeshott can be labelled a pluralist. Nevertheless and in contrast to most of the theorists and theoreticians who describe themselves as pluralist, Oakeshott rejected the idea of facts that somehow speak for themselves. In *Experience and its Modes*, he wrote: 'Fact, whatever else it may be, is experience; without thought there can be no fact . . . Fact is what has been made or achieved; it is the product of judgment . . . Facts are never merely observed, remembered and combined; they are always made'.[9] Accordingly, he sought to understand, and in that sense to explain, why and how pluralities develop and sustain themselves.

His explanation begins with the distinctive aspects of his philosophical Idealism. As analysed in detail in earlier chapters in this volume, Oakeshott's Idealism posited a level of experience that encompassed experience as a whole, experience without qualification, reservation or arrest. He modified, however, previous versions of Idealism in two ways. First, from a philosophical perspective the

Whole was divided into three 'modes' of experience, namely Science, History and Practice. Second, Oakeshott claimed that the master modes are hermetically sealed off from one another such that knowledge or expertise concerning one of them is categorially irrelevant to the other two. There can be intra-modal investigating, reasoning, judging and the like, but there can be no inter-modal studies, reflections or conclusions. To cross these boundaries is a form of confusion that is an *ignoratio elenchi*.

In *On Human Conduct*, Oakeshott asserts that 'the gross undifferentiated sum (so to say) of what is going on is incapable of being characterized; it prescribes no inquiry, it remains for ever speciously ambiguous and therefore unintelligible'.[10] Whatever can or cannot be said about the 'concrete whole' in his later writings, all inquiry is now predicated on first identifying that which is being understood as either an exhibition of intelligence or not.[11] As with his discussion of the modes of experience, these two 'orders' of inquiry are exclusive of one another.[12] Within each of these orders of inquiry there are further 'idioms' of inquiry that provide a more specified language of understanding. Identifying something (a 'going-on') as an exhibition of intelligence opens the door to such languages of understanding as ethics, the study of law, politics or aesthetics. Identifying something that is not such an exhibition calls upon processual notions such as dominate the languages of physics, chemistry, biology and psychology. Because the distinction between the orders of inquiry are categorial and hence do not allow of thinking (or acting) across their lines of demarcation, they establish deep and rigorous pluralities that organize and properly discipline all thinking and acting. This can be called the first and philosophically deepest level of his pluralism.

Oakeshott's pluralism extends beyond how we go about understanding and theorizing; it is also built into his specific understanding of human agency as an 'exhibition of intelligence'. On this view, all human 'acting' entails the formation of a desire for an 'imagined and wished-for satisfaction', a judgement concerning the circumstances favourable or unfavourable to satisfying that desire and an intention to act so as to satisfy the desire. Each of these components of actions is an exhibition of intelligence in that it requires judgements, choices and decisions concerning matters that were indeterminate prior to the agent's decision or choice. To say that they exhibit intelligence is not to assess them in terms of the merits, qualitatively speaking, of the agent's desires, intentions, purposes or plans of action; it is only but not merely to say that all human action involves judgement and decision.

In addition, this world of action is also a world of evaluation. It can be said to be 'objective' in that it is objectively the case that there are agents who hold beliefs, form desires, intentions and purposes and act upon them. It is also the case that if an action is successful the world will change (or remain the same). But it also has a 'subjective' dimension, namely that there is 'no fact of the matter' that either does or could determine the proper or desirable character or quality of the components of action (i.e. an agent's beliefs, desires, intentions or purposes). In practical life, 'where conduct is the choice and pursuit of substantive conditions of things every achievement is evanescent' and 'every satisfaction is casual and late or soon a casualty'.[13]

The radical character of these last remarks raises the question of how pluralities can form or sustain themselves. Would not we have, rather, what William James called a blooming, buzzing confusion?[14] Oakeshott was aware of this question and took several steps to answer it. As is so commonly the case with his work, the steps he takes entail the formulation of yet another distinction, namely between a 'collective' state of affairs and a 'collected' one. He has harsh words for the notion of a collective state and argues that 'the so-called "social inheritance"' is a collected achievement, the result of individuals who share the same or closely related desires and satisfactions joining together and acting in concert.[15] Moreover, such collected achievements can be passed from generation to generation in the form of traditions and practices. The generation of traditions and practices mitigates the evanescent quality of our choices and transactions. Oakeshott notes that a central feature of human practices is that we do not merely choose satisfactions to pursue when we are interacting, but we also do so in a particular manner. Even the most fleeting of transactions between individuals presupposes a set of more durable relationships or practices that inflect but do not determine the desired outcome of the interaction. If our specific, substantive choices and decisions distinguish us as individuals and potentially divide us into different groups and collectivities to the degree that we happen to share a set of ends and purposes, the adverbial character of our practices serves as a way to both preserve those differences and generate a more or less stable environment for our interactions and transactions. This simple observation regarding the importance of the adverbial is key to understanding much of Oakeshott's legacy as a political theorist and his account of practices and individuality.

FREEDOM AND AGENCY

There is one respect in which the concepts of freedom and agency overlap. Every human being not seriously damaged by illness or injury is capable of exercising agency, that is, forming desires and interests, adopting intentions and framing projects and goals. And to do just these things is to act freely in one important sense of the term. We may call this 'elemental' freedom: it is an element in all acts of human agency, but it must be distinguished from a further form of freedom that can be called 'effective'. Elemental freedom is to form desires, intentions and so on, but does not itself assure the agent of satisfying the desires or achieving the purposes. Having effective freedom is to be successful in doing so.

As Oakeshott saw it, life is full of contingencies and relationships are often competitive and frequently agonal. If Mary has something that Joan wants and vice versa, it will often be easy for them to act cooperatively or in concert with one another. And the possibilities for harmonious interactions are increased when there are moral and other practices in place and respected. As we will see below, they are also increased in a civil society with an effective rule of law.

But competition and conflict will remain, and in order to be regularly successful in them individuals require skills and abilities – powers if you will – that go beyond elemental freedom and the minimal capacities for agency. They must be able to see where their true interests lie and who is likely to oppose their pursuit of those interests. They must develop skills of interpersonal relationships such as speaking effectively, cultivating friends and allies, and the like. And they must prepare themselves for frustrations and disappointments. To the extent that they are able to do so – and have some good fortune – they will sometimes achieve effective freedom.

THE PRACTICES OF SELF-ENACTMENT AND SELF-DISCLOSURE

As suggested by familiar terms such as the practice of medicine, law and other professions, the idea of a 'practice' connotes a more or less integrated body of beliefs, customs and rules that prescribe or proscribe (albeit rarely if ever determinately) modes and patterns of conduct that practitioners come to understand and respect in their day-to-day conduct. A practice evolves and 'becomes recognizable' when, through the course of time and continuing interactions, 'it has acquired a certain degree of authority or acknowledged utility'.[16] When this has taken place, practitioners can usually be identified and their actions approved or disapproved by reference to the customs and rules (the latter sometimes codified, interpreted and applied by an agent or agencies invested with the authority to do so). As noted above and discussed in other chapters in this volume, the customs, conventions and rules qualify but do not determine the actions of practitioners.

The enormous importance of practices to human life will concern us momentarily. In order to appreciate Oakeshott's estimation of their value, however, we must consider a distinction he draws between two different species of moral practices: moralities of 'self-disclosure' and moralities of 'self-enactment'. As we shall see below, moralities of self-enactment play a central role in Oakeshott's legacy as a theorist of individuality. First, however, consider moralities of self-disclosure. Actions of this type typically take place in transactional engagements whose success depends heavily on the responses of other agents. These sorts of action aim at achieving an imagined and wished-for satisfaction, but they are properly judged, by the agent herself and by others, not by the particulars of the satisfaction sought but by the extent to which they conform to the relevant moral criteria. A student's wished-for goal may be a higher mark in a course of study. Achieving that grade by cheating is to violate the criteria of self-disclosure associated with how one does well in a classroom setting. In these sorts of cases, to act badly is to disregard or to violate such criteria; notable failure to do is to be '*guilty*'.[17]

To the extent that the moral criteria are respected, interactions among participants may help to achieve one of the great values that

Oakeshott claims for moral practices, namely a degree of stability and mutual trust. Nevertheless, because the satisfactions sought are typically fleeting, and because success in achieving them so often depends on the uncertain responses of others, self-disclosure, while invariably and unavoidably a part of all actions *inter homines*, 'is a hazardous adventure; it is immersed in contingency, it is indeterminable and it is liable to frustration, disappointment and defeat ... *Don Juan lui-même n'acheve pas sa liste*'.[18] The ordinary and extraordinary events of one's life may simply defeat one's ability to do well in school, even when one abides by the criteria of self-disclosure.

Notwithstanding these dark remarks, it is no part of Oakeshott's purpose to discourage self-disclosure. Human beings just are satisfaction-seeking creatures, and Oakeshott welcomed the diversity of initiatives to which this proclivity leads. It is an important part of his pluralism that he believed that doing so is compatible both with the pursuit of a wide variety of substantive satisfactions and with a considerable quantum of decency in human affairs.

Action in the sub-practice of self-enactment is distinguished from self-disclosure by the 'motives' or 'sentiments' from or in or out of which the agent 'permits himself to act'.[19] Motives and sentiments concern an agent 'thinking as he chooses to think and enacting or re-enacting himself as he wishes to be'.[20] What the agent chooses to think and to do is related 'to the integrity of his character' and the 'sentiments in which he acts must be emblems of his self-command'.[21] The quality of those sentiments rests on how well they meet the terms of a moral practice: 'In worthy self-enactment the *meum* of the agent, his "authenticity", is subscription to an *honestum*'.[22] What is achieved on a final examination by a grade-grubber as opposed to someone with a genuine interest in the course material may be indistinguishable in terms of self-disclosure – they may both receive a legitimate, passing grade. Where they differ is in the sentiment and spirit in which they approached the material. The language of virtue (and more especially the language of virtuosity) is appropriate to self-enactment, but its virtues (or *virtus*) are oriented less towards others and more towards the 'demands an agent makes upon himself'. A failure to live up to these demands is shameful. In this instance, I am not shamed by others, I am ashamed of myself.

Despite his rejection of the view that virtuous self-enactment requires no more than an agent's 'good opinion of himself', it might be thought that Oakeshott's commitment to it leads to a preoccupation with self so intense and exclusive as to border on narcissism. The most important response to this objection is that self-enactment and its morality are distinct but not exclusive. In fact, every action, whether aiming at self-disclosure, self-enactment, or both, seeks a satisfaction. What distinguishes self-enactment is that the agent has a threefold concern: first, for the wished-for satisfaction; second, for the requirements of self-disclosure; and third for the quality of character that her action enacts. The second and third concerns may occasionally make conflicting demands, but there is no reason to think that they are always incompatible.

INDIVIDUALITY

We are now in a position to understand why Oakeshott esteems these several practices (and traditions) so highly. On the one hand, they mitigate the contingencies of human life, particularly when they compose what Oakeshott calls civil association. On the other hand, the sub-practice of self-enactment is crucial to his ideal of individuality: an ideal that embraces and celebrates the very elements that augment and intensify those unpredictable facets of our day-to-day existence and thereby enlarges the pluralisms that exist. This section will take up his idea/ideal of individuality. Subsequently sections will consider Oakeshott's views on the meaning and nature of civil association.

Individuality is part of a sensibility of seeing life, with Cervantes who Oakeshott greatly admired, as an adventure instead of a quest. It conveys Oakeshott's profound appreciation of the historical turn in which being effectually rather than merely elementally free became central to human dignity and not merely a burden to be borne. While the idea of oneself as an agent is quite old in the West, the ideal of individuality is of more recent vintage. And just as the condition of agency was greeted 'with various mixtures of revulsion, anxiety, and confidence', the ideal of individuality received varied reviews. For some it was a brisk, energetic ideal and for which there was no substitute. For others it was a disappointing, costly replacement for a more communal, assured way of a life that had been lost.[23]

Oakeshott locates individuality within the sub-practice of self-enactment.[24] As such, part of individuality demands attending to how one pursues one's desires and satisfactions, that is, self-disclosure. But this is not the whole of the story. The indications of an individuality in the making are not nonconformity or 'a resolution to be different at all costs'.[25] It is not something that is achieved solely in one's relationships to others, even though it does require that one subscribes to 'practices whose resources [one] … has made [one's] … own'.[26] Equally if not more important than the relationship to practices, is the claim that individuality involves one's relationship to oneself. In *this* relationship, individuality entails making one's beliefs, thoughts and desires 'one's own'.[27] Making the resources of practices as well as one's own desires 'one's own' is a rather nuanced and fairly disciplined vision of individuality. Oakeshott says that it is 'a difficult achievement', not to be confused with simply following one's whims and inclinations. Although it is a kind of autonomy, it is not to be confused with the demand to generate self-made rules.[28]

Given the self-enacted character of individuality, it is a virtuosity that can find its practical expression in any number of ways of life: a 'masterful egoism', or 'an aristocratic recognition of one's own unimportance', or 'a humility devoid of humiliation' or as moral virtue within a moral practice. As important as this virtuosity may be, Oakeshott also believed that it may be exaggerated when it is taken to be 'an exclusive ideal', but notes that 'this is a corruption which every disposition recognized as a virtue is apt to suffer at the hands of fanatics'.[29]

As noted above, in *societas*, individuals celebrate their capacity for agency and are joined together not by the pursuit of a common substantive end but by the recognition of authority. It is an association not of pilgrims but of wandering, perhaps Quixotic, strangers and adventurers who are open to the pursuit and challenges of individuality.

While this notion of self-enacted individuality achieved a certain prominence, it was not the only response to the burdens of agency. The historical break-up of communal relationships and the reassurances that they provided also left others adrift and dispossessed of their economic and spiritual place in the world. At times his description of these individuals seems to bear some resemblance to Hannah Arendt's discussion of the *sans-culottes* and the unfortunate rise of what she called 'the social'.[30] For Oakeshott, however, they are not to be associated with the poor or the proletariat. But, 'if they were to be identified (as if often the case) as "the masses", then it must be understood that what is being referred to is not their numbers but their incapacity to sustain an individual life and their longing for the shelter of a community'.[31] These individuals found themselves in a world in which the forms of conduct that once provided satisfaction were no longer available. Without the presence of those communal bonds, it became difficult to see how they could take ownership or endorse the emerging adverbial conditions that governed their lives.

The individual manqué also suffered a more profound moral defeat. After having lost the protection of a communal identity, he 'suffered a defeat of his own character. What had been no more than an inability to hold his own in belief and conduct became a radical self-distrust'.[32] The desire to cultivate and celebrate one's individuality was dissipated by a sense that the demands of individuality were simply too onerous. For the individual manqué, the supposed ideal of a self-possessed, collected personality was no ideal, either because he did not believe that he was capable of achieving it or capable of achieving it without too great a cost or for very long. From this perspective, there was nothing grand or glorious in the attempt at self-enactment; moreover, the failures to achieve it came too often. The fall-back position for this would-be individual was to cede (as far as possible) any attempt to choose one's sentiments or reflectively assess the given practices of self-disclosure. This fear of freedom suggests a life of drifting into one's feelings and impulses and, more troubling, embracing a heteronomy in which one is willing to be told what to think and desire.

Within this defeat of character was also hidden 'a small seed of resentment'.[33] Unable to see the point of one's own exertions towards individuality, the individual manqué could no longer see the point of others doing so. Out of this seed of resentment grew the anti-individual who is 'intolerant not only of superiority but of difference, disposed to allow in others only a replica of himself, and united with his fellows in a revulsion from all distinctness'.[34] For the individual manqué and the anti-individual, the state as *societas* merely confirmed all that was unsettling about the possibilities for human dignity that was tied to choice. In contrast, the vision of the state as a *universitas* could provide what *societas* was not able to do, namely a chance at reconstructing the communal bonds that provides substantive choices and addresses the question of how and what to think. It is Oakeshott's theoretical formulations of these historical artefacts that compose his central achievements as a political thinker. It is to these attributes of his theory that we turn to next.

THEORIZING HUMAN ASSOCIATIONS

The theoretical exploration of the distinction between and the conditions of *universitas* and *societas* is provided in Oakeshott's account of enterprise and civil associations. In this exploration, Oakeshott joined a conversation that engaged much of western medieval and modern political thought; namely, how can humans who understand themselves as free agents form and maintain any sort of association that disciplines and yet fully respects the character of their agency and the value of individuality? Oakeshott's legacy in this conversation is distinctive in refining and reducing to a bare minimum the assumptions and characteristics of associations that are compatible with this self-conception.

Enterprise associations reflect, express and advance the capacity of human beings to choose their ends and pursue them in company with others. Such associations may be composed of 'believers in a common faith', 'partners in a productive undertaking', 'allies in the promotion of a "cause", colleagues, expeditionaries, accomplices or conspirators'.[35] They are a kind of 'community of choices' that exists as long as the members subscribe to the ends of the association (e.g. promote the faith, enhance the economic climate, protect open spaces, fight against cancer, improve education) and accept the way in which those ends are achieved. If the association is not a temporary arrangement, its continuation requires both the promulgation and management of policies to achieve the association's purpose(s) and a recognition of rules that establish how the members conduct their business. Oakeshott is quite confident that there is virtually no limit to the purposes, ways and means of agents to form such associations. Moreover, if the effective freedom to join with others in the seeking of some common end is an important expression of moral agency, that is, of the ability to conjoin belief with conduct, then the ability to exit such associations is a necessary corollary. For enterprise associations to avoid becoming tyrannical, they *must* permit exit.

Enterprise associations organized around the pursuit of some end or purpose are certainly a familiar type of association. Perhaps for this reason, Oakeshott notes that it is not surprising that we would believe civil associations to be some version or subset of enterprise associations. More strongly, most theoretical and practical accounts of civil, political and legal institutions are framed in terms of certain ends or purposes – flourishing, economic growth, distributive justice, religious salvation, national assertion, cultural preservation. From this perspective a civil association is merely an enterprise association plus an element of coercion.

This is not an unfamiliar way to understand political association. Given the purposive character of government and its undeniably violent character, different traditions have understood and sometimes attempted to reconcile these elements in different ways. Anarchists, realists and some post-modern thinkers have argued that violence (or at least some violent moment) is an inherent part of our understandings of political authority, justice and right. Others argue that the free character of government can be preserved in one of two ways, either by offering a set of common substantive purposes and ends that *all* human beings could, should or would (if given the proper conditions) acknowledge *or* by basing our political and legal institutions on implicit, explicit or hypothetical consent – perhaps even emphasizing the importance of emigration (i.e. exit) to the idea of legitimacy.

Oakeshott's response to this theoretical and practical circumstance may be his greatest achievement as a theorist of civil association and political authority. On his view, the character of civil association (and, as we shall see, the character of political authority) cannot be identified by focusing on notions such as violence (although coercion is an inevitable element of the law), substantive purposes, consent or a variety of other such claims. Instead, civil association rests on the subscription to rules establishing how we go about pursuing our individual and conjoined purposes. In what amounts to the same thing, civil association rests on the recognition of political authority – that is, the recognition of those rules of conduct that coordinate the conduct of participants. It is a view that distinguishes civil from enterprise association and coheres with the idea of moral agency by not assuming a universal purpose or the option of exit. Moreover, it emphasizes a feature that is commonly found in enterprise associations; namely, the importance of rules to govern how the membership conducts its business. In an enterprise association, however, rules do not define the association. Rather, that definitional role is played by the substantive purpose(s) that they are seeking to pursue. Nevertheless, although many of these rules will be exclusive to a particular association (the rules governing a group of radical environmentalists will probably differ from those governing a tennis club), not all of them will be exclusive to themselves. Some rules of enterprise associations set how things will be accomplished and not what will be accomplished. That is, they are adverbial in character.

In a civil association the adverbial character of rules is moved front and centre and effectively displaces the focus on the substantive purposes that define an enterprise association. Individuals in a civil association are joined together by an authoritatively recognized way or manner of doing things and not by a set of goals and desires or the capacity of the sovereign to exercise violence. Much of the force of this idea of 'civil' is captured in the ordinary admonition to act civilly to another. In so doing, we are trying to get the individuals to mind their manners and to conduct themselves in a way that is appropriate to the adverbial requirements of the practices in which they are engaged. The admonition is not one that is necessarily meant to stop the activity itself (say between children who are playing together), but tells them how they should proceed (namely, play nicely). The only thing that matters in a civil association is how people are treating one another. Civil associates or *cives* are individuals who are joined together solely by the recognition of and attention to *how* they will cooperate or interact with one another. Consequently, they are indifferent to the specific ends and purposes that their fellow members are pursuing. The rules that govern the manner of their interactions and pursuits is the law or *lex*. It is the recognition of those rules as authoritative that defines the character of civil association (more on this below).

Oakeshott's conception of civil association provides a way for individuals to be joined together in a manner that, he believes, is fully consistent with their moral agency and also with a wide variety of ever-changing prudential practices. The operative words that Oakeshott employs here are those of recognition and subscription, and not of such things as consent or justice. We subscribe to civil association by recognizing the rules of the association as authoritative. There is no one moment in which we decide whether we are in or out. There is no hypothetical situation that could allow us to determine whether we should be in or out. A civil association is up and running only to the extent that the members continually recognize the rules that govern themselves. It falls apart when that recognition is no longer forthcoming.

Within a civil association, how do *cives* contain and sometimes resolve disputes and disagreements amongst themselves? To answer this question we need to consider some additional concepts that are important to Oakeshott's theory of civil association: authority, *lex*, obligation and 'politics'.

AUTHORITY, *Lex*, OBLIGATION, RULING AND 'POLITICS'

There are two familiar but very different meanings of the word 'authority', namely 'an authority' and 'in authority'. 'An' authority can be attained by persons who are regarded by others as having exceptional knowledge, skill or understanding concerning a particular subject matter, practice or activity. It depends on the readiness of others interested in the subject matter or activity to accept and follow the statements or treat as exemplary the actions of those who claim to be and are recognized by others as having the requisite knowledge or skill. If the statements, advice or actions are not readily accepted and followed, the authority disappears. In short, authority in this sense depends on outcomes; on it being regularly the case that when the statements and advice of the putative authorities are believed and followed then they lead to outcomes superior to those produced by believing the statements and following the advice of oneself or most other people.

In contrast, Oakeshott can be read as arguing that 'in' authority is the only genuine meaning of the term and that it is found only in a *respublica*. It is held and exercised not by persons as such but exclusively by those who occupy offices invested with the authority to issue laws, rules, judicial decisions and the like. The authority of those offices is recognized and subscribed to by *cives* and it is by virtue of their recognition and subscription that they acquire obligations to obey laws, rules and decisions that have been properly promulgated or issued by office holders. Thus in a *respublica* there is what various thinkers call an internal relation between 'in' authority, *lex* and lesser rules, and obligation. There is no *lex* without authority; authority is no more than an empty concept without *lex*; all obligations are to or under *lex*, which, tautologically, is that which is invested with authority.

As with his general discussion of civil association, Oakeshott's primary purpose in analysing authority is to show what it is and is not, a project shared by numerous thinkers on the subject. In rejecting constitutionalism and other 'formal-legal' theories, however, he sets aside (disdains?) an objective that many of his predecessors and other successors have sought – and claimed – to have achieved, namely to identify the origin, sometimes temporally speaking, of authority. The views that have been advanced on this subject are highly diverse. In addition to the consent and contract theories mentioned above, there are also theories of constitutionalism that identify its origination at the historical moment at which a constitution was adopted, which locate it in a succession of historical moments that are claimed to be importantly continuous, which appeal to divine right, natural law, charisma and other theories that ground it in the substantive merits of the decisions of those putatively holding authority, and so on. None of these theories can adequately account for the origin of authority. In most cases they presuppose the recognition of authority in order to bestow further authority. For Oakeshott, civil authority 'cannot be acquired in a once-and-for-all endowment but only in the continuous acknowledgement of *cives* who are familiar with the distinction between recognizing a rule and subscribing to its conditions' on the one hand, and 'discerning its utility, or giving approval to what it prescribes' on the other.[36]

Oakeshott's conclusion, then, is that authority is a 'postulate' of civil association. No authority, no civil association. Period. We must accept this conclusion because all the numerous efforts to provide a, perhaps, more theoretically satisfying conclusion can be shown to be failures. This brings us to the 'correlate' or 'counterpart' of civil authority, namely obligation, and the relation of the latter to an important part of Oakeshott's thinking about freedom and politics.

The obligations undertaken by subscription to civil authority can only be discharged by taking this or that particular action, but the obligation itself creates not a specific act but an injunction to act in a manner that subscribes to the *lex* in question. Inadequately subscribing to the adverbial conditions may lead to some sort of punishment, but, in contrast to disobedience to the law of an enterprise association, it is not in itself an act of disassociation. How agents choose to discharge the obligation is for them to decide. Within the, always somewhat indeterminate, limits set by *lex*, they may act casually or passionately, clumsily or with *delicatesse*, these being matters of concern primarily to those who seek to self-enact themselves so as to become the sort of persons they aspire to become.

Two features of these claims about *lex* and obligation deserve to be highlighted. The first is that the judgements and decisions made by *cives* imply that following the law is not an automatic or thoughtless activity. This is an important part of Oakeshott's rejoinder to those who think that civil association is a form of despotism that demands docile or servile conduct from *cives*. A second point joins this discussion to considerations that Oakeshott raises in his essay 'The Rule of Law' (1983).[37] As in his discussion of *lex* and civil association, the rule of law is understood as an association characterized by rules that are non-purposive, purely adverbial and unavoidably indeterminate. In addition, Oakeshott's discussion in this essay provides another angle for understanding how free agents can be associated to one another through *lex*. On this account, the rule of law can be conceived of as one of many modes of association in which human beings are capable of participating. It is a categorially different association that excludes, but does not deny, other associations. In this respect, it is not unlike other sorts of relationship. For example, Henry's friendship with John neither determines nor precludes whether they are business partners, members of the same synagogue or in a relationship of teacher and pupil. Because each of these relationships is distinct – with its own set of practices, expectations, purposes and so on – no single association or perhaps even group of associations encompasses the whole of oneself. Echoing the thoroughgoing pluralism discussed earlier, each of these modes of association implies distinct, abstract *persona*.[38] From this perspective, the rule of law is an association of *persona* who are related to one another through the adverbial conditions of the law. It is a relationship that does not speak to our substantive purposes but to the procedural conditions that we need to take into account when doing whatever it is that we are doing. It is a relationship that is not sustained by a set of concrete, material institutions, but by the capacity and willingness of *persona* (which we may call *cives* in this role) to think of themselves and their activities in those terms.

In one of the many respects in which Oakeshott agreed with Hobbes, there is an important sense in which he argued that all of the politically organized societies that he theorized are absolutisms. The authority and *lex* of civil association, and the somewhat bogus law of enterprise association, have, in principle, jurisdiction over all the actions of *cives* and subjects. This, of course, follows from his insistence that there neither is nor can be a determinative constitution or other highest law that prescribes or proscribes what *lex* or law that those in authority may adopt.

In this sense, authority and *lex* can regulate the manner in which *cives* and subjects pursue their substantive satisfactions, but how far, for what reasons and in what ways should *lex* do so? This is not a question of the scope of authority or the approval of authority and *lex*, but of the desirability of the conditions prescribed or prohibited by *lex* (not the substantive purposes of *lex* because it has none). As Oakeshott notes: 'The rule of law bakes no bread, it is unable to distribute loaves or fishes (it has none), and it cannot protect itself against external assault, but it remains the most civilized and least burdensome conception of a state yet to be devised.'[39] It is in ruling and 'politics' that these questions of desirability are properly raised and deliberated. These are metaphorical uses of both 'ruling' and 'politics', but Oakeshott scrupulously reserved 'politics' for proposals, deliberations, negotiations and the like, that concern the desirability of the conditions prescribed by *lex* and hence of the *bonum civile* of *respublica*. Participants in 'politics' must continue to subscribe to authority, but they may approve, dissent from or propose changes in *lex*. They address their thoughts and desires to 'rulers', to those who are authorized to promulgate or refuse to promulgate them as *lex*.

There are numerous and familiar desires and objectives that have no proper place in 'politics', engagement in which requires a 'disciplined imagination'.[40] 'Politics', for example, has nothing to do with awards or benefits to suitors for its favours and many other perhaps worthy ideals and objectives. In 'politics' we should put aside the 'cloudy enchantments of *Schlaraffenland*', the 'large consideration of human happiness and virtue' and the best 'means of satisfying current wants'.[41] Of the desires and objectives that ought to be pursued through ruling and 'politics', Oakeshott specified the following further three: first, that 'a civil prescription [one that puts a form of conduct under threat of civil penalty or sentence of civil disability] is undesirable if it be incapable of enforcement';[42] second, 'that subscription to civil conditions should be required of performances only in respect of their capacity to harm other agents'; and third, 'that a projected innovation should be such that the *respublica* concerned can accommodate it'.[43]

As to the first of these, it is not because such prescriptions cannot be enforced but rather because enforcing them requires 'an apparatus of search and inquisition' that 'conflicts with the norms of civil conduct ... plausibly tolerated by the *respublica*'. In this regard, Oakeshott instances Calvin's Geneva as an example of a putatively civil society that featured such overreaching prescriptions and such an apparatus but that could not tolerate them for long; numerous others come readily to mind.

The second consideration is closely akin to J. S. Mill's 'harm principle' and evidences what might be called the 'libertarian' strains in Oakeshott's thinking, but is better regarded as his commitment to effective civil freedom. It is not unconditional because there are no actions that are categorially exempt from prescribed conditions. It is important, however, because 'civil intercourse recognizes [ought to recognize] a circumstantial privacy [that goes] beyond formal autonomy', that is, civil freedom.[44]

The third condition on the desirability of *lex* is also not unconditional, because different *respublicae* can tolerate different rules and their capacity to do so changes over time. This consideration is 'an aid to reflection', one that 'invokes the "toleration" of the *respublica*' and the value it accords to continuity and change in its arrangements.

Oakeshott would have been the last to claim that these considerations provide anything approaching a detailed instruction manual or algorithm that would itself tell rulers and/or *cives* whether it would be desirable to adopt this or that proposal. Beyond and perhaps more important than these, he called not upon constraining and obstructing institutional arrangements, such as checks and balances or federalism, but looked rather to qualities of character, sensibility, thought and judgement of *cives* to choose what should receive the requisite attention to sustain the *bonum civile* of *respublica*. Although this engagement may yield less assurance of desirable decisions than some theorists have hoped and even believed attainable, 'it calls for so exact a focus of attention and so uncommon a self-restraint that one is not astonished to find this mode of human relationship to be as rare as it is excellent'.[45]

We may think of 'ruling' and 'politics' as fail-safe devices or, more in keeping with the estimation signalled by the last passage just quoted, as a *faute de mieux*. When *cives* fail to adequately subscribe to authority and *lex*, rulers may, following established procedures, penalize them for doing so. And when disagreements arise concerning the conditions specified by existing *lex* or the desirability of proposed changes in *lex*, 'politics' may be undertaken to resolve the difficulties. How much is achieved by this undertaking is of course a contingent matter. As with all human conduct, it is contingent on the intelligence, the sensibility, the *savoir faire* and *delicatesse* that participants bring to it. If Oakeshott found little reason for optimism in the experience of the modern European state, he did not despair of the possibilities.

NOTES

1 *HC*, p. vii.
2 *HC*, p. 30.
3 *HC*, p. vii
4 *HC*, p. 11.
5 *HC*, p. 1.
6 *HC*, p. 202.
7 *HC*, p. 201.
8 J. Rawls, *Political Liberalism* (New York: Columbia University Press, 2005), pp. 36–9.
9 *EM*, p. 42.
10 *HC*, p. 12.

11 Unconditional understanding in *HC* is now 'the continuous recognition of the conditionality of conditions' (p. 11), and while Oakeshott did not see this conception of theorizing as denying further 'unconditional critical engagements', he did believe that such engagements had to be deferred in order to present a theory. As he noted, the theorist 'has a heavenly home, but he is in no hurry to reach it' (p. 25).
12 *HC*, p. 15.
13 *HC*, p. 84.
14 W. James, *The Principles of Psychology*, vol. I (New York: Henry Holt, 1890), p. 488.
15 *HC*, pp. 86–7.
16 *HC*, p. 56.
17 *HC*, p. 76.
18 *HC*, p. 73.
19 *HC*, p. 70.
20 *HC*, p. 72.
21 *HC*, p. 73.
22 *HC*, p. 73.
23 *HC*, p. 236.
24 *HC*, p. 236.
25 *HC*, p. 237.
26 *HC*, p. 237.
27 *HC*, p. 237.
28 *HC*, pp. 236–7.
29 *HC*, p. 238.
30 H. Arendt, *The Human Condition* (University of Chicago Press, 1958), pp. 35ff.
31 *HC*, pp. 275–6.
32 *HC*, p. 277.
33 *HC*, p. 277.
34 *HC*, p. 277–8.
35 *HC*, p. 114.
36 *HC*, p. 154.
37 M. Oakeshott, 'The Rule of Law', in *OH*, pp. 119–64.
38 *Ibid.*, p. 120.
39 *Ibid.*, p. 164.
40 *HC*, p. 164.
41 *HC*, p. 164.
42 *HC*, p. 178.
43 *HC*, p. 178.
44 *HC*, p. 179.
45 *HC*, p. 180.

WILLIAM A. GALSTON

10 Oakeshott's political theory: recapitulation and criticisms

INTRODUCTION

For much of his career, scholars – especially in America – did not know quite what to make of Michael Oakeshott. Was he a Burkean conservative? The last gasp of British Idealism? An aesthete with aristocratic sympathies? A quasi-libertarian admirer of Henry Simons? A Hobbesian authoritarian? Or even a hyper-individualist with anarchist leanings?

That so many diverging, or even conflicting, interpretations of Oakeshott exist is partly due to the fact that his own thought significantly evolved over time, if not in content, then at least in form. His early writings are indebted to the legacy of the language of Idealist philosophy; his post-war essays bear a visible mark of revulsion from the changes European society was undergoing in those years and thus take on a distinctively conservative flavour; and in the subsequent period individualistic, even libertarian motives gradually become more prominent.

Previous chapters in this book have focused on analysing those particular stages in Oakeshott's social and political thought. The purpose of this chapter is, however, to examine what can be said about Oakeshott's political theory in general and to make a number of suggestions regarding the degree of satisfactoriness and relevance of its arguments to today's world.

LIBERAL OAKESHOTT?

In the two decades since Oakeshott's death interpreters have increasingly converged on the conclusion that at the theoretical level, anyway, he was a liberal – if of a highly distinctive kind.[1] I do not disagree. If a liberal is someone who puts a conception of individual freedom at the centre of political philosophy and believes that there is a mode of politics consistent with the exercise of freedom, so conceived, then Oakeshott was indeed a liberal.

That so many scholars have viewed him as a non-liberal or even an anti-liberal reflects the ways in which our understanding of liberalism has become intertwined with theoretical perspectives and historical developments that he viewed as inessential to, and often at odds with, liberalism as he understood it. Oakeshott worked for much of his career to disentangle these threads. Liberalism does not require, or imply, the Rationalism he so forcefully rejected. On the contrary, liberalism is entirely compatible with modesty concerning reason's power. As most interpreters now recognize, Oakeshott was neither an historicist nor a relativist, but rather a sceptic in the tradition of Montaigne.

Oakeshott was anything but a Romantic conservative defending pre-modern communal ties. Nor was he straightforwardly Burkean. Nevertheless, he argued (with approving references to Burke), liberalism need not adopt an antagonistic stance towards inherited tradition. Indeed, liberalism is best understood as a tradition that weaves together elements of prior traditions – from the Romans, from the Normans, and from the centuries of struggle to define British society and politics. Nor is there a necessary connection between liberalism and progressivist/Whig assumptions about history as a story of inevitable human progress; the case for liberalism is independent of the propensity of human events to produce liberal orders. Nor does the defence of individual liberty rest on a doctrine of natural rights that protects individuals against government power. In fact, so-called natural rights are at most summary abstractions (which Oakeshott called 'abridgements') of liberty-protecting practices that have developed over time. Natural rights cannot protect liberty in political associations that fail to respect habeas corpus and the rule of law.

What of the other great liberal commitment, to human equality? There are two ways in which Oakeshott embraced equality. First, human beings are equal as free agents. (Indeed, agency freedom forms the core of Oakeshott's understanding of human conduct.) And second, human beings equally enjoy the freedom provided by the rule of law. In another sense, however, Oakeshott denied human equality: the modern freedom of individuality, he argued, is an achievement, not a fact, and not all individuals are up to its demands. Worse, the incapable many may use their power to diminish the freedom of the capable few. In this respect, Oakeshott stands in the tradition of aristocratic liberals – represented by Tocqueville and J. S. Mill, among others – who cherished modern liberty but feared that the mass society spawned by modern egalitarianism might undermine it.

In the economic sphere, Oakeshott found himself at odds with the views of philosophical liberals across the political spectrum. *Pace* Rawls and left-liberalism, he argued, the conception of justice intrinsic to liberalism – formal equality and the rule of law – did not embrace the enforced redistribution of resources to meet some norm of 'fairness'. But he was no more sympathetic to the view – advanced by free-market conservatives, Keynesian liberals and socialists alike – that economic growth was the key objective of social policy and the *sine qua non* for all other social goals. The belief in '"maximum productivity"', he once wrote, 'is one of the most damaging of the moral superstitions of our age'. He rejected as seductive but specious what he called the 'plausible ethics of productivity'. The conception of the good life as 'nothing other than the enjoyment by more and more people of more and more of everything' is, he contended, a 'revolting nothingness, which only has to be successful in order to reduce human life to absolute insignificance'.[2]

Nor did Oakeshott take sides in the running debate between left-liberal advocates of central state power and its right-liberal critics. In his view, individual freedom and rightful authority are not opposed; indeed they go together. The issue is not the strength or weakness of the state, but rather the reasons for which it uses its power. A state that protects freedom must be plenipotentiary in some areas and absent from others.

Many interpreters have wondered how a theorist who so intensely admired and drew so much from Hobbes could possibly be a liberal. Oakeshott deepens the puzzle by rejecting, root and branch, John Locke, the philosopher often regarded as the fount of liberalism:

> The moderate individualism of Locke has no attraction for those who have embraced a radical, an Epicurean individualism. Locke's 'steady love of

liberty' appears worse than slavery to anyone who, like Montaigne, is 'besotted with liberty'. Democracy, parliamentary government, progress, discussion, and the 'plausible ethics of productivity' are notions – all of them inseparable from Lockean liberalism – which fail now to arouse even opposition; they are not merely absurd and exploded, they are uninteresting.[3]

For Oakeshott, Locke's famed moderation amounted to a truncation of true individuality, which is often radical, even extreme. By contrast, Oakeshott saw Hobbes as providing the political philosophy within which the individuality of Epicurus and Montaigne could flourish. As he put it in one of his most arresting formulations:

It is Reason, not Authority, that is destructive of individuality ... Hobbes is not an absolutist precisely because he is an authoritarian. His scepticism about the power of reasoning ... together with the rest of his individualism, separate him from the Rationalist dictators of his or any age. Indeed, Hobbes, without himself being a liberal, had in him more of the philosophy of liberalism than most of its professed defenders. He perceived the folly of his age to lie in the distraction of mankind between those who claimed too much for Authority and those who claimed too much for Liberty.[4]

Oakeshott discerned a similar polarity in the thinkers and activists of his own day, and he sought to provide a coherent middle way between statism and anarchism. He tried to construct a parsimonious liberalism whose alpha and omega is human freedom. His guiding question was like Rousseau's: how can entrance into the civil condition leave human beings and citizens with undiminished freedom? As Rousseau famously put it, the problem is '"to find a form of association that will defend and protect the person and goods of each associate with the full common force, and by means of which each, uniting with all, nevertheless obey only himself and remain as free as before". This is the fundamental problem to which the social contract provides the solution'.[5]

In a similar vein, Oakeshott, writing on Hobbes but also speaking for himself, argued that the problem for which civil association is the solution is not human nature but rather the human condition of multiplicity of wills:

The natural man is the stuff of civil association which, whatever else it is, is an association that can comprehend such individuals without destroying them ... There is in this association no concord of wills, no common will, no common good; its unity lies solely in the singleness of the Representative, in the *substitution* of his one will for the many conflicting wills. It is a collection of wills united in one Sovereign Representative, and in generation and structure it is the only sort of association that does not compromise the individuality of its components.[6]

THE PHILOSOPHICAL CONTEXT OF OAKESHOTT'S POLITICAL THOUGHT

While the edifice of Oakeshott's political philosophy is abstract and even forbidding, its basic structure is straightforward. It is, to begin, embedded in a three-stage metanarrative of the history of political philosophy. In stage one, the guiding concepts are Reason and Nature, and the masterpiece is Plato's *Republic*. In stage two, Will and Artifice – rooted in Roman thought, revealed religion and medieval nominalism – take centre stage and find definitive expression in Hobbes's *Leviathan*. The core idea of stage three is Rational Will, whose implications are best developed in Hegel's *Philosophy of Right*.[7]

Oakeshott rejected outright the classical Greek outlook. In his view, nature cannot provide norms for individual conduct or civil association, and human reason is not so constructed as to mirror or grasp nature's basic structure. His political philosophy can be understood as an effort to systematize the basic structure of Hobbes's *Leviathan* – to take seriously the human and political world as a compound of will and artifice – while deploying Hegel's understanding of the rational will as a corrective to Hobbes's appetitive account.

It is easy to underestimate how radically Oakeshott rejected the Platonic–Aristotelian view. He offered a sympathetic account of Plato's thought, and he took over important elements of Aristotle's account of deliberation and political discourse. But a closer inspection underscores the gulf between them.

For Aristotle, the political association is a compound of nature and artifice: 'there is in everyone by nature an impulse toward this sort of partnership [political association]. And yet the one who first constituted [it] is responsible for the greatest of goods'.[8] To say that the *telos* of human association is the political community is not to say that it will come into being of its own accord; it must be created.

But the creation is guided by, and completes, a template the creator does not create. For Oakeshott, by contrast, the civil or political association is pure artifice: 'The word "civil", in Hobbes, means artifice springing from more than one will ... Civil authority is authority arising out of an agreement of wills, while natural authority ... has no such generation and is consequently of a different character'.[9] Bluntly put, 'the civil condition is an artifact'.[10]

For Aristotle, moreover, every association is purposive. As he announces at the beginning of the *Politics*, 'it is clear that all partnerships aim at some good'.[11] For Oakeshott, by contrast, the association that can reconcile individual freedom and political authority is and must be non-purposive. Civil association is a form of moral association, and morality is inherently non-purposive – a Kantian conception that Aristotle would have found all but unintelligible.

Aristotle contends that the partnership that is 'most authoritative of all and embraces all the others ... aims at the most authoritative good of all. This is what is called the city or the political partnership'.[12] Politics is thus an elevated human activity, though ultimately not the highest. For his part, Oakeshott rejects the very idea of an authoritative good at which politics aims, and his view of politics is decidedly less elevated than Aristotle's:

> politics, we know, is a second-rate form of human activity, neither an art nor a science, at once corrupting to the soul and fatiguing to the mind, the activity either of those who cannot live without the illusion of affairs or those so fearful of being ruled by others that they will pay away their lives to prevent it.[13]

For Aristotle, finally, the rightful claim to political power could not be decoupled from the ability to exercise that power wisely and in the common good. For Oakeshott, following Hobbes, 'the main consideration is not wise but authoritative rule'.[14] There can be no legitimate appeal from that authority to the purposes for which it is or should be exercised. This does not mean, Oakeshott insists, that all are equally fit to rule. The prudent use of political power is based on experience that cannot be reduced to rules. The rule of the 'politically inexperienced' leads to the deformation of politics through ideology, which is the inevitably unsuccessful attempt to replace sound, situated individual judgements with abstractions.[15]

Still, legitimacy is one thing, wisdom another. What matters most is maintaining political authority, rightly understood.

HUMAN CONDUCT AND CIVIL ASSOCIATION

How is it possible to reconcile political authority and the exercise of individuality? In Oakeshott's analysis, to begin, there are two kinds of freedom. The first is inherent in human agency, conduct seen as an expression of intelligence rather than impulse – as an ensemble of beliefs, understandings and meanings. Conduct is always located within a specific situation and is directed towards relieving some inadequacy of that situation. It is always chancy, never wholly calculable in advance; it is subject to contingency of the world and of other agents.

Human conduct is situated, not abstractly in the world of nature and anonymous others, but within some sort of established practice that prescribes conditions for, but does not determine, the substantive choices and performances of agents. Practices are to conduct what languages are to speech: a language does not tell us what to say, but rather how to say it in ways that other speakers can understand and to which they can respond. There are two kinds of practices: the transactional, directed towards achieving some purpose; and the moral, which is non-purposive. As Oakeshott put it:

> Agents ... are, of course, seekers of wished-for satisfactions and providers of such satisfactions as are enjoyed; they are engaged in the transitory transactions which constitute substantive conduct. And they are related also in terms of many prudential practices, the rules and uses of which are designed to promote the success of the activities and transaction they govern ... the common characteristic of these practices is to be instrumental to the achievement of imagined and wished-for satisfactions. But a moral practice is not a prudential art concerned with the success of the enterprises of agents; it is not instrumental to the achievement of any substantive purposes or to the satisfaction of any substantive want ... It is concerned with the act, not the event; with agents as doers making an impact upon one another and not in respect of the particular wants for which they are seeking satisfaction.[16]

As Paul Franco observes, freedom of human agency denotes 'a formal dimension of all conduct recognized to be human'.[17] So understood, agency freedom does not dictate any particular form of human association – including liberalism. As long as the morality of communal ties prevailed, a politics that circumscribed individual choices could coexist with agency freedom.

But as pre-modern Europe gave way to the Renaissance, Oakeshott argued, a new ideal of freedom as individuality emerged. Key thinkers specified the meaning and value of agency freedom as the ability to explore one's own gifts, cultivate one's own outlook and make one's own way in the world. As this ideal spread, ideas of collective wellbeing and the common good lost credibility, and it became increasingly difficult to identify common purposes around which members of a political association could unite.[18]

If Aristotle was right – if every human association was purposive – then there would be an insoluble contradiction between association and individuality. But as we have seen, Oakeshott asserted, against Aristotle, there are forms of conduct and association constituted by non-purposive practices. 'Civil association' is such an association: its practices, codified in the kinds of rules we call law, prescribe, not ends that all citizens must pursue, but only the manner in which they are to be pursued. Laws are recognized as authoritative, not because of their wisdom or utility, but only with regard to their source. Because civil laws are non-purposive, and because accepting their authority does not mean surrendering one's own judgement about what is wise or useful, the rule of law does not undermine individuality. Indeed, it is the only form of political association that does not.

Oakeshott offered a lucid summary of the freedom members of civil associations enjoy. They

> may, at choice, enter into relationships of affection, of discourse, of gainful enterprise, or of playful engagement, but in respect of being civilly associated they cannot be either required or forbidden to do so ... Thus, the 'freedom' inherent in this mode of association lies, first, in the associates *not* being related to one another in the pursue of any substantive purpose they have not chosen for themselves and from which they cannot extricate themselves by a choice of their own, and secondly in their actions and utterances being not even officially noticed or noticeable (much less subjected to examination or direction) in respect of their substantive character but solely in respect of the civil conditions to which they are required to subscribe.[19]

This brings us to Oakeshott's distinction between 'enterprise' and 'civil' associations. Enterprise associations unite individuals in pursuit of purposes they (happen to) share. These associations are consistent with individuality so long as individuals choose to participate in them. It is not purposive action, individual or collective, but rather than the imposition of purposes, that undermines individuality. But civil associations are compulsory in two senses: individuals must belong to at least one such association; and their laws are backed by state power. That is why Oakeshott regarded the purposive political association – a compulsory enterprise association – as a 'moral enormity'.[20] Conversely, only non-purposive civil associations are fully compatible with the freedom to form, join and leave voluntary enterprise associations. If there are political purposes binding on all citizens, then enterprise associations inconsistent with those purposes are bound to be restricted or even banned. For this reason, Oakeshott insisted that the rule of law must not be justified as instrumental to collective purposes such as peace, order, stability, freedom and prosperity. This does not mean giving up on them altogether; most are not consequences of, but rather inherent in, civil association.[21]

Oakeshott contended that laws are not commands in the sense of telling people what to do. Rather, they impose obligations to subscribe to 'adverbial conditions in the performance of the self-chosen actions of all who fall within their jurisdiction'.[22] While this may seem counterintuitive, Oakeshott pressed ahead undaunted. In a well-known footnote to *On Human Conduct*, he remarked:

> The appearance procedures and rules may have of excluding (forbidding), or more rarely on enjoining, substantive choices and actions is illusive. Practices identify actions adverbially; they exclude (forbid) or enjoin them in terms of prescribed conditions. The criminal law, which may be thought to come nearest to forbidding actions, does not forbid killing or lighting a fire, it forbids killing 'murderously' or lighting a fire 'arsonically' ...[23]

Because the rule of law is adverbial rather than categorical, it is subject to substantive constraints. For Oakeshott, measures to promote special interests are not genuine law; nor are efforts to further (allegedly) common goals. And the rule of law is subject to formal conditions as well – for example, publicity, non-retroactivity, impartiality and all the other norms that constitute the 'inner morality' of a legal system.[24]

Theories of natural law typically assert that an unjust law is not really law at all. Hobbes went to the other extreme, contending that there is no criterion of justice outside the law itself. Oakeshott steered between them: while he had no patience for natural law, he stopped short of Hobbes's identification of *jus* with *lex*. Not only are there formal constraints on law, there are substantive constraints as well. In particular, he argued, law should not conflict with a 'prevailing educated moral sensibility' that can distinguish between the conditions of virtue and good conduct on the one hand and, on the other 'those which are of such a kind that they should be imposed by law'.[25] So legitimate political authority is constrained, not only by the distinction between substantive commands and adverbial rules, but also by the difference between those matters that are appropriately subject to law and those that are not. These constraints, not abstract rights, define Oakeshott's conception of limited government. He had no patience for bills of rights or for the constitutional courts charged with applying them to legislative enactments.[26]

Indeed, Oakeshott's antipathy to such abstractions bordered on the ferocious. He described the early history of the United States as 'an instructive chapter in the history of the politics of Rationalism'.[27] The Declaration of Independence, he averred, is 'a characteristic product of the *saeculum rationalisticum* [that] represents the politics of the felt need interpreted with the aid of an ideology'.[28] Abstract principles are postscripts, not prefaces; they are at most heuristics for exploring the intimations of traditions, not standards for amending them.[29] The greatest American statesman took a different position. In asserting human equality, Abraham Lincoln insisted, the authors of the Declaration 'meant to set up a standard maxim for free society which should be familiar to all: constantly looked to, constantly laboured for, and even, though never perfectly attained, constantly approximated, and thereby constantly spreading and deepening its influence and augmenting the happiness and value of life to all people, of all colours, everywhere'.[30] I shall later argue that there are reasons to prefer Lincoln's view.

MODERN CHALLENGES TO INDIVIDUALITY

On Human Conduct contains two distinct elements: the analytical, which develops a conceptual framework that drives, organizes and applies contrasting conceptions of human agency and association; and the judgemental, which offers a strong, morally grounded preference for a particular mode of association. It is easy to get lost in the conceptual architecture and miss the underlying moral point, which is in fact urgent and breaks through the veneer of self-restraint, especially in the concluding essay. Franco, one of Oakeshott's most astute interpreters, argues that the point of the work is not to recommend civil association as against enterprise association, but rather to make clear the distinction between them.[31] I disagree.[32] In fact, Oakeshott saw the enterprise association as perhaps the greatest threat to individuality in modern times; all the more so when it reflected, as it often did, the sentiments of mass publics.

Oakeshott translated his analytical categories into historical terms and used them to comprehend the character of modern European states. The distinction between civil and enterprise associations is rooted in the Roman distinction between *societas* and *universitas*. The tie that binds members of the *societas* is not a common substantive purpose, but rather loyalty to one another. The *universitas*, by contrast, is a 'corporate aggregate' made up of persons 'associated in respect of some identified common purpose'.[33] While medieval statecraft focused principally on the latter, the emergence of a new ideal of individuality beginning in the Renaissance posed a challenge to the state understood as the collective pursuit of shared goals. This gave rise to a (muted) strand of European thought that gestured towards a new conception of the state as *civitas* – that is, as the political version of the non-purposive *societas*. To underscore its distinctiveness, Oakeshott called this form of organization the *civitas peregrina*:

> an association, not of pilgrims travelling to a common destination, but of adventurers each responding as best he can to the ordeal of consciousness in a world composed of others of his kind, each the inheritor of the imaginative achievements (moral and intellectual) of those who have gone before ...[34]

So conceived, individuality offered enormous opportunities for self-exploration and creation. But as Oakeshott's use of 'ordeal' made clear, it was also a challenge, which those unable or unwilling to make choices for themselves experienced as an unwelcome burden.

In an extraordinary essay entitled 'The Masses in Representative Democracy', Oakeshott redescribed modern European history as an epic clash between the proponents of individuality and its enemies. He began with the emergence of individuality in modernity – as he vividly put it, 'not Adam, not Prometheus, but Proteus'.[35] As chronicled in the writings of Pico della Mirandola, Montaigne, Hobbes and Kant, among others, 'the disposition to regard a high degree of individuality in conduct and in belief as the condition proper to mankind and as the main ingredient of human "happiness" had become one of the significant dispositions of modern European character'.[36] The emergence of individuality led to demand for a kind of government capable of transforming the interests of individuality into rights and duties – in short, to liberalism properly understood.[37]

But what some Europeans welcomed as liberation, many others experienced as deprivation. The new dispensation bred resignation in some, but envy, jealousy and resentment in others. This led to militant anti-individualism, to movements disposed to subordinate rising individuals to their own insecure character. (Oakeshott labelled this kind of person the 'individual manqué'.) They demanded a form of government that could protect them against the burdens of individuality – specifically, the responsibility of choice and the weakening of comforting traditional communities.[38] As Oakeshott pungently put it, 'the "masses" as they appear in modern European history are not composed of individuals; they are composed of "anti-individuals" united in a revulsion from individuality'.[39] The character of the 'mass man' is such that he will be moved only by the offer of release from the burden of making choices for himself. 'He is specified primarily by a moral ... inadequacy. He wants "salvation"; and in the end will be satisfied only with release from the burden of having to make choices for himself.'[40]

Because mass men had feelings rather than thoughts, Oakeshott continued, they required leaders. Their natural submissiveness disposed them to accept leaders; and this new type in fact emerged: 'a man who could more easily make choices for others than for himself: a man disposed to mind other people's business because he lacked the skill to find satisfaction in minding his own'.[41]

In Oakeshott's view, this uprising of mass men against individuality yielded two main consequences. The first was a new morality of anti-individualism, a morality not of liberty and self-determination but rather of equality and solidarity, a focus on the 'common good' rather than the goods of individuals. Because private property bolsters individuality, the new morality opposed it. By the nineteenth century this new morality had established itself as a disposition recognized by leading thinkers as 'the image of a new barbarism'.[42] The second consequence was a new mode of government that would make for the anti-individual the choices he was unable to make for himself.[43] Anti-individuals claimed to want the new rights of individuals and the means needed to participate in them. But in fact they wanted different kinds of rights – not to pursue wellbeing, but to enjoy it. The desire pushed anti-individualist governments to impose equality of circumstances.

There was, in short, no historical teleology pushing modernity in the direction of ever-enlarging individuality. Rather, the modern age was the arena of tension between individuality and its enemies, and between civil association and enterprise association as templates for the exercise of public power. Not only did the consolidation of early modern Europe into 'states' retain elements of the pre-modern dispensation, including remnants of communalism and what Oakeshott called lordship; it also brought into being a new capacity for centralized administration and new understandings of how that capacity could be used to satisfy human desires.

Numerous goals offered states the opportunity to act as enterprise associations: cultural integration, economic maximization, the rule of enlightened experts, the therapeutic ideal, and of course war. While Oakeshott rejected most of them as appropriate occasions for the exercise of state power, he could hardly deny states the authority to wage war, especially defensive wars. But he could and did reject the social mobilization war entails as a model with broader implications. He was not interested in finding what William James famously called the 'moral equivalent of war'. He was much closer to Randolph Bourne's equally famous claim that 'war is the health of the state', which Bourne did not intend as an endorsement either of war or of the state that wages it.[44]

Oakeshott left no doubt about where he stood. The state as enterprise association, he said, is 'an understanding of the character of a state which has bitten deep into the civil institutions of modern Europe; it has compromised its civil law and corrupted the vocabulary of civil discourse'.[45] Worse, the enterprise state systematically corrupts its citizens: 'the member of such a state enjoys the composure of the conscript assured of his dinner. His "freedom" is warm, compensated servility'.[46]

While the burdens of individuality create a demand for 'solidarity', that demand is atavistic, a 'relic of servility'. True individuality is an achievement, not a fact; it requires, and in turn fosters, independence and self-determination, as opposed to servility, which puts comfort and security ahead of freedom. That is why 'no European alive to his inheritance of moral understanding has ever found it possible to deny the superior desirability of civil association without a profound feeling of guilt'.[47]

These two ways of living in modernity, and the two modes of association corresponding to them, account for the polarized consciousness of modern Europe – polarized because they are not mutually supportive, but rather fundamentally opposed. And the human stakes are very high:

> for the 'mass man' to have won for himself a position of undisputed sovereignty would entail the complete suppression of ... what must be considered the strongest of our moral and political dispositions and the survival of the weakest ... he remains an unmistakably derivative character, an emanation of the pursuit of individuality, helpless, parasitic and able to survive only in opposition to individuality.[48]

Readers may discern in these comments echoes of the concerns about 'mass society' evoked by the rise of communism and fascism at the end of World War II. (It is unclear whether Oakeshott was acquainted with Erich Fromm's *Escape from Freedom*, but the resonances between that work and 'The Masses in Representative Democracy' are striking, as they are with José Ortega y Gasset's *Revolt of the Masses*.)

But Oakeshott's argument goes deeper, historically and philosophically. As modernity developed, its commitments to human individuality and human equality came to stand in tension with one another. Aristocratic liberals such as Tocqueville feared that the desire for the secure enjoyment of equality of conditions could only be requited at the expense of the liberty that individuality required. The pressure of social conformity might join hands with the coercion of public policy to discourage the development of idiosyncratic excellence.

Oakeshott was unfashionable for many reasons, prominent among them his identification with the tradition of aristocratic liberalism. Yes, he said, as human beings we are all capable of agency – that is, of free undetermined action. But for whatever reason, we are not equally capable of bearing the burdens of freedom, and in particular of accepting the responsibility for oneself that freedom requires. Those who are capable of true individuality will always be resented and threatened by those who are not. And the most essential task of a free society is to protect the opportunity for individuality from policies that would undermine it in the name of egalitarian benevolence.

CRITIQUE

There is much to contest at every stage of Oakeshott's intricate argument, and certainly at its end. One need not be a socialist, or even a social democrat, to believe that Oakeshott radically underplays those aspects of the modern economy that create an inescapable interdependence among individuals and require a collective response. It is too simple to interpret the economic dimensions of the modern enterprise state as evidence of servility.

To go farther down this road, however, would plunge us into a political thicket from which we might not emerge. Instead, I will focus this concluding section on three crucial building blocks of Oakeshott's argument: his distinction between purposive and non-purposive rules; his account of authority; and his claim that abstract principles are at best abridgements of prior practices.

Rules

It is with hesitation that one questions Oakeshott's interpretation of Hobbes. But it is hard to accept his claim that Hobbes develops a theory of civil association. To be sure, Hobbes denies the existence of a *summum bonum*. But he affirms a *summum malum* – namely violent death and the circumstances that permit it. And because all human beings seek to avoid the *summum malum*, they 'agree on this, that Peace is Good, and therefore also the way, or means of Peace' – those 'dictates of Reason' that are 'Conclusions, or Theoremes, concerning what conduceth to the conservation and defence' of each and every individual. Hobbesian political community is human association oriented to the goal of peace, and Hobbesian political morality is the ensemble of conduct that supports such an association.[49]

Oakeshott did not exactly reject this line of argument. Instead, he sidestepped it. Peace and security, and the like, he asserted, 'are not substantive purposes and they do not specify enterprise association'.[50] Although he offered no argument in support of this assertion, one can tease out what he had in mind. After all, Hobbes had observed, without peace it is impossible to attain any other objects of human endeavour. (It was at this point that he interpolated his famous list of objects unattainable in circumstances of war.) So peace is not a purpose of action but rather a condition for successful purposive action. It is Hobbes's version of Rawls's primary goods – namely, an all-purpose means.

While this argument is intelligible, it is hardly persuasive. It is true that if one is no longer alive, one can no longer pursue purposes. But it does not follow that we prize life only as a condition of pursuing purposes or that we fear death only as the cessation of such pursuit. Life is one among many goods sought both for itself and as means to other goods. Because peace preserves life, it is sought as a good in itself and not only as the means to other goods.

If this argument is valid, then (*pace* Oakeshott) Hobbes did not in fact provide a theory of civil association, but rather of a minimally purposive enterprise association. It is consistent with individuality, not because it refrains from promoting public purposes, but because the purpose it promotes is, Hobbes argued, the only purpose freely accepted by all individuals.

It might still be the case that although Oakeshott was wrong about Hobbes, he was right about his more general claim. But was he? Can there be non-purposive 'adverbial' rules that govern, not the substance but only the manner of acting? And if there are such rules, do they offer the most plausible way of understanding public life?

Recall Oakeshott's effort to reinterpret criminal laws as adverbial or modal specifications: prohibitions against murder and arson are actually prohibitions against killing 'murderously' or lighting fires 'arsonically'. The contortion of vernacular speech is a clue that the argument is being forced. But more than that: any action can be subsumed under a more general category. So if a law prohibits that action but not others in the category then it meets Oakeshott's standards for adverbiality, which means that, in principle, all laws are adverbial. If so, the distinction disappears, and with it, Oakeshott's thesis.[51]

If this argument seems too abstract, consider traffic laws, often held up as the paradigm of adverbial specifications because they tell you how to drive, not where. But consider speed limits, which establish a balance between safety and efficiency. There is no obviously best way of achieving that balance: lower limits reduce vehicular deaths and injuries, but at the cost of increasing travel time and (for commercial enterprises such as trucking) costs as well. Every specification of a limit reflects a substantive judgement, at the margin, about the relative importance of safety and efficiency.

Or consider procedures that govern how legislatures debate and enact laws, not which laws they should pass. Multiple streams of scholarship converge on the same conclusion: the line between procedure and substance is impossible to maintain. The debate in the US Senate over filibuster rules is part of a larger argument about the balance to be struck – in a large, diverse, representative democracy – between the ability of a majority to enact legislation and the ability of a minority to ensure that its views are taken into account. Another example: the US Constitution requires a two-thirds majority of the Senate to ratify treaties. The reason is substantive, not procedural: because a treaty represents a binding commitment of the entire nation, it should enjoy broad support across partisan and ideological lines. Conversely, this requirement encodes the view that in deliberating and voting on treaties, senators should be more guided by the national interest, and less by parochial interests, than is typically the case. And senators sometimes rise to their responsibilities. In the face of the most intense party polarization the United States has witnessed in more than a century, fully one-third of the Republicans broke ranks with their leadership late in 2010 to help ratify the New START treaty.

But let us assume, *arguendo*, that non-purposive civil rules do exist. Given Oakeshott's account in 'The Rule of Law', one cannot help wondering how important they are, or could be. Consider his distinction between law and 'policy', by which he means any effort to satisfy interests, either of a part of the community or the community as a whole. So understood, policy contradicts the rule of law. So an American official who, taking his cue from the Preamble to the Constitution, seeks to promote the 'general welfare', is making a moral mistake.[52] The 'common defence' fares no better: a civil association is 'least itself' when it is at war.[53] Lay readers must be forgiven if they conclude that the exclusion of domestic policy and national defence does not leave law with much to do; otherwise put, that describing civil association as the rule of law leaves out the real world of politics.

Considerations of this sort have led so sympathetic an interpreter as Richard Flathman to complain that Oakeshott had gone too far in severing the link between politics and purposive collective action. Despite Oakeshott's insistence to the contrary, peace, security, stability and the like are ends of action, not just conditions for it. When statesman act, as Lincoln did, to preserve the union, or de Gaulle did to avert civil war in France, 'to refuse to use the word "purpose" ... is worse than a quibble'.[54]

These reflections cast a less favourable light on Oakeshott's celebrated depiction of political life: 'there is neither harbour for shelter nor floor for anchorage, neither starting-place nor appointed destination. The enterprise is to keep afloat on an even keel'.[55] If Oakeshott were right, politics would be 'at sea' in more senses than one. But navigators have their pole star; why can't statesman? The fact that a political community never reaches its 'appointed destination' doesn't mean that it can't have one. If I must choose, I will take, without hesitation, Lincoln's characterization of the Declaration as a 'standard maxim' over Oakeshott's, because Lincoln's is truer to the facts of political life, at least in the United States. I must leave it to others to determine whether Oakeshott's is truer to the facts of British politics. However that may be, because the account of civil association developed in *On Human Conduct* does not limit its geographical reach, it is fair to test it against non-British evidence.

Authority

I can deal more briefly with Oakeshott's account of authority, which suffers, I believe, from two deep inadequacies. First, Oakeshott did not explain why authority exists or, otherwise put, why rational individuals would or should accept it. Authority, he said, is a 'postulate' of the civil condition whose validity does not rely on an external appeal; it is 'self-authenticating'.[56] Hobbes had an answer, of course, but Oakeshott could not invoke it without attributing purposes to the civil association. So there is a link between the weakness of Oakeshott's anti-purposive account of politics and his inability to provide an explanation for authority and authority's writ.

Second, Oakeshott divorces authority from all considerations of knowledge, skill or wisdom: the validity of authority is one thing, its exercise quite another. Like Hobbes, Oakeshott wants to rule out any appeal from the fact of authority to the content of law. But here again, the demands of theory lean against the descriptive credibility of his account. In the real world there is always a tension between the formal legitimacy of authority and the actual capacities of those who wield it. Thomas Jefferson argued that the popular election of representatives would not only confer legitimacy but also tend to select individuals of more than ordinary intellectual and moral gifts. The Progressives argued, conversely, that some key positions should be filled by appointed officials who were insulated from popular pressures. But both agreed that legitimacy and fitness could not be neatly separated. And they were right.

Consider platoons of soldiers in the field. From a formal standpoint, the newly minted second lieutenant is in command. But his grizzled sergeant, though technically subordinate, has the experience needed to accomplish the mission and bring the troops through it with minimum losses. Foot soldiers are not required to sacrifice their lives needlessly, simply because a new leader who does not know what he is doing orders them to do so. Hobbes's account of legitimate self-defence permits individuals to invoke self-preservation against otherwise binding authority.[57] Once again, the underlying argument is that membership in the civil association and obedience to authority has a motive – a purpose – that can override authority when its demands contradict the point of membership.

Principles

Oakeshott takes two things from Hegel above all: his understanding of will as rational rather than appetitive; and his conception of abstract principles as derivative from actual experience. Locke's principles, he insisted, were nothing more than a distillation of the

English political tradition, a postscript masquerading as a preface.[58] Americans' belief that these principles stood on the solid ground of reason and nature was at best an energizing illusion.[59] For the most part, abstract principles subtract from rather than add to political understanding. Sundered from their experiential base, they distort, often to the point of brutality, the practice of quotidian politics.

If Oakeshott had looked differently at the implications of his own theory, he might have revised his view. He famously described politics as the pursuit of a tradition's intimations; he insisted that every tradition is 'multi-voiced'; and he acknowledged that some of these voices contradict others.[60] This is where Socratic political philosophy begins, by inquiring into the source of these contradictions and seeking a more satisfactory position that could incorporate what is valid in each of the competing propositions. Although this process of reflection begins within a tradition, it does not end there. For a few, it culminates in an escape from the cave, in philosophy, a form of wisdom that not only probes eternity but also illuminates human affairs.

Oakeshott accepted this story, up to a point. He parted company with Socrates and Plato in denying to philosophy any practical force. Theorizing moral conduct is one thing, engaging in it quite another. The errant theorist mistakes the *postulates* of human conduct – what philosophy discovers to be the grounds of agency – for *principles* from which correct conduct may be deduced. In so doing, he ceases to be a philosopher and becomes a *philosophe*, an intellectual, an imposter.[61]

We have reached the crux of the matter: how can we know that bringing philosophy into practice distorts rather than illuminates? Equally to the point, how can we square Oakeshott's account of philosophy with his own practice? *On Human Conduct*, we have seen, is a philosophical inquiry into the postulates of agency and association that somehow yields specific recommendations for political practice. As Flathman rightly says of Oakeshott, 'his preference for civil association cannot be mistaken, and it is impossible to read his texts without realizing that one of his aims is to persuade his readers to make it their aim as well'.[62] On Oakeshott's own account, then, one of two things must be the case: either his move from philosophic inquiry to political persuasion was illegitimate; or his account of the relation between philosophy and practice was mistaken.

CONCLUSION

Despite his announced antipathy to ideology and his preference for *l'esprit de finesse*, Oakeshott is intransigent in his refusal to compromise individuality. This commitment lends his theory great moral power but also undermines it at key points. The reason is this: given the human condition (or predicament) of diverse multiplicity, we cannot live without ordered association. As members of political associations, we (or at least those of us who care about individuality) must seek the conditions that allow individuality to flower while minimizing the constraints on its exercise. *But there is no ordering that can leave multiplicity untouched or individuality untrammelled.* While polities may organize themselves to reduce the conflict between individual endeavour and collective enterprise, they cannot eliminate it. Shared purposes may be made more or less parsimonious, but no association can do without them altogether.

It was Oakeshott's refusal to accept this reality that led him to cross the line separating philosophical radicalism from outright implausibility. Murder is a noun, not an adverb; peace is not only a condition but also a goal of action. Law prohibits as well as enables; political deliberation always has an end in view. It is not unreasonable to ask a theory so explicitly rooted in concrete practice to attend to these simple truths. As Aristotle said, *tithenai ta phainomena*.

NOTES

1 See, *inter alia*, P. Franco, *The Political Philosophy of Michael Oakeshott* (New Haven, CT: Yale University Press, 1990); R. Flathman, *Pluralism and Liberal Democracy* (Baltimore, MD: Johns Hopkins University Press, 2005), ch. 5; W. J. Coats, Jr, 'Michael Oakeshott as Liberal Theorist', *Canadian Journal of Political Science*, 18 (1985), 773–87; E. Podoksik, 'Overcoming the Conservative Disposition: Oakeshott vs. Tönnies', *Political Studies*, 56 (2008), 857–80.

2 M. Oakeshott, review of H. Selsam, *Socialism and Ethics*, in *CPJ*, p. 273.

3 M. Oakeshott, 'John Locke', in *CPJ*, p. 85.

4 M. Oakeshott, 'Introduction to *Leviathan*' [1975], in *HCA*, p. 63.

5 J.-J. Rousseau, Of the Social Contract, or Principles of Political Right, Book I, ch. 6, in J.-J. Rousseau, *The Social Contract and Other Later*

Political Writings, trans. V. Gourevitch (Cambridge University Press, 1997), pp. 49–50.
6 Oakeshott, 'Introduction to *Leviathan*', pp. 61–2.
7 *Ibid.*, p. 7.
8 Aristotle, *The Politics*, trans. C. Lord (University of Chicago Press, 1984), Book I, ch. 2, 1253a30, p. 37.
9 Oakeshott, 'Introduction to *Leviathan*', pp. 27–8.
10 *Ibid.*, p. 46.
11 Aristotle, *Politics*, Book I, ch. 1, 1252a1, p. 35.
12 *Ibid.*, Book I, ch. 1, 1252a4–6, p. 35.
13 M. Oakeshott, 'Introduction' [1946], in T. Hobbes, *Leviathan*, ed. M. Oakeshott (Oxford: Blackwell, 1946), p. lxiv.
14 Oakeshott, 'Introduction to *Leviathan*', p. 41.
15 M. Oakeshott, 'Rationalism in Politics', in *RP*, p. 23.
16 *HC*, pp. 60–1.
17 P. Franco, 'Michael Oakeshott as Liberal Theorist', *Political Theory*, 18 (1990), 420.
18 P. Franco, 'Oakeshott, Berlin, and Liberalism', *Political Theory*, 31 (2003), 501–2.
19 *HC*, p. 314.
20 M. Oakeshott, 'On Misunderstanding Human Conduct', in *VMES*, p. 279.
21 M. Oakeshott, 'The Rule of Law', in *OH*, p. 161.
22 *Ibid.*, p. 136.
23 *HC*, p. 58n.
24 *HC*, p. 153n.
25 Oakeshott, 'Rule of Law', p. 160.
26 *Ibid.*, p. 143.
27 Oakeshott, 'Rationalism in Politics', p. 26.
28 *Ibid.*, p. 28.
29 M. Oakeshott, 'Political Education', in *RP*, pp. 120–1, 125.
30 A. Lincoln, debate with Stephen Douglass, Alton, Illinois, 15 October 1858, in P. M. Angle (ed.), *Created Equal? The Complete Lincoln–Douglas Debates of 1858* (University of Chicago Press, 1958), p. 379.
31 Franco, *Political Philosophy of Michael Oakeshott*, p. 158.
32 As does Efraim Podoksik, who remarks that Oakeshott 'does not conceal his preference for the civil association (or *societas*)'. Podoksik, 'Overcoming the Conservative Disposition', 873.
33 *HC*, p. 203.
34 *HC*, p. 243.
35 M. Oakeshott, 'The Masses in Representative Democracy', in *RP* [1991], p. 364.

36 *Ibid.*, p. 366.
37 *Ibid.*, pp. 368–70.
38 *Ibid.*, pp. 370–2.
39 *Ibid.*, p. 373.
40 *Ibid.*, p. 381.
41 *Ibid.*, p. 374.
42 *Ibid.*, p. 376.
43 *Ibid.*, p. 377.
44 Bourne, an early twentieth-century American thinker who combined radicalism and individualism, broke with John Dewey and many other liberals of his day over their support for US entrance into World War I.
45 *HC*, p. 312.
46 *HC*, p. 317. Oakeshott goes so far as to blame the conception of the state as enterprise association for the programmes of 'extermination' that disfigured the twentieth century.
47 *HC*, p. 321.
48 Oakeshott, 'Masses in Representative Democracy', pp. 381–2.
49 Hobbes, *Leviathan*, ch. 15.
50 *HC*, p. 119.
51 For a related argument, see E. Podoksik, 'Oakeshott's Theory of Freedom as Recognized Contingency', *European Journal of Political Theory*, 2 (2003), 64–5.
52 Oakeshott, 'Rule of Law', p. 162.
53 *Ibid.*, p. 164.
54 Flathman, *Pluralism and Liberal Democracy*, pp. 156–7.
55 Oakeshott, 'Political Education', p. 127.
56 *HC*, p. 150.
57 For an analysis, see S. Sreedhar, 'Defending the Hobbesian Right of Self-Defense', *Political Theory*, 36 (2008), 781–802.
58 Oakeshott, 'Political Education', pp. 120–1.
59 Oakeshott, 'Rationalism in Politics', pp. 27–8.
60 M. Oakeshott, '*Rationalism in Politics*: A Reply to Professor Raphael', in *VMES*, p. 183.
61 *HC*, pp. 30–1.
62 Flathman, *Pluralism and Liberal Democracy*, p. 159.

PART III

Oakeshott and others

DAVID BOUCHER

11 Oakeshott in the context of British Idealism

INTRODUCTION

In a review of W. M. Urban's book *Beyond Realism and Idealism* Michael Oakeshott captured the essence of the difference between the two competing theories of knowledge: 'the "driving force" of Idealism is the belief that the known cannot be independent of the knower; and the "resistance" of Realism is the belief that what is known must be an antecedent reality'.[1] In the modern era Berkeley developed a form of Idealism that was designed to counter materialism and reveal the ultimate spiritual character of experience beneath our sense impressions. Berkeley contended that there can be nothing but spirits which are active on the one hand and passive sensible objects on the other, and objects do not exist except as perceived by the active spirit.[2] Despite being a sceptic, Berkeley was convinced of the reality of the self in self-conscious activity.

It was this 'subjective' Idealism to which G. W. F. Hegel objected when he claimed that the universe is an undifferentiated indivisible unity in which there is no conception of the self until thought begins to differentiate the I from the Thou. Absolute Idealism begins with the principle of unity, and attempts to account for the differentiations into which this unity has fragmented. This is a reaction, not only against Berkeley but also against the dualism of Descartes' belief that the mind must conform to its objects, and against Kant's contention that reality must conform to the a priori categories of the mind while retaining a dualism between things as they are known to the mind and as they are in themselves.[3] The fundamental principle of Absolute Idealism affirms that all that exists and appears is in and for consciousness. There can be nothing beyond or outside consciousness.

In this chapter I will locate Oakeshott on the philosophical landscape in which he placed himself alongside fellow Idealists for whom the concepts of monism, the Absolute, modality and coherence were paramount to reaching conclusions which were counter-intuitive and at variance with the prevailing theories of naturalism, positivism, utilitarianism and the emerging opposition of Realism.

LOCATING OAKESHOTT

Alfred North Whitehead famously described the history of western philosophy as a series of footnotes to Plato. He was not suggesting, of course, that there is some vague agreement among philosophers on fundamental issues over the centuries, which relies upon authority. He was alluding to the immense wealth of general ideas dispersed throughout Plato's writings, informed by his personal qualities, the opportunities afforded him by experiencing a great moment in European civilization, and his bequest of an intellectual tradition not yet ossified into a rigid system. Whitehead maintained that in Plato we find a wealth of suggestive inspirational ideas developed and transformed by subsequent generations.[4]

It is not surprising, then, that many students of philosophical Idealism have detected in Kant, Fichte, Hegel, Schelling and the British Idealists elements of Platonism. The British Idealists, for example, were, like most students of philosophy in the latter part of the nineteenth century, immersed in Plato and Aristotle, and many contributed substantive studies of their writings to the growing body of critical literature. While John Henry Muirhead may have overemphasized the extent to which the Cambridge Platonists gave root to an indigenous Idealism, he was correct in identifying ancient philosophy, and particularly Plato and Aristotle, as an important source of ideas for British Idealists.[5] In Oxford, Benjamin Jowett's translations and interpretations of the ancients revived scholarly interest in Plato and Aristotle, but his own understanding was not free of Hegelian colouration, nor was that of Edward Caird.

Caird, for example, beautifully illustrates Whitehead's observation about the suggestiveness of Plato's thought. In Caird's first publication, 'Plato and Other Companions of Socrates', he articulated what he takes to be some of the fundamental considerations of Idealism found in Plato. Principally, Plato's theory of ideas, for him and others, was prescient of Idealism. You cannot separate being and knowing, thought and existence, they are a unity, which leads to the question of whether the individual or the universal is the primary reality. In its modern form, Caird thought, the issue may be formulated as follows: to what extent the intellect creates the world, by addressing the issue of whether (a) objective reality may be attained through the exercise of thought, or (b) through the passive experience of sensations. Plato did not resolve the problem, but went some way to doing so in his later writings. Nevertheless, he left a partially unresolved dualism, which if it does not find its resolution in Hegel, finds it nowhere else. The dualism is between the timeless and static world of universals and the transient, concrete, changing world experienced by individuals. Failure to resolve the dualism rendered Plato's forms or ideas in danger of being out of touch with the world we know.[6]

When Michael Oakeshott unequivocally nailed his colours to the mast of Idealism he was by implication attaching himself to the well-understood debt that the movement to which they belonged owed to ancient Greece.[7] Plato, after all, represented the epitome of the tradition that Oakeshott was later to name 'Reason and Nature'.[8] Oakeshott identified the same deficiency in this tradition as Caird had done, that is its tendency, because of its emphasis on the universal, to stand outside the world of experience.[9] It is then an exaggeration to suggest that Oakeshott would have arrived at his philosophical position via Plato had he not encountered Hegel and Bradley.[10] Indeed, Hegel and Bradley pointed the way to the synthesis of the Platonic tradition and Hobbes's form of Epicureanism.

In Oakeshott's view, Plato's intellectualism, finding the springs of action in conformity with transcendent laws, was counterbalanced by the tradition whose masterpiece was the *Leviathan*, that of Will and Artifice, highlighting at once the achievement and the deficiency of Hobbes. Hobbes's debt was to Epicureanism and he began his philosophical inquires with 'will' instead of law, refocusing attention away from the universal to the individual. Hobbes lacked, however, as did the whole Epicurean tradition, an adequate theory of volition. A will without a guiding principle above self-interestedness is in danger of mere caprice. Hobbes attempted to overcome the problem with respect to political obligation by emphasizing that the state is a work of art and not of nature. A work of art is the creature of will, and what is remarkable about civil association is that it is 'artifice springing from more than one will' and 'civil authority is authority arising out of agreement of wills'.[11]

Modern philosophy, in Oakeshott's view, or at least what was valuable in it, was the attempt to reconfigure the theory of natural law with the Epicurean theory of Hobbes, manifesting itself in such phrases as Rousseau's 'General Will' or Hegel's 'Rational Will' or Bosanquet's 'Real Will'. The view that Oakeshott expresses is common among the Idealists. Hegel saw the history of philosophy in terms of the traditions of the objective (Oakeshott's Reason and Nature), subjective (Oakeshott's Will and Artifice) and immanent (Oakeshott's Rational Will). For Hegel, each is partial, and reflects the level of consciousness attained up to its own time. The subjective view of experience is defective because of its excessive concern with finite matter. It reveals to us not the content of philosophy but only its 'formal subjective moment'.[12] The objective moment is deficient because the view of experience offered ignores the subjective moment. Hegel contends: 'philosophy demands the unity and intermingling of these two points of view'.[13] The unity is discovered in the synthesis of these moments, in what is immanent in the history of philosophy. Philosophy as universal thought incorporates both the subjective and objective moments revealing its content incrementally in the history of philosophy. Philosophy and its history are one and the same.

Bernard Bosanquet adopts these Hegelian principles to discuss the philosophical theory of the state. Hobbes, he contended, had a subjective conception of political unity that lay in a will that was actual but not general. For Locke it was objective and lay in a will that was general but not actual. The synthesis of the two was attempted in Rousseau's notion of the general will, which was at once actual and general.[14] Oakeshott contends: 'the most profound movement in modern political philosophy is, as I see it, a revivication of the Stoic natural law theory achieved by the grafting upon it an Epicurean theory; it springs from the union of the two great traditions of political philosophy inherited by Western Europe from the ancient world'.[15] This third tradition's master conception is the Rational Will, 'and its followers may be excused the belief that the truths of the first two traditions are fulfilled and their errors find a happy release'.[16]

Oakeshott himself was one of these followers, partially because the tradition of Rational Will was 'seen on the analogy of human history'.[17] What did he mean? The idea of a criterion for guiding conduct, for example, seen on the analogy of history, means that standards for evaluating and guiding conduct arise in the course of social interactions and are imminent in the practices in which humans engage. The norms that emerge are not so capricious as to be contingent upon subjective human interests, nor so abstract as to be outside the realm of human experience, wants and desires.

Oakeshott's published works are notoriously lacking in references, which makes it difficult to determine the sources that influenced him in the formation of his Idealism. He says that he learnt most from F. H. Bradley's *Appearance and Reality* and G. W. F. Hegel's *The Phenomenology of Spirit*.[18] W. R. Sorley, his tutor at Cambridge, H. H. Joachim and J. S. Boyce-Smith encouraged, read and criticized the chapters which comprise *Experience and its Modes*. Oakeshott's notebooks show that he was a voracious reader of a wide range of philosophical books, many of them written by Idealists such as Edward Caird, J. M. E. McTaggart, Bernard Bosanquet, Henry Jones and J. S. Mackenzie, in addition to works by Bradley and Hegel. Oakeshott's manner of note taking was to copy quotations rather than comment on them, but the quotations are often prescient with a content that was later to become his own. In 1922 his selection indicates the value he was later to place upon activities or practices. He quotes extensively, for example, from Henry Jones's *A Faith That Enquires*, 'a thing is what it does ... A thing that does nothing *is* nothing. Strip an object of its activities, and see what remains: You will find nothing'.[19] The same idea is expressed differently in his selection from McTaggart: 'the inside of two empty boxes are no doubt singularly alike. But the unity of this sort may possibly be over-valued'.[20] This emphasis upon unity, which so characterizes Oakeshott's *Experience and its Modes*, is replicated in the notes he took from a review of *The Life and Philosophy of Edward Caird*: 'at the basis of his whole thought lay a single idea, reaching not by reasoning but by insight, expressed ... (letter 1891) in the words "to me difference always seems to presuppose and explicate unity – which is the fact below all other facts"'.[21]

Although in most other respects Bosanquet and Oakeshott were worlds apart, their conceptions of philosophy were expressed in remarkably similar terms. Bosanquet directly addressed the question of what is implied in a philosophical theory, and contended that everyone knows that a flower is a different thing when understood by the botanist, chemist or artist, and philosophy cannot hope to compete with these specialists on their own ground. Instead, it takes the flower and determines its significance in the totality of experience: 'and this we call studying it, as it is, and for its own sake, without reservation or presupposition'.[22] Oakeshott used almost exactly the same terms: 'philosophical experience, I take to be experience without presupposition, reservation, arrest or modification'.[23] The idea of the modes being arrests of the 'timeless and complete actuality' was something Oakeshott could have found in one of his favourite books, H. H. Joachim's *The Nature of Truth*.[24]

THE ABSOLUTE, MODALITY AND COHERENCE

When Oakeshott argues that all experience is thought or judgement, he is denying an external reality independent of mind, even to the extent of rejecting the distinction between sensations, feelings and thoughts. Thought and judgement are not aspects of reality, they are the concrete totality of experience itself. There can be nothing experienced that is not thought, and nothing thought that is not a world of ideas. In this respect Oakeshott agrees with F. H. Bradley and T. H. Green that there is nothing ready-made and given in experience. He rejects, however, Bradley's view that there is a purely psychical level of experience, complete and undifferentiated, and embraces Green's view that experience properly begins only at the level of thought.[25]

The different modes of experience, such as history, science, practical life and poetry, are worlds of ideas that fall short of the concrete whole but which nevertheless have reached a certain degree of robustness in the conditional intelligibility they offer. They are built upon unquestioned postulates that generate, or create, their own subject matter, or conclusions. In history, for example, the historian's business is not to discover or recapture, or even interpret, the past, 'it is to create and construct'.[26] In other words, much of what the Idealists affirm is counter-intuitive. There is no prior reality that the worlds of ideas interpret. Oakeshott argues: 'interpretation requires something to interpret, but when we speak of it our knowledge slips under our feet, for there is never in experience an *it*, an original, distinguishable from interpretation, and consequently there can be no interpretation'.[27] In other words, 'text and interpretation are one and inseparable'.[28]

The Absolute Idealists, including Green, Bosanquet, Jones and Collingwood, entertain a similar conception of philosophical inquiry. Beginning with the principle that experience is one undifferentiated whole, they are concerned to provide an ontology by which this whole has become differentiated into different worlds of ideas, such as history, aesthetics, science and so on. Each of these modifications of the whole are satisfactory only to the extent that they are able to maintain what they assert, that is, to the degree that the world in which the conclusions are generated is coherent. None is absolutely coherent because each falls short of experience as whole and therefore assumes or presupposes principles that are unquestioned and upon which entire worlds of ideas, such as physics, chemistry and poetry, rest. The philosopher, then, looks at each element in experience from the vantage point of the whole. In this respect they take their lead not only from Hegel but also from Spinoza. In describing his own philosophy in a letter of 1891, Caird epitomizes the manner in which the Idealists viewed experience. He says: 'if I used Spinoza's phrase "looking at things *sub specie aeternitatis*" I would mean looking at them from the point of view of the whole, i.e. recognising the unity which, whether recognised or not, is always presupposed in my knowing them in distinction from, and in relation to, each other'.[29]

The philosopher, unlike the physicist, chemist or poet, cannot be satisfied with the conditionality of the worlds, and instead of enjoying the conditional intelligibility they offer, interrogates their postulates and reveals them to be contradictory and in violation of the principles that characterize the whole of experience, absolute consistency and coherence. Wherever there is contradiction, an ultimately unstable world of ideas is revealed, falling far short of experience without presupposition, reservation or arrest. Oakeshott exemplifies this conception of the nature and aims of philosophy. When considering the historical mode of experience, for example, he concludes: 'pretending to organise and elucidate the real world of experience *sub specie aeternitatis*, history succeeds only in organising it *sub species praeteritorum*'.[30]

To maintain consistently the philosophical manner of mind is an impossibility, and in his or her non-philosophical moments the philosopher may enjoy and even revel in the conditional intelligibility provided by the modes. As Bradley confirms, 'outside of philosophy there is no consistent course but to accept the unintelligible, and to use in its service whatever ideas seem, however inconsistently, to work best'.[31] What is puzzling, Oakeshott suggests, is not that we take advantage of this conditional intelligibility equal to our needs, but that we 'should ever feel the urge to leave this world of satisfying and useful verdicts'.[32]

Oakeshott and Bradley differ from most other Absolute Idealists, such as Hegel and the early Collingwood, in that they do not attribute a logic to the sequence by which successive forms of experience emerge. Bradley quite clearly indicates the world that the mind makes for its habitation and manifestation, suggesting a process in which action comes first and reflection follows the question 'What have I done?' We become aware of what we have unintentionally accomplished and of existences we do not recognize but possess as our own creations.[33]

Oakeshott argues that 'there can be no limit to the number of possible modifications in experience'.[34] They are not at first conceived of, designed and implemented. They emerge indiscriminately and naively 'without premonition' of what they will lead to. From the gropings of human intelligence, a mode eventually exhibits a 'recognisable shape', with participants who are faithful to the conventions of the practice. When such a mode or practice develops 'a certain firmness of character', there comes a point when we may wish to move beyond acquiring and using the skill constitutive of the activity and discern the logic by which the activity is related to others and to the whole.[35]

Oakeshott, like Bradley and in conformity with Hegel, but unlike Green, Jones, Mackenzie and Muirhead, to mention only a few, makes a strong distinction between theory and practice. In *Experience and its Modes* he distinguishes between modes, or languages, of explanation, and the language of practice. Later, in *Rationalism in Politics* and *On Human Conduct* the vocabulary is modified, but the principle remains the same. In the former it is claimed that the languages of explanation 'do not pretend to have injunctive force'.[36] In the latter we have the distinction between 'doing' or conduct and 'theorising', namely that theory and practice are distinct and that the theoretical consideration of an activity has nothing to offer its conduct. Oakeshott contended: 'the theorist of conduct is not, as such, a "doer", and the theoretical understanding of conduct cannot itself be theorized in terms of doing'.[37] The theorist or philosopher has a different concern from the practitioner, 'namely, to investigate the conditions of their enterprises, not to engage in them'.[38] The practitioner is not best placed for understanding an activity in terms of its postulates, and if that person should do so, he or she ceases to be a practitioner and becomes a theorist or philosopher. Anyone who commits the category error of intruding recommendations into an activity on the basis of conclusions reached while considering its postulates has betrayed his or her calling, and is a theoretician or *philosophe* rather than a philosopher. The difficulty the would-be theorist encounters is mistaking postulates for principles from which guides to conduct may be derived and 'correct' performances deduced.

When Oakeshott talked of logic, it was not, of course, what was currently understood as logic. The book he learnt a great deal from was H. H. Joachim's *The Nature of Truth*, which, when it referred to 'current logic' in 1906, was referring to the philosophical study of thought and knowledge, unmistakably allied to Bradley and Bosanquet, which in turn had been handed down by Hegel through Lotze and Sigwart. After the First World War this logic had come under severe assault in Oxford by Realists such as John Cook Wilson, H. H. Pritchard and E. F. Carrit, and in Cambridge by Bertrand Russell, G. E. Moore and Ludwig Wittgenstein.

At Oxford, John Cook Wilson, a former pupil of Green, was an extremely astute reader of idealistic logic, and thoroughly familiar with Kantian methods, and certainly represented their arguments fairly and accurately. It was not that he misunderstood the Idealists, he just could not believe how anyone could subscribe to such counterintuitive nonsense.[39] Cook Wilson suggested that we cannot define, prove or justify the possibility of knowledge, but we are able to exemplify it. Fundamentally, Cook Wilson was convinced of the truth of mathematics as objective knowledge that needed no defence or justification. This put him at odds with the position Bradley maintained in *Appearance and Reality*. Cook Wilson believed that the Idealists were hopelessly confused in their logic of judgement. The mistake lay in the fallacy of maintaining that judgement was a kind of activity distinct from inference, resulting in the logic being indistinguishable from metaphysics.[40] He opposed the Idealist view that logic is about thought, and argued that statements express different types of thought, such as opinion, supposition and inference. We must distinguish, he argued, between apprehension and opinion or belief.[41] Apprehension is not something distinguishable from reality, it is reality. It was therefore absurd to conflate apprehension and opinion in the activity of judgement.[42] Fundamentally, the Idealists put forward a logic of judgement, and Cook Wilson a logic of apprehension. The terms are not equivalents, and in defending the terms they used, their whole philosophies were invoked. To a large extent they were incommensurable logics, and to engage with either in their own terms was to concede the argument.[43]

In Cambridge, Bertrand Russell published two books at the turn of the twentieth century that constituted sustained rebuttals of Idealist logic.[44] Russell was an unremitting empiricist, maintaining that all knowledge results from experience. He applied logic to both mathematics and language. This is what attracted the interest of Rudolph Carnap and Hans Hahn of the Vienna Circle. Russell maintained that it was with profit that the method, and not the results of the sciences, could be imported into philosophy. To get to the heart of it, Russell objected to the Idealist denial of the absolute truth of mathematics. He maintained that mathematical statements are simply and absolutely true. They are not, as the Idealists claimed, partially true; momentarily true as an aspect of dialectical transition; nor true as part of a wider whole; not at once empirically true and transcendentally false; and not just relatively or conditionally true.[45]

Russell's importance at the time Oakeshott was writing was as the precursor of Wittgenstein and the Vienna Circle. Russell and those he influenced emphasized the importance of applying scientific methods to philosophy. They believed that scientific logical rigour would be to the benefit of all disciplines, including philosophy. Ostensibly, the methods of the Cambridge Realists and the Idealists appears to be very similar in one respect. Both believe that philosophy is coming to know better something we already in some sense know. Oakeshott formulates this philosophical principle in the following terms: 'there is no such thing as a transition from mere ignorance to complete knowledge: the process is always one of coming to know more fully and more clearly what is in some sense already known'.[46] L. Susan Stebbing, a follower of the Cambridge School, argues that metaphysical analysis is 'discovering *what it is precisely* which we already in some sense knew'.[47] They are, nevertheless, referring to different methods. The British Idealists employ the 'regressive' method while the Cambridge Realists employ the 'decompositional' method.

The decompositional method entails taking the given and breaking it down into its structure and component parts. G. E. Moore's common-sense philosophy exemplifies this method. Moore maintains most rational people are aware of a common stock of propositions that provide the background to our reflections. Among these would be such propositions as: at some time in the past I was born; at different times relative to other people I have been located in different positions on this earth; many living human beings populate the planet. Such propositions, Moore contends, are indisputable.[48] His method consisted in defending philosophical claims with reference to our conceptual intuitions. In epistemology, he famously attempted to refute scepticism by claiming that we *do* have knowledge of the external world. His 'proof' consisted in holding up his hands and saying here is one hand and here is another, thus demonstrating knowledge and certainty of the external world.[49]

Oakeshott's *Experience and its Modes*, despite its reluctance directly to name its targets, is essentially an exemplification of the regressive method opposed to the method of Moore and Cambridge Realism, and a defence of the Idealist logic of judgement against the various attacks on it.[50]

Oakeshott's enterprise is not with the methodology of the various modes and the methods by which they reach their conclusions. These are not what he means by the conditions or postulates that distinguish each mode from the others. He is concerned not with methodology, but with the logic of inquiry, understood not as a concern with the truth of their conclusions, 'but with the conditions in terms of which they may be recognised to be conclusions'.[51] Oakeshott, following Bradley, Bosanquet and Joachim, reasserted the view that logic was the philosophical study of thought and knowledge, entailing the interrogation of postulates that underpin the modes or arrests in what Joachim called their 'timeless and complete actuality'.[52]

This was not what the term logic had come to mean in 1933. It was at this time not a branch of philosophy as such, but more a science of symbols and forms, detached from what was symbolized or formed. This was especially so with symbolic or formalistic logic and the theory of logical analysis tied to logical positivism.[53] In a clear allusion to logical positivism's dependency of philosophy upon the natural sciences, Oakeshott dismisses their relevance outside their own sphere of activity. He maintained:

> it is scarcely to be expected, in these days, that we should not be tempted to take up the idea of philosophy as, in some sense, 'the fusion of the sciences', 'the synthesis of the sciences' or the *scientia scientiarum*. Yet, what are the sciences that they must be accepted as the datum, and as a datum not to be changed, of valid knowledge? And if we begin with the sciences, can our conclusions be other or more than merely scientific?[54]

The logic of the criterion of truth to which Idealists subscribed, while rejecting the correspondence theory of truth in which the mind conforms to reality, is still a propositional logic. It is not a propositional logic of discrete statements. A proposition brings a whole world of ideas to bear upon it and the truth it presents is dependent, not upon its correspondence to an external reality but upon the non-contradiction and coherence of the whole in relation to the single statement. One fact or statement has no truth value without its relation to a whole range of facts and propositions, which affirm it. Joachim takes this to be a cohering unity of ideas, a significant whole in which all its 'constituent elements reciprocally determine one another's being as contributory features in a single concrete meaning'.[55] G. R. G. Mure confirms this view when he argues truths are the property of judgements in that they are implicated in a coherent unity of judgements.[56] The criterion of truth is internal to a system and there cannot be anything outside it that acts as the arbiter of the truth or falsity of its propositions. Oakeshott is completely committed to this theory in contending: 'coherence is the sole criterion: it requires neither modification nor supplement, and is operative always and everywhere'.[57] Philosophy does not deny the conclusions of the modes, it merely points out their conditionality.

The union of coherence and comprehensiveness constitutes truth. A mode, or significant whole, is the 'arbiter of fact'.[58] This does not sanction any fanciful statement we may wish to make and which is consistent, as having a truth value. For Bradley it is the inconceivability of the opposite within a system of ideas that confers the status of truth.[59] Joachim explains how this works. For him a 'significant whole' is one whose constitutive elements are reciprocally involved and determine one another's being as contributory to a particular meaning. The cohering elements reciprocally adjust and control each other. This is why a centaur is inconceivable because its constituent elements resist entering into reciprocal adjustment.[60] Conceivability means, for Joachim, systematic coherence, which is the determining feature of a significant whole. Oakeshott contended in his 1924 notebook that truth 'cannot rest on any argument to uphold it, it rests solely upon itself – Coherence with the world of experience as the seeker knows it'.[61] For him, coherence is at once the test and definition of truth and it is what the evidence obliges us to believe.[62]

THE CHALLENGE OF PERSONAL IDEALISM

Absolute Idealists, when Oakeshott was a young man, had cleared away the philosophical debris of the past, including that of the British Empiricists, naturalistic evolution and traditional natural rights theories.[63] They then moved on to fight on two principal fronts: against the various Realists who rejected their logic and methods, and against subjective Idealism, a revolt within Idealism by those loosely influenced by Berkeley. Oakeshott displayed a remarkable independence of mind at Cambridge in that he formulated his own arguments for Absolute Idealism against those he looked to for philosophical guidance, McTaggart and Sorley, who were the Personal Idealists critical of the Absolutism of Bradley and Bosanquet, and in an intellectual climate, led by G. E. Moore, Bertrand Russell and Ludwig Wittgenstein, unrelentingly opposed to both Absolute Idealism and Personal Idealism.[64] The first of the British Idealists to express their concern about the implications for the individual of Absolutism was Andrew Seth, at Edinburgh, who later became Andrew Seth Pringle-Pattison, on condition of receiving a bequest.[65] The debate reached its epitome in 1918 at a meeting of the Aristotelian Society that addressed the question: 'Do Finite Individuals Possess a Substantive or an Adjectival Mode of Being?'[66]

The Absolutists and the Personalists, although strongly emphasizing their differences, shared a good deal of common ground. Seth agreed with the modality of experience and accepted the principles of non-contradiction and the coherence theory of truth.[67] In order to attain truth we must have knowledge of the process of its becoming and the end to be realized, and this, he conceded, may be called the Absolute or God. The finite individual, for all the Idealists, both Personal and Absolutist, could not be taken in isolation. The individual depended for its content on an objective system of reason. Seth agreed with Green and Bradley that the individual is inconceivable without society, and philosophically the individual is organic to a universal life or world. Seth contended that the individual 'cannot possibly be regarded as self-contained in relation to that life, for such self-containedness would mean sheer emptiness'.[68] The individual has a universal nature within the whole in which souls are made. So far Seth is almost indistinguishable from the Absolute Idealists. It is perhaps more accurate to see Personal Idealism as 'a development of the mode of thought which has dominated Oxford ... it is not a renunciation of it'.[69]

The key difference between the two schools of thought was the emphasis each gave to the reality of the individual, that is, to 'finite individuality'. In 1885 Seth gave an intimation, in his *Scottish Philosophy*, of his dissatisfaction with an aspect of Absolute Idealism. Hegel was defective, in Seth's view, because he treated man simply as a universal, that is, a perceptive consciousness. Hegel's perceptive consciousness is a spectator of things, occupying a universal standpoint, and merged into the universal. Seth opined: 'a philosophy which goes no further than this in its treatment of the individual, leaves untouched what we may call the individual in the individual – those subjective memories, thoughts, and plans which make each of us a separate soul'.[70] The starting point for Personal Idealism is dissatisfaction with the place of the individual personality in the programme of post-Kantian Hegelianism. Leading the revolt against Absolutism, he now questioned its metaphysical conclusion in the name of Personalism. Seth contended that 'the radical error both of Hegelianism and of the allied English doctrine I take to be the identification of the human and the divine self-consciousness, or to put it more broadly, the unifications of consciousness in a single Self'.[71] The self refuses to admit of other selves, and in this respect it is perfectly impervious. What is more, he adds, 'I have a centre of my own – a will of my own – which no one shares with me or can share – a centre which I maintain even in my dealings with God Himself'.[72]

The emphasis Seth gave to selfhood and the uniqueness of the finite individual differentiated him from the Absolutists. The individual could not be regarded as a mere appearance of reality. Like Berkeley, Seth believed the individual person was an experienced certainty, the very foundation of all action and thought.[73] He reinforces the importance of the self in accounting for the nature of experience. Seth argued that the self exists only through the world, and the world only through the self. Self and the world are the same reality looked at from different points of view. The basic unity, or identity, of reality can only be grasped, however, from the point of view of the subject, or person.[74] The finite individual cannot be negated by the Absolute without denying the reality of finite centres, which give the entire superstructure of experience its foundation.[75]

W. R. Boyce Gibson agrees with this greater emphasis on the point of view of the 'personal experient'. The immediacy of the self, or Being for oneself, is an indubitable fact of personal life, and demands a psychology from the experient's point of view. Personal Idealism maintains the centrality of human life but insists at the same time on the essentially spiritual and infinite.[76] Absolute Idealism and Personal Idealism had a common enemy in naturalism, but Absolute Idealism was deficient in two main respects. First, it criticized human experience, not from the vantage point of human experience itself, 'but from the visionary and impractical standpoint of human nature'.[77] Second, it refused to give adequate recognition to volition in human nature. In Seth's view, Absolute Idealism was in danger of consigning the finite individual to insignificance.[78] Following Rudolph Eucken, Boyce Gibson contended that the central idea of Absolute Idealism, that the real is rational, is upheld by Personal Idealism, but 'from the point of view of the personal experient'.[79]

Both McTaggart and Sorley, in their different ways, were part of the revolt from within against Absolute Idealism. As a student of history from 1920 at Gonville and Caius College, Cambridge Oakeshott avoided a formal philosophical training, although he did take McTaggart's 'Introduction to the Study of Philosophy' and the political thought option in both parts of the tripos.[80] Sorley was largely preoccupied with the debates of the latter part of the nineteenth century, particularly with the relationship between evolution and ethics, and the ethics of naturalism in general.[81] He did, nevertheless, make an important contribution to Personal Idealism. Sorley argues that ethical experience is undeniable, it is part of the very fabric of reality, and stands on its own as a genuine aspect of the Real. No account of Reality can be complete without accounting for its foundational place in the whole. Ethics is at the heart of metaphysics and in it the 'ought' offers us guidance to what truly 'is'.[82] Value, for him, resides, not in universal abstractions but in concrete individuals such as things or persons. Things have value, however, only insofar as they are instrumental with respect to persons. The individual, in Sorley's philosophy, is the sole location for realizing intrinsic value. In the acknowledgement of selves, we must also admit of individual freedom. Seth argues: 'it is the nature of the self to act and thus, in certain circumstances, to choose or select between possible alternatives. This is neither a freak of unmotivated willing nor an irruption of a pure ego into the realm of time. It is simply the real choice of a real self.'[83]

Oakeshott's teacher, J. Ellis McTaggart, inspired to some extent by Seth's *Hegelianism and Personality*, similarly wanted to give emphasis to the experiencing individual. McTaggart believed that the individual was central to philosophical inquiry. The whole has to be understood from the standpoint of the experiencing individual. Because he believed that everything that exists is spiritual, he was an ontological Idealist who placed himself alongside Berkeley, Leibniz and, in his mind, Hegel, yet he added the proviso that the content of spirit must fall within finite selves, with no part whatsoever capable of falling within more than one self.[84] Judgements about whether something is good, bad or worthy have meaning ultimately only for the individual consciousness. Only the individual is capable of giving meaning to judgements about whether something is good, bad or worthy. Value does not consist in relations among individuals, nor in the whole which they comprise. A person who loves another, does not find value or goodness intrinsic to the relation, but in being one of those related. By being one of the terms of the relation value has meaning for the individual.[85]

The question of finite individuality, then, is central to both Absolute Idealism and Personal Idealism, and Oakeshott's *Experience and its Modes* is a full-scale attack on the 'reality' of the finite individual as the Personal Idealists presented it. When exploring the various modes, he does not ask what is real for each, but instead asks what in each is an individual or a thing. For him, each individual is an abstraction constructed on the basis of unquestioned assumptions, or postulates, which are different for each mode. Each 'individual' when weighed in the balance against the Absolute is found wanting, and is exposed as a mere arrest in experience.

Oakeshott's prolonged engagement with the question of 'identity in difference' is unintelligible without reference to the issue of whether the individual or universal is real. The whole idea of identity in difference, or continuity in change, is what enables us to designate an individual. T. H. Green, for example, had argued that to assert an identity at once implies difference or change. There can be no identity unless throughout a process of change there is a unity of principle or law running through it. The different objects which result at difference stages of change exhibit a real identity, even though they may be as different as the acorn and the oak, and 'on the recognition of the difference depends the significance of the assertion of identity'.[86] Green goes on to formulate a distinction between finite individuality in the natural and moral worlds. For the oak tree there is no consciousness of its virtual identity with the acorn. The identity exists not for it, 'but for a consciousness to which oak and acorn are alike relative. But in the process constituting the moral life according to our interpretation of it, the germ and the development, the possibility and its actualisation, are one and the same consciousness of the self'.[87] Both Bradley and Oakeshott go to some pains to emphasize that the kind of identity one finds in human activity is not the teleological kind applicable to the acorn and the oak. They use the same example to illustrate the difficulty of fixing an identity, and to demonstrate that individuality is designated. Sir John Cutler's silk socks were darned with wool, and over time wool replaced the silk until not one shred remained. The conundrum was, were they the same old socks or new ones? The answer Bradley gives is that the 'identity of a thing lies in the view which you take of it. That view seems often a mere chance idea, and, where it seems necessary, it still remains an idea'.[88] This is not, however, an example of personal or historical identity. What constitutes the identity in this instance, Oakeshott argues, is the identity in terms of which the succession of changes – the added wool – is recognizable because of the unchanged item in the situation, namely the shape of the stockings which makes them stockings. It is the shape that identifies the socks that survive, giving them an identity which is not itself composed of the differences.[89] The identity of Oakeshott's historical and practical individuals, for example, is that which Bradley called the 'identity of indiscernibles'. An identity is designated by inference 'on the principle of what *seems* the same *is* the same, and cannot be made different by any diversity, and that so long as an ideal content is identical no change of context can destroy it'.[90] Bradley contends the identity of an individual implies that throughout change identity may persist despite in whatever other ways it differs. Without this assumption, and it is nothing more than an assumption, 'there will neither be selves nor things'.[91]

The problem of individuality and identity is not resolved but merely postponed or 'perfunctorily settled' within each of the modes of experience, or worlds of ideas. Each assumes the principle of a certain type of identity persisting throughout change as an unquestioned postulate. In the world of history this principle of identity is the postulate upon which the historical individual is constructed.[92] The historical individual is an abstraction. It is a mere designation rather than a definition, because not even the axes of birth and death circumscribe the relations in which an individual stands to the world. What came before and what comes after contribute to the coherence of the designation.[93]

What constitutes a fact in each mode is an unquestioned presupposition that differentiates it from the other modes. Science presupposes a world of stable, unchanging, quantitative fact, while in history the assumption is of a world of unchanging past fact. In both worlds, to deprive something of its factual status is to deny that it ever was a fact. In practical life, however, a fact is presupposed to be mutable and transient. What is a present fact has change and instability at its very core, in that practical life is characterized by the desire to change what is into what ought to be. In practical life the issue of finite individuality is at its most acute. In practical life, as in other modes, the thing, or the individual, is designated and presupposed, not defined. The criterion of the designation is not completeness, or self-completion, but what is separate and self-contained. The practical self is the product of practical thought and presupposed in all action. This self in practical life is presupposed to be self-determining, and the consequent implication of freedom requires no demonstration, because by definition it belongs to the practical self. To deny self-determination is to deny the world of practice, and the principle that underpins it, that is, the 'separateness and uniqueness' of the individual, or person. The individual in practical life, for Oakeshott, is equally an abstraction, an arrest or modification of experience, as the individual, or thing, presupposed in all the other modes.[94] This echoes Bradley's contention that the idea of selves as individuals separate from others is a 'mere fancy', a delusion of theory. Individuals are constituted by social relations, outside of which they are nothing.[95]

ABANDONING THE ABSOLUTE?

In *Experience and its Modes* only the Absolute is a self-sustaining individual or identity that is completely self-subsisting. Any identity asserted that falls short of complete coherence is an arrest in the concept of individuality, and falls short of 'what is ultimately satisfactory in experience'.[96] Throughout *Rationalism in Politics*, *On Human Conduct* and *On History* this is the conception of philosophy presupposed. There are many commentators who wish to deny this fundamental continuity in his thinking and suggest that Oakeshott abandoned Absolute Idealism and its associated belief in monism, and embraced instead a pluralism which accepted the integrity of each world of ideas, giving no special status to philosophy among the voices in the conversation of mankind.[97]

The most recent is Luke O'Sullivan, who argues that Oakeshott gradually rejected his 'early belief in the possibility of unconditional knowledge of reality'.[98] O'Sullivan contends that Oakeshott came to reject the monism of Absolute Idealism and adopted, by implication, the plurality of Personal Idealism and its prioritizing of the 'finite individual'. Understanding consists ultimately of an irreducible plurality of modes or 'voices', none of which has priority over any other.[99] The question is, then, did Oakeshott's conception of 'understanding' undergo a transformation?

In the first instance the problem of 'finite individuality', central to Absolute Idealism, continued to be one of Oakeshott's main concerns. In *On Human Conduct*, the essay 'On the Theoretical Understanding of Human Conduct' is principally focused upon the designation of individuality. Each designation depends on postulates, and the coming to know differently and more adequately something we already know. The language has become modified, but the basic principles remain the same. Understanding entails, first, identifying something in terms of an order of inquiry, as either a practice or a process. To understand something in terms of a practice presupposes that it is identified in terms of exhibitions of intelligence, that is, as individuals acknowledging and subscribing to rules and activities. To understand something as a process implies viewing changes as occurrences that happen, or which things undergo, but of which that which changes is not conscious. Each generates different idioms of discourse, which Oakeshott calls platforms of conditional understanding. In each of the platforms finite individuals are designated, adequate for the purpose but unable to sustain themselves when subjected to the interrogation of its postulates.[100] Oakeshott argues that to understand an ideal character in terms of its postulates is to understand it differently from the terms in which it is already understood.[101] The theorist who acknowledges his or her calling to be the interrogation of postulates and the examination of the conditionality of knowledge has submitted to the calling of the philosopher.[102] The philosophy is in fact the victim of thought, because 'philosophy is not the enhancement of life, it is the denial of life'.[103] Oakeshott adds, many years later, 'this engagement to be perpetually *en voyage* may be arrested without being denied'.[104] Coherence is persistently the criterion by which the adequacy of statements is measured.

It is Oakeshott's introduction of the metaphor, and it is nothing more than that, of conversation in order to characterize the relationship between what he calls the different voices that seem to mislead many commentators into thinking a fundamental shift has taken place. He uses the term to indicate the dialectical, rather than the eristic, nature of a conversational relation.[105] The inference from this is that philosophy is merely another voice among all of the others, with no priority or special status.

It is a mistake, in my view, to consider the adoption of the language of conversation as in any way significant, above and beyond clarification of the relation in which the modes stand to each other. Philosophy is in fact unlike the other voices. It springs from the conversation, and is parasitic on the other voices, just as it had been in *Experience and its Modes*. It explores the quality and style of each voice and its relation to the others. In 1983, fifty years after *Experience and its Modes*, Oakeshott explored the distinct modal conditions that constitute the practice of history, and this once again exhibits the continuity I am claiming. The study is concerned not to determine the truth of historical conclusions, only the conditions in terms of which they may be regarded as conclusions. It is not his concern to relate history to experience as a whole, but failure to do so does not indicate he abandoned the principle of absolute coherence as the ultimate criterion of truth. Absolute and unconditional consistency, and not the search for a body of knowledge, is what condemns the philosopher to be perpetually *en route*.

What, then, are the implications for philosophy of Oakeshott's characterization of the relationship between the various worlds of ideas, or imaginings, including philosophy, as conversational? The view that emerges may be described in three propositions, and if it can be shown that they are not new to his understanding of the nature of philosophy, it will at least establish a continuity that does not merit the contention that he abandoned Absolute Idealism. First, philosophy is not eristic, and does not attempt to persuade. Second, it is parasitic on the other voices, and makes no substantive contribution to them. And, third, it is not a body of knowledge. It is a manner of thinking.[106]

On the first point there is a lifelong consistency. Philosophy consists not in 'persuading others, but in making our own minds clear'. It is non-competitive and 'something independent of the futile attempt to convince or persuade'.[107] It is something we may undertake without entering a competition.[108] It sounds, then, very like the philosopher's place in the conversation of mankind.

Nor does Oakeshott deviate on the second contention that philosophy is parasitic on the modes. Understanding involves making identifications in terms of postulates. Philosophical activity questions the postulates, and hence is parasitical on the modes they constitute. It differs from those modes in that they are satisfied with the conditional intelligibility they offer, whereas philosophical inquiry 'is peculiar merely because, in the pursuit of the process it is governed by a radical scepticism with regard to every stopping place that is suggested; it is suspicious of every attempt to limit the enquiry'.[109] What this indicates is that Stephen Gerencser's contention that Oakeshott believed in the attainment of absolute knowledge in his early years and then became a sceptic is unsustainable.[110]

On the third proposition, that philosophy is not a body of knowledge but a manner of thinking, it is entirely consistent with the view expressed in *Experience and its Modes*. There is no suggestion there that philosophy is a body of knowledge. Oakeshott puts the reader straight immediately. He says we will not find in the work a system or universal truths. He offers a provisional point of view. Philosophy is not about absolute certainty versus lesser degrees of truth, but the determination to interrogate every presupposition encountered, in other words, to be permanently *en route*. It is a method, or way of thinking, aimed at achieving intelligibility, not an accumulated body of knowledge: 'it has no peculiar and exclusive source of knowledge'.[111] Put differently, the philosopher is distinguished by 'virtue of having submitted himself to a particular kind of curiosity'.[112] There are no special sources of information at its disposal, philosophy is 'simply thought which has been allowed to follow its own bent with unqualified freedom'.[113] There are no authorities in philosophy, and it is the only activity in which ignorance is considered a virtue. Maurice Cranston, a colleague of Oakeshott's, understood this well when he argued the conception of philosophy in *Experience and its Modes* did not involve the construction of a comprehensive system of knowledge. It was, on the contrary, a method, or way of thinking, aimed at achieving intelligibility.[114]

NOTES

1 M. Oakeshott, review of W. M. Urban, *Beyond Realism and Idealism*, in *CPJ*, p. 321.

2 G. Berkeley, *Treatise Concerning the Principles of Human Knowledge* (Indianapolis: Bobbs Merrill, 1970), §§ 22–3.

3 H. Jones, 'Idealism and Epistemology', in D. Boucher (ed.), *The Scottish Idealists* (Thorverton: Imprint Academic, 2004), pp. 106–40.
4 A. N. Whitehead, *Process and Reality* (New York: Free Press, 1979), p. 39.
5 J. H. Muirhead, *The Platonic Tradition in Anglo-Saxon Philosophy* (London: George Allen & Unwin, 1931).
6 E. Caird, 'Plato and Other Companions of Socrates', *North British Review*, 43 (1865), 351–84.
7 *EM*, p. 6.
8 M. Oakeshott, 'Introduction to *Leviathan*', in *HCA*, p. 7.
9 For an interesting exploration of Oakeshott's relationship to the Ancient Greeks see E. S. Kos, *Michael Oakeshott, the Ancient Greeks and the Philosophical Study of Politics* (Thorverton: Imprint Academic, 2007).
10 A. Botwinick, *Michael Oakeshott's Skepticism* (Princeton University Press, 2011), pp. 5–6.
11 Oakeshott, 'Introduction to *Leviathan*', pp. 27–8. For an extensive discussion of Oakeshott's understanding and use of Hobbes, see I. Tregenza, *Michael Oakeshott on Hobbes: A Study in the Renewal of Philosophical Ideas* (Thorverton: Imprint Academic, 2003). See also Chapter 13 below.
12 G. W. F. Hegel, *Lectures on the History of Philosophy*, trans. E. S. Haldane (London: Kegan Paul, Trench, Trübner, 1892), p. 92.
13 *Ibid.*
14 B. Bosanquet, *The Philosophical Theory of the State* (London: Macmillan, 1923), pp. 98–9.
15 M. Oakeshott, 'Dr Leo Strauss on Hobbes', in *HCA*, p. 148.
16 Oakeshott, 'Introduction to *Leviathan*', p. 7.
17 *Ibid.*
18 *EM*, p. 6.
19 M. Oakeshott, notebook 3, in *NL*, forthcoming, quoting p. 242 of H. Jones, *A Faith That Enquires* (London: Macmillan, 1922).
20 M. Oakeshott, notebook 4, in *NL*, forthcoming.
21 J. Estlin Carpenter, review of J. H. Muirhead and H. Jones, *The Life and Philosophy of Edward Caird*, *Hibbert Journal*, 19 (1922/3), 194.
22 Bosanquet, *Philosophical Theory of the State*, p. 2.
23 *EM*, p. 2.
24 H. H. Joachim, *The Nature of Truth* (Oxford University Press, 1906), p. 176.
25 See A. J. M. Milne, *The Social and Political Thought of the English Idealists* (London: Allen & Unwin, 1962), pp. 177–8.

26 *EM*, p. 93. In his notebook 4, Oakeshott transcribes a quotation from his teacher: 'An intuitive understanding' = 'understanding which, in knowing, creates the objects of knowledge'. W. R. Sorley, *On the Ethics of Naturalism* (Edinburgh: Blackwood, 1885), p. 286.
27 *EM*, pp. 31–2.
28 M. Oakeshott, 'The Concept of a Philosophical Jurisprudence', in *CPJ*, p. 155.
29 E. Caird, letter to Miss Talbot, 28 October 1891, printed in H. Jones and J. H. Muirhead, *The Life and Philosophy of Edward Caird* (Glasgow: MacLehose, 1921), p. 172.
30 *EM*, p. 147.
31 F. H. Bradley, *Essays in Truth and Reality* (Oxford: Clarendon Press, 1914), p. 235.
32 *HC*, p. 8.
33 F. H. Bradley, *The Presuppositions of Critical History and Aphorisms* (Bristol: Thoemmes Press, 1993).
34 *EM*, p. 331.
35 M. Oakeshott, 'The Activity of Being an Historian', in *RP*, p. 137; *OH*, p. 5.
36 M. Oakeshott, 'The Study of "Politics" in a University', in *RP*, p. 328. Here he refers to history and philosophy as 'two modes of thought'.
37 *HC*, p. 35.
38 *HC*, p. 26.
39 J. Cook Wilson, *Statement and Inference with Other Philosophical Papers*, 2 vols. (Oxford: Clarendon Press, 1926).
40 H. A. Prichard, 'Professor John Cook Wilson', *Mind*, 28 (1919), 312–13.
41 Cook Wilson, *Statement and Inference*, vol. I, p. 92.
42 C. R. Morris, *Idealistic Logic: A Study of its Aim, Method and Achievement* (London: Macmillan, 1933).
43 *Ibid.*, p. 224.
44 B. Russell, *A Critical Exposition of the Philosophy of Leibniz* (London: George Allen & Unwin, 1900); *The Principles of Mathematics* (London: George Allen & Unwin, 1903).
45 For an interesting account of the main issues in Logic between Russell and the Idealists, particularly Bradley, see S. Candlish, 'British Idealism: Theoretical Philosophy', in D. Moyar (ed.), *The Routledge Companion to Nineteenth Century Philosophy* (London: Routledge, 2010), pp. 658–88.
46 Oakeshott, 'Concept of a Philosophical Jurisprudence', p. 171.
47 L. S. Stebbing, 'The Method of Analysis in Metaphysics', *Proceedings of the Aristotelian Society*, 33 (1932/3), 93.

48 G. E. Moore, 'The Nature and Reality of Objects of Perception', in G. E. Moore, *Philosophical Studies* (London: Routledge & Kegan Paul, 1922), pp. 31–96.
49 G. E. Moore, 'Proof of an External World', *Proceedings of the British Academy*, 25 (1939), 272–300.
50 Morris, *Idealistic Logic*, pp. 223–4.
51 *OH*, p. 5.
52 Joachim, *Nature of Truth*, p. 176.
53 *Ibid.*, p. vii.
54 *EM*, p. 11.
55 Joachim, *Nature of Truth*, p. 66.
56 G. R. G. Mure, 'Benedetto Croce and Oxford', *Philosophical Quarterly*, 4 (1954), 329.
57 *EM*, p. 37.
58 F. H. Bradley, *Essays on Truth and Reality* (Oxford: Clarendon Press, 1914), p. 218.
59 F. H. Bradley, *Appearance and Reality: A Metaphysical Essay* (London: George Allen & Unwin, 1925), p. 537.
60 Joachim, *Nature of Truth*, p. 68.
61 M. Oakeshott, notebook 6, in *NL*, forthcoming.
62 *EM*, pp. 34–7.
63 See D. Boucher (ed.), *The British Idealists* (Cambridge University Press, 1997); D. Boucher, *The Limits of Ethics in International Relations* (Oxford University Press, 2009), ch. 10.
64 In 1968, as self-deprecating as ever, Oakeshott declared 'true enough though' in response to the view that he was an interesting survival 'out of date before he was born'. Speech on the occasion of the presentation of the *Festschrift Politics and Experience*, Oakeshott Papers, British Library of Political Science, 1/3, Various Speeches.
65 Seth, for example, objected to Absolute Idealism's 'unification of consciousness in a single Self'. A. Seth [Pringle-Pattison], *Hegelianism and Personality* (Edinburgh: Blackwood, 1888), p. 215.
66 Published as J. H. Wildon Carr (ed.), *Life and Finite Individuality: Two Symposia* (London: Williams & Norgate, 1918).
67 A. Seth [Pringle-Pattison], *The Idea of God in the Light of Recent Philosophy* (Oxford University Press, 1917), p. 189.
68 *Ibid.*, p. 259. Compare G. Watts Cunningham, *The Idealistic Argument in Recent British and American Philosophy* (New York: Century, 1933), pp. 162–3.
69 H. Sturt, *Personal Idealism* (London: Macmillan, 1902), p. vi.

70 A. Seth [Pringle-Pattison], *Scottish Philosophy* (Edinburgh: Blackwood, 1907), p. 221.
71 Seth [Pringle-Pattison], *Hegelianism and Personality*, p. 215.
72 *Ibid.*, p. 217.
73 He was nevertheless critical of Berkeley in his *Idea of God*, responding to Henry Jones's charge of subjectivism See W. J. Mander, *British Idealism: A History* (Oxford University Press, 2011), pp. 362–4.
74 A. Seth [Pringle-Pattison], 'Philosophy as Criticism of the Categories', in A. Seth and R. B. Haldane (eds.), *Essays in Philosophical Criticism* (London: Longmans, Green, 1883), p. 38.
75 Watts Cunningham, *Idealistic Argument*, p. 165.
76 W. R. Boyce Gibson, 'A Peace Policy for Idealists', *Hibbert Journal*, 5 (1906/7), 410.
77 Sturt, *Personal Idealism*, p. x.
78 Seth [Pringle-Pattison], *Idea of God*, p. 266.
79 Boyce Gibson, 'Peace Policy for Idealists', 409.
80 J. M. E. McTaggart, *Philosophical Studies* (New York: Books for Libraries, 1966), pp. 183–209. Among Oakeshott's papers is McTaggart's printed syllabus and summary of the lectures. It is heavily annotated.
81 See, for example, W. R. Sorley, *Recent Tendencies in Ethics* (Edinburgh: Blackwood, 1904); Sorley, *On the Ethics of Naturalism*.
82 W. R. Sorley, *Moral Values and the Idea of God* (Cambridge University Press, 1918), p. 6.
83 *Ibid.*, p. 436. Also see Mander, *British Idealism*, pp. 368–9.
84 McTaggart, *Philosophical Studies*, p. 273.
85 *Ibid.*, pp. 97–109.
86 T. H. Green, 'Fragment of an Address on the Text "The Word is Nigh Thee"', in *Works* (London: Longmans, Green, 1888), vol. III, p. 225.
87 *Ibid.*, p. 226.
88 Bradley, *Appearance and Reality*, p. 74; cf. *OH*, pp. 114–15.
89 *OH*, pp. 114–15n.
90 F. H. Bradley, *The Principles of Logic* (Oxford: Clarendon Press, 1922), p. 288.
91 Bradley, *Appearance and Reality*, p. 348.
92 *EM*, p. 124.
93 *EM*, p. 151.
94 *EM*, pp. 268–74.
95 F. H. Bradley, *Ethical Studies* (Oxford: Clarendon Press, 1927), esp. pp. 165–8.
96 *EM*, p. 148.
97 See for example R. Grant, *Oakeshott* (London: Claridge Press, 1990), pp. 65–70; S. Gerencser, *The Skeptic's Oakeshott* (London: Macmillan,

2000), esp. pp. 33–51; T. Nardin, *The Philosophy of Michael Oakeshott* (University Park: Pennsylvania State University Press, 2001), pp. 44–5; P. Franco, *Michael Oakeshott: An Introduction* (New Haven, CT: Yale University Press, 2004), p. 125.

98 L. O'Sullivan, 'Introduction', in M. Oakeshott, *What is History? And Other Essays* (Thorverton: Imprint Academic, 2004), p. 5.

99 *Ibid.*

100 *HC*, pp. 1–8.

101 *HC*, pp. 9–10.

102 *HC*, p. 11.

103 *EM*, p. 355.

104 *HC*, p. 11.

105 M. Oakeshott, 'The Voice of Poetry in the Conversation of Mankind', in *RP*, pp. 197–247.

106 *Ibid.*, pp. 199, 200, 203, 204.

107 *HC*, p. 7.

108 *EM*, pp. 3 and 7.

109 Oakeshott, 'Concept of a Philosophical Jurisprudence', p. 172.

110 Gerencser, *Skeptic's Oakeshott*, pp. 33–51.

111 *EM*, p. 82.

112 Oakeshott, 'Concept of a Philosophical Jurisprudence', p. 181.

113 *Ibid.*, p. 176.

114 M. Cranston, 'Remembrances of Michael Oakeshott', *Political Theory*, 19 (1991), 324.

EFRAIM PODOKSIK

12 Oakeshott in the context of German Idealism

INTRODUCTION

German philosophical culture, as we know, had a pivotal influence on Michael Oakeshott's thought. It was not the first foreign intellectual tradition with which Oakeshott became acquainted in the original language. His first such interest (as a young student) was French thought. He would regularly borrow foreign books in French (Rousseau, Voltaire) from his college library, and one of his earliest essays contains a list of bibliography that testifies to his extensive reading of French authors.[1] From the mid 1920s onwards, however, it was Germany that attracted him more and more. He travelled there quite often; began to read German authors in the German language; taught contemporary German philosophers (such as Heidegger and Husserl); and his works began to be filled with references to German texts.

This in itself is not very remarkable. Germany in the early twentieth century was, in many respects, the centre of the humanities (and of philosophy, in particular), and in terms of that period the prestige of its universities was certainly no less than that enjoyed by certain American universities in more recent times. It is not surprising, therefore, that a young talented Briton would turn his eyes towards Germany. Moreover, British intellectual life itself included traditions that self-consciously followed what were recognized to be German ideas. These ideas were regarded as representing an intellectual alternative to the 'mainstream', characterized, as it were, by sensualism, empiricism or methodological individualism. The counterculture of British intellectual life in the nineteenth century (represented by Coleridge and Romanticism, or by Liberal

Anglicanism) was distinctively 'German'. Moreover, towards the end of that century heterodoxy itself became mainstream: British (Absolute) Idealism, heavily influenced by the German Idealism of Kant and Hegel, conquered the philosophical discourse in British universities for a few decades.

Oakeshott initially was an Absolute Idealist, and his thinking naturally bears the marks of German Idealism. But if this had been the only aspect of German influence on him, it would have been of little significance. It would testify not to the German influence as such, but rather to the influence of a certain native British tradition which itself sprang up out of engagement with German authors. For national intellectual traditions are rarely, if ever, exported as a coherent whole. As these traditions develop in interaction with their social environment, so the meaning of their content usually changes when they are stripped of this environment. Traditions transmit themselves as fragments (through certain thinkers or certain works). These fragments are then assimilated in a foreign landscape and adjust themselves to a different set of questions and intellectual habits.

This, however, was not the case with Oakeshott. He was not merely a British author who borrowed ideas from the German writers he read. My claim is that Oakeshott was, to a great degree, a German philosopher. His debt was not to specific items out of the stock of German intellectual heritage (or not only to them), but rather to the German intellectual tradition as a coherent whole, and on its own terms. This is one of the reasons why his writings were so often ignored in his own land: Oakeshott wrote beautiful English prose, but the content of what he wrote often sounded unintelligible to those who were unfamiliar with the questions that troubled German thinkers. Thus, in order to understand the significance of Oakeshott's ideas it is important to take him not as a British thinker who somehow absorbed elements from German thought, but as a German thinker who had something of importance to say to the world.

MODES OF EXPERIENCE

There was one philosophical idea to which Oakeshott ardently subscribed (with terminological variations) throughout his entire life: the notion of the plurality of the forms of human experience. He envisaged these forms, modes or images as absolutely independent ways of experiencing reality as a whole, each limited though by its own specific postulates (or presuppositions).

The idea that experience may exist in a variety of forms was not unfamiliar in the history of philosophy. F. H. Bradley and R. G. Collingwood have been mentioned as Oakeshott's immediate predecessors in this respect. More generally, philosophical attempts at making sense out of the categorial plurality of human experience can be traced back to Kant and Hegel. Indeed, in *Experience and its Modes* Oakeshott himself named Hegel and Bradley as his sources of inspiration.[2]

The affinities between Oakeshott and the aforementioned thinkers do exist. Yet they are too general. When Oakeshott's idea of modes of experience is examined closely, it appears to be significantly different, especially in two respects. First, his modes are parallel worlds that neither meet nor clash; they are simply irrelevant to each other. In this sense they are not like Kant's categories (or Bradley's attributes of the Absolute), nor can they be seen as different stages in the hierarchy of experience, and therefore they do not supersede each other dialectically (as in Hegel or Collingwood). They are parallel (even if partial) reflections of the same unity of the world, a unity that cannot be divided into parts. This description resembles Spinoza's delineation of the modes of 'thought' and 'extension'.[3] Yet Spinoza acknowledged only two such modes as accessible to man (even though in principle their number is infinite), whereas Oakeshott allowed for several. The reason is (and here lies the second important feature of his approach) that the Oakeshottian modes are not general categories of logic or intuition, but rather historically emerging spheres of cultural activity, such as history or science.

These two features – the idea that the modes are parallel worlds irrelevant to each other, and the view of them as cultural activities (some of which specifically belong to advanced modern civilization) – is what makes Oakeshott's theory initially appear to stand apart. Yet, in fact, this view belongs to a philosophical tradition, and the tradition is distinctively German. The problem of the manifoldness of experience dividing itself into separate types was a central concern of German thought and culture since

Leibniz,[4] appearing in different forms in the works of almost every German author. It occasionally appears also in other philosophical traditions. Yet nowhere does it reach the degree of centrality that it reached in Germany, and much of what is said on this subject in other traditions is often just an echo of debates in German philosophy.

To explain: the German philosophical tradition did not influence neighbouring traditions in its entirety. It was classical German Idealism, represented by Kant and Hegel, that received most attention. Therefore, when the subject of the plurality of forms of experience was addressed in other philosophical traditions, it was addressed in terms of classical Idealism. Oakeshott, however, tackles this question in the manner of the German philosophers of later generations, which turned out to be significantly more idiosyncratic. In the late nineteenth and early twentieth centuries it came to dominate German thought, but it did not readily export itself abroad. The thinkers most significant for our story here are Arthur Schopenhauer, Georg Simmel and Heinrich Rickert.

The Schopenhauerian moment in Oakeshott's philosophy is still unexplored territory. Oakeshott knew and occasionally referred to Schopenhauer's writings.[5] Yet, perhaps because his most famous mention of Schopenhauer in 'The Voice of Poetry' is critical, significant affinity between Oakeshott's views and many of Schopenhauer's insights has until now remained unnoticed. Oakeshott must have rejected Schopenhauer's metaphysics. But Schopenhauer's ideas and his philosophical style were of such force that they often provoked philosophical imagination even in those philosophers who did not buy his metaphysical presuppositions.

In respect of the modality of experience, the relevant aspect of Schopenhauer's philosophy is his understanding of how the will objectifies itself. The central and best-known idea of Schopenhauer is that the world can be conceived of by philosophy in a double way. On the one hand, it is the phenomenal world of representation. On the other hand, it is the world *in itself* (or more precisely – that part of *in itself* which is accessible to philosophical vision), that is, the world as will. The world as it appears to us, as representation, is a world of plurality; it consists of individual items and is governed by the '*principium individuationis*'.[6] The will, on the contrary, is one; it 'remains indivisible'.[7] Its oneness is not numerical. Rather, it stands beyond the very possibility of conceiving 'one' as a separate item; the world of will is beyond the very idea of plurality.

Now, each particular representation is an objectification of the will. Phenomena appear to be distinct and different from each other. Yet all of them objectify what is in essence one and the same thing. They objectify not aspects of the will, or parts of it, but the will as a whole: 'the will reveals itself just as completely and just as much in *one* oak as in millions'.[8] In other words, 'the inner being itself is present whole and undivided in everything in nature, in every living being'.[9]

How can the difference between items in experience be made intelligible? For Schopenhauer, the difference that matters is not the one between individual items but that between the types to which these items belong. For the will, in fact, objectifies itself not directly but in two stages, so to speak. It first objectifies itself into eternal forms, or types (which Schopenhauer calls 'Ideas'). These Ideas (which are themselves inaccessible to us in terms of the categories of perception yet can be contemplated in aesthetic intuition) in their turn objectify themselves into individual phenomena. Ideas objectify one and the same indivisible will. Yet they objectify it in different degrees (grades) of distinctiveness, starting from the forces of nature and ending with objectification at its highest grade: an individual human character. Thus, for Schopenhauer, Idea is 'every definite and fixed *grade of the will's objectification*, in so far as it [the will] is thing-in-itself and is therefore foreign to plurality'.[10]

This is the metaphysical scheme that comes closest to Oakeshott's way of grasping modes of experience. It is true that Oakeshott refuses to arrange his modes of experience according to their degree of approximation to reality. But this point should not lead us to exaggerate the difference between Oakeshott and Schopenhauer, for although Schopenhauer does speak about the grades of objectification, his system is a stranger to the idea of development. It does not presuppose any progress from lower to higher forms of the will's objectification. Schopenhauer's world is timeless, since time for him is an illusion in our representation. When we perceive the world as representation, we may believe that, historically speaking, higher forms of objectification appear later than lower forms. Yet this is immaterial: each and every Idea is presupposed from the very beginning.

The crucial point connecting Oakeshott with Schopenhauer is that both envisage plurality in such a way that each aspect of it is understood not as a part of the whole but as a certain mode of reflecting the whole in all its completeness. What follows from this and sets their theories apart from the mainstream Kantian–Hegelian tradition is that the world they both describe implies radical plurality, which is irreducible to unity, explicitly so in Oakeshott and implicitly in Schopenhauer (hence the latter's pessimism: what he envisions as unity – the will – is always at conflict with itself; its objectifications cannot be brought into a coherent harmony).

Schopenhauer's insight can be thus seen as a scheme for the view of modes of experience as imperfect reflections of the whole. Schopenhauer considers these objectifications as fighting with each other. Yet it is quite easy to replace the notion of struggle with that of mutual irrelevance, especially when one begins to consider the modes in terms of various cultural activities, which is the second feature of Oakeshott's theory. This step is first taken, however, not by Oakeshott but by a German philosopher who himself was deeply influenced by Schopenhauer: Georg Simmel. Simmel was not a Schopenhauerian in the full sense of the term. To a significant degree he was a Neo-Kantian. It is indeed Kant's philosophy rather than Schopenhauer's that implies the plurality of cultural spheres, the motive elaborated by the Neo-Kantian philosophy of culture. Yet Simmel's peculiarity is that he succeeds in addressing this Neo-Kantian motive in a very similar way to Schopenhauer.

Simmel argued that our life constantly creates forms, some of which are capable of composing a system that may reflect the entire reality through its specific system of postulates. Simmel called these forms 'worlds'. Among such worlds he counted, for example, 'the world in the form of art, in the form of knowledge, in the form of religion, in the form of gradation of value and significance in general'.[11] These worlds are 'mutually incapable of any mixture, any overlap, any intersection, because each already expresses the entire stuff of the world in its special language'.[12] Simmel's notion of worlds therefore presupposes plurality which in its essence stands contrary to the principle of unity.

This view sounds identical to Oakeshott's, including the use of the term 'world'. This is hardly a coincidence. Oakeshott read

Simmel,[13] and in my opinion Simmel can be named as Oakeshott's immediate philosophical predecessor. For what is common to them is not only the general recognition of the variety implied in human experience, but also the nuances of this recognition. Both conceive of forms of experience as mutually irrelevant reflections of the entirety of the world; and both classify them in terms of cultural activities.

Now, there is an additional point that Oakeshott and Simmel appear to share: they are both more interested in the analytical description of this variety than in providing the historical account of its emergence. Yet both think that this phenomenon of variety is characteristic especially of modern western civilization. Oakeshott, for example, suggests that the well-developed voices of science, poetry and especially history are a relatively recent achievement.[14] This idea, again, is one of the major motives of the German intellectual tradition in general. Among the thinkers who elaborated on it, one can count Max Weber. He argued that what triggered the emergence of modernity was the increasing tension between religious experience, which turned towards the ascetic rejection of the world, and other spheres of human activity (economic, aesthetic and so forth). This tension led, in the end, to the subsequent emancipation of these spheres from religion.[15] Simmel and Weber both stood close to the Southwest (Baden) School in Neo-Kantianism, and it is the thinkers of this school who emphasized the specifically *modern* character of this cultural variety.

Heinrich Rickert, a leading representative of the Southwestern School, is mentioned and quoted by Oakeshott on several occasions.[16] Rickert offered one of the most elaborate statements on the modern character of the pluralism embedded in modern experience in his book *Kant as the Philosopher of Modern Culture*. He argued that modernity started with the disintegration of the synthesis that characterized the Middle Ages, the synthesis of three spheres: thinking, will, and feeling. Modern culture is that in which each of these spheres demands complete autonomy for itself (in the sphere of thinking, truth is now sought only for its own sake; in the sphere of will [statesmanship], politics is pursued for its own sake; similarly, in the sphere of feeling, the religious man looks for God for God's sake).[17] Rickert's classification of spheres is not identical to those of Simmel or Oakeshott. He tries to follow the order of Kant's three critiques (pure reason is signified by him as 'truth'; critical reason as 'will'; judgement as 'feeling') in order to argue that Kant was the first philosopher to grasp the full implications of the change. But the nuances of his classification are less important for our discussion than his account of the plurality of cultural forms as a product of the historical development of the specifically modern times: for him, the modern post-Renaissance post-Reformation world is the world of plurality in which each cultural sphere demands for itself complete autonomy and is valued to the extent that it establishes such an autonomy. What is most important here is that Rickert's point is not idiosyncratic and original; he merely made explicit the presupposition that was, at that time, shared basically by every thinker who philosophized in terms of the notion of the variety of forms of experience. Hence, when considered in this context, Oakeshott's theory of modes of experience appears as a theory of modernity, even if he did not elaborate this point at length.

Conceiving the philosophy of modes of experience as a statement about modernity has important implications for our interpretation of Oakeshott's stance vis-à-vis German philosophy in particular, and of his philosophical vision in general. This point will be addressed in the concluding section of this chapter, after I deal with the two other aspects of Oakeshott's thought that bear marks of German influence – his philosophy of practical life and his theory of the state and human association.

PRACTICE

Some commentators consider practice as the main thread of Oakeshott's thought and see him as pre-eminently a philosopher of practice.[18] I do not share this view. I believe that the importance of 'practice' in Oakeshott's thought recedes in the course of time, as he becomes apprehensive about the subversive potential of an exaggerated emphasis on it. Yet he explores the subject extensively, especially in his early and middle periods, and to the extent that the voice of 'practice' finds its place in his thought, its outline and main characteristics appear to be influenced by the German intellectual tradition.

One of the most significant features of this tradition in the late nineteenth and early twentieth centuries was a gradually increasing feeling of crisis, provoked by the fear of the irretrievable loss of a unified world view. In Britain, utilitarianism or Absolute Idealism satisfied the need for unity. But Germany was allergic to comprehensive utilitarianism, whereas Absolute Idealism was a non-starter precisely because it was an Hegelian system, and in Germany Hegelianism was then broadly perceived as a thing of the past and its tools of combating intellectual and cultural fragmentation were regarded as naive. Neo-Kantianism became popular partly because it acknowledged this condition of fragmentation.

This does not mean, however, that attempts at rejecting or overcoming modern fragmentation ceased. Yet those attempts that acquired cultural significance came from a very different direction: they challenged the very idea that unity could be restored through philosophical reflection. Rather, it was argued, unity could be restored only if one abandoned all attempts at conceptualization: unity can be grasped only intuitively, through immediate present experience, that is, through 'life', which stands above reason and reflection.

The position to which I am referring came to be known as 'life-philosophy'. It was not only a philosophical current; towards the 1920s it developed into a fashionable cultural trend that appealed especially to the young generation nurtured in the neo-Romantic tradition of the youth movement. But a number of major philosophers of the preceding generations were generally considered as its intellectual lights. Three names can be mentioned here: Friedrich Nietzsche, Wilhelm Dilthey and, again, Georg Simmel. Nietzsche became a powerful cultural symbol for almost all those who in the early twentieth century protested against the mediocrity and complacency of the mainstream bourgeois culture.[19] Dilthey's work bestowed on this drive a measure of philosophical respectability, as he developed his notion of experience, grounded in the totality of human life rather than in the dry rationalistic formulae of European philosophy from Locke to Kant.[20] Finally, Simmel attempted towards the end of his life to combine 'life-philosophy' with the Neo-Kantian notion of modal plurality.

'Life-philosophy' was not an exclusively German phenomenon. One of its major proponents was a French philosopher, Henri

Bergson, with whose writings Oakeshott had been familiar even before he immersed himself in studying German culture.[21] Yet, when Oakeshott deals with the notions of life and practice, he does this in an unambiguously German idiom.

Take Oakeshott's early essays from the mid 1920s. They are full of references to German writers, having been written under the influence of his own German experience in those years, including participation in the activities of the German youth movement. Many of his statements appear to be perfectly *lebensphilosophisch*. He puts emphasis on the value of 'life' in itself, praises the cult of youth and speaks a lot about the importance of present immediate experience. Consider the following statements: 'in the place of the world's external standard of value, we should adopt a more personal standard'.[22] 'Though to live in the present may appear frivolous, to live for the future is certainly vain'.[23] Or:

> we have, I think, in the natural beliefs of youth, undimmed by the sordid demands of age and experience, a motive and foundation strong enough to produce and sustain it [life]. In youth, before we consented to take life as it is, before prudence has taught us the unwisdom of living ahead of ourselves, before we have succumbed to the middle-class passion for safety, regularity and possession, we believe that the most important thing is to preserve, at all costs, our integrity of character ... Religion ... is *simply life itself*, life dominated by the belief that its value is in the present, not merely in the past or the future, that if we lose ourselves, we lose all.[24]

'Life-philosophy' was not unchallenged in Germany. One of its most vocal critics was Rickert, who became afraid of the spirit of irrationality it carried with it.[25] Oakeshott often referred to Rickert's works in other contexts, though we do not know what he thought about Rickert's critique. Yet, in any case, towards the early 1930s this kind of 'life-philosophy' rhetoric begins to lose its appeal for Oakeshott. In *Experience and its Modes* he relegates the conduct of life to practical experience, considered as a defective mode alongside others. At the same time, the 'life-philosophy' motives still influence parts of the book. First, the very notion of total experience appears to be an echo from the tradition of 'life-philosophy', and the emphasis on present insight is still felt throughout the volume.[26] Second, and more substantially, Oakeshott's analysis of the specific features of the mode of practical experience is very indebted to the

German 'life-philosophy', even if he now separates practical experience from total experience. In particular, his outline of practical experience seems to be very close to that presented by Georg Simmel in his philosophy of the 'individual law'.[27]

Simmel conceived of the notion of the individual law as an alternative to Kantian morality. The main problem of that morality was, for him, the identification of moral law with the principle of universality: any maxim of human conduct should be capable of being applied universally, whereas any universal maxim should be regarded as moral. Simmel rejected this view, arguing that one can imagine a moral law valid only for a specific individual and derived out of the totality of the life of that individual. The individual law is then nothing other than the imperative to be true to oneself. This does not mean that *ought* should be identical to *is*, so that every personal action would be, by definition, considered as 'moral'. There can be a gap between the sphere of *is* and the sphere of *ought*, but this is because they are just different lines implied in the same process of life. Neither comes from outside. Life is a constant process of reconciling itself with its own norm (ought). *Is* and *ought* are like two modes in which the same life proceeds.[28]

Oakeshott describes the mode of practical experience in a similar manner, conceiving it in terms of the fundamental discrepancy between 'what is here and now' and 'what ought to be'.[29] These are two different modes (within the mode of practical experience), governed by their own presuppositions. Practice itself is a constant attempt at transforming what is into what ought to be, an attempt that never reaches a satisfactory end.

Thus in his analysis of practical experience Oakeshott employs the scheme and philosophical tools outlined by Simmel. This should not be surprising. As I pointed out earlier, Simmel tried to develop a world view that would accommodate striving for the totality and integrity of life experience alongside the Neo-Kantian emphasis on the pluralism of cultural spheres. When Oakeshott was writing *Experience and its Modes*, he stood at a similar junction, though he was looking in the other direction. Whereas for Simmel this combination meant departing from Neo-Kantianism and moving towards life-philosophy, for Oakeshott it signified precisely the opposite: his departure from life-philosophy and adoption of the Neo-Kantian pluralism of spheres.[30]

This departure was, nevertheless, gradual. Motives of 'life-philosophy' continued to play an important role in his works over the following two decades, becoming especially salient in the post-war essays dedicated to the critique of Rationalism. Oakeshott attacked the rationalistic conception of knowledge and rationalistic morality, arguing that these were merely abstractions from the totality of human behaviour based on practical knowledge and the morality of custom.[31]

The philosophical roots of this attack can also be found in the German philosophical tradition. Oakeshott's general sentiment clearly resembles the aforementioned attacks of Dilthey and Simmel on the spirit of Rationalism. German authors also appear to be the source of many of his specific claims. Consider, for example, the story of the transformation of moral life in Christianity: Oakeshott suggests that for early Christians religion was basically the way of life and morality was a matter of habit, whereas later, Christianity became a moral ideology governed by dogmas.[32] Oakeshott just repeats here a very influential view of the leading German Protestant theologian Adolph Harnack about the origin of the Christian dogma.[33]

This and other parallels between Oakeshott and German thinkers may offer a lot of fascinating material for various research projects. In this chapter, however, I will limit myself to what I regard as the major philosophical source of Oakeshott's central epistemological distinction: that between the knowledge of *what* and the knowledge of *how*, or technical versus practical knowledge. The former, according to him, is inferior to the latter and should be seen as an auxiliary to it rather than as its master. The knowledge of *what* is always an abstraction from practised activities. Knowing how to cook is something more than acquainting oneself with a book about cooking.

It is often claimed that Oakeshott was influenced by Gilbert Ryle's similar distinctions.[34] It is rarely noticed, however, that the origin of this idea can be found in a specific branch of German Idealism, perhaps because this branch is not Hegelian, as one is used to expect from Oakeshott, but again Schopenhauerian. It is possible that Ryle's article triggered Oakeshott's formulation of the idea. Yet Ryle's ideas themselves 'came straight out of Schopenhauer',[35] and Oakeshott was hardly unfamiliar with Schopenhauer's main writings.

Schopenhauer's philosophy as a whole was not 'empiricist', but his theory of representation was strictly so. He argued that the sciences are merely convenient reflective tools for bringing to our awareness what we already know by perceiving. Concepts, he said, are representation, although they are not representations of immediate perceptions. They are representations of the second order, 'representations of representations', abstract representations, and as such they stand in a necessary relation to perceptions: 'without this they would be nothing'.[36] Therefore, concepts do not add anything essentially new to our knowledge; they just put our knowledge in order. This may be of some use in some cases, but often (for example, in geometry) abstract thinking is an impediment; for the theorems of geometry, proved in an artificial way, do not let us perceive the truth of their assertions immediately. This is also true of logic:

> Although it might be said that logic is related to rational thinking as thorough-bass is to music, and also as ethics is to virtue, if we take it less precisely, or as aesthetics is to art, it must be borne in mind that no one ever became an artist by studying aesthetics, that a noble character was never formed by a study of ethics, that men composed correctly and beautifully before Rameau, and that we do not need to be masters of thorough-bass in order to detect discords . . . [Logic] . . . is merely knowing in the abstract what everyone knows in the concrete.[37]

Rational knowledge indeed 'has its greatest value in its communicability'.[38] But 'when one man alone is supposed to execute something in an uninterrupted course of action, rational knowledge, the application of reason, reflection, may often be even a hindrance to him'.[39] Reflection makes behaviour uncertain, and its ability to discriminate between tiny shades of difference is significantly weaker than that of practical intuition. The application of reason, Schopenhauer concedes, 'is necessary for the pursuit of a virtuous way of living'. But 'its function is a subordinate one; to preserve resolutions once formed, to provide maxims for withstanding the weakness of the moment, and to give consistency to conduct'.[40]

Now, it is not only the views of Schopenhauer and Oakeshott that appear similar, but also possible (and actual) misconceptions that these views provoke. The most likely misconception is that this approach replaces reason with some irrational intuition. The answer to this misconception is identical in both cases: neither Oakeshott nor Schopenhauer postulates here some supernatural intuitive insight. Schopenhauer's philosophy includes, of course, the possibility of super-sensual intuition (rejected by Oakeshott). But it is related to a completely different subject: that of aesthetic contemplation providing access to Ideas.[41] Here, in the realm of actual phenomenal perception, nothing is truly 'intuitive' in that sublime mysterious sense. Practical knowledge is no less certain and true in the ordinary sense than reflective knowledge. It is just that our conceptual reflection is never so finely tuned as to be capable of encompassing the totality of details required for correct practical judgement. Our practical habits are simply a better guide when nuanced discrimination is required.

STATE AND HUMAN ASSOCIATION

The third major theme of Oakeshott's philosophy is his view of the state and human association. In this respect, Oakeshott's thought can be roughly divided into two periods: one includes his writings on politics up until the mid 1950s; the other starts with the essay 'On Being Conservative' and culminates in *On Human Conduct* (1975).

Before the mid 1950s Oakeshott tackled the notion of the state from a broadly Hegelian perspective. He subscribed to the general vision of British Idealism and advocated transcending usual dichotomies such as society versus individual, freedom versus authority and so on. Each of these terms taken separately was, for him, just an abstraction from the 'concrete' (in the Hegelian sense) whole. For this reason he expressed uneasiness with methodological individualism, for example.[42]

This yearning for the concrete 'third' found its expression in Oakeshott's triadic vision of the history of European political thought. In the 'Introduction' to Hobbes's *Leviathan*, he distinguished between three traditions – Reason and Nature (exemplified by Plato); Will and Artifice (Hobbes); and the third, whose most outstanding representative was Hegel, that of Rational Will.[43] The followers of this third tradition, Oakeshott remarked, 'may be excused the belief that in it the truths of the first two traditions are fulfilled and their errors find a happy release'.[44] It appears that at the time when Oakeshott was writing this introduction (1946) he regarded himself as standing close to this synthesizing tradition, despite his growing interest in Hobbes.

A less familiar application of this pattern of thought can be found in Oakeshott's *Lectures in the History of Political Thought*. There he distinguished between three possible views of the bond that ties the members of a modern European state. On the one hand, the state could be and was perceived as an entity that gives expression to the 'natural' ties between its citizens, exemplified, for example, by kinship. On the other hand, it could be and was seen as an artificial collectivity based on contract. Yet a third interpretation is also possible, in which the state is 'neither "natural" nor "artificial"; neither "necessary" nor "designed"'.[45] It is an historical association: more contingent than a natural community, but at the same time more substantial than a joint stock company.[46] The members of this association are united by 'the experience of living together which they have enjoyed over the years'.[47]

Like the tradition of Rational Will in respect of the two other traditions, the 'historical' conception of the state is the most recent of the three conceptions, having emerged in European thought 'only with great difficulty'. Among those who first explored it, Oakeshott names Vico, Ferguson, Hume and Burke and also 'several German writers – Herder, Savigny, and Hegel, for example'.[48] There is indeed a very clear indebtedness to the German intellectual tradition in Oakeshott's conceptualization of the separate category of 'historical', for it was the German humanities of the nineteenth century that were especially prone to proclaiming themselves as governed by the category of 'historical', developing, for example, the 'historical' approach to law, economics or other disciplines.

To what extent Oakeshott himself subscribed to this third conception of the state is difficult to say. He certainly sympathized with it. Yet the *Lectures* were given during the 1960s, and at that time Oakeshott was already labouring on producing his own theory of human association. The *Lectures* themselves contain some rudiments of what was to be elaborated on in *On Human Conduct*. Oakeshott's ideas in this period differ in content and form from those marking his earlier triadic vision. They are characterized by the dichotomous (rather than triadic) exposition, by a less qualified acceptance of individualism and by a stronger influence of Hobbes.

It is important, of course, to be aware that the distinction between the two periods in Oakeshott's social thought is not absolute. One should speak about a tendency and change in emphasis rather than a clear-cut break. Oakeshott's earlier writings already contain some germs of his later individualism, whereas his later writings do occasionally employ his initial Hegelian idiom. On the whole, however, the change is undeniable.

While it is readily accepted that Oakeshott's earlier Idealist writings are heavily influenced by German social and political philosophy, German influences on the theory outlined in *On Human Conduct* are rarely acknowledged. Even though Oakeshott provides in it an extensive interpretation of Hegel as a theorist of civil association, this interpretation bears strong liberal or even libertarian overtones, which fit in more easily when the overall context of Oakeshott's theory is seen as Anglo-American. Yet I believe it is impossible to realize the significance of *On Human Conduct* unless this work is acknowledged as a sort of dialogue with the theorists of society of nineteenth-century Germany. First, Oakeshott's choice of perspective and his style point to that direction. One could consider his emphasis on the categories of 'state' and 'association', his legalistic rhetoric and his Latinisms (such as *universitas*), all of which draw on the tradition of German legal and social philosophy, represented, for example, by Otto von Gierke[49] and Ferdinand Tönnies. But even more importantly, the fundamental vision of Oakeshott's volume can be understood only when this work is juxtaposed with those theories. To show why this is so, I will briefly recapitulate the argument I developed elsewhere regarding the parallels and differences between Tönnies and Oakeshott.[50]

Tönnies famously distinguished between 'community' (*Gemeinschaft*) and 'society' (*Gesellschaft*).[51] He conceived of them not as two separately existing kinds of human organization, but rather as ideal types found in different degrees in every society. Yet he also believed that in general the historical process leads away from a society in which the *Gemeinschaft* elements are predominant towards the one in which the *Gesellschaft* elements enjoy preeminence. Modern society, in his view, is mainly a *Gesellschaft* containing islands of *Gemeinschaft*.

The main difference between the two is this: *Gemeinschaft* is a natural organic association, based on the concord of wills between its members; *Gesellschaft*, on the contrary, is a mechanical collection of separate individuals rationalistically pursuing their ends. The distinction between the two is based on the distinction between two modes of life and conduct predominant among their members, or (in Tönnies's language) two kinds of will. Tönnies conceived of the human being as an organic entity whose life should constitute harmonic process. Thinking is the crown of this process; nevertheless, it is only one aspect of the totality of life. The aspect of thinking should therefore be subservient to life as a whole. This characterizes life in *Gemeinschaft*, where the harmonic totality of one's own life is naturally immersed in the harmonic interrelationship of the 'natural' wills of its members.

It happens, however, that, when the rational element of human will reaches a certain degree of sophistication, it is no longer prepared to tolerate its relative dependence on the whole. Rather, it detaches itself from the whole of the personality and, aware of its intrinsic intellectual superiority, tries to dictate to conduct its own terms. It formulates goals to achieve, the means to achieve them, and then instigates the activity required for achieving them. *Gesellschaft* is an association of such purpose-minded rationalistic individuals.

Tönnies considered this latter type of will and the type of society associated with it – *Gesellschaft* – as overturning the proper order of conduct. Consequently, it continuously falls into inner discord. The emancipation achieved through the liberation of *ratio* turns out to be illusive, for it imposes the tyranny of abstract purpose, to the achievement of which the whole conduct is dedicated. The natural stream of life, by contrast, is unburdened by any such abstractly formulated purpose; it is more flexible, more susceptible to nuances, and thus more truly free. Hence, Tönnies's critique of the modern individualistic society. As an artificial *Gesellschaft* it precludes the possibility of harmonic existence. Being governed by the rationality of purpose(s), it presupposes discord. The rationality of purpose promises absolute autonomy to everyone; yet society composed of rational individuals is always under the shadow of absolute dictate, for the purpose of the association can never be fully reconciled with the sum of the individual purposes of its members.

An important point to notice here is that Tönnies considered *Gesellschaft* as *one* type, which constantly vacillates between two poles: freedom and tyranny. Herein lies the significance of Oakeshott's theory, which basically suggests that these two poles account for two different *kinds* of *Gesellschaft* (though, of course, he does not use this term). Oakeshott shares Tönnies's interpretation of European history, considering the dissolution of 'the morality of communal ties'[52] and its gradual replacement with a more individualistic arrangement as one of the central aspects of the transformation of the medieval world into the modern one. Or, one could say, this was a transformation from *Gemeinschaft* to *Gesellschaft*. Yet Oakeshott conceives of not one but two types of *Gesellschaft*: civil association and enterprise association. Both are products of modern times; both are essentially 'rational'; both suit the modern personality driven out of the cosiness of communal warmth. Yet they reflect two opposing attitudes to the modern state. There are people who perceive the modern opportunity to develop one's own individuality as a burden. To them, enterprise association appears to be a refuge, since it offers them a shared purpose. There are, however, others who embrace the possibilities offered by this condition whole-heartedly, and it is they who are apt to consider the state in which they live in terms of civil association: association with no common purpose but with a common system of law.

Tönnies would not allow for this last option. The reason is that, for him, individualism, rationality and purposiveness were intrinsically linked: an autonomous individual is someone whose mind is emancipated, and the sign of this emancipation is the ability to formulate purposes for oneself. Any *Gesellschaft* therefore must be an enterprise association. Oakeshott, by contrast, thinks that an association (and the kind of conduct upholding it) can be rational without being 'purposive'. This rationality finds its expression in subscription to the explicitly formulated non-purposive rules of civil association. And if this is so, then life in the modern *Gesellschaft* does not need to lead to discord and the loss of individual integrity; on the contrary, civil association is a truly emancipatory type of human organization.

CONCLUSION

I hope that I have sufficiently demonstrated that Oakeshott's thought owes much to German philosophy. I would like to conclude this chapter by explaining what, in my opinion, makes this fact extremely important for the proper appreciation of Oakeshott's ideas.

I believe that considering Oakeshott in the context of German philosophy does not merely reveal the sources of many of his ideas. Rather, it helps us to understand the driving passion of his vision. The fundamental feature of German intellectual life of the late nineteenth and early twentieth centuries was its ambivalent disposition towards modernity, which occasionally led to cultural pessimism. Two aspects of modern life appeared especially disturbing to German thinkers: the loss of an integrated world view, and the growing rationalization and individualization of society. This does not mean that these two features were always interpreted negatively. Yet they rarely provoked unambiguous acceptance. Moreover, it was often believed that these problems are intrinsic to modernity, and therefore they cannot be solved by incremental adjustments. Rather, if one looked for a solution, it had to be (at least, philosophically) utopian and revolutionary. Hence the philosophical radicalism of 'life-philosophy'.

These three motives (lack of unity, rationalization, and 'life'), played major roles in Oakeshott's philosophy. And if one can properly assess what their roles were, one can understand where Oakeshott stood vis-à-vis German thought, and what message he wanted to transmit.

We have seen that Oakeshott started his intellectual career by adopting a kind of rhetoric that is clearly recognizable as belonging to 'life-philosophy'. For him, 'life-philosophy' was not the result of a long and painful search for redemption, but something that he adopted almost instinctively. It just was in the air, it was fashionable. Yet he soon abandoned the main tenets of this teaching, even if some parts of it survived until the 1950s. Instead, he began to organize his thought around two other motives: the lack of unity, and rationalization/individualization.

But why did he abandon 'life-philosophy', which offered an answer to these two motives? In my view, the reason is that he came to the conclusion that plurality and rational association do not need an answer; that they are their own answer. In other words, he stopped seeing them as a problem. And this is what distinguishes him from the mainstream German intellectual tradition. He shares its view that modernity entails the plurality of cultural spheres and individualism. But he does not share its fear that this brings unhappiness. The radicalism of Oakeshott's approach is that he turns radical plurality and radical individualism into an opportunity for enjoyment. Therefore, whereas for German philosophy and sociology the basic question was how the modern condition can be superseded, or at least modified, for Oakeshott it was: how can modernity be maintained and enjoyed? The German context reveals Oakeshott as one of the most important advocates of modernity in twentieth-century philosophy.

NOTES

1 M. Oakeshott, 'An Essay on the Relations of Philosophy, Poetry and Reality', in *WH*, pp. 114–15.
2 *EM*, p. 6.
3 On this point, see also Chapter 6 above.
4 See my unpublished draft '*Bildung*: A Tradition in Crisis'.
5 See M. Oakeshott, 'The Voice of Poetry in the Conversation of Mankind', in *RP*, pp. 218–19; M. Oakeshott, 'Talking Politics', in *RP* [1991], p. 460.
6 A. Schopenhauer, *The World as Will and Representation*, 2 vols., trans. E. F. J. Payne (New York: Dover Publications, 1966), vol. I, ch. 22, p. 127.
7 *Ibid.*, p. 128.
8 *Ibid.*
9 *Ibid.*, p. 129.
10 *Ibid.*, p. 130.
11 G. Simmel, *The View of Life: Four Metaphysical Essays with Journal Aphorisms*, trans. J. A. Y. Andrews and D. N. Levine (University of Chicago Press, 2010), p. 20.
12 *Ibid.*, p. 21.
13 See M. Oakeshott, notebook 12, in *NL*, forthcoming. I analysed numerous parallels between Simmel and Oakeshott in E. Podoksik, 'Ethics and the Conduct of Life in the Old Georg Simmel and the Young Michael Oakeshott', *Simmel Studies*, 17 (2007), 197–221; 'From Differentiation to Fragmentation: Oakeshott, Simmel and Worlds of Experience', in M. Henkel and O. Lembcke (eds.), *Vernunft und Ethik im politischen Denken Michael Oakeshotts* (Darmstadt: Wissenschaftliche Buchgesellschaft, forthcoming). On Simmel's and Oakeshott's philosophies of religion, see also E. Corey, 'Religion and the Mode of Practice in Michael Oakeshott', *Zygon*, 44 (2009), 144–6.

14 Oakeshott, 'Voice of Poetry', p. 197; cf. M. Oakeshott, 'The Activity of Being an Historian', in *RP*, pp. 137–8.
15 For example M. Weber, 'Religious Rejections of the World and their Directions', in H. H. Gerth and C. W. Mills (eds.), *From Max Weber: Essays in Sociology* (London: Routledge, 1991), pp. 323–59.
16 See *EM*, p. 282n; Oakeshott, 'Activity of Being an Historian', p. 72; M. Oakeshott, 'The Study of "Politics" in the University', in *RP*, p. 314.
17 H. Rickert, *Kant als Philosoph der modernen Kultur* (Tübingen: J. C. B. Mohr, 1924), p. 110.
18 For example A. Sullivan, *Intimations Pursued: The Voice of Practice in the Conversation of Michael Oakeshott* (Thorverton: Imprint Academic, 2007).
19 S. E. Aschheim, *The Nietzsche Legacy in Germany: 1890–1990* (Berkeley: University of California Press, 1994).
20 See W. Dilthey, *Introduction to the Human Sciences*, trans. R. J. Betanzos (London: Harvester Wheatsheaf, 1988), p. 73.
21 See Oakeshott, 'Essay on the Relations of Philosophy, Poetry and Reality', pp. 114–15.
22 M. Oakeshott, 'Religion and the World', in *RPML*, p. 32.
23 *Ibid.*, p. 33.
24 *Ibid.*, pp. 33–4; italics the present author.
25 H. Rickert, *Die Philosophie des Lebens: Darstellung und Kritik der philosophischen Modeströmungen unserer Zeit* (Tübingen: J. C. B. Mohr, 1920).
26 On this point, see J. Liddington, 'Oakeshott's Temporal Solipsism', paper presented at the Michael Oakeshott Association inaugural conference, 3–5 September 2001, London School of Economics.
27 See Simmel, *View of Life*, pp. 99–154.
28 Compare G. Simmel, 'Das individuelle Gesetz', in *Georg Simmel Gesamtausgabe* (Frankfurt-on-Main: Suhrkamp, 2001), vol. XII, p. 438.
29 *EM*, p. 281.
30 For a more extended discussion of the parallels between Oakeshott and Simmel in this aspect, see Podoksik, 'Ethics and the Conduct of Life in the Old Georg Simmel and the Young Michael Oakeshott'.
31 M. Oakeshott, 'Rationalism in Politics', in *RP*, pp. 1–36; M. Oakeshott, 'The Tower of Babel', in *RP*, pp. 59–79.
32 Oakeshott, 'Tower of Babel', pp. 76–7.
33 Compare A. Harnack, *Lehrbuch der Dogmengeschichte*, vol. I, *Die Entstehung des kirchlichen Dogmas* (Freiburg im Breigsau: J. C. B. Mohr, 1894), pp. 141–2, 156.
34 G. Ryle, 'Knowing How and Knowing That', *Proceedings of the Aristotelian Society*, 46 (1945), 1–16.

35 B. Magee, *Confessions of a Philosopher: A Personal Journey through Western Philosophy from Plato to Popper* (New York: Modern Library, 1999), p. 298. According to Magee, Ryle read Schopenhauer as a student but later forgot about him; writing his *Concept of Mind* (1949) fifty years later, he was unaware that he was repeating Schopenhauer.

36 Schopenhauer, *World as Will and Representation*, vol. I, ch. 9, p. 40.

37 *Ibid.*, vol. I, ch. 9, p. 45.

38 *Ibid.*, vol. I, ch. 12, p. 55.

39 *Ibid.*, vol. I, ch. 12, p. 56.

40 *Ibid.*, vol. I, ch. 12, p. 58.

41 Oakeshott, 'Voice of Poetry', pp. 218–19.

42 For example M. Oakeshott, review of J. D. Mabbott, *The State and the Citizen*, in *CPJ*, pp. 248–59.

43 M. Oakeshott, 'Introduction' [1946], in T. Hobbes, *Leviathan*, ed. M. Oakeshott (Oxford: Basil Blackwell, 1946), p. xii.

44 *Ibid.*

45 *LHPT*, p. 421.

46 *LHPT*, p. 423.

47 *LHPT*, p. 423.

48 *LHPT*, p. 423.

49 See M. Henkel, 'A Conservative Concept of Freedom: Otto von Gierke's "*Genossenschaftslehre*" and Oakeshott's Philosophy of Practice', in C. Abel (ed.), *The Meaning of Michael Oakeshott's Conservatism* (Thorverton: Imprint Academic, 2010), pp. 77–96.

50 E. Podoksik, 'Overcoming the Conservative Disposition: Oakeshott vs. Tönnies', *Political Studies*, 56 (2008), 857–80.

51 F. Tönnies, *Community and Civil Society*, trans. J. Harris and M. Hollis (Cambridge University Press, 2001).

52 *MPME*, pp. 19–20.

IAN TREGENZA

13 Oakeshott's contribution to Hobbes scholarship

INTRODUCTION

The figure of Thomas Hobbes held a special fascination for Michael Oakeshott. Over a period of about four decades from the 1930s to the 1970s Oakeshott wrote a series of essays and reviews on Hobbes that remains an important touchstone in the world of Hobbes scholarship. At first glance it might appear odd that Oakeshott the philosophical idealist and critic of rationalism would be attracted to a philosopher such as Hobbes, whose place in the formation of modern rationalism and materialism is the stuff of legend. The fact that this materialist/rationalist reading of Hobbes, to the extent that it is still maintained, is so only in a qualified form, is in no small part due to the work of Oakeshott and a few others, such as Leo Strauss, A. E. Taylor and Howard Warrender, who, in the middle years of the twentieth century overturned many of the traditional assumptions about Hobbes and set the modern Hobbes industry on its course.

One of the central features of this literature was the endeavour to uncover the unity that was believed to lie at the heart of Hobbes's thought. For all of their differences, Strauss, Warrender and Oakeshott offered readings of Hobbes that sought to bring together the disparate parts into a unified vision. For Oakeshott, this could be found by identifying the 'single passionate thought' which, like Ariadne's thread, ties the various parts together.[1] Specifically, this involved a certain understanding of the nature of philosophic thought in Hobbes, which, when appreciated, puts paid to some of

My thanks are due to Stephen Chavura for valuable comments on an early draft of this chapter.

the cruder materialistic readings of Hobbes, as well as enabling a proper account of Hobbes's individualism and in turn his theory of authority. In this chapter I will endeavour to establish these links, indicating how Oakeshott understood the connections between Hobbes's theory of knowledge, his conception of the individual and his theory of authority. While there are some important changes in Oakeshott's writings on Hobbes, there is also a basic continuity between these works. Elsewhere I have made the case that the changes ought to be understood in relation to broader developments in Oakeshott's political theory itself.[2] While I will discuss some of these changes and developments, my principal aim in this chapter is to present a broad synoptic account, indicating the logical connections between the different aspects of Oakeshott's reading of Hobbes.

Undoubtedly Oakeshott's two most substantial works on Hobbes are the 'Introduction' to Hobbes's *Leviathan*, first published in 1946, then revised and republished in the 1975 collection *Hobbes on Civil Association*, and 'The Moral Life in the Writings of Thomas Hobbes', which was delivered as a lecture in 1960.[3] But before considering these works in detail, it is worth making a few observations to set the context.

During the 1930s a renewal of interest in the writings of Hobbes was under way that saw a number of studies call into question some of the received images of Hobbes and his place in the history of philosophy. Oakeshott responded to this literature with two lengthy reviews, one which surveyed a selection of the current literature,[4] and one that was an appreciative but critical review of Leo Strauss's 1936 book on Hobbes.[5] In both of these reviews Oakeshott makes a number of claims that he would subsequently change or modify, yet he also lays down lines of interpretation that he would later pursue in greater detail. In general terms, he welcomed the new literature for the way it challenged some of the cruder stereotypes – Hobbes the materialist, egoist or apostle of fear – as well as resituating Hobbes in the history of thought. He praises, for instance, John Laird's (1934) work for emphasizing Hobbes's debt to late scholastic thought rather than to Bacon and the new experimental science, as well as Frithiof Brandt's detailed study (1928) of the development of Hobbes's conception of nature.[6] While welcoming these studies, Oakeshott also indicated that more work was yet to be done – 'the true nature of Hobbes's individualism has yet to find its expositor'.[7]

Holding out some promise in this regard was Leo Strauss's seminal *The Political Philosophy of Hobbes* (1936). Of all the works of this period, Oakeshott thought Strauss's was 'of the first importance' and he described it 'as the most original book on Hobbes which has appeared for many years'.[8] In this work Strauss famously made the case that Hobbes's political theory was not derived from his science but from a new moral attitude springing from fear of violent death. This new 'bourgeois' attitude, for Strauss, represented a decisive break with traditional political philosophy and is the basis, not only of liberalism but of all modern political thought. While Oakeshott thought there was much to be said for Strauss's rejection of any simple naturalistic reading of Hobbes, he was not convinced by Strauss's depiction of Hobbes's account of the individual, nor with his claim that Hobbes made a decisive break with previous political philosophy. Strauss underplays Hobbes's debt to the medieval tradition as well as to the revival of Epicureanism of the sixteenth and seventeenth centuries. I will return to Oakeshott's engagement with Strauss below, since there is not much doubt that Oakeshott absorbed many of Strauss's insights even as he sought to correct others.[9] The point to make here is that in these early reviews we can see the germ of Oakeshott's distinctive contribution to Hobbes scholarship. Some old unhelpful myths about Hobbes had been overturned, but there was more work to do to properly determine the nature of Hobbes's philosophical system, his conception of the individual, and his place in the history of thought.

CONTEXTS: PHILOSOPHICAL, MORAL, POLITICAL

In spirit (if not in detail) Oakeshott would follow Strauss in seeking to provide a broad synoptic account of Hobbes's thought and its place in the history of political philosophy. In his 1946 'Introduction' he would famously describe *Leviathan* as

> the greatest, perhaps the sole, masterpiece of political philosophy written in the English language. And the history of our civilization can provide only a few works of similar scope and achievement to set beside it. Consequently, it must be judged by none but the highest standards and must be considered only in the widest context.[10]

The context is nothing short of the history of western political philosophy. Political reflection, Oakeshott suggests, operates at different levels of abstraction, from the purely practical (the concern with means and ends), the doctrinal, to the philosophical. Political philosophy is a kind of reflection that has not been arrested or foreshortened at an earlier stage of development, but seeks to view political life in the *speculum universitatis*. It involves establishing 'the connections, in principle and in detail, directly or mediately, between politics and eternity'.[11] *Leviathan* is one of the few works that consistently reaches such heights, and in this respect it stands alongside Plato's *Republic*, Augustine's *City of God* and Hegel's *Philosophy of Right*.

However, the history of western political philosophy is not singular but contains three distinct sub-traditions, which Oakeshott labels 'Reason and Nature', 'Will and Artifice' and 'Rational Will'. The first of these finds its greatest exponent early on in the philosophy of Plato, but it runs through Aristotelianism and the natural law tradition. The second also has an ancient lineage stemming from Epicurus and Judaic-Christian conceptions of 'will and creation', through Roman legal ideas and Augustine. But it was reinvigorated in the late medieval period in the ideas of late scholastic nominalism:

> The displacement of Reason in favour of will and imagination and the emancipation of passion were slowly mediated changes in European thought that had gone far before Hobbes wrote ... and the greatness of Hobbes is not [*contra* Strauss] that he began a new tradition in this respect but that he constructed a political philosophy that reflected the changes in the European intellectual consciousness which had been pioneered chiefly by the theologians of the fifteenth and sixteenth centuries.[12]

Leviathan for Oakeshott is the great exemplar of this tradition of 'Will and Artifice'. The final tradition, 'Rational Will', is a relative latecomer – 'not appearing until the eighteenth century' – and it involves an historical synthesis of the first two traditions. Its greatest exponent is Hegel, and Oakeshott observes that 'its followers may be excused the belief that in it the truths of the first two traditions are fulfilled and their errors find a happy release'.[13] Here Oakeshott is repeating, though in a more detached form, a claim he had made in his earlier review of Strauss, that Hobbes 'never had a satisfactory or coherent theory of volition' and that the defects in Hobbes's theory of volition were only remedied in the 'Rational Will' tradition running through Rousseau, Hegel and Bosanquet.[14]

Oakeshott would not make such a bold criticism of Hobbes's individualism again, and indeed, he would come to view Hobbes's conception of the individual in positive terms and as the basis for a theory of civil association not unlike his own. This change is indicative of broader developments in Oakeshott's political theory itself, but the point to stress here is that Oakeshott's earlier writings on Hobbes bear the imprint of his Idealist inheritance. The tripartite conception of the history of political philosophy is Hegelian in inspiration and can be found in various forms in the work of many of the British Idealists.

In the early section of Oakeshott's other major contribution to Hobbes scholarship – 'The Moral Life' – we also find some consideration of context. Yet here the focus has shifted from a philosophical context that encompasses the entire history of political philosophy, where the distinction between past and present is of minor significance – the *speculum universitatis* – to a kind of historical explanation that concerns the moral and political experience of post-medieval Europe. Here he also employs a tripartite schema in which the three forms of the moral life are the 'morality of communal ties', the 'morality of individuality' and the 'morality of the common good'. Since the first of these lapsed with the gradual breaking up of the medieval order, the second and third 'idioms' of moral conduct are the crucial ones for understanding modern moral and political experience. They are also central to Oakeshott's account of the distinction between civil and enterprise association, which is given its consummate expression in the final essay of *On Human Conduct* (1975). Here individuality is an historic achievement that emerged with the breaking up of the tightly integrated communities of medieval Europe, 'and since the emergent character of Western Europe was one in which a feeling for individuality was becoming preeminent ... this unavoidably became for Hobbes, as it was for his contemporary moralists, the subject matter of moral reflection'.[15] For Oakeshott, Hobbes is said to be the master exponent of the morality of individuality and 'the first moralist of the modern world to take candid account of the current experience of individuality'.[16] The experience of individuality provoked a reaction in the form of the 'morality of the common good', where 'individuality is suppressed whenever it conflicts, not with the individuality of others, but with the interests of a "society" ... engaged in a single common enterprise'.[17]

Both these forms of the moral life gave rise to two specific understandings of authority in the modern state, namely, civil and enterprise association. The first is a legal and procedural conception of the state concerned to protect the experience of individuality, and the second, the morality of the common good, gave rise to the enterprise conception of the state. Whereas in his early work Oakeshott could criticize Hobbes from the perspective of the 'Rational Will' tradition, such criticism disappears and his later theory of civil association is intimately linked to the morality of individuality given an early and systematic articulation in the philosophy of Hobbes. Before exploring more closely the relationship between authority and individuality in Oakeshott's Hobbes, some discussion of Oakeshott's reading of Hobbes's philosophical system is in order.

THE SYSTEM

Having determined that the *philosophical* context for *Leviathan* is the tradition of 'Will and Artifice' that had undergone something of a revival in the centuries before Hobbes wrote, Oakeshott proceeds to outline Hobbes's philosophical system. This context is crucial for understanding the system, because on Oakeshott's reading Hobbes's philosophy owes little to the new experimental science and much to the late medieval nominalists and early modern fideists. Appreciating this goes part of the way to correcting the claim made in some readings that Hobbes's theory was ultimately a failure because the doctrine of materialism is at odds with his theory of political obligation. On this reading, 'The joints of the system are ill-matched, and what should have been a continuous argument, based on a philosophy of materialism, collapses under its own weight'.[18] For Oakeshott, this view stems from a misunderstanding of the nature of Hobbes's system, which is not to be thought of in terms of an architectural analogy where the materialistic foundation is made to support a theory of moral and political obligation. Rather, it is held together by a 'single passionate thought' or 'guiding clue' that involves 'the continuous application of a doctrine about the nature of philosophy'. Hobbes's philosophy, Oakeshott suggests, is like a mirror held up to the world so that what is seen is determined by the nature of the mirror itself. The philosophic mirror is the mirror of reason and its categories are cause and effect. Such a world is a circumscribed world or a world of material objects. This means that philosophy, as an inquiry into the relationship between such objects, is to be distinguished from theology or faith, empirical science and experience or sense.[19]

Philosophy, then, can only deal with those things that come within its domain, which therefore leaves to one side everything concerning matters of theology and faith. For Oakeshott, Hobbes 'denies, not the existence of these things, but their rationality'.[20] A contrast is also to be drawn between philosophy and science. Though, as Oakeshott points out, Hobbes tends to use the terms 'science' and 'philosophy' as synonyms owing to the fact that in the seventeenth century they had yet to be prized apart, nevertheless he well understood the important distinction between 'knowledge of things as they appear and enquiry into the fact of their appearing, between a knowledge (with all the necessary assumptions) of the phenomenal world and a theory of knowledge itself'.[21] Hobbes's concern with the latter distinguishes him from Bacon and the experimental work of the Royal Society and points the way to Locke and Kant. Moreover, when Hobbes describes the world in mechanistic terms it is not because he thought it was in fact a machine, but because this was a fitting analogy for considering the world of cause and effect. The machine analogy is generated by reasoning rather than observation. Hobbes is therefore, according to Oakeshott, 'a scholastic, not a "scientific" mechanist'.[22] Hobbes's philosophy, then, does not lie in any doctrine about the nature of the world but in his understanding of the nature of philosophical knowledge. And while humans as seen through this lens can be understood in mechanistic terms, it is inaccurate to find in Hobbes's thought the origins of anything like a science of politics or more generally a unified model of the natural and human sciences.[23] Later in his career Oakeshott would take this further (in a way that reflects the practice–process distinction outlined in *On Human Conduct*) and suggest that the predicament Hobbes 'is considering is uniquely human although the condition it generates is, in some respects, common to all moving bodies; it calls for an answer in terms of uniquely human conduct ... [which] has no counterpart in a universe composed of bodies characterized solely by inertial motion'.[24]

The final distinction to be noted is that between philosophy and experience. Hobbes famously begins *Leviathan* with the claim that all thought begins in sense experience – 'there is no conception in a man's mind, which hath not at first, totally, or by parts, been begotten upon the organs of sense'.[25] As senses accumulate they generate imagination (decaying sense) which gives rise to memory. This in turn produces prudence in the individual and history, a record of past events, in the life of society. Such experience can be considered 'absolute' since it deals with particulars or 'facts', but it is to be contrasted with philosophical knowledge, which is 'conditional' and concerned with universals. For Oakeshott, 'philosophical knowledge [in Hobbes] ... (because it is reasoned) is general and not particular, a knowledge of consequences and not of facts, and conditional and not absolute'.[26] Moreover, this science of universals is fundamentally a linguistic, creative act involving the fixing of names. 'From beginning to end,' Oakeshott claims, 'there is no suggestion in Hobbes that philosophy is anything other than conditional knowledge, knowledge of hypothetical generations and conclusions about the names of things, not about the nature of things.'[27] Or as Hobbes himself expressed it,

> No man can know by Discourse, that this, or that, is, has been, or will be; which is to know absolutely: but only, that if This be, That is; if This has been, That has been; if This shall be, That shall be: which is to know conditionally; and that not the consequence of one thing to another; but of one name of a thing, to another name of the same thing.[28]

This nominalist reading of Hobbes, where philosophical truth is both a product of the mind as well as distinct from other forms of knowledge, is not so far removed from Oakeshott's own particular form of Idealism, which famously distinguishes between different modes of experience. J. L. Auspitz aptly observed about Oakeshott's early work, *Experience and Its Modes*, that it 'reads as if William of Occam had undertaken to redo Hegel'.[29] This goes part of the way to explaining Oakeshott's attraction to a philosopher such as Hobbes. It would be a mistake to claim, however, that Oakeshott simply read his own philosophy into Hobbes. Indeed, Hobbes's early interpreters and critics made much of his nominalism and it formed a central part of the theological polemic against him.[30] Leibniz, for instance, observed that even 'Ockham himself was not more nominalistic than is Thomas Hobbes'.[31] This connection was lost sight of through the nineteenth century as Hobbes's apparently hedonistic individualism was read as laying the moral groundwork for utilitarianism. He was also believed to have been a forerunner of the attempt to build a unified model of the natural and human sciences. In more recent times the link between Hobbes and nominalism (and late scholastic thought more generally) has been re-established. The contextualist turn in the history of political thought is an important reason for this, but there is little doubt that Oakeshott's reading of Hobbes paved the way for much of the more recent recovery work. Integral to this nominalist, sceptical conception of knowledge is a thoroughgoing individualism, and alongside a determination to get Hobbes's philosophical system right, Oakeshott sought to provide a proper account of the Hobbesian individual.

INDIVIDUALISM: EPISTEMOLOGICAL AND MORAL

As outlined earlier, Oakeshott's early Hobbes writings, and most emphatically the 'Introduction', were concerned with establishing Hobbes's correct philosophical pedigree. This is the tradition of 'Will and Artifice' that flowered in the late medieval and early modern period. These two terms, will and artifice, are intimately connected. Both God and man are creatures of will rather than reason, and the human construction of both knowledge and political order, as Hobbes announces in the introduction to *Leviathan*, is akin to God's creation of the natural world. Furthermore, in Hobbes's system, according to Oakeshott, 'The human being is first fully an individual, not in respect of self-consciousness, but in the activity of willing ... [and Hobbes's] civil philosophy is based, not on any vague belief in the value or sanctity of the individual man, but on a philosophy for which the world is composed of *individuae substantiae*'.[32]

This insight enabled Oakeshott to break the link between Hobbes's individualism and psychological egoism, which tended to dominate nineteenth-century Hobbes studies.[33] Hobbes's apparent depiction of human will in hedonistic terms was thought to have led to utilitarianism and associationist psychology. Other British Idealists, such as Green, Bosanquet and Collingwood, all had Hobbes firmly pinned down as a hedonist and proto-utilitarian,[34] and as such Hobbes failed, it was claimed, to articulate a fully convincing theory of the will. Though as we have seen, in Oakeshott's early work there is a suggestion that Hobbes's theory of volition is inadequate, he does not base this judgement on a hedonistic reading of Hobbesian man. Rather, Hobbes's premise 'is a doctrine of solipsism, a belief in the essential isolation of men from one another, and expounded as a theory of knowledge ... when this genuine premise of Hobbes's argument is appreciated, the attribution to him of the doctrine of the essential selfishness of man is seen at once to be mistaken'.[35] This conception of the individual both generates the chaos of the state of nature but it also gives rise to a particular conception of civil authority where individuality is preserved. Moreover, the creation of civil order out of chaos is the political analogue of the philosopher's method of fixing names in order to construct philosophical truth. In both cases, the method resembles 'that of the creation'.[36]

As well as correcting the hedonistic reading, Oakeshott is also concerned to refute the popular view that Hobbes's individualism gave rise to a form of absolutism 'designed precisely to destroy individualism'.[37] Writing immediately after the Second World War, this criticism had a particular political edge since at this time the apparent connection between Hobbes and modern totalitarianism was often drawn.[38] But for Oakeshott, this misconception again arose from a failure to grasp the nature of Hobbes's conception of reasoning. According to Oakeshott,

> Hobbes is not an absolutist precisely because he is an authoritarian. His scepticism about the power of reasoning, which applied no less to the 'artificial reason' of the Sovereign than to the reasoning of the natural man, together with the rest of his individualism, separate him from the rationalist dictators of his or any age. Indeed, Hobbes, without being himself a liberal, had in him more of the philosophy of liberalism than most of its professed defenders ... *Autres temps, autres folies*: if Hobbes were living today he would find the universal predicament appearing in different particulars.[39]

Further refinement of Oakeshott's account of the Hobbesian individual is to be found in 'The Moral Life'. But as noted earlier, here the picture is slightly different owing to the different framework Oakeshott deploys. Hobbes is presented here as a theorist who generalizes the experience of individuality, which by the seventeenth century had profoundly affected the moral, political and intellectual life of European society. It is Hobbes's moral theory – his theory of human conduct – that overtakes the epistemological nominalism. Though there is substantial overlap between the two views and there is no 'break' from one picture to another, Hobbes is now presented as a moralist of *individuality* rather than a philosopher of *individualism*. In this essay and in a number of other works from the same period, Oakeshott is concerned with individuality as an historical experience that gave rise to a certain conception of political order – civil association – but that is a precarious achievement always threatened by the anti-individualist reaction it provoked. Certain readings of Hobbes – notably those of Strauss and Macpherson[40] – seem to carry the suggestion that his form of individualism is little more than a 'bourgeois' morality and that the true Hobbesian man is one concerned above all with safety, security and material comfort.

The problem here is not so much a failure to get the epistemology right, but a failure to strike the right balance between the competing elements of pride and fear in Hobbes's writings. Strauss had made the case that fundamental to Hobbes's new morality was a rejection of pride or aristocratic honour and its replacement with fear of violent death. Pride or vanity is the dangerous passion because it leads us to assert our misplaced sense of superiority even to the point of endangering our lives. Fear on the other hand is the great civilizing passion, as it enables us to see the human predicament without illusion. According to Strauss's reading, 'vanity is the force which makes men blind, fear is the force which makes men see'.[41] Fear is also the constructive passion that generates reason, pointing the way to a solution of the war of all against all.

Oakeshott acknowledged that Hobbes tended to talk in negative terms about pride and that he appealed to fear as the great motivating passion. But to focus solely on the passion of fear in Hobbes is to overlook a central ingredient in his moral theory. As early as 1935, Oakeshott welcomed the new research that demonstrated 'that Pride, and not Fear, is the master conception of his political philosophy'.[42] In 'The Moral Life' he would write that Hobbesian man's 'supreme and characteristic passion is Pride; he wishes above all else to be convinced of his own superiority'.[43] The desire to be first, to achieve eminence, is in large part wherein 'felicity' consists. Oakeshott describes this race for precedence in Hobbes in terms reminiscent of the struggle for recognition in Hegel's master–slave dialectic. Though in the state of nature men are enemies of each other, they nevertheless need each other – 'without others there is no recognition of superiority and therefore no noticeable felicity'.[44] Moreover, it is not death itself that is the *summum malum*, but violent death at the hands of a competitor in the race for precedence: 'desire is directed, not towards survival, but towards being first (and thus being "honoured" and meriting "honour"); and aversion is directed towards being dishonoured. This is what it is to be a man and not an animal'.[45]

Pride, however, must be tamed, since 'when a man is among men, pride is more dangerous and death more likely'.[46] The problem with pride is that it is volatile and all too easily descends into what Hobbes calls vainglory. Oakeshott thinks that Hobbes follows in the Augustinian tradition by recognizing 'the twofold meaning which the word [pride] has always carried'. The first, symbolized by Satan, involves the hubristic and delusory endeavour to usurp God and thereby take control of 'the world of men and things'. The second meaning of pride does not involve taking God's place, but merely imitating him. Here, according to Oakeshott, 'self love appears as self-knowledge and self-respect, the delusion of power over others is replaced by the reality of self-control, and the glory of the invulnerability which comes from courage generates magnanimity and magnanimity, peace'.[47] Hobbes, it seems, did not base his argument on such grounds because he realized that 'this is a generosity too rarely to be found to be presumed on, especially in pursuers of Wealth, Command or sensual pleasure; which are the greatest part of Mankind'.[48] On Oakeshott's reading, Hobbes downplayed pride and 'recalled man to his littleness'[49] because 'he felt constrained to write for those whose chief desire was to "prosper"', even though he 'understood human beings as creatures more properly concerned with honour than with either survival or prosperity'.[50]

On this reading, Hobbes is no defender of the 'bourgeois' morality that Strauss discerns, nor of the 'possessive individualism' of nascent capitalism as he appears in Macpherson's reading, nor even of the 'privatized' individual outlined by others such as Hannah Arendt and Sheldon Wolin.[51] The true Hobbesian ideal of individuality, Oakeshott suggests, is that of the self-reliant, magnanimous, almost heroic character who is contemptuous of injustice and has no need to 'prove' his superiority over others.

Oakeshott alludes to this idea of the aristocratic individual to circumvent a problem over which much ink has been subsequently spilt in the rational choice literature on Hobbes; namely, how is it possible for rational, fearful actors to move from the insecurity of the state of nature to the civil state? Or, to put it otherwise, why should any individual in the state of nature be the first to agree to a covenant when the conditions for 'mutual trust' have not been secured? Oakeshott suggests that while there might be many in the state of nature who succumb to 'avarice, ambition, and the like', there are, nevertheless, others who are prepared to take the risk and support the covenant in the reasonable hope or expectation that enough others will do the same. It is not necessary that all must always keep the terms of the covenant, but 'it is enough if enough may on any occasion be reasonably depended upon to endow by their willing obedience the sovereign with enough power to terrify into obedience those who on that occasion are not disposed to obey'.[52] At the end of 'The Moral Life' Oakeshott alludes to Hobbes's good friend Sidney Godolphin – a man of 'pride' rather than 'reason' – as the kind of character likely to make covenants stick and provide a way out of the state of nature.[53]

AUTHORITY AND CIVIL ASSOCIATION

When it comes to the issue of authority in Hobbes, Oakeshott is less interested in its cause or generation than in its structure. This is because it is not Hobbes's social contract that it is of central importance to Oakeshott, but the conception of authority that lies at the heart of Hobbes's theory of civil society, or, to use Oakeshott's preferred term, civil association.[54]

As with the theory of knowledge, and of the individual, Oakeshott from an early stage thought that Hobbes's theory of authority had not been given the treatment it deserved; it 'has suffered from its being isolated from the system of his thought'.[55] Though his early writings on authority drew on Idealist themes reminiscent of Green and

Bosanquet, Oakeshott never followed their claim that Hobbes's sovereign ruled merely by force – 'in a will which is actual, but not general', in Bosanquet's phrase.[56] Hobbes's conception of the need for civil authority, Oakeshott argued, stemmed not from a moral belief or from practical expediency but from the perception of the solipsistic predicament of man. In this respect it is of a piece with his belief that science begins by first of all fixing the meaning of names.[57]

In attempting to give a properly systematic account of Hobbes's theory of authority, Oakeshott recognizes a central difficulty that has plagued Hobbes scholars over the years. It is the problem of consistency, or whether there is in fact a unified moral and political theory in Hobbes at all. In keeping with most writers of his time, Hobbes uses terms such as 'obligation' in a variety of contexts and for different purposes. In some places Hobbes suggests that the laws of nature are hypothetical theorems of natural reason that show humans the way to peace. And since there is no 'obligation on any man, which ariseth not from some Act of his own'[58] such theorems do not become laws 'properly so-called' until they are authorized by the sovereign. This is the sense Oakeshott attributes to Hobbes.[59] At other times, however, Hobbes suggests that the 'Lawes of Nature are Immutable and Eternall',[60] and this has led some commentators, most notably Warrender, to the conclusion that they are authentic laws that oblige all men at all times. Even in the state of nature, such laws are obligatory. They can be suspended, but never invalidated, in conditions of insecurity. On this reading, 'the function of the sovereign is not to make valid a covenant that was previously invalid, but to prevent (by taking away subsequent causes of fear) what is already a valid covenant from becoming invalidated'.[61] Warrender makes the claim that despite his undoubted novelty, 'Hobbes is basically a natural law philosopher'.[62] If this reading is correct, then Hobbes could more appropriately be considered a representative of Oakeshott's tradition of 'Reason and Nature'.

The disagreement between Warrender, Oakeshott and, indeed, Strauss is emblematic of the difficulties interpreters face when trying to extract a consistent theory of obligation from Hobbes's writings. As Oakeshott points out in 'The Moral Life', there are many discrepancies in Hobbes's theory that cannot be put aside. Based on various key passages in Hobbes, Warrender has shown the possibility of extracting a plausible natural law reading of Hobbes at variance with both the traditional reading that views Hobbes's argument solely in terms of self-interest, and the particular moral theory that Oakeshott discerns.

Though Oakeshott and Warrender have different readings of the status of natural law in Hobbes's writings, they are nevertheless in agreement that there is a genuine moral theory to be discerned, and consequently, civil association does not involve the simple conflation of authority and power. Moreover, Oakeshott's reading of Hobbes's theory of authority was refined through his engagement with Warrender's work. In an appendix to *The Political Philosophy of Hobbes* (1957), Warrender criticized Oakeshott's reading of Hobbes's theory of authority on certain points.[63] Oakeshott's response to these criticisms can be seen both in the extensive treatment of Hobbes's moral theory in 'The Moral Life', where Warrender's reading receives considerable attention, as well as in the subsequent revision to the section on obligation in the 1975 version of the 'Introduction' to *Leviathan*.[64] Not only are these changes a response to the criticisms of Warrender, and perhaps J. M. Brown,[65] they can also be understood in terms of Oakeshott's own emerging theory of civil association, which comes to converge with some of the themes contained in his Hobbes writings. I have discussed these alterations at length elsewhere,[66] so here I will briefly mention one important element.

In the first version of the 'Introduction' Oakeshott identified four senses of obligation in Hobbes – physical, rational, moral and political – each arising from a different motivation. The fourth sense, political, is not a separate category but involves a combination of the first three.

> Civil society is a complex of authority and power in which each element creates its own appropriate obligation. There is the moral obligation to obey the authorised will of the Sovereign; there is the external physical obligation arising from force or power; and there is the internal rational obligation of self-interest arising from fear of punishment and desire of peace.[67]

Warrender rejected Oakeshott's fourfold account of obligation, suggesting that only two of them can be found in Hobbes. The first is physical obligation, which Warrender thinks is to be understood metaphorically, and the second is moral obligation. For Warrender, political obligation is not a new type of obligation but is simply a short expression for the citizens' duty to obey civil laws. Moreover, Oakeshott's rational or pre-civil obligation does not accommodate Hobbes's crucial distinction between obligation *in foro interno* and *in foro externo*. On Oakeshott's original reading, in the state of nature the laws of natural reason, since they are theorems, or pieces of prudential advice, 'oblige merely *in foro interno*'.[68] For Warrender, as mentioned above, the laws of nature are obligatory in both the 'internal' as well as the 'external court', even though in conditions of insecurity they might be suspended. Brown also presses the criticism against Oakeshott that in trying to create a moral obligation where none formerly existed he distorts Hobbes's intended meaning that the laws of nature are commanded by God and on that account are morally compelling.[69]

In both 'The Moral Life' as well as the revised version of the 'Introduction' the distinctions between physical, rational, moral and political obligation are discarded and replaced by moral and civil obligation. Whereas in the original version of the 'Introduction' Oakeshott claimed that a covenant only becomes morally obligatory 'if and when the Sovereign authority commands its observation',[70] he now claims that there are genuine moral obligations in the state of nature. In situations of insecurity the laws of natural reason can still not be considered laws in the proper sense, as per Warrender's account, but nevertheless the covenants that these laws lead us to make are 'examples of pure but imperfect "moral" obligation'.[71] Not only is this an important change in Oakeshott's reading of Hobbes, it is also very close to the argument developed in *On Human Conduct*, where civil association is understood to be a particular kind of moral practice.

Oakeshott does not think that these tensions in Hobbes were the product of mere confusion. Rather, he invokes the distinction made famous by Strauss between exoteric and esoteric knowledge. Briefly, Strauss suggested that a great many political philosophers disguise their true or esoteric doctrine behind a public or exoteric teaching in order to avoid the kind of persecution that the promulgation of dangerous, sceptical ideas invariably arouses. Understanding the great works of political philosophy involves knowing how to read the concealed message between the lines.[72] Oakeshott wants to make the case that the discrepancies in Hobbes arise from his strategy of 'artful equivocation', where one moral theory – that which Oakeshott believes to be the most authentically Hobbesian – was directed to the initiated 'whose heads were strong enough to withstand the giddiness provoked by his scepticism', and the other moral theory, couched in a traditional natural law vocabulary of duties and rights, was addressed to the ordinary man.[73] While there is little doubt that Oakeshott is alluding to Strauss, this insight about Hobbes's audience(s) could also be seen as pointing the way to a theme that has been widely treated in much of the recent work on Hobbes's rhetoric.[74]

Before concluding with some remarks on the legacy of Oakeshott's reading for Hobbes scholarship, it should be noted that Oakeshott's engagement with Hobbes went beyond a straightforward philosophical or historical interest in his work. On more than one occasion he would observe that *Leviathan* is nothing short of a retelling of the underlying Pauline and Augustinian myth of western civilization. Where most of us are passive participants in the 'collective dream' that constitutes our civilization, occasionally great artists or philosophers, those 'whose work reaches the level of literature', come along who reimagine the dream and give it a new impetus. In such a work 'we shall be reminded of the common dream that binds the generations together, and the myth will be made more intelligible to us'.[75] For Oakeshott, *Leviathan* is a work of such grandeur. It is,

> like any masterpiece ... an end and a beginning: it is the flowering of the past and the seed-box of the future. Its importance is that it is the first great achievement in the long-projected attempt of European thought to reembody in a new myth the Augustinian epic of the Fall and Salvation of mankind.[76]

But whereas the older version of the myth tended to exalt man by pointing to his original fellowship with God, *Leviathan* 'recalls man to his littleness, his imperfection, his mortality, while at the same time recognizing his importance to himself'.[77]

THE LEGACY

As mentioned at the outset, Oakeshott was one of a handful of mid-twentieth-century interpreters who laid the groundwork for the explosion of Hobbes scholarship of the past three to four decades. One of the notable features of the scholarship over this time is its increasing fragmentation. While Oakeshott was aware of the tensions and ambiguities in Hobbes, he nevertheless sought, like Strauss and Warrender, to disclose the unity that he believed a close reading of Hobbes's work could yield. There is much less conviction today that Hobbes's thought contains such unity, and this (along with the specialization that is probably the inevitable corollary of the professionalization of the political theory community) is reflected in the tendency of scholars to focus on isolated aspects of Hobbes's thought in lieu of a reading of the whole.[78]

Despite this broad shift in scholarly approaches to Hobbes, Oakeshott's legacy – understood either in terms of direct influence or simply as opening up lines of interpretation that have been pursued in greater detail by others – is considerable. Oakeshott's brief but suggestive observations on Hobbes's debt to late medieval nominalism and early modern scepticism have been explored in numerous historical works. One of the best such examples is Richard Tuck's demonstration that Hobbes's civil science incorporates at the same time as it attempts to transcend the pervasive scepticism that shaped the European consciousness in the late sixteenth and early seventeenth centuries.[79] Other studies that emphasize Hobbes's modal conception of knowledge deriving from his nominalism include Conal Condren's *Thomas Hobbes* (2000) and, in relation to Hobbes's theology, Arrigo Pacchi's essay 'Hobbes and the Problem of God' (1988).

One of the hallmarks of Oakeshott's reading of Hobbes is the individualism, which, as we have seen, has an epistemological as well as a moral dimension. W. H. Greenleaf[80] made the case some time ago that Hobbes scholarship could be broken into three broad camps: the traditional (based on a materialistic/scientistic reading); the individualist; and the natural law. Oakeshott, along with Strauss and John Watkins, were said to be the foremost examples of the individualist reading of Hobbes. The important connections and differences between Oakeshott's and Strauss's view of the Hobbesian individual have been referred to. Watkins's work is also worth mentioning, as it develops a reading of Hobbes's individualism and its relation to political obligation that owes much to Oakeshott.[81] Patrick Riley's work *Will and Political Legitimacy* (1982) likewise contains an interpretation of Hobbes's theory of authority inspired by Oakeshott. An explicit defence of Oakeshott's reading of Hobbes's moral conception of the individual can be found in Alan Ryan's essay 'Hobbes and Individualism' (1988), while Gabriella Slomp's *Thomas Hobbes and the Political Philosophy of Glory* (2000) discusses in great detail the important role of pride in Hobbes's writings, which, as has been noted, is an important feature of Oakeshott's account. But of all the contemporary works on Hobbes conveying both the spirit and much of the detail of Oakeshott's reading, none offers a better example than Richard Flathman's *Thomas Hobbes: Skepticism, Individuality and Chastened Politics* (1993). Flathman's approach to Hobbes, which contains both philosophical interpretation as much as appropriation, is thoroughly Oakeshottian in inspiration and is an important source of his own distinctive brand of voluntarist liberalism.[82]

These works constitute a small sample of studies indicating the influence of Oakeshott on Hobbes scholarship. To do this full justice, however, one would have to look in much greater detail at the whole topic of the connection between Hobbes and liberalism, which has been one important strand of Hobbes scholarship since the nineteenth century, but which Oakeshott did so much to consolidate. It has been claimed, for instance, that Oakeshott was engaged in a project of 'sanitizing' Hobbes's fundamentally 'despotical' doctrine.[83] It is certainly the case that Oakeshott's reading is highly creative and that certain features of Hobbes's thought are emphasized and others – notably the utilitarian, the scientistic, perhaps even the 'despotical' – are minimized, reinterpreted or ignored. Hence I have made the case elsewhere that to see Oakeshott's reading in its brilliant complexity involves situating it in terms of his broader philosophical vision.[84] Viewed from this perspective, we can see that what Oakeshott was doing in constructing a certain reading of the past to pursue his own philosophical and political agenda is something that political philosophers have always done, and none more effectively than Hobbes himself.

NOTES

1 M. Oakeshott, 'Introduction to *Leviathan*' [1975], in *HCA*, p. 16.
2 I. Tregenza, *Michael Oakeshott on Hobbes: A Study in the Renewal of Philosophical Ideas* (Thorverton: Imprint Academic, 2003). I will be drawing on this work as well as on my earlier article, 'The Life of

Hobbes in the Writings of Michael Oakeshott', *History of Political Thought*, 18 (1997), 531–57.

3 The 'Moral Life in the Writings of Thomas Hobbes' was first published in the 1962 edition of *RP*. It was republished in *HCA*. I will refer to the 1962 edition.

4 M. Oakeshott, 'Thomas Hobbes', in *CPJ*, pp. 110–21.

5 M. Oakeshott, 'Dr Leo Strauss on Hobbes', reprinted in *HCA*, pp. 132–49.

6 J. Laird, *Hobbes* (London: Benn, 1934); F. Brandt, *Thomas Hobbes' Mechanical Conception of Nature* (Copenhagen: Levin & Munksgaard, 1928).

7 Oakeshott, 'Thomas Hobbes', p. 117.

8 Oakeshott, 'Dr Leo Strauss on Hobbes', p. 133.

9 See J. Boyd, 'The Lion and the Ox: Oakeshott's Engagement with Leo Strauss on Hobbes', *History of Political Thought*, 29 (2008), 690–716.

10 Oakeshott, 'Introduction to *Leviathan*', p. 3.

11 *Ibid.*, p. 5.

12 *Ibid.*, p. 58.

13 *Ibid.*, p. 7.

14 Oakeshott, 'Dr Leo Strauss on Hobbes', pp. 147–8.

15 Oakeshott, 'Moral Life', pp. 250–1.

16 M. Oakeshott, 'The Masses in Representative Democracy', in *RP* [1991], p. 367.

17 Oakeshott, 'Moral Life', p. 250.

18 Oakeshott, 'Introduction to *Leviathan*', p. 15.

19 *Ibid.*, p. 17.

20 *Ibid.*

21 *Ibid.*, p. 19.

22 *Ibid.*, p. 18.

23 *Ibid.*, p. 20.

24 M. Oakeshott, 'Logos and Telos', in *RP* [1991], pp. 357–8.

25 T. Hobbes, *Leviathan*, ed. M. Oakeshott (Oxford: Blackwell, 1946), p. 7.

26 Oakeshott, 'Introduction to *Leviathan*', pp. 21–2.

27 *Ibid.*, p. 25.

28 Hobbes, *Leviathan*, p. 40.

29 J. L. Auspitz, 'Individuality, Civility, and Theory: The Philosophical Imagination of Michael Oakeshott', *Political Theory*, 4 (1976), 288.

30 See M. Goldie, 'The Reception of Hobbes', in J. H. Burns and M. Goldie (eds.), *The Cambridge History of Political Thought 1450–1700* (Cambridge University Press, 1991), pp. 589–615.

31 Leibniz, cited *ibid.*, p. 593.

32 Oakeshott, 'Introduction to *Leviathan*', p. 60.

33 M. Francis, 'The Nineteenth-Century Theory of Sovereignty and Thomas Hobbes', *History of Political Thought*, 1 (1980), 517–40.
34 For further discussion of Oakeshott's departure from other Idealists on this matter, see Tregenza, *Michael Oakeshott on Hobbes*, pp. 55–62. For Collingwood's reading of Hobbes, see D. Boucher, *The Social and Political Thought of R. G. Collingwood* (Cambridge University Press, 1989), ch. 3.
35 Oakeshott, 'Thomas Hobbes', p. 120.
36 T. Hobbes, *De Corpore*, Author's Epistle to the Reader, in *The English Works of Thomas Hobbes* (London: J. Bohn, 1839), vol. I, p. xiii.
37 Oakeshott, 'Introduction to *Leviathan*', p. 62.
38 A. D. Lindsay, for instance, wrote that Hobbes was 'the first totalitarian philosopher', *The Modern Democratic State* (Oxford University Press, 1943), p. 81. Compare also Hannah Arendt's treatment of Hobbes in *The Origins of Totalitarianism* [1951] (New York: Harcourt Brace Jovanovich, 1973), pp. 139–47.
39 Oakeshott, 'Introduction to *Leviathan*', pp. 63–4.
40 Oakeshott clearly had Strauss in mind in this essay, but the criticisms extend to Macpherson's 'possessive individualist' Hobbes, who makes his appearance in 1962, in C. B. Macpherson, *The Political Theory of Possessive Individualism: Hobbes to Locke* (London: Clarendon Press, 1962). Compare Oakeshott's dismissive comment in *HC*, p. 242n.
41 L. Strauss, *The Political Philosophy of Hobbes: Its Basis and its Genesis* [1936] (University of Chicago Press, 1952), p. 130.
42 Oakeshott, 'Thomas Hobbes', p. 117.
43 Oakeshott, 'Moral Life', p. 254.
44 Oakeshott, 'Introduction to *Leviathan*', p. 36. This comes from a paragraph added to the revised version of the 'Introduction'.
45 M. Oakeshott, 'Letter on Hobbes', *Political Theory*, 29 (2001), 834–5. Strauss also invokes Hegel in his discussion of fear of violent death as the elementary form of self-consciousness in Hobbes. See Strauss, *Political Philosophy of Hobbes*, pp. 57–8.
46 Oakeshott, 'Introduction to *Leviathan*', p. 35.
47 Oakeshott, 'Moral Life', p. 291.
48 Hobbes, *Leviathan*, p. 92; Oakeshott, 'Moral Life', p. 291.
49 M. Oakeshott, '*Leviathan*: A Myth', in *HCA*, p. 154.
50 Oakeshott, 'Moral Life', p. 294.
51 For a defence of Oakeshott's reading of Hobbesian man, see A. Ryan, 'Hobbes and Individualism', in G. A. J. Rogers and A. Ryan (eds.), *Perspectives on Thomas Hobbes* (Oxford: Clarendon Press, 1988), pp. 81–105.
52 Oakeshott, 'Moral Life', pp. 298–9.

53 *Ibid.*, pp. 299–300. Historical works that provide some support for the kind of 'prideful' or aristocrat individual that Oakeshott sees in Hobbes's writings (as opposed to the rational, bourgeois calculators implied by Strauss and Macpherson) can be found in I. Coltman, *Private Men and Public Causes: Philosophy and Politics in the English Civil War* (London: Faber & Faber, 1962), and K. Thomas, 'The Social Origins of Hobbes's Political Thought', in K. C. Brown (ed.), *Hobbes Studies* (Oxford: Blackwell, 1965), pp. 185–236.

54 One of the changes Oakeshott makes in the revised version of the introduction is the systematic replacement of the term 'civil society' with 'civil association'. For some discussion of the way Oakeshott minimizes notions such as contract and consent in Hobbes, see S. Gerencser, *The Skeptic's Oakeshott* (London: Macmillan, 2000), pp. 111–18.

55 Oakeshott, 'Thomas Hobbes', p. 120.

56 B. Bosanquet, *The Philosophical Theory of the State* (London: Macmillan, 1923), p. 98.

57 Oakeshott, 'Thomas Hobbes', p. 120.

58 Hobbes, *Leviathan*, p. 141.

59 See also J. W. N. Watkins, *Hobbes's System of Ideas* (London: Hutchinson, 1965), pp. 85–99.

60 Hobbes, *Leviathan*, p. 104.

61 H. Warrender, *The Political Philosophy of Hobbes: His Theory of Obligation* (Oxford: Clarendon Press, 1957), p. 44.

62 *Ibid.*, p. 57.

63 *Ibid.*, pp. 330–5.

64 Oakeshott, 'Introduction to *Leviathan*', pp. 64–72.

65 J. M. Brown, 'A Note on Professor Oakeshott's Introduction to the *Leviathan*', *Political Studies*, 1 (1953), 53–64; cf. Oakeshott, 'Moral Life', p. 273n.

66 See Tregenza, *Michael Oakeshott on Hobbes*, ch. 3, on which I am drawing; cf. Gerencser, *Skeptic's Oakeshott*, ch. 5.

67 M. Oakeshott, 'Introduction' [1946], in Hobbes, *Leviathan*, p. lxi.

68 *Ibid.*, p. lix.

69 Brown, 'Note', 56. See also Tregenza, *Michael Oakeshott on Hobbes*, p. 96, for further discussion of this matter.

70 Oakeshott, 'Introduction', p. lx.

71 Oakeshott, 'Introduction to *Leviathan*', p. 68.

72 See L. Strauss, *Persecution and the Art of Writing* (University of Chicago Press, 1952).

73 Oakeshott, 'Moral Life', p. 287–8. See also Boyd, 'Lion and the Ox'.

74 See, for instance, D. Johnston, *The Rhetoric of Leviathan: Thomas Hobbes and the Politics of Cultural Transformation* (Princeton

University Press, 1986); Q. Skinner, *Reason and Rhetoric in the Philosophy of Hobbes* (Cambridge University Press, 1996).

75 Oakeshott, '*Leviathan*: A Myth', p. 151.

76 Oakeshott, 'Introduction to *Leviathan*', p. 58.

77 Oakeshott, '*Leviathan*: A Myth', p. 154. For further discussion of the 'mythic' aspects of Oakeshott's reading of Hobbes, see my *Michael Oakeshott on Hobbes*, ch. 5, and '*Leviathan* as Myth: Michael Oakeshott and Carl Schmitt on Hobbes and the Critique of Rationalism', *Contemporary Political Theory*, 1 (2002), 349–69.

78 See K. Minogue, 'Parts and Wholes: Twentieth-Century Interpretation of Thomas Hobbes', *Annales de la Catedra Francisco Suarez*, 14 (1974), 77–108.

79 R. Tuck, 'Optics and Sceptics: The Philosophical Foundations of Hobbes's Political Thought', in E. Leites (ed.), *Conscience and Casuistry in Early Modern Europe* (Cambridge University Press, 1987), pp. 235–63; and *Philosophy and Government, 1572–1651* (Cambridge University Press, 1993).

80 W. H. Greenleaf, 'Hobbes: The Problem of Interpretation', in R. Peters and M. Cranston (eds.), *Hobbes and Rousseau: A Collection of Critical Essays* (New York: Anchor Books, 1972), pp. 5–36.

81 Watkins, *Hobbes's System of Ideas*.

82 See especially R. Flathman, *Willful Liberalism: Voluntarism and Individuality in Political Theory and Practice* (Ithaca, NY: Cornell University Press, 1992).

83 C. Tarlton, 'The Despotical Doctrine of Hobbes, Part 1: The Liberalization of *Leviathan*', *History of Political Thought*, 22 (2001), 587–618.

84 Tregenza, *Oakeshott on Hobbes*.

DANA VILLA

14 Oakeshott and the Cold War critique of political rationalism

INTRODUCTION

Viewed from a certain angle, the rise of post-structuralist and post-modernist theorizing in the 1980s and 1990s seemed to signal a return to an intellectually dubious (and politically dangerous) cult of irrationalism. Jürgen Habermas's *The Philosophical Discourse of Modernity* (1987) stands as perhaps the most sophisticated defence of ethical-political rationalism in the face of the broad but diffuse 'rage against reason' symbolized by post-structuralist thought.[1] Lesser figures such as Richard Wolin and Zeev Sternhell have recently added their voices to warn against the 'seductions of unreason' and the renaissance of the 'anti-Enlightenment tradition'.[2] Habermas worried about the levelling of the genre distinction between philosophy and literature, as well as post-modernism's apparent repudiation of normative foundations. Wolin and Sternhell are cruder but more direct. The critique of Enlightenment rationality, they assert, can lead only to fascism or some form of romantic nationalism. To doubt the rational foundations of 'the rights of man' was to join the forces of darkness represented by Gobineau, de Maistre, Schmitt and Heidegger.

The reader of the contemporary 'reason versus unreason' literature will be struck by how this literature evades (or suppresses) the powerful critiques of political rationalism that emerged during the 1940s and 1950s in the English-speaking world. These critiques – offered by Michael Oakeshott, Hannah Arendt, Isaiah Berlin, Jacob Talmon and Karl Popper – were diverse in approach, form and motivation. They did, however, share one thing: a firm sense that dogmatic political rationalism (whether in 'Platonic', Jacobin or

Marxist form) was as big a threat to civilization as were the racist and nationalist ideologies of the fascists and their fellow travellers. This shared sensibility flowed from the clear recognition that not just the Nazis, but the Soviets as well, were totalitarian, the latter's genealogical connection to the work of Karl Marx and the Enlightenment tradition notwithstanding.

This chapter presents Oakeshott's critique of 'rationalism in politics', comparing and contrasting it with the cognate critiques of Hannah Arendt and Isaiah Berlin. My purpose is twofold. First, I want to show how Oakeshott's critique is both original and distinct. It is not reducible to criticisms made by famous predecessors (such as Edmund Burke), nor to those made by his contemporaries. Second, I want to show how Oakeshott's critique of political rationalism, while both complex and elegant, pales in comparison to the more probing criticisms made by Arendt and Berlin. Both Arendt and Berlin were more inclined to seek out 'proto-totalitarian' elements in western philosophical and political thought, in part because they narrowly escaped totalitarian persecution themselves. The traumas of Auschwitz and the Gulag led them to question the rationalist demand – evident since Plato – for 'final solutions' to moral-political problems and the conflict of values.[3]

OAKESHOTT'S CRITIQUE OF RATIONALISM IN POLITICS

The best place to start the consideration of Oakeshott's critique of political rationalism is with his essay 'Rationalism in Politics' (1947). 'Almost all politics today have become Rationalist or near-Rationalist', Oakeshott observes. This statement clearly implies a target at once broader and narrower than the pathological rationalism (or pseudo-rationalism) of Soviet Marxism. What Oakeshott has in mind is the rise of a technocratic or engineering mentality in politics. This mentality transcends substantive ideological differences. It approaches virtually all political issues as technical problems susceptible to rational solution by the appropriate experts. The solution of problems demands someone educated not in the practices, institutions and traditions of the past, but rather in the up-to-date administrative and technical innovations of the present. Indeed, the 'sovereignty of technique' is one, if not *the*, defining characteristic of 'rationalism in politics'.

The political rationalist, then, reduces politics to a set of problems, and assumes that all problems have one (and only one) rational solution.[4] A number of consequences flow from this reduction and from this assumption. First, reducing politics to 'problem-solving' has the effect of draining off most of its (controversial) ethical content. Rightly or wrongly, but usually tacitly, the political rationalist will assume the correctness of a certain account of justice. Second, such a problem-solving perspective frames everyday political debate and deliberation – the ideologically charged argument of ordinary citizens and politicians alike – as so much static or white noise. Argument and debate simply gets in the way of the serious business of rectifying society's problems. In this sense, political rationalism is inherently undemocratic: it makes political judgement a function of specialized or 'expert' knowledge (an idea first broached in the Platonic dialogues). Third, the assumption that there is one and only one rational solution to every 'real' problem radically devalues both plurality and pluralism in the public realm. As Oakeshott puts it, 'there can be no place for preference that is not rational preference, and all rational preferences necessarily coincide'.[5] Finally, the problem-solving perspective encourages the false belief that 'political machinery can take the place of moral and political education'.[6]

Oakeshott is convinced that this Rationalist optic on politics has its basis less in a particular historical or ideological movement (the Enlightenment, say, or utopian socialism) than in a 'certain doctrine about knowledge'. This doctrine Oakeshott describes as the 'hidden spring' of political rationalism and 'the pre-eminent source of its endurance'.[7] What is this doctrine, and how is it responsible for the predominance and continued vitality of 'rationalism in politics'?

Oakeshott's answer is framed in terms of the old Aristotelian distinction between *praxis* and *phronesis* (on the one hand) and *techne* (on the other). Every activity – cooking, painting, making music or poetry, conducting scientific inquiry – has, we might say, its 'technical' and its 'practical' side. The former is often abstracted and presented as a set of rules, steps or techniques for making an experiment, painting a picture, composing a sonata and so on. The crucial point for Oakeshott, however, is that *knowing what* to do is never a substitute for *knowing how* to do it. Indeed, the knowledge required in all arts dealing with human beings – whether it be medicine, management, diplomacy or politics – has a dual character, one in which knowing *how* turns out to be inseparable from knowing *what*. The very distinction between technical and practical knowledge, while useful for thinking about how knowledge guides human activity, can thus be profoundly misleading. It suggests, falsely, that the two sides of activity-guiding knowledge can be sundered, or that one side (the technical) can stand in totally for the other (the practical). As Oakeshott puts it, 'nowhere, and pre-eminently not in political activity, can technical knowledge be separated from practical knowledge, and nowhere can they be considered identical with one another or able to take the place of one another'.[8]

The political rationalist is someone who starts with a predetermined end in mind, and then goes about looking for the proper (most effective or expeditious) means or techniques for achieving it. In his essay 'Rational Conduct' Oakeshott argues that such a reified means–end distinction cannot coherently guide any skilled conduct: 'A cook is not a man who first has a vision of a pie and then tries to make it; he is a man skilled in cookery, and both his projects and achievements spring from that skill'.[9] The point here, however, is that the political rationalist thinks that it *can* provide such a guide. He acts accordingly, turning a blind eye to practical know-how. The 'certain doctrine about knowledge' that guides him on to this dubious path is, in Oakeshott's view, the Cartesian-Baconian one. Both Descartes and Bacon equated genuine knowledge with certainty, and both saw the attainment of certainty as hinging upon a rigorous purging of all knowledge that is 'merely' traditional or handed down.[10] Once the storehouses of our minds have been cleared of the accumulated lumber of received ideas and inherited prejudices, the acquisition of solid, methodically grounded and indubitable knowledge – knowledge such as we find in geometry or mathematical physics – can begin.

For Oakeshott, the fundamental error of the Rationalist is precisely this equation of *knowledge* with *certainty*. Deployed as an epistemological standard, it demands the elimination of all that is merely traditional in character, the better to build upon 'the unshakeable rock of absolute ignorance'.[11] It is this fundamental error that leads the Rationalist to fetishize *technique*, which, unlike practical knowledge, appears to be both self-contained and to satisfy the standard of certainty. Hence the rationalist's assertion that what Oakeshott (and Aristotle) calls 'practical knowledge' is not knowledge at all, and his assumption that the 'sovereignty of reason' entails the 'sovereignty of technique'.[12]

Oakeshott contends that the rationalist's belief in the sovereignty of technique flows from a powerful but mistaken image of 'true' knowledge. But it also flows from a forgetting of the practical understanding or 'sight' that guides us in various contexts of use (using a tool, baking a cake, composing a sonata, writing a book). Technique is something the rational ('sovereign') subject can be sure of and manipulate. He can deploy it in pursuit of his predetermined ends, the better to achieve domination of the natural or social world. Technique thus appears self-contained, firmly grounded in nothing that cannot be demonstrated.

According to Oakeshott, this set of Rationalist prejudices undergirds the modern hegemony of ideology in politics. Like technique, an ideology gives the appearance of certainty and self-containedness. It relies on nothing handed down from the past, and it claims to provide all the knowledge necessary for reforming society and achieving a just or well-ordered polity. Just as with Bacon's rules for research, an ideology is to be applied in deductive, mechanical fashion, subsuming whatever concrete historical particulars happen to be at hand.[13] Such 'methodical' application flows from the ideology's statement of first principles (whether these be human equality, racial purity, individual freedom, social justice or class struggle). Once the leading idea of the ideology is posited, the rest apparently flows automatically (a point Arendt also makes in her 1951 essay 'Ideology and Terror').[14]

Oakeshott's linkage of ideological politics to the rationalist's faith in technique and his fondness for 'first principles' will be persuasive to those who have an instinctive aversion to programmatic and/or radical political movements. What is original (and somewhat disturbing) in 'Rationalism in Politics', however, is the way he equates virtually *all* contemporary politics with the Rationalist mindset. The 'conversion of habits of behaviour, adaptable and never quite fixed or finished, into comparatively rigid systems of abstract ideas' is the norm, not the exception.[15] Thus Oakeshott's characterization of Friedrich Hayek's *The Road to Serfdom* (1944) as itself a 'doctrine'. 'A plan to resist all planning may be better than its opposite, but it belongs to the same style of politics'.[16] Even more disturbing is Oakeshott's projection of this tendency back into the early modern period. Machiavelli and Locke – two very different theorists, with very different concerns and moral outlooks – turn out to both be representatives of the Rationalist tendency. Machiavelli provides the 'new man' lacking in political education with a set of tried and true techniques for the gaining and keeping of political power; Locke's *Second Treatise of Civil Government* is described as a 'long-lived' and 'valuable' political 'crib' for those lacking both political education and inculcated habits of political behaviour (the rising middle classes of the so-called 'bourgeois' revolutions).[17]

The characterization of Machiavelli as a technical adviser and Locke as a crib provider underlines one primary reason for the appeal of simple, doctrinaire or ideological approaches to the political domain in modern times. That appeal resides less on a conscious or unconscious conversion to Cartesian habits of mind than it does upon the pressing need of new classes of political actors to have a kind of orientation guide, one that helps them act and judge in the public realm, a realm from which they had been previously excluded. Oakeshott hardly shares the Plato-flavoured elitism of a Leo Strauss. However, his overarching point – that doctrinaire or technical approaches, based on the repudiation of tradition and practical wisdom, come into their own in the modern period – bears an eerie resemblance to Strauss's indictment of universal 'technical' education in his essay 'Liberal Education and Responsibility'.[18]

For Strauss, the masses can never be the recipients of a 'gentlemanly' education in moderation and practical wisdom since they lack leisure and the requisite philosophical (or 'liberal') tutor. For Oakeshott, the lack of political education of the rising middle and working classes – their lack of habituation to established habits of political behaviour – dictates an abstract, simplified, 'principle and technique' approach to politics. It is no accident that Marx and Engels provided the 'most stupendous of political rationalisms' to the least politically educated (and least politically experienced) social class. Similarly, Oakeshott argues, 'the early history of the United States of America is an instructive chapter in the history of the politics of Rationalism', the colonists being called upon to exercise political initiative without much prior preparation.[19]

Because independence began with an 'admitted illegality, a specific and express rejection of a tradition', the Americans had to defend it with 'an appeal to something which is itself thought not to depend upon tradition'. Hence, the Americans

> were disposed to believe ... that the proper organization of a society and the conduct of its affairs were based upon abstract principles, and not upon a tradition which, as Hamilton said, had 'to be rummaged for among old parchments and musty records'. These principles were not the product of civilization; they were natural, 'written in the whole volume of human nature'. They were to be discovered in nature by human reason, by a technique of inquiry available alike to all men and requiring no extraordinary intelligence in its use ... The Declaration of Independence is a characteristic product of the *saeculum rationalisticum*. It represents the politics of the felt need interpreted with the aid of an ideology. And it is not surprising that it should have become one of the sacred documents of the politics of Rationalism, and, together with the similar documents of the French Revolution, the inspiration and pattern of many later adventures in the rationalist reconstruction of society.[20]

Stepping back from this breezy rejection of doctrines of natural right, we can see that Oakeshott has in fact offered us a metanarrative, one on roughly the same scale as Strauss's story about the struggle between the ancients and moderns (albeit lacking the melodrama built into the latter). Machiavelli, Locke, the American revolutionaries, the French revolutionaries, Marx and Engels, utopian socialists, liberal planners, welfare state constructors: all are cut from the same cloth, that of Rationalism. They all reject the practical wisdom contained in established institutions and modes of political behaviour, in the mistaken belief that the self-consciously formulated and technically implemented (by violence, if necessary) is to be preferred to anything established and traditional.

While Oakeshott's narrative may be on the same scale as Strauss's, it is obviously different. Oakeshott chastises the moderns for their rationalism and worship of technique, while Strauss chastises them for their repudiation of *classical* political rationalism (the 'moderate' yet aristocratic rationalism of Plato, Aristotle and – Strauss thinks – Socrates). But how is Oakeshott's story different from, say, that of Burke, his most obvious predecessor?

The answer to this question is found in Oakeshott's qualified acceptance of the legitimacy of the modern age. Modernity is overwhelmingly rationalist in its approach to politics. However, Oakeshott maintains, it has also established certain distinctions and patterns of life we challenge only at great peril. There is in Oakeshott a palpable (Burkean) nostalgia for established ways of doing things and a 'living' or organic political culture. But the reader of Oakeshott will search in vain for anything approximating to the more familiar nostalgia of 'post-liberal' anti-secularists. Unlike Strauss, Erich Voegelin and the more recent work of Charles Taylor, there is no longing in Oakeshott for 'the world we have lost'. This was a theologically integrated world in which the value spheres of science, art, poetry, private life and economic activity lacked any genuine autonomy.

Thus, whereas Burke was a traditionalist and an anti-modernist, Oakeshott is a traditionalist and an idiosyncratic modernist. He is at one with Constant, Mill and Berlin when it comes to the 'liberty of the moderns'. He is surprisingly libertarian with respect to business and economic affairs.[21] And he is surprisingly pluralist (in Berlin's sense) when it comes to the relative autonomy of the different vocabularies of scientific inquiry, historical explanation and poetic 'image-making'.[22] The 'partnership between the past and the present' (the phrase is Burke's) that Oakeshott wishes to maintain in the face of Rationalist social restructuring does not entail the rolling back of modern achievements (the priority of individual liberty; freedom of association; the 'dis-embedding' of the economy; religious and political pluralism). Rather, it entails the recognition of these achievements as defining characteristics of *our* political and cultural reality.

These achievements did not spring out of pure reason but out of a constitutionalist tradition whose roots extend back to the Middle Ages.[23] Combined with the end of feudalism and the emergence of market society, this constitutionalism gave birth to an English liberal tradition that Oakeshott largely endorses (despite its occasional self-misunderstandings, as evidenced, for example, by Lockean natural rights and Mill's faith in progress). The animating idea behind his liberal conservatism is not that progress or evolution be arrested or repudiated, but that it take place on the basis of consensus and continuity, where possible.

For Oakeshott, then, 'the right conduct of policy' does not involve the application of abstract principles of freedom (or anything else) to society. Rather, it involves teasing out those possibilities, tendencies and patterns of behaviour that are already immanent in society itself. Politics rightly conducted is never more that 'the pursuit of intimations; a conversation, not an argument'.[24] It is a conversation that, ideally, takes places amongst politically educated human beings: human beings with a deep knowledge of the present condition of their polity as well as its particular traditions and established patterns of behaviour.

Framed in such a manner, Oakeshott's 'anti-rationalist' conception of politics apparently has much to recommend it. Rejecting bogus 'recipes', pseudo-universalist principles and a mechanical-deductive approach to political judgement, it brings us down to earth, to a particular place and a particular time. The point of this particularism is not the rejection of our common humanity but the exploration of the complex patterns of institutional and political behaviour that make up a given nation state's political inheritance. For Oakeshott, it is the richness of this inheritance that the 'rationalist' consistently overlooks. His fixation on abstract principles, on 'clear and distinct ideas', leads him to put the cart before the horse. In fact, principles emerge from patterns of behaviour, not the other way round. They are not discovered by pure reason but by the patient and informed elucidation of the possibilities contained in a particular political culture and tradition.

PROBLEMS WITH OAKESHOTT'S CRITIQUE

Viewed from our contemporary globalized perspective, Oakeshott's critique of Rationalism appears insular and reactive, if not reactionary. It is one thing to criticize the excesses of the Jacobins or the technocrats, another to reduce modern ideas of freedom and human rights to reflections of local context and practice. If all *real* critique is immanent critique, then how do we begin to uphold human dignity in those parts of the world where the vocabulary of human rights is only now beginning to take hold? Oakeshott would most likely respond that 'human dignity' is an empty ideal if it is detached from any and all local cultures and traditions. Yet while it is no doubt true that human dignity can take on flesh, as it were, only in terms of specific cultures and patterns of behaviour, it is not true that our sense of injustice and insults to human dignity is so constrained. To be mildly Socratic about it: we may not know, or agree, upon what 'Justice' with a capital 'J' is. However, we can agree – thanks to liberal tradition, the vocabulary of human rights and conceptions of human dignity implicit in a variety of philosophical and religious traditions – about what gross *injustice* looks like. That 'negative' knowledge is enough.

This leads me to consider two points that apply to Oakeshott as well as to the similarly tradition-based thought of Alasdair MacIntyre and Hans-Georg Gadamer. The first is that it is all too easy to endow cultures and traditions with a bogus wholeness or self-containedness. This is a natural tendency of conservative thinkers, who tend to see fairly well defined or organic 'wholes' where others see an array of contingent, permeable and ever shifting constellations. A focus on the richness of any tradition – whether it be the English political tradition, Thomism or German humanist *Bildung* – has the effect of creating a kind of aesthetic pseudo-object, one that is self-contained, harmonious and largely coherent.

Rejecting all forms of abstract universalism, the conservative connoisseur of tradition will endow his or her favourite tradition with resources and 'intimations' that are less immanent than they are the result of a larger and more cosmopolitan view of the world. The 'English political tradition', for example, has many strands, some Rationalist, others proudly not. The point is that the construction of this tradition always involves a work of active (and contestable) interpretation. And such interpretation, if it is to lay claim to even minimal validity, will invariably be informed (as Oakeshott's writing was informed) by acquaintance with divergent strands of western and non-western, Rationalist and non-Rationalist, philosophical and political thought. To pretend otherwise is to surrender to the siren song of reification.

My second point has to do with Oakeshott's stated preference for continuity, consensus and 'conversation'. Even if one allows, as Oakeshott does, that traditions evolve, change and absorb a number of 'non-native' influences (the English case, for example, involves the assimilation of republicanism, socialism and 'rationalism', broadly construed), the question is the manner of their change and 'evolution'. Politics, as J. G. A. Pocock observed long ago, is the realm of the contingent, not the eternal, the necessary, the gracefully developmental or self-same.[25] Contingency, allegorized as *fortuna*, implies the likelihood of the unprecedented and the unforeseen.

It is not surprising that writers like Arendt and Berlin, responding to ideologies of historical necessity and the totalitarian catastrophe they helped bring about, also emphasize the central role played by contingency and the human capacity to begin, to initiate. And it is not surprising that more recent writers, like Thomas Kuhn and Michel Foucault, have emphasized the role discontinuity plays in the history of ideas. Politics, as the realm of the contingent, is also the realm of new beginnings, of revolutionary breaks, new foundations and 'paradigm shifts'. Oakeshott's preferred image of an ongoing conversation, rooted in established tradition and patterns of political behaviour, is suited only for what, following Kuhn, we might call 'normal' politics.[26] Confronted by genuine novelty or discontinuity – such as we find in revolutionary situations – the conversation metaphor breaks down. It must either read the new back into what was already there (as Oakeshott himself does in his characterization of Locke's *Second Treatise*) or frame it as an unfortunate importation from 'alien' sources.

A third point concerns the nature and extent of Oakeshott's critique of political rationalism. Viewed from one angle, this critique seems, if anything, to be hyper-inclusive. Oakeshott's incomplete catalogue of the 'progeny of rationalism' includes (amongst other things) 'the Beveridge Report, the Education Act of 1944, Federalism, Nationalism, Votes for Women, the Catering Wages Act, the destruction of the Austro-Hungarian Empire, the World State ... and the revival of Gaelic as the official language of Eire'.[27] As noted above, it also includes the revolutionary traditions of France and America, doctrines of natural right and social contract, and the administrative mindset generally. However, as I suggested at the outset, this apparent capaciousness masks a certain shallowness.

In part, this lack of depth is a function of Oakeshott's conception of what a proper (non-ideology-driven, non-Rationalist) politics looks like. If politics is 'the activity of attending to the general arrangements of a set of people whom chance or choice have brought together'; and if 'attending to the arrangements of a society' is an 'activity that has to be learned' not by absorbing ideologies, statistics or programmes but only by initiation into the activity itself as it is currently (and has been traditionally) practised – *then* it follows that local context and practice trump all other considerations, effectively circumscribing our notion of what politics is and can be.[28] The optic of the Oakeshottian political theorist will, as a result, be confined to pointing out how the prevalence of ideology and instrumental rationality negatively impacts upon his or her own political culture. The latter is reified into a self-contained 'tradition' of political behaviour and activity, one which frames novel ideas and practices as alien excrescences. Hence Oakeshott's definition of politics as 'the art of where to go next in the exploration of an already existing traditional kind of society'.[29]

What is wrong with this? I would suggest that it leaves the more profoundly disturbing aspects of political rationalism – its characteristic separation of knowing from doing, its positing of a hierarchical relationship between theory and practice, its worship of the means–end category, and its deep hostility to either political or moral pluralism – underinterrogated and relatively unexplored. Constrained by such a conception of 'proper' politics, the Oakeshottian political theorist will stop well short of probing the full range of dangers – to liberalism, to democracy and to politics itself – that the Rationalist tradition in politics represents. For that exploration, we need to turn to two of Oakeshott's contemporaries, Hannah Arendt and Isaiah Berlin.

ARENDT AND THE RATIONALIST TRADITION IN POLITICS

Arendt's first major work of political theory, *The Origins of Totalitarianism* (1951) is famous for several reasons. First, there is Arendt's insistence that totalitarianism is a genuinely novel form of political regime. It is not simply dictatorship or the state blown up to monstrous proportions. Second, there is her insistence that the set of practices, events and *mentalités* that made totalitarianism possible (such as race-thinking, imperialism, tribal nationalism and bureaucratic authoritarianism) were *pan-European* phenomena, and not simply the peculiar properties of either Germany or Russia. Third, there was her articulation of what historians have since come to call the 'blowback' thesis. This is the idea that practices of race-based domination evolved and perfected in the various imperial colonies came home to roost in Europe itself. Finally, there was her identification of the concentration camp – whether the Nazi *lagers* or the Soviet Gulag – as 'the central institutions' of totalitarian rule. These were institutions in which 'experiments in total domination' – specifically, the attempt to eliminate the human capacity for spontaneous action, to render human beings mere bundles of reflexes – were carried out.[30]

It was this last theme, with its associated insight that totalitarian rule was the attempt to refashion the polity as 'one man of gigantic dimensions', devoid of human plurality and spontaneity, that led Arendt to investigate certain deeply set patterns in the western tradition of philosophy and political thought. Initially, she was quite dubious about *Geistesgeschichte*-type genealogies of totalitarianism formulated by intellectual historians. However, as she set about researching a project on the 'proto-totalitarian elements' in the thought of Karl Marx, she came to see just how deep the western tradition's hostility to plurality and spontaneous, 'unruly' action actually was. In *The Human Condition* (1958), the work that subsumed the proposed Marx study, she provided an in-depth critique of the western tradition of political thought. This tradition, she claimed, installed a hostility to plurality, spontaneity, opinion and open-ended argument at its commencement, in its Platonic-Aristotelian origins.

In *The Human Condition* and other writings Arendt presents the origin of the western tradition of political philosophy as directly traceable to Plato's vehement hostility to Athenian democracy. Plato famously juxtaposed reason to opinion, dialectic to rhetoric, the realm of the intelligible to that of the sensible, and eternity to the temporal and worldly. He did this, Arendt argues, because he wanted to escape the apparent 'futility, boundlessness, haphazardness and moral irresponsibility' that beset political speech and action undertaken in a context of robust plurality (such as we find in the Athenian democracy), where every actor is 'also a sufferer'.[31] Plato thought he could escape this lack of control and sovereignty by positing a set of trans-temporal, rationally intelligible standards (the forms) for human action and conduct. If such standards existed, only the wise – those whose philosophical education habituated them to thinking abstractly, in terms of essences – could potentially grasp them. Action in this world – the creation, articulation and preservation of a just or rational polity – would follow deductively from the eternal standards intuited by the wise. Theory would loom over practice, reducing the latter to the status of a *means* by which to realize the *ends* philosophy had gleaned from the order of the cosmos itself. Those who know would rule over those who do, inserting a radical and irreducible *hierarchy* into what had been (previously) the realm of equality: the public-political realm.[32]

The reader might well acknowledge that this is what Plato does, yet express scepticism towards the Arendtian idea that it tells us a lot about our tradition of political thought *as a whole*. Indeed, it is possible to see Arendt's story about the 'great tradition' from Plato to Marx as itself a reification, different from, yet comparable to, Oakeshott's more Burkean hypostatization. The fact remains, however, that a politics of Truth (whether given by reason or revelation) is the norm rather than the exception in the western tradition, and that every iteration of such a politics is intrinsically hierarchical and (thus) anti-democratic. Those who know what Reason or God demand impose it on their less rational or pious brethren, viewing the plurality of opinion as a vice harmful to the (supposedly healthy) unity of society. Thus, wherever we look – whether it be Aristotle or Augustine, Calvin or Luther, Descartes or Hobbes, Rousseau or Voltaire, Hegel or Marx – we find a dubious privileging of a truth given by reason (dialectic, science or theory) or revelation, and an even more dubious repudiation of pluralism or perspectivism in politics. Even Kant, the moral high point of the Enlightenment, insisted on Reason's unquestionable law-giving prerogatives (a practical reason that was the same for all), as well as the monarch's right to be the 'master' that a creature such as man needs.

The Rationalist tradition in western political thought, then, largely follows Plato's lead in radically devaluing pluralism and the conflict of opinion. It seeks a firmer ground on the basis of which reason or science commands, or upon which all should 'rationally' be able to agree (assuming they have the full use of their reason). The former option, apparent in such diverse thinkers as Plato, Hobbes, Hegel and Marx, reduces a large proportion of the polity to the status of children in need of philosophical-theoretical guidance. The latter option, evident in the less scientistic social contract thinkers (Locke, Rousseau and Kant), sets severe constraints on both democratic practice and disagreement. Even worse, from Arendt's perspective, is the way the Platonic model encourages us to think of political *action*, which is plural and non-sovereign in character, as a form of *making* or fabrication. Plato suggested this analogy to his fellow, democratically inclined Greeks because fabrication presented a form of activity in which the initiator (a) began with a pre-given idea of the end or product in mind, and (b) remained in full command of the activity itself, from conception through concrete realization. If political action is like making – that is, if it starts with an idea or blueprint, and then simply needs the right materials, tools and procedures to bring about the final product – then diverse opinions are extraneous. Only the specialized knowledge of the moral or political expert (the ruler) is essential.

The 'action as making' analogy produces other pathologies as well. Most obviously, it encourages the real or would-be ruler to view the concrete individuals making up the community as so much raw material awaiting his shaping hand and the imposition of political-moral form. The matter–form topos is explicit in thinkers as diverse as Plato and Machiavelli, and has both its Nazi and Soviet variants. Whatever version it takes, human dignity and human rights are predictably denied. Moreover, the analogy provides ample support for our tendency to view political action *not* as a many-voiced debate expressing a diversity of perspectives, but rather as something intrinsically *instrumental* in character. The 'means–end' category, as Arendt repeatedly pointed out, comes to dominate. This further marginalizes the politically constitutive phenomenon of human plurality, encouraging us to assimilate political action to *violence* (which, as Arendt also notes, is inherently instrumental in character).[33] The result is a turn away from Platonic or architectonic politics towards a Machiavellian conception of political action as primarily *strategic* in character, as well as a Weberian conception of political *power* as consisting in the ability to enforce one's will on others.

How is Arendt's critique of political rationalism different from Oakeshott's? First, it points us to a number of *anti-political prejudices* built into the western rationalist tradition, in all its variants. Second, it is based upon from a phenomenological conception of authentic politics that frames *beginning* (or initiation) as a central aspect of all genuine political action. Politics is not the 'art of where to go next in an already existing kind of traditional society'. Rather, it encompasses both open-ended debate (the deliberative constitution of both political ends and means) *and* radical beginning or 'revolutionary turns in the conversation'.

The latter is, of course, the theme of Arendt's 1963 work *On Revolution*. This study of *modern* political action proceeds by means of a contrast between the French and American revolutionary experiences. Both traditions centre on the problem and possibility of 'starting anew' in politics, a possibility Arendt celebrates but which Oakeshott sees as a kind of category mistake or Rationalist illusion. Are all 'new beginnings' in politics merely *continuations* of what went before? Oakeshott would answer yes, with the caveat that any attempt to create real discontinuity will lead to disaster. Arendt, alive to the deformations of the Rationalist French and Marxist revolutionary traditions, would answer no, and point to the success of the American Founders in creating something entirely new: in constituting a new public space of freedom.

Arendt and Oakeshott are closer when it comes to their critiques of instrumental or bureaucratic rationality in politics. But even here there are notable divergences. Oakeshott is not really concerned with the damage an inclusive concept of *Zweckrationalität* inflicts on the political sphere. Rather, he wants to show that our general conception of 'rational' conduct, which involves the prior specification of the end at which we aim, as well as the choice of the most rational or efficient means to that end, is always an *abstraction* from the more inclusive field of a particular activity. Specific projects and specific goals spring from the context of a particular form of activity, not the other way round. A cook does not begin with an abstract idea of a cake and then select the appropriate means by which to make it, any more than a scientific practitioner begins with an abstract, context-independent hypothesis that he then attempts to prove or disprove via experiment. In both cases, the actions of the practitioner are 'determined not solely by his premeditated end, but by what may be called the traditions of the activity to which his project belonged'.[34]

The political and moral implications of such a stance are fairly clear. To be 'rational' when it comes to moral and political conduct does not mean (*pace* Weber and the Rationalist reformer) first bracketing the established context or tradition of behaviour, then specifying a moral or political end, and then (finally) selecting the appropriate means to realize that end. Rather, political rationality means recognizing that moral and political coherence derive from our established traditions and ways of doing things. With this recognition secured we can then attempt to remedy or correct incoherence, rupture and anachronism by drawing upon the very tradition that the Cartesian or technocratic rationalist views as moribund. Reform, in other words, is never a matter of seeking out new foundations or instrumentally rational ways of doing things. Rather, it flows from refreshing our pre-theoretical knowledge of moral and political behaviour, a pre-theoretical knowledge that is woven into, and inseparable from, a particular 'way of living'.[35]

Reweaving the fabric of a particular mode of life or pattern of behaviour was never Arendt's concern. The threat posed by ubiquitous means–end rationality was not, in her view, that we misconceive our activities and how to go about resolving the problems that they generate. Rather, the threat has to do with a flattening or one-dimensionalization of the public sphere. Where moral-political problems are framed in terms of the 'rational choice' of efficient means or utility-maximizing ends, the ruler, bureaucrat or political technician can step in and take the place of a 'noisy', ' irrational' and 'ill-informed' public. A political world framed by the horizon of means–end rationality is one that necessarily privileges expert knowledge while devaluing democratic speech and deliberation. Arendt's critique of the 'tyranny' of the means–end category in politics is thus undertaken in defence of a robust democratic politics, one that makes room for radical beginning and revolutionary turns in the conversation. In contrast, Oakeshott's critique is undertaken not in the name of plurality or democracy, but in the name of tradition. He wants us to appreciate the richness (if that's the right word) of what is already there.[36]

BERLIN AND THE CRITIQUE OF MONISM

Like Arendt, Berlin's critique of Rationalism in politics emerged from his reading of leading figures of the western tradition of philosophy and political thought. His youthful reading of the great nineteenth-century Russian authors revealed to him a widespread belief that

> solutions to the central problems [of poverty, oppression, cruelty and human degradation] existed, that one could discover them, and, with

sufficient selfless effort, realize them on earth. They all believed that the essence of human beings was to be able to choose how to live: societies could be transformed in the light of true ideals believed in with enough fervour and dedication.[37]

The assumption that a set of 'final solutions' to man's most vexed social and political problems existed was not one limited to morally indignant Russian authors of the nineteenth century. As Berlin's subsequent reading at Oxford made clear, a parallel assumption animated western moral and political thought from Socrates through Condorcet and beyond.

Stated somewhat broadly, the great figures of the western tradition all believed that human reason, employing the methods of science or deductive logic, could establish an objective knowledge of 'how to live, what to be'. Rational argument and/or scientific investigation could reveal to us the 'correct solution to personal and social problems'.[38]

This faith – the faith of occidental rationalism – has proved remarkably strong and long-lasting, sceptical critics like Nietzsche and Max Weber notwithstanding. It is premised, Berlin thought, on the idea that

all genuine questions must have one true answer and one only, all the rest being necessarily errors; in the second place, that there must be a dependable path towards the discovery of these truths; in the third place, that the true answers, when found, must necessarily be compatible with one another and form a single whole, for one truth cannot be incompatible with another.

Thus, 'in the case of morals, we could then conceive what the perfect life must be, founded as it would be on a correct understanding of the rules that governed the universe'.[39] There may be disagreements about the right path to the answer (churches, laboratories, experiment, calculation, intuition, etc.) but, the Rationalist assumes, 'the answers must exist, otherwise the questions were not real'. This assumption is so strong that it even undergirds those nineteenth-century thinkers (like Hegel, Comte, Marx and Mill) who deny that there *are* such things as 'eternal' questions. Such questions do not exist abstractly in the manner of Platonic forms. They – along with the rationally correct answers – will be revealed to mankind through the progress of history itself.

Western rationalism, then, is deeply 'monist' in character. A single set of true, mutually compatible answers to all genuine questions concerning the ranking of human ends and a 'rational' or just form of social organization *must* exist, or else reason is 'merely' an instrument of calculation. Of course, faith in such a morally substantive reason is edifying. But it is also deeply illiberal. Like the religious man, the Rationalist allows for the appearance of many 'errors'. There is, however, only one Truth, *unum verum*. From Berlin's pluralist vantage point, it does not require a great deal of imagination to see how the Enlightenment tradition, enamoured of classical rationalist pretensions and the new scientific method, could give rise to both authoritarian socialism and technocratic welfare democracies.

The usual response to such broad-brush critiques of western rationalism is to charge the critic with promoting irrationalism, relativism, or worse. If Reason cannot tell us how to rank our values and ends, or how to organize our common life, then we are thrown back on tradition, local prejudice and unmoored ('decisionist') choice. This strategy does not really work in the case of Berlin, whose commitment to liberal values is well known. What alternative, then, does Berlin offer in place of the monism of the rationalist tradition? And how does this alternative escape the charge of irrationalism or relativism?

Berlin upholds a variety of moral pluralism, one that derives from his reading of Machiavelli, Vico and Herder. It also owes much to the tragic view of the world of value offered by Nietzsche and Weber (though Berlin is much less explicit about his debt here). All of these thinkers thought in terms of *moralities*, not Morality. Machiavelli was crucial to Berlin insofar as his thinking presented a stark contrast between a *political*, neo-Roman set of ultimate values and the central values of Christianity. On the one hand, we have patriotic, aggressive, manly citizens who love their country and liberty; on the other, we have humility, acceptance of suffering, unworldliness and the hope of salvation in an afterlife. As Berlin writes, Machiavelli 'does not condemn Christian virtues. He merely points out that the two moralities are incompatible, and he does not recognize an overarching criterion whereby we are enabled to decide the right life for men. The combination of *virtù* and Christian values is for him an impossibility. He simply leaves you to choose'.[40]

To this incompatibility between rival tables of ultimate values Berlin adds Vico's historicism and Herder's cultural holism. Both Vico and Herder emphasized the idea that a particular culture can embody a set of values that is irreconcilable with other cultures or civilizations. Each culture, each civilization has its own vision of reality, its own dominant conception of the good life. This would seem to land us in the kind of historicism or relativism that a political rationalist like Leo Strauss reviles. Berlin, however, insists that his moral pluralism is not tantamount to relativism, nor does it begin and end with the 'anthropological' observation of historical and cultural variation in the world of values. Rather, it is an *objective* form of moral pluralism, one whose deepest thought concerns the nature of value itself. Values are 'objective' when they are ultimate for a given culture or public form of life. It is not, as the relativist thinks, a question of individual preference, taste or decision. Moreover, it is not simply the case that different tables of value can be irreconcilable, or that cultural values can collide. The tensions also run through particular sets of ultimate values, and through individual value concepts themselves.

With respect to the last point, Berlin's most famous example is found in his celebrated essay 'Two Concepts of Liberty'. Not only is liberty a value in tension with other values (equality, justice, order, etc.), it turns out to be in tension with itself. While historians of ideas have identified over two hundred meanings for 'liberty', within the western tradition two dominant senses have emerged. Berlin identifies these (famously) as 'negative' and 'positive' liberty. The former refers to an inviolate sphere of personal freedom, a sphere free from interference by governing authorities, the state or any public, social or ecclesiastical power. Negative liberty is a 'freedom from' undue interference by such powers, powers that always tend to overstep their proper boundaries in the pursuit of a paternalistic (and usually moralizing) agenda. The locus of such liberty is the individual and his or her 'freedom of motion', understood in a broad sense. The all-important boundary for proponents of negative liberty, such as Constant, Mill and Berlin himself, is that between the public and private realms. The right of public authority to exercise its power is never in principle questioned. Rather, the matter centres on where we draw the *frontier* between the reach of public authority (concerning activity that impacts the rights and vital interests of others) and our individual sphere of free choice and motion (freedom of thought, expression and what Mill called 'self-regarding actions').

Positive liberty, on the other hand, focuses on the possibility of being one's own master. It focuses, in other words, on the achievement of genuine autonomy or rational self-direction. One can, after all, be guaranteed a relatively large field of 'negative' liberty (and the freedom from external impediments this implies), yet still feel constrained by a variety of internal obstacles to self-mastery. Such internal obstacles may have their origin in the 'weakness of will' and the over-mastering strength of our passions; or they may be the result of individual psychological factors (a domineering father or a remote mother, for example) that create a propensity for self-loathing and neurosis. And – as a variety of neo-Marxist and feminist critics have pointed out – such internal obstacles may also take the form of ideologies (market individualism, patriarchal authority), which colonize our minds and determine a good part of how we understand ourselves. Whatever their nature or source – whether they are appetites we cannot control, neurotic behaviours we cannot overcome or self-conceptions that help reinforce subordination and a feeling of failure – we recognize such internal impediments to self-direction as cheating us of a full or positive sense of liberty.

Berlin's point in making the distinction between negative and positive liberty is not to laud the former and utterly anathematize the latter. Rather, it is to underline that both senses of the word 'liberty' are rooted in authentic experiences, and that neither is reducible to the other. As Berlin puts it, 'the answer to the question "who governs me?" is logically distinct from the question "how far does government interfere with me?"'[41] Yet both questions help shape our sense of how much liberty we, as individuals, actually have. And both questions have alternatively driven western political, philosophical and religious thought – from the Stoics and early Christianity, through Locke and Mill, and through the parallel Rousseau–Hegel–Marx sequence – down to the present day.

However – and this is where Berlin's point about internal value conflict links back up with his overarching critique of political rationalism – there is a strong, almost overwhelming tendency in the western tradition of political thought to *socialize* or *politicize* the quest for self-determination or autonomy. The perfectly acceptable (from a liberal standpoint) Kantian idea that persons should be autonomous beings, 'authors of value, or ends in themselves', quickly devolves into the notion that rational self-direction must apply to our outer, social lives – our relations to others – if it is to be more than a fiction. The real sources of impediments to our self-mastery are to be found in the social-political world. We are enslaved, as the Marxists would say, by our own creations: by the pseudo-objectivities of the state and the capitalist labour market. Only when these are dissolved and the coordination of our social life is brought within the ambit of a *collective* form of self-legislation will an *authentic* form of autonomy be possible.

As a general theoretical point, this socialization of the conditions of autonomy may well be allowed. The Stoic's retreat to the 'inner citadel' was, after all, unsatisfying on a number of levels. The real hitch, however, is found in the Hegelian-Marxist identification of 'rationality' with 'conformity to the rational or necessary structure of things'. As Berlin writes, channelling the Hegelian-Marxist logic:

> We are enslaved by despots – institutions or beliefs or neuroses – which can be removed only by being analysed and understood. We are imprisoned by evil spirits which we have ourselves – albeit not consciously – created, and can exorcize them only by becoming conscious and acting appropriately: indeed, for Marx understanding is appropriate action. I am free if, and only if, I plan my life in accordance with my own will; plans entail rules; a rule does not oppress or enslave me if I impose it on myself consciously, or accept it freely, having understood it, whether it was invented by me or others, providing that it is rational, that is to say, conforms to the necessities of things.[42]

Here we approach the heart of the matter. It is one thing for the Stoic advocate of self-governance to counsel mastery of the passions and conformity to the necessity of things, quite another for the revolutionary reformer to do so. What happens in the latter case is that the 'higher' and 'lower' selves – a division presupposed by all doctrines of positive liberty – are split into distinct social groups. Reason/intellect is identified with the theoretically informed vanguard party, which – through Marxism or some other ideology – claims insight into the rationally necessary course of social evolution. Freedom and autonomy will result from conformity to the laws of social development. However, the masses in a society confronted with a revolutionary situation cannot be expected to comprehend the rational necessity of either historical progress or social-political transformation. They will continue to be trapped in the ideological illusions of the 'heteronomous' society. Therefore, they must be 'forced to be free'. The logic here – a logic Berlin detects in Rousseau, Fichte, Hegel, Comte and Marx – is simple:

> The sage knows you better than you know yourself, and you are the victim of your passions, a slave living a heteronomous life, purblind, unable to understand your true goals. You want to be a human being. It is the aim of the [revolutionary] state to satisfy your wish. 'Compulsion is justified by education for future insight'.[43]

In this development, not only has positive freedom been socialized and human faculties apportioned, Plato-like, to different social groups. Reason becomes tyrannical because it *no longer recognizes the legitimacy of individual choice unguided by theoretical insight*. Negative liberty presumes, simply, the attainment of minimal rational adulthood, an attainment open to everyone without serious cognitive or psychological defect. A socialized form of positive liberty, on the other hand, presumes an 'education to autonomy', an education in which there are distinct groupings of teachers and taught, and in which the mass of the people 'cannot be expected to understand or cooperate with the purposes of their educators'.[44] Coercion of an almost limitless variety is justified by the appeal to autonomy, the need to conform to rational necessity, and the monist desire to find a 'final solution' to value conflict and do away with the social sources of heteronomy. The politicization of the pursuit of autonomy renders 'negative' liberty more or less unreal, at best one more obstacle to the achievement of genuine freedom.

CONCLUSION

Berlin's diagnosis of the persistent monism of the western tradition – coupled with his analysis of the way the drive to autonomy converts into a socio-political project in which rational insight is effectively monopolized by a theoretical avant-garde – yields a profound and disturbing vision of the latent pathologies animating political rationalism. In the twentieth century these pathologies came to the fore, and political rationalism ran amok. Berlin's point, of course, is that this running amok has deep roots in some of the most respected (and respectable) philosophical doctrines of our culture. Arendt performs a parallel critique by revealing how, at the beginning of our tradition, a metaphoric of fabrication was used to recode political action as a form of making. Those who know – Truth, the forms, God, the science of society or the logic of history – command those who do, all in the effort to *produce* a socio-political reality that conforms to the ideal ('scientific') blueprint. Of course, neither Berlin nor Arendt conceive of some abstract entity called 'Reason' to be the enemy. Their point – and it seems an obvious one in light of the horrors of the twentieth century – is that an hubristic political rationalism, a rationalism that pretends to know *the* truth beyond all opinion, is one sure path to hell.

Oakeshott's criticism of political rationalism, on the other hand, is aimed more at understanding a broad tendency of our age rather than a potentially pathological dimension of our tradition. The rationalist flavour (in Oakeshott's sense) of much of our politics is undeniable. But the tendency to think in terms of programmes, pregiven ends and efficient means to those ends is not – in and of itself – pathological. Nor does it necessarily blind us to the resources of our own (native) political cultures. What it does do – and this is the strongest element of Oakeshott's critique – is prevent us from robustly and imaginatively appropriating these resources. Reduced to 'problem-solving' and ideological cribs for competing ideals of justice, politics ceases to be a bridge to a *productive* encounter with the past. The resources remain, but – to be Gadamerian for a moment – their effective historical potential is cancelled out. The resulting loss is ours alone.

NOTES

1 See J. Habermas, *The Philosophical Discourse of Modernity*, trans. F. Lawrence (Cambridge, MA: MIT Press, 1987).

2 R. Wolin, *The Seduction of Unreason: The Intellectual Romance with Fascism from Nietzsche to Post-Modernism* (Princeton University Press, 2004); Z. Sternhell, *The Anti-Enlightenment Tradition* (New Haven, CT: Yale University Press, 2009).

3 See I. Berlin, *The Crooked Timber of Humanity* (Princeton University Press, 1998), pp. 3–4.

4 M. Oakeshott, 'Rationalism in Politics', in *RP*, p. 6.
5 *Ibid.*
6 *Ibid.*
7 *Ibid.*, p. 7.
8 *Ibid.*, p. 9.
9 M. Oakeshott, 'Rational Conduct', in *RP*, p. 91.
10 Oakeshott, 'Rationalism in Politics', pp. 14–17.
11 *Ibid.*, p. 12.
12 *Ibid.*, p. 11.
13 *Ibid.*, p. 15.
14 H. Arendt, *The Origins of Totalitarianism* (New York: Harcourt Brace Jovanovich, 1973), pp. 460–79.
15 Oakeshott, 'Rationalism in Politics', p. 21.
16 *Ibid.*
17 *Ibid.*, pp. 24–5.
18 L. Strauss, 'Liberal Education and Responsibility', in *Liberalism Ancient and Modern* (New York: Basic Books, 1968), pp. 9–25.
19 Oakeshott, 'Rationalism in Politics', p. 26.
20 *Ibid.*, p. 28.
21 See M. Oakeshott, 'The Political Economy of Freedom', in *RP*, pp. 37–58.
22 See M. Oakeshott, 'The Voice of Poetry in the Conversation of Mankind', in *RP*, pp. 197–247.
23 M. Oakeshott, 'Political Education', in *RP*, pp. 120–1, with respect to Locke.
24 *Ibid.*, p. 125.
25 See J. G. A. Pocock, *The Machiavellian Moment: Florentine Political Thought and the Atlantic Republican Tradition* (Princeton University Press, 2003), pp. 156–218.
26 Oakeshott, 'Political Economy of Freedom', p. 48; 'Political Education', pp. 126 and 129.
27 Oakeshott, 'Rationalism in Politics', pp. 6–7.
28 Oakeshott, 'Political Education', pp. 112–13, 121.
29 Oakeshott, 'Political Economy of Freedom', p. 58.
30 Arendt, *Origins of Totalitarianism*, p. 436.
31 H. Arendt, *The Human Condition* (University of Chicago Press, 1958), pp. 181–91.
32 *Ibid.*, pp. 220–9.
33 H. Arendt, *On Violence* (New York: Harcourt, Brace & World, 1970), p. 46.
34 Oakeshott, 'Rational Conduct', p. 99.
35 *Ibid.*, p. 109.
36 See M. Oakeshott, 'On Being Conservative', in *RP*, pp. 168–96.
37 Berlin, *Crooked Timber of Humanity*, pp. 3–4.

38 *Ibid.*
39 *Ibid.*, p. 6.
40 *Ibid.*, p. 8.
41 I. Berlin, *Liberty: Incorporating Four Essays on Liberty* (Oxford University Press, 2002), p. 177.
42 *Ibid.*, p. 190.
43 *Ibid.*, p. 196.
44 *Ibid.*

BIBLIOGRAPHY

OAKESHOTT'S WORKS

Publication details of titles authored solely by Michael Oakeshott can also be found in the list of abbreviations above, pages xiv–xv.

'The Activity of Being an Historian', in *Rationalism in Politics and Other Essays*. London: Methuen, 1962, pp. 137–67.

Address to the History Society, London School of Economics, n.d., unpublished, Oakeshott collection: 1/3, LSE Archives.

'The Character of a University Education', in *What is History? And Other Essays*. Thorverton: Imprint Academic, 2004, pp. 373–90.

'The Claims of Politics', in *Religion, Politics, and the Moral Life*. New Haven, CT: Yale University Press, 1993, pp. 91–6.

'The Concept of a Philosophical Jurisprudence', in *The Concept of a Philosophical Jurisprudence: Essays and Reviews 1926–51*. Thorverton: Imprint Academic, 2007, pp. 154–83.

'The Concept of a Philosophy of Politics', in *Religion, Politics, and the Moral Life*. New Haven, CT: Yale University Press, 1993, pp. 119–37.

'The Concept of Government in Modern Europe', in *The Vocabulary of a Modern European State*. Thorverton: Imprint Academic, 2008, pp. 93–105.

'Contemporary British Politics', in *The Concept of a Philosophical Jurisprudence: Essays and Reviews 1926–51*. Thorverton: Imprint Academic, 2007, pp. 203–19.

'Dr Leo Strauss on Hobbes', in *Hobbes on Civil Association*. Oxford: Basil Blackwell, 1975, pp. 132–49.

'Education: The Engagement and Its Frustration', in *The Voice of Liberal Learning: Michael Oakeshott on Education*. New Haven, CT: Yale University Press, 1989, pp. 63–94.

'An Essay on the Relations of Philosophy, Poetry and Reality', in *What is History? And Other Essays*. Thorverton: Imprint Academic, 2004, pp. 67–116.

Experience and its Modes. Cambridge University Press, 1933.
'The Idea of "Character" in the Interpretation of Modern Politics', in *What Is History? And Other Essays*. Thorverton: Imprint Academic, 2004, pp. 255–77.
'The Idea of a University', in *The Voice of Liberal Learning: Michael Oakeshott on Education*. New Haven, CT: Yale University Press, 1989, pp. 95–104.
'Introduction', in T. Hobbes, *Leviathan*. Oxford: Basil Blackwell, 1946, pp. vii–lxvi.
'Introduction to *Leviathan*', in *Hobbes on Civil Association*. Oxford: Basil Blackwell, 1975, pp. 1–74.
'John Locke', in *The Concept of a Philosophical Jurisprudence: Essays and Reviews 1926–51*. Thorverton: Imprint Academic, 2007, p. 85.
'Learning and Teaching', in *The Voice of Liberal Learning: Michael Oakeshott on Education*. New Haven, CT: Yale University Press, 1989, pp. 43–62.
Lectures in the History of Political Thought. Thorverton: Imprint Academic, 2006.
'Letter on Hobbes', *Political Theory*, 29 (2001), 834–5.
'*Leviathan*: A Myth', in *Hobbes on Civil Association*. Oxford: Basil Blackwell, 1975, pp. 150–4.
'Logos and Telos', in *Rationalism in Politics and Other Essays*, new and expanded edition. Indianapolis, IND: Liberty Fund, 1991, pp. 351–9.
'The Masses in Representative Democracy', in *Rationalism in Politics and Other Essays*, new and expanded edition. Indianapolis, IND: Liberty Fund, 1991, pp. 363–83.
Morality and Politics in Modern Europe: The Harvard Lectures. New Haven, CT: Yale University Press, 1993.
'Mr Carr's First Volume', in *The Concept of a Philosophical Jurisprudence: Essays and Reviews 1926–51*. Thorverton: Imprint Academic, 2007, pp. 325–33.
Notebooks and Letters 1922–90. Thorverton: Imprint Academic, forthcoming.
'On Being Conservative', in *Rationalism in Politics and Other Essays*. London: Methuen, 1962, pp. 168–96.
On History and Other Essays. Oxford: Basil Blackwell, 1983.
On Human Conduct. Oxford: Clarendon Press, 1975.
'On Misunderstanding Human Conduct', in *The Vocabulary of a Modern European State*. Thorverton: Imprint Academic, 2008, pp. 267–79.
'A Place of Learning', in *The Voice of Liberal Learning: Michael Oakeshott on Education*. New Haven, CT: Yale University Press, 1989, pp. 17–42.
'Political Discourse', in *Rationalism in Politics and Other Essays*, new and expanded edition. Indianapolis, IND: Liberty Fund, 1991, pp. 70–95.

'The Political Economy of Freedom', in *Rationalism in Politics and Other Essays*. London: Methuen, 1962, pp. 37–58.

'Political Education', in *Rationalism in Politics and Other Essays*. London: Methuen, 1962, pp. 111–36.

'Political Laws and Captive Audiences', in *The Vocabulary of a Modern European State*. Thorverton: Imprint Academic, 2008, pp. 168–77.

'Preface to *The Form of Ideology*', in *The Vocabulary of a Modern European State*. Thorverton: Imprint Academic, 2008, pp. 293–4.

'Rational Conduct', in *Rationalism in Politics and Other Essays*. London: Methuen, 1962, pp. 80–110.

'Rationalism in Politics', in *Rationalism in Politics and Other Essays*. London: Methuen, 1962, pp. 1–36.

'*Rationalism in Politics*: A Reply to Professor Raphael', in *The Vocabulary of a Modern European State*. Thorverton: Imprint Academic, 2008, pp. 181–6.

'Religion and the World', in *Religion, Politics, and the Moral Life*. New Haven, CT: Yale University Press, 1993, pp. 27–8.

Review of F. H. Bradley, *Collected Essays*, in *The Concept of a Philosophical Jurisprudence: Essays and Reviews 1926–51*. Thorverton: Imprint Academic, 2007, pp. 140–2.

Review of *Conservative Essays*, in *The Vocabulary of a Modern European State*. Thorverton: Imprint Academic, 2008, pp. 280–2.

Review of *The Conservative Opportunity*, in *The Vocabulary of a Modern European State*. Thorverton: Imprint Academic, 2008, pp. 187–9.

Review of *Conservative Thoughts*, in *The Vocabulary of a Modern European State*. Thorverton: Imprint Academic, 2008, pp. 295–7.

Review of R. Kirk, *The Conservative Mind*, in *The Vocabulary of a Modern European State*. Thorverton: Imprint Academic, 2008, pp. 81–4.

Review of J. D. Mabbott, *The State and the Citizen*, in *The Concept of a Philosophical Jurisprudence: Essays and Reviews 1926–51*. Thorverton: Imprint Academic, 2007, pp. 248–59.

Review of H. E. Read, *Anarchy and Order*, in *The Vocabulary of a Modern European State*. Thorverton: Imprint Academic, 2008, pp. 73–7.

Review of H. Selsam, *Socialism and Ethics*, in *The Concept of a Philosophical Jurisprudence: Essays and Reviews 1926–51*. Thorverton: Imprint Academic, 2007, pp. 271–4.

Review of Q. Skinner, *The Foundations of Modern Political Thought*, in *The Vocabulary of a Modern European State*. Thorverton: Imprint Academic, 2008, pp. 287–92.

Review of W. M. Urban, *Beyond Realism and Idealism*, in *The Concept of a Philosophical Jurisprudence: Essays and Reviews 1926–51*. Thorverton: Imprint Academic, 2007, pp. 321–2.

'The Rule of Law', in *On History and Other Essays*. Oxford: Basil Blackwell, 1983, pp. 119–64.
'Science and Society', in *The Concept of a Philosophical Jurisprudence: Essays and Reviews 1926–51*. Thorverton: Imprint Academic, 2007, pp. 240–7.
'Scientific Politics', in *Religion, Politics, and the Moral Life*. New Haven, CT: Yale University Press, 1993, pp. 97–110.
'The Study of "Politics" in a University', in *Rationalism in Politics and Other Essays*. London: Methuen, 1962, pp. 301–33.
'Talking Politics', in *Rationalism in Politics and Other Essays*, new and expanded edition. Indianapolis, IND: Liberty Fund, 1991, pp. 438–61.
'Thomas Hobbes', in *The Concept of a Philosophical Jurisprudence: Essays and Reviews 1926–51*. Thorverton: Imprint Academic, 2007, pp. 110–21.
'The Tower of Babel', in *On History and Other Essays*. Oxford: Basil Blackwell, 1983, pp. 165–94.
'The Tower of Babel', in *Rationalism in Politics and Other Essays*. London: Methuen, 1962, pp. 59–79.
'The Universities', in *The Voice of Liberal Learning: Michael Oakeshott on Education*. New Haven, CT: Yale University Press, 1989, pp. 105–35.
'The Vocabulary of a Modern European State', in *The Vocabulary of a Modern European State*. Thorverton: Imprint Academic, 2008, pp. 232–66.
'The Voice of Conversation in the Education of Mankind', in *What is History? And Other Essays*. Thorverton: Imprint Academic, 2004, pp. 187–99.
'The Voice of Poetry in the Conversation of Mankind', in *Rationalism in Politics and Other Essays*. London: Methuen, 1962, pp. 197–247.
'Work and Play', in *What is History? And Other Essays*. Thorverton: Imprint Academic, 2004, pp. 303–14.

SECONDARY SOURCES

Adorno, T. and M. Horkheimer. *Dialectic of Enlightenment: Philosophical Fragments*, trans. E. Jephcott. Stanford University Press, 2002.
Alexander, J. 'Oakeshott on Hegel's "Injudicious" Use of the Word "State"', *History of Political Thought*, 32 (2011), 147–76.
Anderson, P. 'The Intransigent Right', in *Spectrum: From Right to Left in the World of Ideas*. London: Verso, 2005, pp. 3–28.
Angle, P. M. (ed.) *Created Equal? The Complete Lincoln–Douglas Debates of 1858*. University of Chicago Press, 1958.

Arcilla, R. V. *For the Love of Perfection: Richard Rorty and Liberal Education*. New York: Routledge, 1995.
Arendt, H. *The Human Condition*. University of Chicago Press, 1958.
On Violence. New York: Harcourt, Brace & World, 1970.
The Origins of Totalitarianism. New York: Harcourt Brace Jovanovich, 1973.
Aristotle. *Nicomachean Ethics*, trans. M. Ostwald. Indianapolis, IND: Bobbs-Merrill, 1962.
The Politics, trans. C. Lord. University of Chicago Press, 1984.
Arnold, M. *Culture and Anarchy*. Cambridge University Press, 1966.
Aschheim, S. E. *The Nietzsche Legacy in Germany: 1890–1990*. Berkeley: University of California Press, 1994.
Auspitz, J. L. 'Individuality, Civility, and Theory: The Philosophical Imagination of Michael Oakeshott', *Political Theory*, 4 (1976), 261–94.
Ayer, A. J. *Philosophy in the Twentieth Century*. London: Weidenfeld & Nicolson, 1982.
Baillie, J. B. *The Origin and Significance of Hegel's Logic: A General Introduction to Hegel's System*. London: Macmillan, 1901.
Barth, K. *Protestant Theology in the Nineteenth Century: Its Background and History*. London: SCM Press, 1972.
Bédarida, F. (ed.) *The Social Responsibility of the Historian*, Diogenes no. 168. Oxford: Berghahn Books, 1994.
Bennett, J. B. 'Liberal Learning as Conversation', *Liberal Education*, 87 (2001), 32–9.
Berkeley, G. *Treatise Concerning the Principles of Human Knowledge*. Indianapolis: Bobbs-Merrill, 1970.
Berlin, I. *The Crooked Timber of Humanity*. Princeton University Press, 1998.
Liberty: Incorporating Four Essays on Liberty. Oxford University Press, 2002.
Bevir, M. *The Logic of the History of Ideas*. Cambridge University Press, 1999.
Bloch, M. *The Historian's Craft*. Manchester University Press, 1984.
Blumler, J. G. 'Politics, Poetry and Practice', *Political Studies*, 12 (1964), 355–61.
Bosanquet, B. *The Philosophical Theory of the State*. London: Macmillan, 1923.
Botwinick, A. *Michael Oakeshott's Skepticism*. Princeton University Press, 2011.
Boucher, D. *The Limits of Ethics in International Relations*. Oxford University Press, 2009.
'Overlap and Autonomy: The Different Worlds of Collingwood and Oakeshott', *Storia, Antropologia e Scienze del Linguaggio*, 4 (1989), 69–89.

The Social and Political Thought of R. G. Collingwood. Cambridge University Press, 1989.

Boucher, D. (ed.) *The British Idealists*. Cambridge University Press, 1997.

Boyce Gibson, W. R. 'A Peace Policy for Idealists', *Hibbert Journal*, 5 (1906/7), 407–24.

Boyd, J. 'The Lion and the Ox: Oakeshott's Engagement with Leo Strauss on Hobbes', *History of Political Thought*, 29 (2008), 690–716.

Bradley, F. H. *Appearance and Reality: A Metaphysical Essay*. London: George Allen & Unwin, 1925.

Essays on Truth and Reality. Oxford: Clarendon Press, 1914.

Ethical Studies. Oxford: Clarendon Press, 1927.

The Presuppositions of Critical History and Aphorisms. Bristol: Thoemmes Press, 1993.

The Principles of Logic. Oxford: Clarendon Press, 1922.

Brandt, F. *Thomas Hobbes' Mechanical Conception of Nature*. Copenhagen: Levin & Munksgaard, 1928.

Brown, J. M. 'A Note on Professor Oakeshott's Introduction to the *Leviathan*', *Political Studies*, 1 (1953), 53–64.

Bullough, E. *Aesthetics*. Stanford University Press, 1957.

Burckhardt, J. *The Civilization of the Renaissance in Italy*, trans. S. G. C. Middlemore. Harmondsworth: Penguin, 1990.

Butterfield, H. *The Whig Interpretation of History*. New York: W. W. Norton, 1965.

Caird, E. 'Plato and Other Companions of Socrates', *North British Review*, 43 (1865), 351–84.

Candlish, S. 'British Idealism: Theoretical Philosophy', in D. Moyar (ed.), *The Routledge Companion to Nineteenth Century Philosophy*. London: Routledge, 2010, pp. 658–88.

Cassirer, E. *An Essay on Man: An Introduction to a Philosophy of Human Culture*. New Haven, CT: Yale University Press, 1992.

'Hermann Cohen and the Renewal of Kantian Philosophy', *Angelaki*, 10 (2005), pp. 95–108.

Substance and Function and Einstein's Theory of Relativity, trans. W. B. Swabey and M. C. Swabey. New York: Dover Publications, 1953.

Catlin, G. Review of *Rationalism in Politics, and Other Essays*, in *Western Political Quarterly*, 16 (1963), 259–61.

Churchill, W. 'Consistency in Politics', in W. Churchill, *Thoughts and Adventures*. Wilmington, DE: ISI Books, 2009, pp. 35–44.

Clark, S. R. L. *God's World and the Great Awakening*. Oxford: Clarendon Press, 1991.

Coats, J. W., Jr. 'Michael Oakeshott as Liberal Theorist', *Canadian Journal of Political Science*, 18 (1985), 773–87.

Oakeshott and his Contemporaries. London: Associated University Presses, 2000.
Cobban, A. J. 'History and Sociology', *Historical Studies*, 3 (1961), 1–8.
Cohen, H. *Das Princip der Infinitesimal-Methode und seine Geschichte*, Berlin: Ferd. Dümmler, 1883.
Collingwood, R. G. *An Autobiography*. Oxford University Press, 1939.
The Idea of History. Oxford University Press, 1946.
The Idea of Nature. Oxford University Press, 1945.
Speculum Mentis. Oxford: Clarendon Press, 1924.
Coltman, I. *Private Men and Public Causes: Philosophy and Politics in the English Civil War*. London: Faber & Faber, 1962.
Cook Wilson, J. *Statement and Inference with Other Philosophical Papers*. 2 vols. Oxford: Clarendon Press, 1926.
Copleston, F. *A History of Philosophy*, vol. VIII, *Bentham to Russell*. 11 vols. London: Burns & Oates, 1966.
Corey, E. 'Religion and the Mode of Practice in Michael Oakeshott', *Zygon*, 44 (2009), 139–51.
Cornford, F. M. *Micro-Cosmographia Academica*. Cambridge: Bowes & Bowes, 1908.
Cranston, M. 'Remembrances of Michael Oakeshott', *Political Theory*, 19 (1991), 323–6.
Croce, B. *History: Its Theory and Practice*, trans. D. Ainslie. New York: Russell & Russell, 1960.
Dallmayr, F. 'Conversation Across Boundaries: Political Theory and Global Diversity', *Millennium: Journal of International Studies*, 30 (2001), 331–47.
Davies, M. L. *Historics: Why History Dominates Contemporary Society*. London: Routledge, 2006.
Davis, H. 'Poetry and the Voice of Michael Oakeshott', *British Journal of Aesthetics*, 15 (1975), 59–68.
DeGirolami, M. O. 'The Problem of Religious Learning', *Boston College Law Review*, 49 (2008), 1212–75.
Devigne, R. *Recasting Conservatism: Michael Oakeshott, Leo Strauss, and Conservative Political Thought's Response to Postmodernism*. New Haven, CT: Yale University Press, 1994.
Dilthey, W. *Hermeneutics and the Study of History*, ed. R. A. Makkreel and F. Rodi. 6 vols. Princeton University Press, 1996.
Introduction to the Human Sciences, trans. R. J. Betanzos. London: Harvester Wheatsheaf, 1988.
Droysen, J. G. *Outline of the Principles of History*, trans. E. B. Andrews. Boston: Ginn & Co., 1875.
Estlin Carpenter, J. Review of J. H. Muirhead and H. Jones, *The Life and Philosophy of Edward Caird*, in *Hibbert Journal*, 19 (1922/3), 189–95.

Flathman, R. *Pluralism and Liberal Democracy*. Baltimore, MD: Johns Hopkins University Press, 2005.

Willful Liberalism: Voluntarism and Individuality in Political Theory and Practice. Ithaca, NY: Cornell University Press, 1992.

Francis, M. 'The Nineteenth-Century Theory of Sovereignty and Thomas Hobbes', *History of Political Thought*, 1 (1980), 517–40.

Franco, P. *Michael Oakeshott: An Introduction*. New Haven, CT: Yale University Press, 2004.

'Michael Oakeshott as Liberal Theorist', *Political Theory*, 18 (1990), 411–36.

'Oakeshott, Berlin, and Liberalism', *Political Theory*, 31 (2003), 484–507.

The Political Philosophy of Michael Oakeshott. New Haven, CT: Yale University Press, 1990.

Freeden, M. *Ideologies and Political Theory: A Conceptual Approach*. Oxford: Clarendon Press, 1996.

Fukuyama, F. *The End of History and the Last Man*. New York: Free Press, 1992.

Gaddis, J. L. *The Landscape of History: How Historians Map the Past*. Oxford University Press, 2002.

Gamble, A. *Hayek: The Iron Cage of Liberty*. Cambridge: Polity, 1996.

Gerencser, S. A. *The Skeptic's Oakeshott*. London: Macmillan, 2000.

Gide, A. *The Immoralist/L'Immoraliste*. New York: Dover Publications, 2003.

Goldie, M. 'The Reception of Hobbes', in J. H. Burns and M. Goldie (eds.), *The Cambridge History of Political Thought 1450–1700*. Cambridge University Press, 1991, pp. 589–615.

Goldstein, L. *Historical Knowing*. Austin: University of Texas Press, 1976.

Gordon, L. *Eliot's Early Years*. Oxford University Press, 1977.

Grant, R. *Oakeshott*. London: Claridge Press, 1990.

'Oakeshott on the Nature and Place of Aesthetic Experience', in C. Abel and T. Fuller (eds.), *The Intellectual Legacy of Michael Oakeshott*. Thorverton: Imprint Academic, 2005, pp. 293–305.

Gray, J. 'Oakeshott as a Liberal', in *Post-Liberalism: Studies in Political Thought*. London: Routledge, 1983, pp. 40–6.

Green, T. H. 'Fragment of an Address on the Text "The Word is Nigh Thee"', in *Works*. 3 vols. London: Longmans, Green & Co, 1888, vol. III, pp. 221–29.

Greene, M. 'Imagining Futures: The Public School and Possibility', in W. Carr (ed.), *The Routledge Falmer Reader in Philosophy of Education*. London: Routledge, 2005, pp. 161–73.

Greenleaf, W. H. *The British Political Tradition*. 4 vols. London: Methuen, 1983.

'Hobbes: The Problem of Interpretation', in R. Peters and M. Cranston (eds.), *Hobbes and Rousseau: A Collection of Critical Essays*. New York: Anchor Books, 1972, pp. 5–36.

Habermas, J. *The Philosophical Discourse of Modernity*, trans. F. Lawrence. Cambridge, MA: MIT Press, 1987.

Harnack, A. *Lehrbuch der Dogmengeschichte*, vol. I, *Die Entstehung des kirchlichen Dogmas*. 3 vols. Freiburg im Breisgau: J. C. B. Mohr, 1894.

Hegel, G. W. F. *Lectures on the History of Philosophy*, trans. E. S. Haldane. London: Kegan Paul, Trench, Trübner, 1892.

The Philosophy of History, trans. J. Sibree. New York: Dover Publications, 1956.

Philosophy of Right, trans. T. M. Knox. Oxford University Press, 1967.

Heidegger, M. *Hegel's Phenomenology of Spirit*, trans. P. Emad and K. Maly. Indianapolis, IND: Indiana University Press, 1988.

Hempel, C. 'The Function of General Laws in History', *Journal of Philosophy*, 39 (1942), 35–48.

'Reasons and Covering Laws in Historical Explanation', in S. Hook (ed.), *Philosophy and History: A Symposium*. New York University Press, 1963, pp. 146–63.

Henkel, M. 'A Conservative Concept of Freedom: Otto von Gierke's "Genossenschaftslehre" and Oakeshott's Philosophy of Practice', in C. Abel (ed.), *The Meaning of Michael Oakeshott's Conservatism*. Thorverton: Imprint Academic, 2010, pp. 77–96.

Himmelfarb, G. *The New History and the Old*. Cambridge, MA: Harvard University Press, 1987.

Hirschman, A. *The Rhetoric of Reaction: Perversity, Futility, Jeopardy*. Cambridge, MA: Harvard University Press, 1991.

Hobbes, T. *De Corpore*, in *The English Works of Thomas Hobbes*, vol. I. 11 vols. London: J. Bohn, 1839.

Leviathan. Oxford: Basil Blackwell, 1946.

Houlgate, S. *The Opening of Hegel's Logic: From Being to Infinity*. West Lafayette, IND: Purdue University Press, 2006.

Huntington, S. *The Clash of Civilizations and the Remaking of World Order*. London: Simon & Schuster, 1998.

'Conservatism as an Ideology', *American Political Science Review*, 51 (1957), 454–73.

Inglis, F. 'Ideology and the Curriculum: Value Assumptions of System Builders', in M. Golby, J. Greenwald and R. West (eds.), *Curriculum Design*. London: Open University Press, 1975, pp. 36–47.

James, W. *The Principles of Psychology*, vol. I. 2 vols. New York: Henry Holt, 1890.

Jay, M. *The Dialectical Imagination: A History of the Frankfurt School and the Institute of Social Research 1923–1950*. Berkeley: University of California Press, 1973.

Joachim, H. H. *The Nature of Truth*. Oxford University Press, 1906.

Johnston, D. *The Rhetoric of Leviathan: Thomas Hobbes and the Politics of Cultural Transformation*. Princeton University Press, 1986.

Jones, H. *A Faith that Enquires*. London: Macmillan, 1922.

'Idealism and Epistemology', in D. Boucher (ed.), *The Scottish Idealists*. Thorverton: Imprint Academic, 2004, pp. 106–40.

Jones, H. and J. H. Muirhead. *The Life and Philosophy of Edward Caird*. Glasgow: MacLehose Press, 1921.

Kaldis, B. 'Oakeshott on Science as a Mode of Experience', *Zygon*, 44 (2009), 169–96.

Kant, I. 'Idea for a Universal History with a Cosmopolitan Purpose', in *Political Writings*, trans. H. B. Nisbet. Cambridge University Press, 1991, pp. 41–53.

Kellner, H. *Language and Historical Representation: Getting the Story Crooked*. Madison: University of Wisconsin Press, 1989.

Kierkegaard, S. *Fear and Trembling*. Cambridge University Press, 2006.

The Point of View for my Work as an Author: A Report to History, trans. W. Lowrie. New York: Harper, 1962.

Kos, E. S. *Michael Oakeshott, the Ancient Greeks and the Philosophical Study of Politics*. Thorverton: Imprint Academic, 2007.

Kristol, I. *The Neoconservative Persuasion: Selected Essays 1942–2009*. New York: Basic Books, 2011.

Kukathas, C. *Hayek and Modern Liberalism*. Oxford University Press, 1989.

Laird, J. *Hobbes*. London: Benn, 1934.

Lawn, C. 'Adventures of Self-Understanding: Gadamer, Oakeshott and the Question of Education', *Journal of the British Society for Phenomenology*, 27 (1996), 267–77.

Liddington, J. 'Oakeshott's Temporal Solipsism', paper presented at the Michael Oakeshott Association inaugural conference, 3–5 September 2001, London School of Economics.

Lindsay, A. D. *The Modern Democratic State*. Oxford University Press, 1943.

McCarney, J. 'Edifying Discourses', in R. Edgley (ed.), *Radical Philosophy Reader*. London, Verso, 1995, pp. 398–405.

McEwan, I. *The Child in Time*. London: Picador, 1988.

Macpherson, C. B. *The Political Theory of Possessive Individualism: Hobbes to Locke*. Oxford: Clarendon Press, 1962.

McTaggart, J. M. E. *A Commentary on Hegel's Logic*. Cambridge University Press, 1910.

Philosophical Studies. New York: Books for Libraries, 1966.
Studies in the Hegelian Dialectic. Cambridge University Press, 1896.
Magee, B. *Confessions of a Philosopher: A Personal Journey through Western Philosophy from Plato to Popper*. New York: Modern Library, 1999.
Mander, W. J. *British Idealism: A History*. Oxford University Press, 2011.
Manning, D. J. and T. J. Robinson. *The Place of Ideology in Political Life*. London: Croom Helm, 1985.
Marx, K. 'Manifesto of the Communist Party', in A. M. Wood (ed.), *Selections*. New York: Macmillan, 1988, pp. 141–68.
Matthews, R. *The Marxist Theory of Schooling*. Brighton: Harvester, 1980.
Meiland, J. W. *Scepticism and Historical Knowledge*. New York: Random House, 1965.
Midgley, M. *Beast and Man: The Roots of Human Nature*. London: Methuen, 1980.
Milne, A. J. M. *The Social and Political Thought of the English Idealists* London: Allen & Unwin, 1962.
Minogue, K. 'Parts and Wholes: Twentieth-Century Interpretation of Thomas Hobbes', *Annales de la Catedra Francisco Suarez*, 14 (1974), 77–108.
Modood, T. 'Oakeshott's Conceptions of Philosophy', *History of Political Thought*, 1 (1980), 315–22.
Moore, G. E. 'The Nature and Reality of Objects of Perception', in G. E. Moore, *Philosophical Studies*. London: Routledge & Kegan Paul, 1922, pp. 31–96.
'Proof of an External World', *Proceedings of the British Academy*, 25 (1939), 272–300.
Morris, C. R. *Idealistic Logic: A Study of its Aim, Method and Achievement*. London: Macmillan, 1933.
Muirhead, J. H. *The Platonic Tradition in Anglo-Saxon Philosophy*. London: George Allen & Unwin, 1931.
Mulcahy, D. G. *The Educated Person: Toward a New Paradigm for Liberal Education*. Lanham, MD: Rowman & Littlefield, 2008.
Mure, G. R. G. 'Benedetto Croce and Oxford', *Philosophical Quarterly*, 4 (1954), 327–31.
Nardin, T. *The Philosophy of Michael Oakeshott*. University Park: Pennsylvania State University Press, 2001.
Newman, J. H. *The Idea of a University: Defined and Illustrated*. London: Longmans, Green & Co., 1901.
Nietzsche, F. *Writings from the Early Notebooks*, ed. R. Geuss and A. Nehemas. Cambridge University Press, 2009.
O'Sullivan, L. 'Introduction', in M. Oakeshott, *What is History? And Other Essays*. Thorverton: Imprint Academic, 2004, pp. 1–36.

Parekh, B. 'The Political Philosophy of Michael Oakeshott', *British Journal of Political Science*, 9 (1979), 481–506.

Paton, H. J. *Kant's Metaphysics of Experience: A Commentary on the First Half of the Kritik der reinen Vernunft*. London: George Allen & Unwin, 1932.

Pocock, J. G. A. 'The Concept of a Language and the Métier d'Historien: Some Considerations on Practice', in A. Pagden (ed.), *The Languages of Political Theory in Early-Modern Europe*. Cambridge University Press, 1987, pp. 19–40.

The Machiavellian Moment: Florentine Political Thought and the Atlantic Republican Tradition. Princeton University Press, 2003.

Podoksik, E. *In Defence of Modernity: Vision and Philosophy in Michael Oakeshott*. Thorverton: Imprint Academic, 2003.

'Ethics and the Conduct of Life in the Old Georg Simmel and the Young Michael Oakeshott', *Simmel Studies*, 17 (2007), 197–221.

'From Differentiation to Fragmentation: Oakeshott, Simmel and Worlds of Experience', in M. Henkel and O. Lembcke (eds.), *Vernunft und Ethik im politischen Denken Michael Oakeshotts*. Darmstadt: Wissenschaftliche Buchgesellschaft, forthcoming.

'Oakeshott's Theory of Freedom as Recognized Contingency', *European Journal of Political Theory*, 2 (2003), 57–77.

'Overcoming the Conservative Disposition: Oakeshott vs. Tönnies', *Political Studies*, 56 (2008), 857–80.

'The Scientific Positivism of Michael Oakeshott', *British Journal for the History of Philosophy*, 12 (2004), 297–318.

'The Voice of Poetry in the Thought of Michael Oakeshott', *Journal of the History of Ideas*, 63 (2002), 717–33.

Popper, K. *Objective Knowledge: An Evolutionary Approach*. Oxford: Clarendon Press, 1972.

Prichard, H. A. 'Professor John Cook Wilson', *Mind*, 28 (1919), 297–318.

Prickett, S. 'Polyphony, the Idea of Education and Social Utility', in S. Prickett and P. Erskine-Hill (eds.), *Education! Education! Education!: Managerial Ethics and the Law of Unintended Consequences*. Thorverton: Imprint Academic, 2002, pp. 85–101.

Quine, W. 'Two Dogmas of Rationalismsm', in *From a Logical Point of View*. Cambridge, MA: Harvard University Press, 1980, pp. 20–46.

Rawls, J. *Political Liberalism*. New York: Columbia University Press, 2005.

A Theory of Justice. Cambridge, MA: Harvard University Press, 1971.

Rickert, H. *Kant als Philosoph der modernen Kultur*. Tübingen: J. C. B. Mohr, 1924.

The Limits of Concept Formation in Natural Science, trans. G. Oakes. Cambridge University Press, 1986.

Die Philosophie des Lebens: Darstellung und Kritik der philosophischen Modeströmungen unserer Zeit. Tübingen: J. C. B. Mohr, 1920.
Rorty, R. *Philosophy and the Mirror of Nature*. Oxford: Blackwell, 1998.
Rousseau, J.-J. *The Social Contract and Other Later Political Writings*, trans. V. Gourevitch. Cambridge University Press, 1997.
Russell, B. *A Critical Exposition of the Philosophy of Leibniz*. London: George Allen & Unwin, 1900.
The Principles of Mathematics. London: George Allen & Unwin, 1903.
Ryan, A. 'Hobbes and Individualism', in G. A. J. Rogers and A. Ryan (eds.), *Perspectives on Thomas Hobbes*. Oxford: Clarendon Press, 1988, pp. 81–105.
Ryle, G. 'Knowing How and Knowing That', *Proceedings of the Aristotelian Society*, 46 (1945), 1–16.
Sandburg, C. 'Nocturn Cabbage', in *Rainbows are Made: Poems by Carl Sandburg*. Orlando, FL: Harcourt, 1982, p. 55.
Schelling, F. W. J. *On the History of Modern Philosophy*, trans. A. Bowie. Cambridge University Press, 1994.
Schiller, F. *Aesthetical and Philosophical Essays*. Boston: Francis A. Niccolls, 1902.
Schopenhauer, A. *Parerga and Paralipomena: Short Philosophical Essays*, trans. E. F. J. Payne. Oxford: Clarendon Press, 1974.
The World as Will and Representation, trans. E. F. J. Payne. 2 vols. New York: Dover Publications, 1966.
Sellars, W. 'Empiricism and the Philosophy of Mind', in W. Sellars, *Science, Perception and Reality*. Atascadero, CA: Ridgeview, 1963, pp. 127–96.
Seth [Pringle-Pattison], A. *Hegelianism and Personality*. Edinburgh: Blackwood, 1888.
The Idea of God in the Light of Recent Philosophy. Oxford University Press, 1917.
'Philosophy as Criticism of the Categories', in A. Seth and R. B. Haldane (eds.), *Essays in Philosophical Criticism*. London: Longmans, Green & Co., 1883, pp. 8–40.
Scottish Philosophy. Edinburgh: Blackwood, 1907.
Shelley, P. B. *Shelley's Poetry and Prose: A Norton Critical Edition*. New York: W. W. Norton, 2002.
Simmel, G. 'Das individuelle Gesetz', in *Georg Simmel Gesamtausgabe*. 24 vols. Frankfurt-on-Main: Suhrkamp, 2001, vol. XII, pp. 417–70.
The Problems of the Philosophy of History: An Epistemological Essay, trans. G. Oakes. New York: Free Press, 1977.
The View of Life: Four Metaphysical Essays with Journal Aphorisms, trans. J. A. Y. Andrews and D. N. Levine. University of Chicago Press, 2010.

Skinner, Q. *Reason and Rhetoric in the Philosophy of Hobbes*. Cambridge University Press, 1996.

Sorley, W. R. *Moral Values and the Idea of God*. Cambridge University Press, 1918.

On the Ethics of Naturalism. Edinburgh: Blackwood, 1885.

Recent Tendencies in Ethics. Edinburgh: Blackwood, 1904.

Spengler, O. *The Decline of the West*, trans. C. F. Atkinson. New York: Random House, 1962.

Spinoza, B. *A Spinoza Reader*, ed. E. Curley. Princeton University Press, 1994.

Sreedhar, S. 'Defending the Hobbesian Right of Self-Defense', *Political Theory*, 36 (2008), 781–802.

Stanford, M. *A Companion to the Study of History*. Oxford: Blackwell, 1994.

Sternhell, Z. *The Anti-Enlightenment Tradition*. New Haven, CT: Yale University Press, 2009.

Stebbing, L. S. 'The Method of Analysis in Metaphysics', *Proceedings of the Aristotelian Society*, 33 (1932/3), 65–94.

Stove, D. C. *The Plato Cult and Other Philosophical Follies*. Oxford: Blackwell, 1991.

Strauss, L. 'Liberal Education and Responsibility', in *Liberalism Ancient and Modern*. New York: Basic Books, 1968, pp. 9–25.

Persecution and the Art of Writing. University of Chicago Press, 1952.

The Political Philosophy of Hobbes: Its Basis and its Genesis. University of Chicago Press, 1952.

'Preface to *Spinoza's Critique of Religion*', in *Liberalism Ancient and Modern*. New York: Basic Books, 1968, pp. 224–59.

Strawson, P. F. *Individuals: An Essay in Descriptive Metaphysics*. London: Methuen, 1959.

Sturt, H. *Personal Idealism*. London: Macmillan, 1902.

Sullivan, A. *Intimations Pursued: The Voice of Practice in the Conversation of Michael Oakeshott*. Thorverton: Imprint Academic, 2007.

Tarlton, C. 'The Despotical Doctrine of Hobbes, Part 1: The Liberalization of *Leviathan*', *History of Political Thought*, 22 (2001), 587–618.

Thomas, K. 'The Social Origins of Hobbes's Political Thought', in K. C. Brown (ed.), *Hobbes Studies*. Oxford: Basil Blackwell, 1965, pp. 185–236.

Tönnies, F. *Community and Civil Society*, trans. J. Harris and M. Hollis. Cambridge University Press, 2001.

Tregenza, I. '*Leviathan* as Myth: Michael Oakeshott and Carl Schmitt on Hobbes and the Critique of Rationalism', *Contemporary Political Theory*, 1 (2002), 349–69.

'The Life of Hobbes in the Writings of Michael Oakeshott', *History of Political Thought*, 18 (1997), 531–57.

Michael Oakeshott on Hobbes: A Study in the Renewal of Philosophical Ideas. Thorverton: Imprint Academic, 2003.
Tuck, R. 'Optics and Sceptics: The Philosophical Foundations of Hobbes's Political Thought', in E. Leites (ed.), *Conscience and Casuistry in Early Modern Europe*. Cambridge University Press, 1987, pp. 235–63.
Philosophy and Government, 1572–1651. Cambridge University Press, 1993.
Tucker, A. *Our Knowledge of the Past: A Philosophy of Historiography*. Cambridge University Press, 2004.
Warrender, H. *The Political Philosophy of Hobbes: His Theory of Obligation*. Oxford: Clarendon Press, 1957.
Watkins, J. W. N. *Hobbes's System of Ideas*. London: Hutchinson, 1965.
Watts Cunningham, G. *The Idealistic Argument in Recent British and American Philosophy*. New York: Century, 1933.
Weber, M. 'Religious Rejections of the World and their Directions', in H. H. Gerth and C. W. Mills (eds.), *From Max Weber: Essays in Sociology*. London: Routledge, 1991, pp. 323–59.
Westphal, K. R. *Hegel's Epistemological Realism: A Study of the Aim and Method of Hegel's Phenomenology of Spirit*. Dordrecht: Kluwer Academic, 1989.
White, H. *The Content of the Form: Narrative Discourse and Historical Representation*. Baltimore, MD: Johns Hopkins University Press, 1987.
White, J. 'Wellbeing and Education: Issues of Culture and Authority', *Journal of Philosophy of Education*, 41 (2007), 17–28.
Whitehead, A. N. *Process and Reality*. New York: Free Press, 1979.
Religion in the Making. Cambridge University Press, 1926.
Wilde, O. *The Major Works*, ed. I. Murray. Oxford University Press, 1989.
Wildon Carr, J. H. (ed.) *Life and Finite Individuality: Two Symposia*. London: Williams & Norgate, 1918.
Williams, K. *Education and the Voice of Michael Oakeshott*. Thorverton: Imprint Academic, 2007.
Windelband, W. 'Rectorial Address', *History and Theory*, 19 (1980), 169–85.
Wittgenstein, L. *Philosophical Investigations*, trans. G. E. M. Anscombe. New York: Macmillan, 1968.
Wolin, R. *The Seduction of Unreason: The Intellectual Romance with Fascism from Nietzsche to Post-Modernism*. Princeton University Press, 2004.
Worthington, G. 'The Voice of Poetry in Oakeshott's Moral Philosophy', *Review of Politics*, 64 (2002), 285–310.

INDEX